Queering the Pitch

Queering the Pitch

The New Gay and Lesbian Musicology

Edited by
Philip Brett
Elizabeth Wood
Gary C. Thomas

ROUTLEDGE NEW YORK & LONDON

Published in 1994 by
Routledge
29 West 35 Street
New York, NY 10001

Published in Great Britain by
Routledge
11 New Fetter Lane
London EC4P 4EE

Copyright © 1994 by Routledge

Printed in the United States of America on acid free paper.

Library of Congress Cataloging-in-Publication Data

Queering the pitch: the new gay and lesbian musicology/
    Philip Brett, Gary Thomas, Elizabeth Wood, editors.
    p.   c.m.
    ISBN 0-415-90752-7.—ISBN 0-415-90753-5 (pbk.)
    1. Homosexuality and music. 2. Sexuality in music. 3. Gay musi
    cians.   I. Brett, Philip. II. Thomas, Gary. III. Wood,
Elizabeth.
    ML55.Q44   1993
    780'.8'664—dc20   93-15025
                                               CIP
                                             MN

British Library Cataloging-in-Publication also available.

CONTENTS

PREFACE   *vii*

1   **Queering the Pitch:**
    A Posy of Definitions and Impersonations   *1*
    Wayne Koestenbaum

Part One ∾ CANONS AND ARIAS

2   **Musicality, Essentialism, and the Closet**   *9*
    Philip Brett

3   **Sapphonics**   *27*
    Elizabeth Wood

4   **On a Lesbian Relation with Music:**
    A Serious Effort Not to Think Straight   *67*
    Suzanne G. Cusick

5   **A Conversation with Ned Rorem**   *85*
    Lawrence D. Mass

Part Two ∾ CHRONICLES

6   **Henry Lawes's Setting of Katherine Philips's Friendship**
    Poetry in His *Second Book of Ayres and Dialogues*, 1655:
    A Musical Misreading?   *115*
    Lydia Hamessley

7   **Unveiled Voices: Sexual Difference and the Castrato**   *139*
    Joke Dame

8   **"Was George Frideric Handel Gay?":**
    On Closet Questions and Cultural Politics   *155*
    Gary C. Thomas

9   **Constructions of Subjectivity in Schubert's Music**   *205*
     Susan McClary

10   **Eros and Orientalism in Britten's Operas**   *235*
     Philip Brett

11   **Queer Thoughts on Country Music and
     k.d. lang**   *257*
     Martha Mockus

Part Three ⁓ CONSORTS

12   **Lesbian Compositional Process:
     One Lover-Composer's Perspective**   *275*
     Jennifer Rycenga

13   **Growing up Female(s):
     Retrospective Thoughts on Musical
     Preferences and Meanings**   *297*
     Karen Pegley and Virginia Caputo

14   **Authority and Freedom:
     Toward a Sociology of the Gay Choruses**   *315*
     Paul Attinello

INDEX   *347*

CONTRIBUTORS   *357*

PREFACE

*I*N 1989, AFTER SOME YEARS of informal social gatherings and organizational initiatives led by Philip Brett, the American Musicological Society sponsored on the official program of its annual national meeting the first Gay and Lesbian Study Group. At the AMS's Oakland meeting a year later, over one hundred young scholars signed on as members and appointed officers to a steering committee and editors for a newsletter. At the first AMS session devoted to "Composers and Sexuality" and chaired by Elizabeth Wood the same year, the essays by Brett, Gary C. Thomas, and Susan McClary that appear in this volume received a standing ovation. Following these events, meetings of professional societies for music theory, ethnomusicology, college music, and popular music also began to include in their discussions issues of sexuality alongside those of gender, race, class, and nationality.

Queering the Pitch, the first collection of lesbian and gay musicology, is a reflection of this new visibility and energy. It will doubtless upset the more conservative elements whose primary business is to gather and interpret historical facts or to exercise judgment upon the canon of Western music according to certain well-established principles. The academic priesthood, in unusual alliance with mainstream music critics, has already reacted with alarm to the work of the more progressive practitioners of the "new" musicology (which our title both salutes and gaily usurps). Scorn has been heaped on what is seen by many as an "ideological crusade" laying siege to the fortress of musicology as usual, and on the "shrill marauders" who are stampeding its sacred cows. But we believe we have a part to play in diversifying our discipline and rescuing it from the rigid ideology and hidden agendas to which only a few years ago it seemed unduly attached.

Analysts and theorists who assume music's autonomy from society and culture are apt to prize the material of music (its grammar, syntax, semantics) over the people who work on it, assume a reverential authority over what constitutes evidence, and take for granted that *facts* can be interpreted according to widely held principles, as if what is *there* is real and those who present the evidence are, or should be, professionally aloof and invisible.

As a group of mostly gay and lesbian scholars whose sexual preferences and acts (or support for diversity in such matters) give us a special relation to and perspective on our society, the contributors to this book choose to incorporate our selves as subjects in our work, including those parts of our-selves that have been kept invisible and thought unacceptable and unspeak-able, both by ourselves and others. To bring new insights and intuitions to the study of music, we have needed to unearth our personal, private, and pleasurable relations with the musical and the sexual in order to "queer" our own business with music. Like feminist studies twenty years ago, ours is a field seeking to define itself, still in the process of uncovering our meth-ods, materials, and terrain. Because this work is by nature cross-disciplinary (our contributors bring to musicology academic training in anthropology, sociology, religion, medicine, comparative literature, women's studies, and cultural studies as well as music), we are also discovering how gay and les-bian scholars in other fields fashion their approaches and differently chal-lenge the assumptions of their disciplines.

If there is one aim that unites us it is to help renovate the study of Western music and its scholarly discourse, which for many of us had become not only unresponsive to our persons, but also insular and unten-able as an intellectual pursuit. More traditional musicologists have assumed we are engaged in outing composers and making unproblematized connec-tions between sexual identities and musical works. While we fully respect outing as a legitimate militant act in gay and lesbian history and modern culture, uncovering "facts" of sexual preference is not the point here. The emphasis in these essays is not on identity politics, although, since critical or scholarly writing is always to some extent involved with self-identity and its attendant politics, no less when it is undeclared (i.e., white, heterosexual, and male) than otherwise, we can at least claim the virtue over most tradi-tional musical scholarship of writing from a declared position. In the debate over essentialism that bedevils and increasingly regulates gender studies, the attitude most of these essays adopt is more or less constructivist. It is for our authors less interesting to assert that Handel or Schubert was "gay" than to reveal the homophobia, as well as the pathetically limited terms, of a scholarly inquiry terrified that either might have been, or to examine and attempt to revalue models of musical difference that these composers repre-sent and to which we can relate. There is a concomitant sense among us that a whole system of judgment grounded on the elevating of "Handel" or "Schubert" into a special category, and the downgrading of other interest-ing musical phenomena, might itself be overdue for renovation.

The concern in this book, then, is less with identities than with representa-tions, performances, and roles. Its emphasis is on throwing into question old labels and their meanings so as to reassociate music with lived experience and the broader patterns of discourse and culture that music both mirrors and actively produces. Its contributors cull from a postmodernist vocabulary of violation, disruption, decentering, contradiction, confrontation, and dislocation new terms and different interpretive strategies, speculations, impressions, and improvisations, which we can bring not only to our study of musical works and their production, but also to musical education, biography, and history.

The risk, the treat that "queering" represents may be to uncover for music's lovers what it is we generally repress in thinking about our experience of music: our emotional attachments to music, our needs met by music, our accommodations to society through music, our voices, our bodies. Musicology's old pitch may never sound quite the same again.

We wish to thank The Haworth Press, Inc. for their kind permission to reprint "A Conversation with Ned Rorem," and the editors of *repercussions* no. 1 in which "Growing Up Female(s): Retrospective Thoughts on Musical Preferences and Meanings" first appeared.

We owe particular thanks to Bill Germano, our peerless and courageous editor, and his assistants Stewart Cauley, Seth Denbo and Jason Dewees; Wayne Koestenbaum, who read the entire book and offered an introduction of extraordinary grace and imagination; Kevin Stevens, for skillful and attractive music examples; Martha Mockus, for her enthusiastic, meticulous "fact" checking; Barbara Engh, Jennifer Horne, and Jonathan Sterne for their help in the final preparation of the manuscript; and above all, our colleagues and friends who contribute their work, their courage, and their commitment.

Philip Brett
Elizabeth Wood
Gary C. Thomas

QUEERING THE PITCH
A Posy of Definitions and Impersonations

Wayne Koestenbaum

To queer the pitch: to interfere with or spoil the business (of a tradesman or showman)....

1866 M. MACKINTOSH *Stage Reminisc.* The smoke and fumes of "blue fire" which had been used to illuminate the fight came up through the chinks of the stage, fit to choke a dozen Macbeths, and—pardon the little bit of professional slang—poor Jamie's "pitch" was "queered" with a vengeance.

1875 T. FROST *Circus Life* The spot they select for their performance is their "pitch," and any interruption of their feats, such as an accident, or the interference of a policeman, is said to "queer the pitch."

S AYS A LESBIAN FRIEND, who wants to write unconventionally about Clara Schumann:

May music escape, for good, the fate of presumed straightness. May music at last be subject to the critic's seduction.

By soda machines in the library's basement the faces of fellow musicology students (my sometime cohort) look cloudy with ambition and compromise—even the queer ones, suspicious of what they consider my tortuous conduct, my betrayal of the musical closet's heart- and head- and limb-constricting pact of silence. Though it's flagrant to expect to earn a degree in my desires, I wish to enforce no separation between my musical and my sexual passions.

When I told my advisor about my passion for Clara Schumann, and the irregular manner in which I intend to express it, he scowled. I can't deny the eerie magnetism of prohibition. I pit myself against it. His naysaying inspires me to declare, within earshot of music, "Dyke."

I dreamt that the music department caught fire; outside it, I cavorted like

Bertha Rochester in sultry, vindicated, mystic dance. In the dream, no scores burned, and the police, when they arrived, applauded.

My musical and my sexual passions are not necessarily identical, but I wish to assume no distinction between them.

     queer, v. slang. To spoil, put out of order. Also, with a person as object:
    to spoil the reputation of, to put (a person) in bad odour (with someone);
    to spoil (a person's) undertaking, changes, etc.
    1913…"That *queered* me with the teacher."

Says a male friend who has been working, for a decade, on a monograph of uncertain subject, perhaps Beethoven, or an ethnographic project that takes him to distant places, or a philosophical treatise on the nature of the composer's voice (my friend is never specific about his interminable quest):

The night I saw my gods, the famous pianist _____, the famous conductor _____, the famous biographer of _____, at the St. Marks Baths, I began my book. After sex that night I felt the usual emptiness, a plainsong loss, as if I had been looted, ransacked; and then, in the midst of enervation I heard a phantom melody, a call to arms I'd heard many times but never until now understood, and I suddenly knew I had to explode and expose my life. In my monograph I speak about music's origins in physiological patterns of tension and release; I don't mention sex, but sex is there between the lines, waiting to be rescued by the right readers. And yet I lack the language to say all this effectively, properly; I lack conceptual tools. A new era is beginning and I am paradoxically saddened by this moment of regeneration, puzzled by the stacks of yellowed, thwarted pages on my escritoire, beside the glowering portrait of Beethoven, and the portrait of my mother and father on their wedding day.

I had not the luxury of saying "gay" in print or in the classroom. In my life I had not the luxury.

The spot they select for their performance is their "pitch," and any interruption of their feats, such as an accident, or the interference of a policeman, is said to "queer the pitch."

Says a woman friend, who specializes in American song:

I gave a talk on lesbian composers (the possibility, the prohibition) at a works-in-progress colloquium, and though no one usually attends these events, this time the whole department showed up in force. They came to quibble, to enforce standards. I could see standards in the smile of the lovely young straight woman, a scholarly star who teaches the Schoenberg seminar. She told me (in rarefied diction I dare not imitate) that music was independent of the body. In response I wanted to strip her naked and lick her body head to toe while humming Bessie Smith's "I've Been Mistreated and I Don't Like It." The upholder of standards used the word *civilized*, a word which usually means I will soon be mortified.

My colleagues listened politely, phrased their objections respectfully: "Of course you understand my rebuttal's reasonableness." I pretended assent to the graduate student who chortled, "Your methodology is highly problematic."

And the Wagnerian with the overbite said I was a lemming, that all of us in queer musicology were Susan McClary's callow disciples, swallowing whole her dead-wrong assumptions. Mr. Overbite thought I was the enemy of music, the enemy of beauty. He misunderstood. My purpose is to return beauty, after long exile, to its rightful place in the discussion—to begin, at last, to speak about the beautiful.

The word "queer" opens beauty's floodgates, enables a serious consideration of aesthetics. We are not the enemies of beauty. We want to speak, at last, about the beautiful.

In U.S. colloq. phr. *to be queer for* (someone or something): to be fond of or 'keen on'; to be in love with.

1956 J. BALDWIN *Giovanni's Room* Actually, I'm sort of queer for girls myself.

Says a straight male professor, tenured, who works on Tchaikovsky:

When, as a child, I heard a local orchestra play the "Pathétique", I stared at the scroll above the stage, and ever since, I have connected Tchaikovsky with hiddenness, circularity, and entrapment. Most concert halls have similar scrolls, like rolled-up diplomas, or utopian sheaves of wheat in old-time Soviet propaganda drawings. These scrolls enjoin me to listen to echoes, hidden inscriptions, and to devote myself—a straight man, out of place, pensive and huge, with the wrong haircut and the wrong shoes and the wrong tastes—to the involuted discourse of homosexuality.

I am not queer but the word explains me. I am not queer but the concept abuts my life. It will be a miracle if the neglected inscriptions are not, by now, illegible.

Hence, *queerdom.*

1977 Daily Express This is a groin-directed compound of mime, ballet and freak show which, as a mere heterosexual, I take to be a celebration of the erotic imagery of queerdom.

Says a distinguished scholar of my acquaintance:

These "queer" characters have no solid musicological schooling. And anyone without the proper training should simply keep his mouth shut. Far too much is published. Best if these charlatans confessed their sexual secrets and left it at that. One can't crudely transpose *sexuality*—the history of which none of these people, Foucault's dupes, truly understands—onto *music;* one can't reduce music to the wet, pat, slick generalizations that these cheaply politicized gonzos go for. I say, purge 'em.

In nightmares these arrivistes prod me; I see their sticky, uncredentialed, overreaching fingers moving toward the musicological pie.

Purge 'em.

To put (one) out; to make (one) feel queer.

1845 W. CORY *Lett. & Jrnls.* Hallam was rather queered (it not being in his line to do anything so conspicuous).

1894 Outing It queered me to think what would happen if they were to lose foothold.

Says a chorister friend, an endearingly femme bass:

The two coming-outs rhyme. "I'm musical" hurts—and heals—as much as "I'm queer." With delight and horror I introduce myself as a musician, an identity (an inkling, a structure) I wear next to my skin. Music takes me back: in grammar school I learned recorder, and those first piping notes, antecedents of everything I've grown to love, remain the scariest, sexiest, most compromising emanations ever to rush from my body, though for years I denied the power of sound—like spunk, but diffuse, emerging slowly and continuously, not in a rash jet. I've never heard anyone explain how music is shadowed by the sexual, or why "I'm a musician" seems as rude, queer, and necessary as "Blow me." Do I need proof that I'm a musician? Can musicianship be revoked? Was I born musical? Were you? Aren't your instincts intertwined—folkways too knotted and abysmal to articulate—with music?

Were you born musical? Is it a proclivity you wear next to your skin?

queerister, obs. form of CHORISTER.

Says a semi-retired professional accompanist, a lesbian assumed by many to be closeted, though in conversation with me she has been consistently unbuttoned and frank:

I, too, wanted to shove the norm off its throne: I hearkened to any ruination, to any smart troublemaking, but in the accompanist's life there is scant space for reversal. The soloist can flounder, but the accompanist must keep perfect time.

Screw the old boys. Ignore their condemnations, in advance. If you listen for the soon-to-come dismissal, you will never say a word.

Think instead of the queer students: silently queer, bruised and attentive, faithful to the full phrase, to the metronome and the composer's intention. To you, queer music students of 1948, this book is retrospectively dedicated.

And to you, present-day scholars, dreamers in and out of the university, I extend only this mild injunction:

Explain why I am an accompanist; explain these soaring episodes I've spent a lifetime fitting into my fingers. Explain the art of listening, of voicing, of blending; of imposing variations on sameness, and sameness on variation. Explain why I am musical. Explain "musical." Leave me out of the picture entirely, if you wish, but explain the hole that's left in music when my kind are missing.

Part One

CANONS AND ARIAS

2

MUSICALITY, ESSENTIALISM, AND THE CLOSET

Philip Brett

*I*N 1968, A YEAR BEFORE STONEWALL and the emergence of gay resistance, the sociologist Mary McIntosh published a remarkable article entitled "The Homosexual Role" embracing a position that would now be called antiessentialist.[1] Noting the difficulties that science had encountered in its efforts to promote the conception of homosexuality as a medical condition, she proposed that

> this conception and the behaviour that it supports operate as a form of social control in a society in which homosexuality is condemned. Furthermore, the uncritical acceptance of the conception by social scientists can be traced to their concern with homosexuality as a social problem. They have tended to accept the popular definition of what the problem is, and they have been implicated in the process of social control.[2]

An antiessentialist approach to homosexuality was further developed in gay studies as a result of a similar thrust in the feminist criticism of gender. It received a powerful endorsement from Michel Foucault, whose position has recently been outlined by David Halperin as follows:

> Foucault did for "sexuality" what feminist critics had done for "gender." That is, Foucault detached "sexuality" from the physical and biological sciences (just as feminists had detached "gender" from the facts of anatomical sex, of somatic dimorphism) and treated it, instead, as "the set of effects produced in bodies, behaviors, and social relations by a certain deployment" of "a complex political technology." He divorced "sexuality" from "nature" and interpreted it, instead, as a cultural production.[3]

There is of course one major problem with this approach. In an age in which public discourse surrounding homosexuality has become increasingly dominated by right-wing rhetoric, institutionalized philistinism, and AIDS panic, it seems to be a way of encouraging oppression by offering a view of gay identity, and furthermore desire, as merely a cultural production—with the implication that this production can simply be unproduced, erased, silenced. Not surprisingly there have been several attempts to find substitute terms. Eve Kosofsky Sedgwick, pointing to the radical condensation of sexual categories in our century to the two species homosexual and heterosexual (and more importantly to the resulting incoherence surrounding those terms), offers the terms "minoritizing" versus "universalizing" as alternatives to essentialist/constructivist because they respond to the question, "In whose lives is homo/heterosexual definition an issue of continuing centrality and difficulty?"[4] In a recent book Diana Fuss attempts the rehabilitation of essentialism by insisting that "interrogating essence wherever we may find it does not necessarily entail simultaneously dismissing it."[5] But essentialism has peculiar new dangers for gay people in a world in which the fantasy of genetic engineering threatens to become a reality: as Sedgwick points out, no medical technologist is talking positively about the proper biological conditions for gay generation.[6] And what antiessentialism has done for the gay movement is at least positively to open up broader vistas of understanding. For part of the very substance of accepting a gay identity in Western culture in our time is by implication the cultivation of that sense of difference, of not subscribing to the straight world's tendency to project itself onto everything it encounters and to assimilate everything to its own idea of itself, but instead valuing, exploring, and trying to understand different things, people, and ideas, in terms that are closer to the way in which they perceive themselves. It is, in other words, worth the risk.

In this paper I want to compare "homosexuality," that abstract, minoritizing, nineteenth-century label for a set of practices, to another word ending in those same three abstracting syllables—a word of which the first use recorded in the *Oxford English Dictionary* occurs in 1853, some twenty years before "homosexuality" itself was coined.[7] What happens when we separate the word "musicality" from the word "music" is comparable to what happens when we separate "homosexuality" (or "sexuality") from "sex." An attribute, a social role, is filtered out of a term that has socially negotiated meanings which differ according to context. The labeling of this role can have striking consequences. To continue quoting McIntosh:

> The practice of the social labelling of persons as deviant operates in two ways as a mechanism of social control. In the first place it helps to provide a clear-cut, publicized and recognizable threshold between permissible and impermissible behaviour. This means that people cannot so easily drift

into deviant behaviour. Their first moves in a deviant direction immediately raise the question of a total move into a deviant role with all the sanctions that this is likely to elicit. Second, the labelling serves to segregate the deviants from the others, and this means that their deviant practices and their self-justification for these practices are contained within a relatively narrow group. The creation of a specialized, despised and punished role of homosexual keeps the bulk of society pure in rather the same way that the similar treatment of some kinds of criminals helps keep the rest of society law-abiding.[8]

It may seem unduly provocative to propose the substitution of musicality for homosexuality in this context, for its identification and demarcation depend more on skill than behavior. Though it is highly "specialized," and sometimes "despised," musicality does not denote a noticeably "punished role," but, rather, a privileged one. I shall, however, be arguing that it is a deviant role—for all those who identify with the label, not merely for the sexual deviants who populate the various branches of its profession.

The application of a labeling perspective to musicality will moreover allow us—as a first step—to get at some of the otherwise inexplicable questions surrounding music and gay identities. These two things are often associated, and not only in the popular imagination: it is surely no coincidence that among the many code words and phrases for a homosexual man before Stonewall (and even since), "musical" (as in, "Is he 'musical' do you think?") ranked with others such as "friend of Dorothy" as safe insider euphemisms.[9] They lacked the openly oppressive hostility of "faggot," "fairy," "nancy-boy," "pansy," "poof," "queer," or "sissy."[10] In reality, and quite apart from the coincidence of these euphemisms, musicality and gay identity exist in an uneasy relation one to the other, as any politically conscious lesbian or gay man trying to make a living in the musical profession will usually admit.

Though it is not proscribed in the same way as homosexuality, music has often been considered a dangerous substance, an agent of moral ambiguity always in danger of bestowing deviant status upon its practitioners. Both Plato and Aristotle saw it in these terms. Theirs was a legacy of moral doubt that infected much of the writing about music in the West, from St. Augustine's anguish about being moved more by the voice than by the words to the attacks of the Calvinists and the counterattacks of the various apologists of the Renaissance. Lurking beneath the objections against music, the ethical question surrounding it, is the long tradition of feeling that it is different, irrational, unaccountable.

In medieval and early modern times beauty in music was commonly described as having the effect of "ravishing" the sense or the soul. A study of this metaphor is long overdue. With its more subjective approach, modern psychology has tended to see music as short-circuiting the defenses and making the subject more receptive to fantasy. Post-Lacanian French psychoanalysts have gone further by developing the idea of the mother's voice as a "sonorous envelope" surrounding the newborn infant—a blanket of sound alternatively regarded as "the first model of auditory pleasure" or an "umbilical net." Guy Rosolato suggests "that music finds its roots and its nostalgia in [this] original atmosphere, which might be called a sonorous womb, a murmuring house, or *music of the spheres*."[11] He goes on to outline the image of the child attempting to "harmonize" with the mother once its voice has been differentiated, and this differentiation is what ultimately stimulates the "dream of recovery" of a "lost object." Kaja Silverman, connecting this theory with the subject's symbolic castration, emphasizes the ambivalence with which the maternal voice is regarded. Relating it to Lacan's category of things that are first distinguished from the subject's self—feces, the mother's breast, the mother's gaze—but whose "otherness" is not strongly marked, she writes: "it is either cherished...as what can make good all lacks...or despised and jettisoned as what is most abject, most culturally intolerable— as the forced representative of everything within male subjectivity which is incompatible with the phallic function, and which threatens to expose discursive mastery as an impossible ideal."[12] If musical pleasure can indeed be linked to this primordial experience then here at another level is a possible explanation for patriarchal societies' ambivalence toward it. Nonverbal even when linked to words, physically arousing in its function as initiator of dance, and resisting attempts to endow it with, or discern in it, precise meaning, it represents that part of our culture which is constructed as feminine and therefore dangerous.

I do not need to rehearse the numerous attempts to contain that danger over the ages. The notion that such efforts belong to a benighted past is potently contradicted everywhere today—from attempts to regulate the popular music record industry to Allan Bloom's best-selling book, *The Closing of the American Mind*.[13] The attempts to appropriate music for the enforcement of patriarchal order, to anesthetize listeners from its effects, and to defeminize it, lie most notably, however, within its own domain and in particular in its educational institutions. The careful listener will have noted the customary synecdoche, which I intend ironically: my "music" refers to the dominant model in Anglo-American music education, that of Western European music. The elevation of this strain of music as "serious," and the devaluing of other kinds of music, is of course part of the process I am talking about.

Let us look briefly at the means of self-policing. For the very reason that it does not readily convey specific meaning, music could not so easily be co-opted for a rational, masculine, heterosexist program, as, for instance, literature or drama were in the later nineteenth century. In these realms, Sue-Ellen Case, summarizing Michael Bronski, isolates "naturalism and realism as strategies that tried to save fiction from the accusation of day-dream, imagination, or masturbation, and to affix a utilitarian goal to literary production—that of teaching morals."[14] Naturalism and realism do not work that way in music. Carl Dahlhaus's thoughtful and thorough examination of these categories in the music of the nineteenth century fails to reveal more than a theoretical model, an "ideal type," which assembles a number of phenomena observed haphazardly and in different combinations (such things as simple tone-painting, the musical representation of speech intonation and rhythm, the development of a musical "prose," the adoption of folk tunes or a folklike tone, the opposition of an aesthetics of the true to that of the beautiful).[15] None of these things, save the last, is notably utilitarian or didactic, and "the accusation of daydream, imagination, or masturbation" could be, and possibly was, leveled at an art so largely concerned with transcendence, the sublime, the sentimental, and with "that infinite yearning which is the essence of Romanticism," to quote E. T. A. Hoffmann's most famous phrase.[16]

From Hoffmann and his generation stems the notion of the superiority of instrumental music, which depends precisely on a lack of specificity: "might this explain why [Beethoven's] vocal music is less successful," continues Hoffmann, "since it does not permit a mood of vague yearning but can only depict from the realm of the infinite those feelings capable of being described in words?"[17] It was the spirit of Romanticism itself, then, that elevated absolute music to a pinnacle from which it was never dislodged even by Wagner's mystical theatricalism. Realism and naturalism were therefore not available as corrective forces in music, except marginally (as in the things described by Dahlhaus and in operatic verismo). Rather, abstraction, formalism, and organicism, given a further boost by Eduard Hanslick's aesthetics, proved the best way to rescue music from its own irrationality. Modernism, when it arrived, simply intensified the principle of abstraction by eliminating from music all imitative "expression," thus removing it further in the direction of pure form and pattern.

Initiation into this largely German ideology of the absolute is a very potent part of what it means to become a musician in the Western tradition. The education of musicians in our society is popularly supposed to consist of the realization of the potential of an inherent, possibly inherited quality, "talent." More realistically, as Henry Kingsbury has so elegantly shown, musical talent, even "musicality" itself, is inextricably linked with power relations in the conservatories where it is negotiated and, in a word, constructed.[18] But the controlling nature of the conservatory regime, intent on preserving itself, differs little from that of other cultural institutions where young people identified as possessing "talent" are trained for some ritualized activity—spectator sports are an obvious parallel. Even more interesting is the way in which cultural values are inculcated in "academic" liberal arts music programs in such a way as to produce a certain understanding of what music is.

Let me simply point to what happens to an undergraduate in the earliest stages of the curriculum. The first courses she is liable to encounter are ones in musicianship and harmony. The exercise material in musicianship is likely to be drawn from the canon of German music (Bach to Brahms) toward which the syllabus generally leans. The acquisition of skill is dependent on the tacit understanding of the superiority of this repertory: it is here that the "masterwork" ideology is first and most effectively instilled. Teutonic abstraction is further emphasized in the harmony course, in which the chief ingredient is likely to be the four-part chorale settings of J. S. Bach. Perhaps for a moment you will indulge my view of these as questionable operations by the master upon a set of simple, defenseless tunes rendered all but unrecognizable by the often excessive harmonic detail forced upon them. Looked at this way they become a paradigm for the patriarchal appropriation of music. If this won't do for some readers, then at least it may be allowed that in concentrating within relatively short and regular phrases a large complement of chromatic harmonies that are usually heard over a longer time span and endowed with texture to make them interesting, these works lean heavily toward abstraction. The student, who is rarely made fully aware of the historical or stylistic context of these hymn-tune arrangements, then imbibes theirs as a "normal" technique rather than the concentration of elaboration that it represents and is thus encouraged to see them as miniature organisms. The stage is set for the enormities of the Schenker system, in which masterworks are, as it were, Bach chorales writ large, or "prolonged."

Ethnomusicology courses, if our undergraduate has enrolled in a department that acknowledges music as a worldwide phenomenon, are likely to come as something of a relief from the regimen of the history, theory, and composition of Western music that follows the basic instruction outlined above; and they probably are. As it stands, however, ethnomusicology is still associated in the popular imagination with the study of primitive forms and peoples. Its application to the highly developed musical traditions of, say, India or Japan, therefore betokens a certain air of patronization. And however self-conscious the approach, there is always the lingering sense of appropriation and control, the hint of the postcolonial whip in the master's hand. I begin to understand why I have resolutely ignored the dictates of musicological fashion by studying the music of my own tribes (that is, the English and homosexuals, insofar as they can be distinguished in the American imagination). In a paper on recent approaches in ethnomusicology, Bruno Nettl characterizes each by seeing how they would work if their object of study was the University of Illinois Music Department.[19] Interestingly enough, his observer was represented as a Martian, a rhetorical ploy that seemed involuntarily to give away the game of ethnomusicology's being something done by a superior person to an inferior one—no less than an extraterrestrial being is required to operate upon musical institutions of the U.S.A. The fetishizing of the great composer and the masterwork in historical musicology is replaced by a truly cultural perspective, but the love of transcription and glorification of fieldwork often make ethnomusicology as positivistic as historical musicology—and the frequent recourse to jargon is a sign of the desire for mystification and abstraction.

With such agendas spread across such vast areas of musical scholarship, it is no wonder that feminism, gender studies, and gay and lesbian perspectives have taken so long to surface. Even now that the ramparts of traditional musicology are constantly assailed by the trumpet call of words like homophobia, misogyny, cross-dressing, and homosocial desire, gay and lesbian studies by gay and lesbian subjects are still rare. The appearance of this work is hampered by our knowing very little about the social experience of those composers who are known or suspected to have been heavily involved sexually or emotionally with others of their own sex. At the Baltimore conference of the American Musicological Society in 1988, Maynard Solomon delineated the homosexual world and experience of Schubert in early nineteenth-century Vienna.[20] Susan McClary is the first to have made anything of this in relation to the music in a paper printed in this volume. The one composer we have been allowed to "know" about in the period is Tchaikovsky. But the disclosing of the Russian composer's sexuality and the careful covering over (or ignoring) of the tracks around Schubert has surely to do with the processing of music by scholarship as a male and predominantly German art. A Russian composer could be homosexual, indeed one so close to Teutonic mastery probably had to be homosexual, because that would allow the exotic, decadent, and effeminate quality of the music to be held up (as I remember it being held up to me in my youth) as a warning. The central German canon must at all costs be preserved in its purity. The closeting of Schubert is of a similar order as the papering over of Wagner's anti-Semitism.

In the twentieth century homosexuality becomes such a tremendous presence in music that its obliteration by silence constitutes one of the most crushing intellectual indictments of positivistic musical scholarship. Apart from a few high priests of modernism, such as Schoenberg, Berg, Webern, Stravinsky, and Bartók, there are many important composers who have been by and large homosexual—or, as in the special case of Ives, so thoroughly saturated in homosexual panic as to be part of the same social phenomenon. And yet we had to wait until 1991 for an accurate and straightforward documentary account of Henry Cowell's sentencing to a long period of imprisonment (including hard labor) in San Quentin as a first offender in a case involving homosexual sex.[21]

Please note that neither Solomon, author of the Schubert paper, nor Michael Hicks, who researched the Cowell case so painstakingly, is gay. As Lawrence Mass indicated in the interview he conducted with me in *Christopher Street* in 1987, and which has recently been reprinted in one of his books,[22] homosexuals, especially those who do not consider themselves so much closeted as "discreet" or who maintain the separation of "art" from "life," are likely to be among the first to dismiss such efforts as being undesirable or to pooh-pooh them as being of little importance. Indeed, one could go further. The presence of homosexuals who do not fully identify as gay in positions of power in the music profession is, as the British composer Nicola LeFanu pointed out to me, one reason why alternative voices such as those of women composers have so hard a time getting heard.[23] It is also one (but not the only) reason why scholarship and criticism from a gay or lesbian perspective has been so late in making an appearance in music.

In order to account for the phenomenon just described, that of the disengagement of homosexuals from questions of gay identity and homosexual and female oppression in music, we may first turn back to McIntosh. Again in quoting her I would like to substitute or bracket musical/homosexual and musicality/homosexuality:

> It is interesting to note that homosexuals themselves welcome and support the notion that homosexuality is a condition. For just as the rigid categorization deters people from drifting into deviance, so it appears to foreclose on the possibility of drifting back into normality and thus removes the element of anxious choice. It appears to justify the deviant behaviour of the homosexual as being appropriate for him as a member of the homosexual category. The deviancy can thus be seen as legitimate for him and he can continue in it without rejecting the norms of society.[24]

This was in fact true of most homosexuals before Stonewall. To realize why this has not changed much since in music, why expressions of gay identity and liberation in music are confined rather to marching bands and choruses, one has only to realize how powerful has become the construction of musicality in the "classical music" world. For the musician in general, and particularly for the gay or lesbian musician, there is an involvement in a social contract that allows comforting deviance only at the sometimes bitter price of sacrificing self-determination. The situation is comparable to, though of course not identical with, that of the woman who exchanges degrees of selfhood for the authority and position afforded by marriage and motherhood in patriarchal society. Deviance from the norm and loss of selfhood, however, are not the sole items at issue. Looked at another way (along the lines of Allan Bloom), the contract also offers elite status in exchange for something more like a commodity: bohemia, "a respectable place for marginality...had to justify its unorthodox practices by its intellectual and artistic achievement."[25] But that achievement only reached its full power and potential in his analysis (as deduced by Sedgwick) through the homoerotic/homophobic process in which desire is stimulated and simultaneously repressed: the musician is fully caught in the erotic double-binding effect of the closet.

Comforting deviance and elite status: why do so many people willingly pay such dues for them? That surely has to do with one aspect of music that I have so far notably avoided: performance. It is performance that attracts and entices most people to become musicians in the first instance. If then later they become scholars, critics, or composers, it is rare that they start out that way without first having been drawn to music by the piano, some other instrument, or by singing. Music is a perfect field for the display of emotion. It is particularly accommodating to those who have difficulty in expressing feelings in day-to-day life, because the emotion is unspecified and unattached. The piano, let us say for example, will thus become an important means for the attempt at expression, disclosure, or communication on the part of those children who have difficulties of various kinds with one or both parents. To gay children, who often experience a shutdown of all feeling as the result of sensing their parents' and society's disapproval of a basic part of their sentient life, music appears as a veritable lifeline. But full participation in the constructed role of musician in our society can only be accomplished by recognizing its deviance and acknowledging the norms of society itself. The powerfully attractive privilege of a sentient and expressive life enabled by the more exclusive forms of artistic endeavor comes at the cost of our tacit agreement not merely "to continue in [deviancy] without rejecting the norms of society" but also to play the deviant role in such a way that those norms are tacitly reinforced: to recall the terms of my second quotation from McIntosh, our public demonstration of feeling serves the function of keeping the rest of society in a state of decorum and restraint. These terms, moreover, are not demanded exclusively of gays or lesbians in the profession. *All* musicians, we must remember, are faggots in the parlance of the male locker room. Hence the immense investment by musical scholarship and by certain types of composition in competitiveness, rigor, masterfulness, and those qualities that reveal the castration anxiety that is so strong in our deviant profession. When Ned Rorem says that he feels more discriminated against as an artist than as a homosexual, this is really what he is referring to.

The prevalence of homosexual panic in musical circles must of course go deeper than the labeling perspective suggests. In her recent work on the epistemology of the closet, Sedgwick has discerned a dynamic impasse between universalizing and minoritizing views of homo/heterosexual definition (between, for instance, Freud's open view of sexual possibility and "third sex" or gay separatist models) and between separatist and transitive tropes of homosexual gender (between, for instance, the super male gay image and the nelly queen). These ambiguities and tensions are revealed by Sedgwick in what is primarily a project of literary criticism focusing on the late nineteenth and early twentieth centuries. Such a significant advance in perceiving the central importance of sexual definition (or lack of it) in modern culture needs testing in other areas, and music provides a particularly interesting field for the project. It is an enclave in our society—a sisterhood or brotherhood of lovers, music lovers, united by an unmediated form of communication that is only by imperfect analogy called a language, "the" language of feeling. In such an unspoken place, the incoherencies and dramas of the closet may be played out in particularly revealing and suggestive ways simply because of the lack of rational verbal discourse.

Let us take, as a brief example, the relation of Benjamin Britten to the phenomenon of the "open secret," which is so crucial to the tensions surrounding homosexual identity even after (one might say especially after) Stonewall. As D. A. Miller has pointed out, secrecy itself, that very instrument of the closet, can function as

> the subjective practice in which the oppositions of private/public, inside/outside, subject/object are established, and the sanctity of their first term kept inviolate. And the phenomenon of the "open secret" does not, as one might think, bring about the collapse of those binarisms and their ideological effects, but rather attests to their fantasmatic recovery. In a mechanism reminiscent of Freudian disavowal, we know perfectly well that the secret is known, but nonetheless we must persist, however

ineptly, in guarding it.[26]

It was this phenomenon of the open secret that peculiarly pushed Britten's sexual identity into the foreground throughout his life. His not acknowledging his homosexual identity in so many words, though it was universally known by some sort of bush telegraph, allowed him to maneuver effectively in British society. It enabled him not only to live openly with Peter Pears, but also to set for Pears and perform with him songs whose texts were unambiguous in their celebration of homoeroticism. Moreover, it allowed him to return again and again in the operas to the themes of the social experience of homosexual oppression, homosocial and homosexual bonding, even man-boy love. And it gave him social and business advantages, allowing him to pursue a highly successful career as an entrepreneur, to be on warm terms with the royal family, and to collect his nation's top set of honors.

Much of what it takes to be a successful composer is bound up in a good reading of one's surroundings and an inventive response to them, whether it be a question of a Josquin learning to play with the expectations of the court patrons of the late fifteenth century or the postwar American composer trading on the obscurantism favored in academic circles in the 1950s and 1960s. Britten tapped a peculiar characteristic of British society that allows any kind of social deviance and ambiguity so long as it is not named, is not published, and does not make claims against the behavioral norm. To appreciate the fact that there was considerable tension surrounding not only Britten's homosexuality, but also the success that he enjoyed despite it, one has to dig a little deeper beneath such blatant attacks as that against "bachelor composers" in the Craft/Stravinsky conversation books.[27] What is revealed is a curious set of opposite and equally loaded critical terms. On the one hand Britten's music was characterized as "mere cleverness," "devilish smart." On the other it was accused of sentimentality. Behind both attitudes, of course, lay the unspoken fascination with Britten's homosexuality, both labels being the reverse sides of the oppositions craft/cleverness, sincerity/sentimentality, which belong among a whole plethora of binarisms that Sedgwick has claimed as "epistemologically charged pairings, condensed in the figures of 'the closet' and 'coming out.'"[28]

Furthermore, critics also embraced a strategy of choosing an approach to the themes of Britten's operas that would mask, parry, or render ridiculous their homosexual content. What is truly amazing about the initial music-critical reception of *Grimes*, given the lack of specific information about the internal nature of the title figure, is its failure to discern an allegory of oppression; a slightly later generation confused the issue even further by

Well, Benjamin **Britten** & Peter **Pears** first **met** when they were quite **young**.. & as they **got on** quite **well**, they decided to go into **partnership** & **work** together. This lasted **quite** a **long time**. When Lord Britten **died** the **Queen** sent Sir **Peter** a **telegram** of **sympathy** ...

Kate Charlesworth, "Benjamin Britten Met Peter Pears ..." (1988)

Issued as a postcard by the Organisation for Lesbian and Gay Action (OLGA), with the following caption: "Clause 28 of the Local Government Bill states that: local authorities cannot fund or 'intentionally promote' homosexuality, and that state schools cannot promote 'the acceptability of homosexuality as a pretended family relationship.'"

discerning a man-boy hate/love theme, all traces of which were rigorously and consciously flushed out of the libretto by the composer. When *Death in Venice* appeared a quarter of a century later, however, allegorization became the only way to neutralize Aschenbach's potent cry to Tadzio of "I love you" at the climax of act 1; and so music critics fell over themselves to adopt and elaborate upon the Apollonian/Dionysian allegory with which Mann himself had clouded some central questions. Such a strategy has not, however, survived Section 28 of the Local Government Act of 1988. In a stroke that demonstrated how simple it is to short-circuit the wiring of the open secret, the Kent and Sussex Education Committees canceled a performance of *Death in Venice* by the Glyndebourne touring company for schools because they sensed that it would be seen to promote homosexuality and thus contravene the law.

As I pointed out in an exchange of letters at the time, the authorities would in fact have been serving government extremists well by showing this opera because of the stereotypical warnings it appears to give against being gay or pederastic: that you will stoop to any indignity (such as painting your face) to lure your young prey, and will die alone, rejected and in misery.[29] In real life, ironically, Britten was a first-rate conventional role model for the youth of Kent and East Sussex, gay, lesbian, or straight. He lived a fruitful, constructive, social, well-ordered life, with a mate who was equally productive. As a hardworking, successful, middle-class citizen who incidentally contributed not insignificantly to the invisible balance of payments, he was in all other respects than his sexuality and pacifism a model of Thatcherite citizenship. In Aschenbach, Britten created a doppelgänger—the dark side of the person he always at some level imagined himself to be. If, as many critics insist, *Death in Venice* is a testament, then it is a testament to the power, not of love, but of the distinctive effects on the personality of the dynamics of the closet.

To what effect did Britten tread the narrow line in order to write music that directly addressed the view of society held from the closet, one might ask, if twenty years later the collusion between the closet and the role of the musician remains virtually unchanged, save for (even in spite of) the decimating effect on our community of AIDS? What was the point of all those coded messages about homosexual oppression and pederasty if they prompted only further denial of their meaning, further entrenchment of the universalism and transcendentalism that make Western classical music a weak substitute for religion in capitalist society and divorce it from meaning? What good is the "discretion model" Britten maintained, and musicians still maintain today, if it merely reinforces dominant culture by confining homosexuality to the private sphere while making it obscurely present in public discourse as an unthinkable alternative? How many of us have offered something better to any musical adolescent who thinks her/himself unique in feeling different, alone, and ashamed?

These are questions for a lesbian and gay musicology not to lose sight of. There are wider implications to them than may at first appear. The collusion of musicality and the closet has also, for example, been intensified by the essentialist myth of musical creativity as a force deriving from the "eternal feminine" in man. The appropriation of the feminine and privatization of "the muse" in the figure of the male composer, who therefore seems in a special way to reflect the trope of the woman's soul trapped in a man's body (in the famous phrase of Karl Heinrich Ulrichs), often seems to demand a compensating amount of energy spent in holding up the facade of masculinity. This lethal combination in turn helps to augment the legendary misogyny of the profession, in which homosexual musicians like Aaron Copland have been especially implicated.[30] In this light, Charles Ives perhaps deserves some small credit for at least being blatant in his abuse of European composers as homosexuals or women. The fact that the terms he uses (playing into and trading off the very gender liminality stemming from Ulrichs's "inversion" model) do not distinguish the one category from the other shows how intertwined are homophobia and misogyny, and how the struggle against the recognition of women in certain roles in music is bound up with homosexual panic.[31]

Since striking a tiny blow at the open secret by knocking politely at the door of the Britten closet in the year of the composer's death, I have become increasingly convinced that the special dedicated role signified by the word musicality is comparable to, and linked with, the role of homosexuality in our societies (at least those of Britain and North America in which I have spent long periods).[32] Neither label is up to much good. They are tools of social control dressed up in one case as "talent" in the other as "condition." And they are outmoded. "Composer," for instance, no longer has much usefulness as a contemporary label outside the institutions of classical music because of the new variety of modes of musical production and the dying force of an ideology constructed around a single (male) originating force and a concept of "art" as an elite and segregated human activity. And it is doubtful whether a "musicality" defined by a bunch of conservatory teachers will play as much part as it has in the past in the social rituals of a music dominated by personality, media, and marketing.[33] Similarly, "homosexual," with its overtones of medicalized essentialism, no longer conveys the richness and variety of the forms of same-sex desire that are manifest in different class, race, age, and even local situations within the West. A lesbian and gay musicology will want to interrogate both terms unceasingly as it re-searches our history, proposes new theories of music, and devises a new pedagogy. It is not the evidence, but the right to interpret it, to which we have to lay claim. "The question was, and is," as Neil Bartlett says of the trial of 1895 in his moving book about Oscar Wilde, "who speaks, and when, and for whom, and why."[34]

Notes

The first version of this paper was delivered at the second annual Sager Symposium at Swarthmore College, March 1990; the second at the first session on "Composers and Sexuality" at the annual meeting of the American Musicological Society in Oakland, November 1990. I wish to thank the many people who have written to me about it or who have made suggestions. It was written from my personal perspective as a gay male and did not set out to explore the relations of musicality to lesbian experience.

1. "Stonewall" refers to the riots in New York City in June 1969, when the patrons of a gay bar fought back against police harassment; these events mark the inauguration of the gay liberation movement.

2. Mary McIntosh, "The Homosexual Role," *Social Problems* 16, no. 2 (Fall 1968); reprinted in *The Making of the Modern Homosexual,* ed. Kenneth Plummer (London: Hutchinson, 1981), 32.

3. David M. Halperin, *One Hundred Years of Homosexuality and Other Essays on Greek Love* (New York: Routledge, 1990), 7.

4. Eve Kosofsky Sedgwick, *Epistemology of the Closet* (Berkeley: University of California Press, 1990), 40. She adds the pertinent observation that "there currently exists no framework in which to ask about the origins or development of individual gay identity that is not already structured by an implicit, trans-individual Western project or fantasy of eradicating that identity."

5. Diana Fuss, *Essentially Speaking* (New York: Routledge, 1989), xiv.

6. Sedgwick, *Epistemology of the Closet,* 43.

7. The *Trésor de la langue française* (Paris: Éditions du centre national de la recherche scientifique, 1971–) prints a usage dating from 1835.

8. Mary McIntosh, "The Homosexual Role," 32.

9. I am indebted for other musical euphemisms for gay men to Robert Dawidoff ("Does he play in the orchestra?") and Byron Adams ("Does he sing in the choir?"); none of us knows the origin of the expressions, needless to say. Robert Dawidoff also drew my attention to A. T. Fitzroy's *Despised and Rejected* (London: C. W. Daniel, 1918; reprinted London: GMP Publishers, 1988). The novel is phenomenal in its openness about what one of its early reviewers called "abnormality in the affections" and allows its characters

to explain many of the familiar codes. As the tortured composer hero Dennis writes to his lesbian friend Antoinette, "When I was at school, I was terrified of my musical gift; I hated it, and did my utmost to suppress it, because I thought it was that which made me different from the other boys. I loathed being 'different'..." (78). The book shows the influence of Edward Carpenter, not only on questions of sexuality ("what had nature been about, in giving him the soul of a woman in the body of a man?" [107]), but also in making connections between the oppression of homosexuals and of Jews, the Irish, women, and the working class; it was banned on account of its fierce advocacy of pacifism, another marker. The author was Rose Allatini, married for twenty years to the composer Cyril Scott before leaving him in 1941 to set up house in Rye with another woman, according to Jonathan Cuthill's informative preface to the GMP reprint.

10. "Queer" of course has been rehabilitated for political purposes. "Faggot" is often used self-deprecatingly among gay men—but its widespread and indiscriminate use in American society as *the* term by which members of any group express their contempt for members of another, and vice versa, indicates the degree to which homophobia is the (often unremarked) common denominator in situations of hatred and aggression.

11. "La voix: entre corps et langage," *Revue française de psychanalyse* 37, no. 1 (1974): 81. It is quoted by Kaja Silverman, with the interesting comment that "the maternal voice not only wraps the child in a soothing and protective blanket, but bathes it in a celestial melody whose closest terrestrial equivalent is opera": *The Acoustic Mirror: The Female Voice in Psychoanalysis and Cinema* (Bloomington: Indiana University Press, 1988), 84–85. Chapter 3, "The Fantasy of the Maternal Voice," discusses the relevant literature. See also Claudia Gorbman, *Unheard Melodies: Narrative Film Music* (Bloomington: Indiana University Press, 1987), 60–63.

12. Silverman, *The Acoustic Mirror*, 86.

13. Allan Bloom, *The Closing of the American Mind* (New York: Simon & Schuster/ Touchstone, 1988).

14. "Toward a Butch-Femme Aesthetic," in Lynda Hart, ed., *Making a Spectacle: Feminist Essays on Contemporary Women's Theatre* (Ann Arbor: University of Michigan Press, 1989), 287, 288, *et passim*.

15. Carl Dahlhaus, *Realism in Nineteenth-Century Music,* trans. Mary Whittall (Cambridge: Cambridge University Press, 1985). For a critique of Dahlhaus's model, see Philip Gossett, "Carl Dahlhaus and the 'Ideal Type,'" *Nineteenth-Century Music* 13 (1989): 49–56.

16. E. T. A. Hoffmann, "Beethoven's Instrumental Music," from *Kreisleriana* in David Charlton, ed., *E. T. A. Hoffmann's Musical Writings*, trans. Martyn Clarke (Cambridge: Cambridge University Press, 1989), 98.

17. Hoffmann, "Beethoven's Instrumental Music," 98.

18. Henry Kingsbury, *Music, Talent, and Performance: A Conservatory Cultural System* (Philadelphia: Temple University Press, 1988).

19 "Mozart and the Ethnomusicological Study of Western Culture: An Essay in Four Movements," in Katherine Bergeron and Philip V. Bohlman, eds., *Disciplining Music: Musicology and its Canons* (Chicago: University of Chicago Press, 1992), 137–155.

20. Maynard Solomon, "Franz Schubert and the Peacocks of Benvenuto Cellini," *Nineteenth-Century Music* 12 (1989): 193–206.

21. Michael Hicks, "The Imprisonment of Henry Cowell," *Journal of the American*

Musicological Society 44 (1991): 92–119.

22. *Homosexuality as Behavior and Identity: Dialogues of the Sexual Revolution Volume II* (New York: Haworth Press, 1990), 36–54.

23. The series known as the Henry Wood Promenade Concerts, the BBC's annual free-form music festival broadcast from London's Albert Hall each summer, has not improved its abysmally low women-to-men ratio of composers.

24. Mary McIntosh, "The Homosexual Role," 34.

25. Allan Bloom, *The Closing of the American Mind*, 235. I am grateful to Fred Maus for exhorting me to develop the "social contract" idea along the lines suggested by Sedgwick's analysis of Bloom, *Epistemology of the Closet*, 54–59.

26. *The Novel and the Police* (Berkeley: University of California Press, 1988), 206.

27. Delivering an opinion on Menotti's *The Last Savage*, Stravinsky is represented as saying, "The predatory female idea might have possibilities, though—I am thinking of Mr. Robbins's ballet about her to the music of my String Concerto—especially to talented bachelor composers such as Britten, Henze, Tchaikovsky, and Menotti" in Igor Stravinsky and Robert Craft, *Themes and Episodes* (New York: Alfred A. Knopf, 1967), 100–101.

28. Sedgwick, *Epistemology of the Closet*, 72.

29. See the exchange between Howard Rogers and myself in the Letters section of *The Musical Times* 130, no. 1758 (August 1989): 450–51, and 131, no. 1763 (January 1990): 10–11. What prompted me to write was Mr. Rogers's assertion, along lines mentioned above, "that the opera is *actually* about the crisis in Aschenbach's creative personality, not a Teach-Yourself-Homosexuality guide" (my italics). According to British terminology, by the way, "clause" and "bill" refer to a law before it has received the Royal assent, after which those terms are replaced by "section" and "act" respectively.

30. In an appreciation of his composition teacher, Nadia Boulanger, written for *Harper's Magazine* (October 1960): 49–51, and reprinted in Carol Neuls-Bates, ed., *Women in Music*, (New York: Harper & Row, 1982), Copland states: "in so far as she composed at all she must of necessity be listed in that unenviable category of the woman composer. Everyone knows that the high achievement of women musicians as vocalists and instrumentalists has no counterpart in the field of musical composition. ...Is it possible that there is a mysterious element in the nature of musical creativity that runs counter to the nature of the feminine mind? And yet there are more women composers than ever writing today...." (240–42). Britten, who would never have been so gratuitously nasty in print, nevertheless treated many of the women characters in his operas with little sympathy: see Ellen McDonald, "Women in Benjamin Britten's Operas," *Opera Quarterly* 4, no. 3 (1986): 83–101.

31. The long-standing dominance of males in the composition of Western classical music exemplifies to a particular degree the situation Greg Bredbeck discerns in his challenging theoretical diagnosis of "ped(erast)agogy" (building on work by David Halperin, Luce Irigaray, and Teresa de Lauretis): "the presence of one self-reproductive gender (man) subsumes both gender and sexual difference"; "Anal/yzing the Classroom: On the Impossibility of a Queer Pedagogy," in George E. Haggerty and Bonnie Zimmerman, eds., *Professions of Desire: Lesbian and Gay Studies in Literature* (forthcoming).

32. My "Britten and Grimes," *Musical Times*, 118 (1977): 955–1000, reprinted in *Benjamin Britten: Peter Grimes* (Cambridge: Cambridge University Press, 1983), 180–89, was first delivered at the American Musicological Society's meeting in Washington, D.C., in

November 1976.

33. Even the BBC now has a glossy monthly (packaged with a CD)—*BBC Music Magazine.* The first editorial (September 1992) pointedly drew attention to "Shopfront and Diversions, which will keep you abreast of new products, music education, jobs and so on" (5). The commercial radio station "Classic FM," also appearing in September 1992, applies British light-music disc-jockey presentation (brash chat, mispronounced foreign words) to classical music in a manner still uncommon in the United States, where announcers' affected voices and precious pronunciations underline the up-market snob appeal of the commodity.

34. Neil Bartlett, *Who Was That Man: A Present for Mr Oscar Wilde* (London: Serpent's Tail, 1988), 149.

3

SAPPHONICS

Elizabeth Wood

I hear the high mezzo voice of the Enigma. Because it is the Enigma: it doesn't explain itself, it makes itself heard.[1]
—Hélène Cixous, *Tancredi Continues*

*T*HE SINGING VOICE as a musical instrument is inexactly understood because its mechanism of production is invisible. Voice is vibration: an exhaled stream of air passes from lungs to larynx, where it opens muscles like valves that regulate it, resist its escape and, vibrating, produce sound;

to resonating cavities of the upper body and head; and to the pharynx, where sound and tone quality is shaped, pitched, projected— "placed" by mouth, tongue, palate, lips.[2]

Sapphonics, this rubric I devised, has overtones and resonances in and beyond voice production and hidden vestibules of the body. I mean to use it as a mode of articulation, a way of describing a space of lesbian possibility, for a range of erotic and emotional relationships among women who sing and women who listen. As an opera lover who is not a trained singer, I stage an imaginary intimacy between voices: theirs singing, being heard; mine listening and, with other listeners writing, being read. Like the writers who read Sappho of Lesbos as poetic precursor of modern lesbian identity, my act of naming claims Sappho the singer for a "lesbian continuum" of listening that itself engendered Sapphonic performances and Sapphonic operas.[3] My sonic outing traces the history and biography of a lesbian music that, like other "fictions of Sappho," is an intertextual legend in fragments: lost, unnamed, buried in opera's Orphic origins and traditions.[4]

I also call Sapphonic a particular voice that thrills and excites me. If this trained female singing voice I speak of, an embodied and acoustic instrument, is no longer audible as material sound, it is visible and resonant as presence in historical contexts and imaginary representations that once shaped and projected it: in performance records and auto/biographies of singers with this voice; narrative traditions of opera and the female voice as these are represented by women writers; opera and voice traditions as these are shaped by women composers and singers. I speak of this voice metaphorically: as vessel of self-expression and identity, channel for a fluid stream that "speaks" for desire in living human form, a lure that arouses listening desires.

I call this voice Sapphonic for its resonance in sonic space as lesbian difference and desire. Its sound is characteristically powerful and problematic, defiant and defective. Its flexible negotiation and integration of an exceptional range of registers crosses boundaries among different voice types and their representations to challenge polarities of both gender and sexuality as these are socially—and vocally—constructed. Its refusal of categories and the transgressive risks it takes act seductively on a lesbian listener for whom the singer serves as messenger, her voice as vessel, of desire.[5]

Si tu veux que je reste auprès de toi
Disperse moins ta voix,
Prends le diapason
De l'intime durée.

("If you want me to stay with you,
Do not disperse your voice,
Pitch it
To the intimate moments.")[6]

—Natalie Barney

My preface is an anecdote from the lesbian life of Natalie Barney (1877–1972). In Paris-Lesbos in the early 1900s, Barney lost her lover, writer Renée Vivien, to the Baroness Hélène van Zylen de Nyevelt. In an attempt to win Vivien back, the Amazon of Letters sent a vocal emissary to avenue du Bois, where the baroness lived, to serenade Vivien. The Leporello who voiced Giovanni-

Barney's desire was her friend the opera diva and reigning "Carmen," Emma Calvé (1858–1942). Calvé's serenade began with the celebrated lament "J'ai perdu mon Euridice" from Gluck's opera *Orfeo ed Euridice.*

Gluck's Orfeo was originally sung in 1764 (in Italian) by a castrato, a decade later (in French) by a tenor. For the opera's revival at the Théâtre Lyrique in 1859, Berlioz transposed Orfeo's tenor part down from F major to C for the voice of Pauline Viardot-Garcia (1821–1910). Berlioz's description then of Viardot's performance in "virile antique costume," weeping by the side of her dead lover, conveys messages a Barney *abbandonata* meant her unseen lover to hear:

> Madame Viardot makes of [the lament] one of the prodigies of expressions...delivered in three different ways: firstly, with a contained grief and in slow movement; then in sotto voce, pianissimo, and with a trembling voice choked by a flood of tears; finally, after the second adagio...with a more animated movement...throwing herself, mad with despair...with bitter cries and sobs of a distracted grief.[7]

Initially, it seems, Barney's Orphic emissary failed her. Only when Calvé sang Carmen again did windows open and Vivien appear to a waiting Barney on the street below.[8] In the opera, Orfeo's lament serves as epilogue to a reunion and rescue that also failed. It inscribes Orfeo's suffering and loss. But given the private context of Calvé's performance the lament succeeded: as epilogue to a contested, but only temporarily interrupted, love affair; prelude to renewed seduction; and ironic warning to every woman involved. In the opera, Orfeo had been prohibited both from looking at the beloved and from explaining to her why he was required to exert such "unnatural" control over what he so "naturally" desired. Orfeo may not see the thing he wants or he will lose it. As metaphor, as myth, the opera's conventional meaning is both emphasized and subverted by the lesbian context a travesty Orfeo represents: her embodiment of a desire between women that society and culture prohibit and silence, her longing for what women may not have, makes visible the experience of lesbian invisibility as it gives voice to forbidden desire.

Both the female Orpheus and her lesbian listener divine difference. Pauline Viardot's daughter, the composer Louise Héritte-Viardot, recalls: "My mother had been much worried about the opera, for she did not know how to treat the part. She had thought out all the details most carefully, had studied the classic sources and had sketched her whole costume herself. But Orpheus *the man* had been as a sealed book to her until [during the dress rehearsal] her hour of inspiration came." Because the singer's daughter finds

Orpheus *the woman* "difficult to speak of," she produces two unnamed listeners as evidence and mute witnesses to its Sapphonic effect. One, "a young girl, fell in love with Orpheus. She grew thin and pale, and her mother in despair resolved to ask my mother's help" to "cure" her. The two mothers conspired to disillusion the girl. "Trembling with excitement at the prospect of seeing her beloved," she met instead a monstrous reversal, a fake: Viardot's siren Orpheus disguised as harpy "in dressing-gown, unkempt hair, cross, irritable, thoroughly disagreeable." The other, a widowed goldworker who lived with her sister, had anonymously left flowers in Viardot's dressing room during every performance, having "spent most of her earnings on flowers and theatre tickets, as to see and hear Orpheus was her idea of bliss." When Viardot discovered this admirer's identity, she embraced and visited her: the diva and her fan became lifelong friends.[9]

While in modern opera practice the substitution of female mezzo or contralto for castrato voice is well established, some men still find the female Orpheus unsettling and inauthentic. John Eliot Gardiner deplores the habit as "alien, fudged, distorted." For Tom Hammond, "the deep maternal contralto...cannot approach dramatic conviction. A woman's voice inevitably deploys entirely extraneous and disturbing sexual overtones which are not only inappropriate to the personality of Orfeo but...do little to conjure up the elegiac and other-worldly character of the castrato voice."[10] Their reactions suggest it is the sound as much as spectacle of desire in the body of the female Orpheus that disturbs because it sends the wrong message. How did Viardot or Calvé sound?

Contemporary reports suggest a big, strong voice with an exceptional 3- to-3½ octave range from G below C to the high F of the Queen of the Night.[11] Whether defined as dramatic soprano or coloratura mezzo, I call Sapphonic this type of voice that refuses standard categories and is today considered a rare phenomenon.[12] Its flexibility, versatility, and power cross over and integrate the physical (and psychological?) boundaries of sites that produce vocal pitch and tone and are commonly distinguished in the female voice as head (soprano), middle (mezzo), and chest (contralto) registers.

In the contralto register, Viardot's lower octave and Calvé's "voix de poitrine" could produce a powerful "masculine" sound, or what Paul Robinson calls in Verdi's mezzo roles a "baritonal fierceness": "It would be a mistake to call them mannish, but they are indelicate in the extreme."[13] In defiant political roles such as Lady Macbeth, Verdi exploits in the female chest voice its paradoxical effects of sexual ambiguity, overpowering vocal authority, and potential for violence.[14]

As this voice makes its sudden ascent from chest to head register, its break through sonic and anatomical boundaries is technically hazardous. "The peculiar quality of Madame Viardot's voice—its unevenness, its occasional harshness and feebleness, consistent with tones of the gentlest sweetness," suggested to Henry Chorley "that nature had given her a rebel to subdue, not a vassal to command. From the first she chose to possess certain upper notes which must needs be fabricated, and which never could be produced without the appearance of effort."[15] Calvé's octave ascent to a high pianissimo D flat, which reached and sustained a floating tessitura for an extraordinary duration, produced what Desmond Shawe-Taylor describes as "certain curious notes—strange, sexless, superhuman, uncanny."[16] Calvé called this her "fourth" voice and claimed that a castrato singer in Rome's Sistine Chapel choir, Domenico Mustafa (1829–1912), taught her how to produce it—a fascinating historical moment of transvestic vocal exchange between differently sexed and gendered bodies: a literally unsexed "fourth" voice for a "third" sex.[17]

The high head or fourth voice "fabricated" by Viardot and Calvé is "false" (falsetto): an artificial or "unnatural" sound, signifying to some the uncannily queer lost sound of a castrato or male falsetto, to others a "sexless" boy chorister. Where the castrato had a comparable three-octave range to Viardot and Calvé (an octave higher than the baritone), the falsettist must extend the upper register to take on boy alto or soprano roles. Both male and female falsetto, using Viardot's technique of "covered tone" or *sotto voce* (literally "under the voice"), suppress head and chest resonance to produce a clear, light, high sound. This fourth voice, says Isaac Nathan, a nineteenth-century music theorist and composer, is a "species of ventriloquism," "an inward and suppressed quality of tone, that conveys the illusion of being heard at a distance."[18]

Castrato and falsetto have been theorized mostly in terms of male voice and male desire.[19] Wayne Koestenbaum, who cites Nathan, proceeds brilliantly to connect theories of production in voice manuals with the discourse of homosexuality.[20] He suggests the so-called "unnatural" male falsetto (especially in its ornamental trill, vibrato, and tremolo), which sounds outside a "normal" range and requires long discipline, work, and training to produce, is "part of the history of effeminacy," a fourth voice "for a fourth sex, not properly housed in the body."[21]

Is singing itself "natural"? asks Koestenbaum. Are vocal registers "a fact of nature," or constructed categories of gender and sexuality? Whether "register represents a zone of opportunity or of prohibition, register-theory expresses two central dualities: true versus false, and male versus female. It is only loosely accurate to say that manuals privilege chest production as male and true, and dismiss head production as female and false," but register-theory "gives most weight to the difference between natural and unnatural," a duality that reflects, even foreshadows, he thinks, distinctions between hetero- and homosexuality.

Voice theories of the falsetto as a defective and degenerate "break" with "natural" singing are linked to medical theories of sexual perversion. As Sander Gilman remarks on "vocal stigmata": "The change of voice signaled the masculinization of the male; its absence signaled the breaking of the voice, the male's inability to assume any but a 'perverted' sexual identity."[22] Gilman notes that clinical case studies of men in the 1890s by sexologist Richard Krafft-Ebing, among others, that "regularly record the nature of the patient's voice," considered the high breaking voice a standard sign of homosexuality. More recently another medical expert, John Money, finds in the fabricated voice a defining characteristic of transsexualism: the female-to-male transsexual modulates intonation and pitch in the voice "to be more baritonal and mannish"; the male-to-female transsexual "to a feminine-sounding husky falsetto."[23]

Koestenbaum suggests the "break" between registers "(called Il Ponticello, the little bridge) is the place *within* one voice where the split between male and female occurs, and that failure to disguise this gendered break is, like falsetto, fatal to the art of 'natural' voice production."[24] Calvé and Viardot valued the break—a place of risk, of break-down, which training usually seeks to disguise or erase—as an asset.[25] So did admirers: Turgenev prized Viardot's "defective" voice for its mental as well as technical risks over "a beautiful but stupid one, a voice in which beauty is only superficial."[26] The extreme range in one female voice from richly dark deep chest tones to piercingly clear high falsetto, and its defective break at crossing register borders, produces an effect I call sonic cross-dressing: a merging rather than splitting of "butch" authority and "femme" ambiguity, an acceptance and integration of male and female.[27]

This border-crossing voice I call Sapphonic is a transvestic enigma, belonging to neither male nor female as constructed—a synthesis, not a split. Having this voice entails risk, but not a necessary loss: it can be *both* butch and femme, *both* male and female.[28] Its challenge is to the polarities of both gender and sexuality as these have been socially constructed and as stable, unchallengeable binary symmetry, for it suggests that both gender and sexuality are transferable. In acoustic effect, its combination of different registers refuses vocal categories and natural/unnatural polarities, and confounds simplistic messages about female desire (and relationships among female desire, class, age, sexual status, and identity) in music's texts and opera's roles conventionally assigned to specific female voice-types. For listeners, the Sapphonic voice is a destabilizing agent of fantasy and desire. The woman with this voice, this capacity to embody and traverse a range of sonic possibilities and overflow sonic boundaries, may vocalize inadmissible sexualities and a thrilling readiness to go beyond so-called natural limits, an erotics of risk and defiance, a desire for desire itself.

I base these observations, first, on a narrative tradition of opera and the female singing voice as these are represented by women writers in musical fictions set in European opera's so-called "Golden Age" in America, 1890 to 1915. Three of the four novels I discuss have as their central character an opera diva modeled on Olive Fremstad (1868–1951), a singer who fascinated these writers much as Viardot inspired the fiction and friendship of George Sand and George Eliot.[29] Since Sand began *Consuelo*, these writers' fictional model, with Viardot's voice, I begin with the sound of Fremstad.[30]

At the outset of her career Fremstad, a Swedish-born Minnesota immigrant, was a "deep-throated, velvet" and "luscious" contralto.[31] But like Viardot and Calvé, Fremstad resisted conventional female vocal, cultural, and sexual categories. Determined to sing Wagner's athletic Viking soprano roles to which she was physically and temperamentally suited, she went to Berlin in 1893 to study with the renowned singer and voice teacher Lilli Lehmann. By effort of will and intellect, and as Viardot, Calvé, and Lehmann herself had done, Fremstad worked her range upward tone by tone to fabricate a different, or what she called a "long," voice: "I do not sing contralto or soprano," she told writer Willa Cather. "I sing Isolde [or Carmen, Brünnhilde, Kundry, Salome]. What voice is necessary for the part I undertake, I will produce."[32] The big, defiant voice she produced was for Carl Van Vechten problematic; he called it a "refractory...not altogether tractable organ" that, like Viardot's, risked hoarse or husky intonation as it broke into head register.[33] Cather, a lesbian, heard it differently: for her its powerful range and mysterious breaking quality were magnetic and thrilling. Paradoxically, the "unnatural" voice communicates to a Sapphonic listener an effect of "wholeness and wellbeing."[34]

Fremstad gives voice to Margarethe Styr in Gertrude Atherton's *Tower of Ivory*; Thea Kronberg in Cather's *The Song of the Lark*; and Lena Geyer, actually a composite of Fremstad and singer Alma Gluck, in Marcia Davenport's *Of Lena Geyer*.[35] In Fremstad's wake, each fictional singer studies opera and voice in Berlin with Lehmann, "the greatest Norma, Fidelio, and Isolde" of her time (Davenport: 69). Each becomes successful and famous, the professional peer of turn-of-the-century divas on Maurice Grau's spectacular payroll at the New York Metropolitan Opera House.[36]

These writers represent the enormous range and flexibility in Fremstad's voice as enigmatic, border-crossing sexual allure. Styr, a Wagnerian mezzo, could sing "with the sexless, silvery sweetness of a boy chorister, which made the tremendous volume of her voice and its noble quality the more remarkable by contrast...[as it] emphasized the sensuousness of the music, and eliminated the richness from her voice" (Atherton: 411). Kronberg's voice "was as flexible as her body, equal to any demand, capable of every nuance...[it] was vitality; a lightness in the body, and a driving power in the blood" (Cather: 572, 381). Geyer was a powerful soprano with "a contralto range in her chest voice....Critics used to go wild looking for terms in which to describe it," writes Davenport. "It was pure earth, female, sex if you want to call it that. You might say that where her high tones were enchanting to the imagination, her low ones warmed the body like an embrace" (Davenport: 55).

To produce and perfect the voice they want and know they can have, in the "Künstlerroman" tradition of lesbian novels of formation, each singer must first conceal and remake an obscure or troubled past to reinvent herself as strong and independent.[37] Styr was Margaret Hill, a prostitute; Geyer a poor peasant born in Czechoslovakia; Kronberg a midwestern child of provincial Scandinavian immigrants.[38] Despite public fame, each remains a social outsider whose personal life is "kept shut up in the closet" (Cather: vi).[39] Her few male friends are safely married or professional musicians who seem to be gay.[40] The singer's most intense intellectual and emotional attachments seem to be with the "strange women" she voices onstage (Atherton: 38).

Men experience the voice as exclusion, an acoustic barrier between the singer and men who desire her. In *Song of the Lark*, when Thea returns to New York from Berlin her old friend Doctor Archie is paralysed by his sense of "dread and disappointment when she begins to sing: she was not there—for him....What he felt was admiration and estrangement" (Cather: 499–500).[41] In *Tower of Ivory*, men find Styr "an ivory fortress....Majestic, frozen....Not a man can boast that he has been received by her alone. I believe she hates men—but mortally!" (Atherton: 18, 21). Rejecting personal love, Styr seeks only "to give intense reality to impossible romance." As she becomes her roles, "her artistic imagination on fire," an avenging female desire ignites her art: "Passion is the stimulant, the drink, the food, the fertilizer for art," cries Styr. "Nurse this! Nurse this!...Let the passions of all womankind tear my heart as they tore Isolde's when they transformed her into a fate and the avenger of her sex" (Atherton: 95, 110, 281).

Lena Geyer is "suspicious and harsh" toward men whom she rejects (Davenport: 213). Her one intimate relationship is with a shy, devoted fan, Elsie deHaven, who in 1907 becomes Lena's live-in and touring companion, beloved confidante, and "invisible necessity" (216). As the fictional Elsie observes, "the world has since said many cruel things about this strange, almost passionate friendship" (208) that, in terms of its model, the intimate relationship between Fremstad ("Livan") and her biographer Mary Cushing ("Tinka"), has kept "invisible" its lesbian "necessity."[42]

If men feel estranged from the Sapphonic voice, young women who hear it are sexually aroused. On first hearing Geyer, Elsie records "how the pulse in my throat choked me. I sat letting it rush through me like electricity, completely unconscious of ever having lived before. It was exactly like the unlocking of a prison door. The voice poured into me, and from that moment it became the only thing I cared to live for....All the barriers built up by convention and habit seemed to shrivel, and I felt in those few moments a free and purposeful individual. I did not even know I was repressed, or inarticulate, yet once I felt freed, I knew that I had never lived before....The sound of her voice stayed with me, and became a physical sensation, almost like a taste, that one can recall at will" (Davenport: 225–7).

"Singing is a stream," Lilli Lehmann told singing pupils.[43] The liquid lure of Geyer's voice, its "power to conquer" and liberate, becomes for Elsie an erotic obsession: she must follow this voice no matter where and what it sings.[44] Elsie's orgasmic sensation suggests lesbian fetishism: the powerful female singing throat as phallus, its sonic stream seminal, her own throat a thirsting orifice: "The same physical thrill was there, that thing that gripped me and made something inside me leap into my ears and throat....The sensation I had was like fresh water pouring into the throat of someone nearly dead of thirst" (Davenport: 232–3).[45] Elsie acts as receptor and mediating narrator between subject and reader, singer and listener, of an erotics of same-sex desire.[46]

For Cather, too, the singing voice is vessel for a fluid stream that gushes from, and overflows, her metaphor for art as a sheath or mold that imprisons for a moment desire for life itself (Cather: 367). The voice of Cather's Thea Kronberg is a Sapphonically performative "second self": a hidden, secret, desiring self embodied in both the singer and listener who share the voice.[47] "What if one's second self could somehow speak to all these second selves in the people who cared, believed in her? It was to music, more than to anything else, that these hidden things in people responded" (273). Thea's voice teachers know that "passion" is key to her elusive and seductive vocal power (570), but in adolescence she keeps hidden even from herself the knowledge that she possesses such a voice: "It was as if she had an appointment to meet the rest of herself, sometime, somewhere" (272). Thea "meets" her second self and acknowledges eros in the voice that emerges in the "Panther Canyon" episode (367–400). Alone in a forest, sheltered in a high cliff cave, she begins to throw stones across the deep canyon, a metaphor for projecting the voice in time as well as space, for the projectiles, she learns, are broken bits of ancient clay water vessels made by Southwest Navajo women. Like the poet Sappho's textual fragments, these represent the memory of female desire and matriarchal myth, the clay vessel Cather's metaphor for the female voice as "shaping receptacle" that "speaks for desire in living human form."[48]

The Sapphonic voice as "an act of remembering" female desire (Cather: 373) is acoustically and metaphorically located and projected by Cather and Atherton in powerful female sites. These may appear to replicate man-made romantic opera's settings for the sexually powerful phallocentric woman who invites male desire (and for Fremstad's Wagnerian roles as warrior-goddess, huntress, siren-witch), but men are missing here, or are, at best, mere observers. It is matriarchal memory in Cather's forest, cave, and water vessel that awakens Thea's desire. A dark, impenetrable forest (in the opening chapter of *Tower of Ivory*) conceals Margarethe Styr from the male gaze, protecting her from men who can hear but who are themselves unseen. Here Styr, like Fremstad the Wagnerian diva of the Munich Opera House, may sing not for men but for herself alone.[49]

In these narratives of the solo singing voice as female desire and intertextual channel of mimetic desire—a desire fostered by desire among the woman who sings, her fictional listener, the woman who writes, her fiction reader—lesbianism is "the thing not named," as Sharon O'Brien observes of Cather herself.[50] A greater challenge to patriarchal stories in the cultural context of turn-of-the-century opera in Europe is the novel *As Music and Splendour* by Irish writer Kate O'Brien, which shows Sapphonics at work in two voices and *within* an openly acknowledged lesbian relationship between lovers who are both also opera singers.[51]

While I have been speaking of Sapphonics as integration of sameness and difference in one solo and undivided voice, what happens when there are two? Women's paired like-voices produce a bivocal Sapphonic effect especially, but not only, in travesty/transvestic duets formerly sung by castrati. (By "bivocal" I mean having two like-voices that inhabit like-bodies that together produce bisexual illusion: the sonic effect of having both sexes in one.) The castrato, argues musicologist Joke Dame, voiced sexual difference in going against the grain of a dominant oppositional male-female pairing.[52] Modern substitution of male tenor and female soprano in duets for castrati cannot match the interchange and interweaving of body, timbre, and pitch paired castrati produced, because their registers are too far apart. When we exchange two female like-voices for castrati configurations, and their "two equal voices rub up against each other, pressing into dissonances that achingly resolve only into yet other knots," we experience female desire differently.[53] If the castrato, the borderline man, subverts desire for symmetrical binary difference, two paired castrati reinstate desire for symmetrical bivocal sameness. If the travesty female, the borderline woman, voices female desire as Sapphonic transgression, two paired women in symmetrical bivocal sameness voice Sapphonic desire as lesbian difference: a doubly subversive symmetry in redoubled vocal drag.[54]

Kate O'Brien's explicit lesbian voices are neither competitive with one another nor separable from roles they share, both those in her plot and those they sing. As Music and Splendour tracks two vocal paths that meet and bond in travesty duets, endure tests in travesty lament, are avenged and reunited "as one" in warrior-goddess roles, and part only as two solo careers demand. O'Brien represents lesbian desire as equal, mutual, like-voiced, in three distinctive musical contexts: Bellini's opera Norma and the travesty laments and duets of Gluck's opera Orfeo and Pergolesi's Stabat Mater.

When Clare Halvey and Luisa Carriãga meet as students in a Paris convent singing school, Luisa is a "natural" mezzo who "always...has been attracted to women—and afraid of that attraction" (O'Brien: 293), but Clare's voice and sexuality are in mysterious "armoured" contest: her voice "a vessel, a battlefield, a pausing place for argument between spirit and flesh, union or divorce" (13). After they become lovers, Clare's voice changes. Men now find it "unusual...a bit too cold, perhaps? It's like a boy's voice...she sang like a castrato" (248). Refusing opera's conventional mad/bad "feminine" roles as inauthentic "lunatic" excess (212), Clare casts herself in "grave, or tragic, or royal" roles "disguised as a boy or man" (240). Although each is loved by a man, the lovers are separated by neither male desire nor lesbian stigma, but their profession as singers. "As your life is, so is hers commanded by her singing voice" (293), and to love a singer is to share that voice: O'Brien leaves open the possibility that lesbian voices reunite.

As Music and Splendour represents the travesty Orfeo as lesbian continuum. As Calvé was a vocal stand-in for Natalie Barney, Viardot, "master in her art" (79), is both vocal model and travesty tradition for Luisa and Clare. At La Scala, where Clare hears a long-lost Luisa as Orfeo singing Viardot's own cadenzas, she moves toward the voice, shocked by its beauty, to embrace her.[55] When Clare is invited to sing Euridice to Luisa's Orfeo, they become lovers for whom the opera Orfeo represents a transcending mask between private revelation of forbidden desire and its necessary public concealment: "The disguise of myth in which they stood [hand in hand] was their mutual reality, their one true dress wherein they recognized each other, and were free of that full recognition and could sing it as if their very singing was a kind of Greek, immortal light, not singing at all" (113).

In this novel's travesty context, the lament, a female song tradition, voices lesbian loss and suffering. When Tom, a composer in love with Clare, and Iago Duarte, Clare's voice teacher who loves Luisa, intervene to oppose their relationship, the embattled lovers sing Pergolesi's *Stabat Mater*, a sequence of instrumentally accompanied vocal solos and duets on a medieval mourning text that Pergolesi scored in 1736 for paired castrati. As Philip Brett observes, the *Stabat Mater* is "a musical paraliturgical version of the Pietà, the true representation in Christianity of castration and its complexes."[56] Its performance represents for Clare and Luisa a "public ordeal" to be shared and endured after "private shame"(299), but their interwoven voices, in sustained and ornamented counterpoint above slowly ascending harmonic steps and throbbing pulse, effect in grief a kind of ecstatic victory.

As metaphor for female resistance to male desire, Kate O'Brien and Cather each position in their narratives a major opera aria (one central to the repertories of Viardot, Calvé, and Fremstad) from Bellini's *Norma*. In the "Casta Diva," the Druid warrior-priestess prays to the moon goddess for peace between Romans and Gauls only to discover that Pollione, her Roman lover, has been unfaithful. O'Brien places the "Casta Diva" at a decisive crossroad for the lovers, reunited once again at La Scala, the site of their first travesty *Orfeo*. Luisa listens in tears to Clare sing the "Casta Diva," her "breast and brain lighted within by the fire-clear singing" (244), but while they are afraid that the men who desire them will divide them, this aria anticipates lesbian renewal and bonding. It also marks a defining scene in Cather's novella, *My Mortal Enemy*.[57] Richard Giannone interprets Cather's use of the "Casta Diva" as a metaphor for Myra Driscoll's personality, division of loyalties, decision, and fate: the story and opera "both treat a heroine's reconciliation of the opposing obligations of sacred and profane love."[58] An alternative reading suggests the "Casta Diva" may encode an unacknowledged lesbian bond in narrator Nellie Birdseye's passion for Myra. For, in the opera, where the aria represents division (man between women), it precedes the like-voice duet for Norma and Adalgisa, "Mira, O Norma" in act 3, scene 1, that represents synthesis and symmetry (between two women): the breaking point at which these former rivals become confidantes who renounce men and vow lasting friendship:

> I shall be your friend and companion
> The world is wide enough to shelter us both

I shall look destiny steadily in the face
While I can feel your heart beating close to mine.

Kate O'Brien's adaptation of Orphic myth differs markedly from Cather's in *The Song of the Lark*, but in both narratives lesbian desire recognizes in the disguise of opera its "one true dress" and "reality." O'Brien ends her novel with Clare's physical and sonic separation from Luisa, her lover and "second self." In the vocal and travesty tradition flowing from Viardot, Calvé, and Fremstad, Gluck's opera *Alceste* inscribes that loss: "She would sing the cold high story for herself, and for one who could not hear" (O'Brien: 328). Thea Kronberg, however, sings her opera story for a "second self" who could and did hear: her living vocal model, Olive Fremstad.

When Cather first met and interviewed this notoriously private and reclusive singer before she began the novel and they became close friends, Cather reassuringly allowed that "the opera glass will never betray any of Madame Fremstad's secrets."[59] Making Thea's story a composite of her own youth in Red Cloud, Nebraska, and Fremstad's in Minnesota, Cather devised a bivocal counterpoint between writer and subject that "does not simply describe an opera or its effects but creates an imaginary opera."[60] Paradoxically, the disguise of opera as it intrudes on fiction may reveal a private reality both this writer and this singer, the writer's opera-singing subject, concealed in public and from their public. In effect, the cross-dressing "William Cather, Junior," who dared not openly name herself or her relationships lesbian, voiced *her* Orphic myth as *Fremstad's* Sapphonic code.[61]

Thea's first music teacher is Professor Wunsch, a tragic figure whose name means desire, but whose desire falls short of the discipline music demands. A failure professionally, Wunsch gives Thea what she emotionally needs: his score of Gluck's *Orfeo* and his memory of Viardot's voice in "the most beautiful opera ever made" (Cather: 89). Orfeo's lament is Wunsch's sad adieu to music, Thea's awakening desire in and for music. "When Wunsch plays, and Thea sings of a life without the thing one needs most, the reader is invited to participate aurally at the moment when two talents, following separate paths on the Orphic landscape, intersect."[62] Thea's voice, I think, invites the reader to participate aurally in the landscape of lesbian operatic life and listening.

Olive Fremstad, the living voice of literary narratives that create imaginary operas, participated like the fictional singers Clare and Luisa in operatic narratives that create Sapphonic space. In opera, Viardot, Calvé, and

Fremstad voiced travesty and transgressive female roles. What if Sapphonic voices belong to lesbian bodies? Does the question of lesbian biography matter only to lesbians who trace traditions?

I mean next to "hear" Sapphonics in opera and social contexts: turn-of-the-century opera roles that venture into unconventional sexualities, and a lesbian artistic milieu centered on Paris.

Facts don't exist. The sole truth lies in a tone of voice.[63]
—Ned Rorem, *The Later Diaries of Ned Rorem*

In a biographical tradition of the female celebrity, especially the opera diva, that stresses marriage and maternity as much as gossip about scandalous heterosexual liaisons, an absence of data may imply sexual nonconformity or difference. Lacking information, or refusing to name evidence at hand, biographers regard the private lives of Calvé and Fremstad as "elusive." Calvé apparently never married. A close friend of Colette, obviously known to the Paris-Lesbos circle of Barney and Vivien, she plays no part in their biographies, nor they in hers. Fremstad is shown to have married in 1906 and separated soon afterward; a second marriage in 1916 to a much younger man lasted six weeks and was apparently not consummated. Between "marriages," Fremstad lived with Mary Cushing, her "buffer" and secretary-companion, closet code words for a lesbian partner. Nothing at all is told of Fremstad in later life except that she was "difficult" and reclusive. Unacknowledged butch-femme implications in Cushing's blithe account of her relationship with Fremsted seem obvious to a lesbian reader today. Cather, too, had been immediately and powerfully attracted on first hearing, then meeting Fremstad—and Fremstad unusually accessible and attentive—as they embarked on an intense, enduring friendship. No biographer of Cather or Fremstad has named that lesbian.

Significant in these Sapphonic intertexts, although not my main focus here, is the voice of Fremstad's contemporary, Mary Garden (1874–1967).[64] What did Garden, who never married, mean in saying "I never really loved anybody. I had a fondness for men, yes, but very little passion and no need"?[65] What does it mean that Fremstad and Calvé "may have belonged, like Garden, to those who live in the parts they play"?[66] What can we learn of the Sapphonic landscape from roles these singers "lived" in public?

In both standard and new repertory, Calvé, Fremstad, and Garden built careers as actor-singers on powerful, seductive interpretations of transgressive heroines and travesty "breeches" roles. Each defied stage convention in her uses of dramatic realism, revealing costume, and often scandalous publicity.

Garden's repertory was especially sexually adventurous: as Chrysis in Camille Erlanger's *Aphrodite* (1906), an opera with two lesbian roles and based on the novel by Pierre Louÿs; as the cross-dressed Egyptian queen of Massenet's *Cléopâtre* (1914) who, disguised as a boy, visits a brothel and makes love to another boy. Famed for her overtly sexual Mélisande, Thaïs, and Salome, Garden also sang Mozart's travesty Cherubino and Massenet's travesty title role as *Le Jongleur de Notre Dame*, a tenor part as a fifteen-year-old boy for which she produced a light, pure, high voice.[67]

Calvé's most notable roles were the travesty Cherubino, Salome's mother Hérodias in *Hérodiade* (Massenet's version of Salome), Salome herself, and Carmen.[68] A "volcanic" stage personality, Calvé's Carmen was admired by George Bernard Shaw for its "power of seduction," display of "naked animality," and passionate method acting. Shaw found her interpretation neither romantic, noble, nor sentimental, but intense, truthful, brave, temperamental, and direct. Her death scene was "horribly real."[69] Calvé had studied genuine gypsy dance to prepare for Bizet's fake ones, just as Fremstad visited a morgue to practise handling a severed head for her role as Strauss's Salome.

Listeners who thought Fremstad's "an introverted art" were astounded at her Kundry in *Parsifal* for its wild physical ferocity and "dangerous" seductiveness. Her "lascivious" Salome so outraged New York society ladies that it was withdrawn after one performance.[70] Lesbians saw this diva as Amazon warrior. On holiday with Fremstad in her Bridgeport, Maine, summer house and watching the singer catch and clean fish, swim, row, tramp, chop wood, Cather felt she was "living with the wife of the dying gladiator in her prime in deep German forests," while Cushing saw "an athletic young Goddess. With her fine legs and lean haunches [she] would have made a handsome boy."[71] In Munich early in her career, Fremstad played travesty roles; wearing breeches, her Carmen (Munich, 1902) was a seductive "masculine" woman who made "no physical approach" to Don José. At forty-three, she was still drawn to youthful woman-as-boy cross-dressed roles: in 1911, after seeing the premier in Vienna of *Der Rosenkavalier*, it was Octavian, not the Countess, she wanted to sing.[72]

These singers were especially known for their title roles in *Carmen* (1875) and *Salome* (1905), axes of a repertory of late nineteenth-century French opéras comiques that are named for their transgressive heroines. Created by Massenet, Delibes, Charpentier, Chabrier, and others, these include *Lakmé*

(1883), *Manon* (1884), *Gwendoline* (1886), *Thaïs* (1894), *Louise* (1900), *Hérodiade* (1904), *Aphrodite* (1906), *Thérèse* (1907), and *Cléopâtre* (1914).[73] Two, named for Sappho and now little known, convey a sense of the way a fictional tradition has been kept alive and shaped both by male fantasies of Sappho's voice as political defiance, sexual excess, and risk, and—even more buried and unnamed—by female singers and listeners who heard that voice Sapphonically.[74]

Emile Augier derived the libretto for Gounod's first opera, *Sapho* (1851), from Théophile Gautier's novel, *Mademoiselle de Maupin* (1835). While musically Gounod was influenced by Gluck's operas, his heroine is no tragic Lesbian of Mytilene playing her lyre alongside Gluck's travesty Orfeo or Alceste. Nor is she the cross-dressed seducer of Gautier's fiction with both a male and a female lover. Gounod's Sappho is a thoroughly bourgeois hetrosexual fiction: the scandalous schoolmistress doomed to suicidal despair when she sacrifices her love of Phaon the boatman for a greater political cause; who identifies with the myth of Hero and Leander before hurtling off a cliff to drown.

Henri Cain and Artur Bernede based their libretto for Massenet's *Sapho* (1897) on the novel by Alphonse Daudet (1884). Daudet's contemporary temptress and whore is in Massenet's opera the bohemian prostitute Fanny Legrand, a commodified artists' model for a statue titled "Sapho." When a chaste country lad, Jean Gaussin, falls in love with her, she tries to remake herself as the virtuous Sappho with fantasies of married love until a former lover, La Borderie (sic), and the sexual subculture Fanny has spurned, disclose to Jean her true identity. Fanny is doomed to lose Jean and return to her old ways.

Both operas are an exciting trove of Sapphonic intertextualities. Gounod created the role of Sappho specifically for the voice of Viardot.[75] Massenet's Fanny was written for Calvé, for which she used her fourth voice.[76] Before the premier at the Paris Opéra Comique on 27 November 1897, Calvé studied the role with novelist Daudet, whose son Lucien and his lovers Proust and Cocteau were among her friends. Before the opera disappeared from the repertory, Garden sang Fanny for the Manhattan Opera House production in New York on 17 November 1909. Fanny Legrand, I believe, may be a composite portrait of two lesbians: Clotilde Legrand ("Cloton"), the model for Proust's fictional Madame Leroi and onetime lover of Barney's lover, the artist Romaine Brooks; and the singer Georgette Leblanc, who recorded scenes from this opera accompanied by Massenet. Leblanc, a feminist and lesbian, and onetime mistress of Maurice Maeterlinck, was vocal and dramatic model for *Ariane et Barbe Bleue* (1907), Maeterlinck's opéra comique composed by Paul Dukas.[77]

However these operas when first performed may have been received by lesbian listeners, the novels of Gautier and Daudet "gripped the imagination" of opera-loving Cather in her cross-dressing "bohemian" phase as a journalist in the 1890s. Daudet's *Sappho*, a "cult item" among Cather's select circle of friends in Lincoln, Nebraska, confused as much as it confirmed her lesbian identity. It "involves shades and semitones and complex motives, the struggling birth of things and burnt-out ghosts of things," Cather wrote, "that it baffles psychology to name."[78] Sharon O'Brien, discussing Cather's review of a song recital by contralto Clara Butt, whose "The Enchantress" was "Circe-like" and "unnatural," suggests that what Cather may have thought she heard Butt envoice was the familiar "femme fatale" of French Sapphic fictions: an enticing but deadly and degenerate lesbian as viewed through male eyes. The envoicing in French Sapphic opera and song of a female desire at erotic odds with the voice in Sappho's poetry may baffle the lesbian listener—unless, that is, the singer (a Viardot, Calvé, Garden, or Marilyn Horne) queers the text.

The *statue* of Sappho in Massenet's opera (as much as the portrait of Sand that Cather enshrined in her room) is a recognizably transvestic emblem with a queer sense of history. Daudet derived for his novel the stone image of the woman cross-dressed as a man to seduce another woman from Gautier's poetic transposition in his novel of the Sapphic statue in an earlier novel, *Fragoletta* (1829) by Henri Latouche. In Gautier's poem, the (presumably male) narrator who gazes at the statue wonders "Is it a young man? Is it a woman?" The Enigma doesn't explain itself. It makes itself heard as the Sapphonic *voice* the poem's title encodes. That is: "Contralto."[79]

French opéras comiques are a promising source for lesbian and feminist study of narratives based on contemporary novels and plays, and contextualized by political, religious, social, and psychological realism, that vocalize the powerful female Other as a threat to patriarchal order.[80] Arguably the most controversial of these are Bizet's *Carmen*, based on Prosper Mérimée's Spanish gypsy tale, and Strauss's *Salome*, Oscar Wilde's pseudobiblical and Oriental drama. Carmen and Salome represent renegade figures of unbridled sexual passion: gypsy and Jew as the exotic, feminized, non-Western Other, the object of the male gaze whose return of the gaze with teasing defiance, scorn, or indifference enhances her allure for male desire.[81]

Carmen, chronologically the first, is important to my argument on several counts. First, *Carmen* marks a Sapphonic shift in power and gender in opera, a takeover by the female body and the female voice made inevitable by the disappearance of the castrato, when the vocal dominance of the high coloratura soprano of bel canto singing is displaced by the dramatic mezzo of contemporary verismo.

Like Bellini's Norma and Adalgisa, the role of Carmen was created for the strong but flexible middle register of the dramatic soprano, a compass similarly required in the lighter textured female travesty roles of Cherubino, Octavian, Bellini's Romeo, Orlovsky in *Die Fledermaus*, Siebel in Gounod's *Faust*, and the Composer in *Adriadne auf Naxos*, but also exploited in heavier mezzo roles that call for great agility and power: the travesty Leonore in *Fidelio*, Saint-Saëns's Dalila, Puccini's Minnie, the barkeeping pioneer in *La Fanciulla del West*, and the explicitly lesbian role of Countess Geschwitz in Berg's *Lulu*. Vocally, however, only Carmen, Dalila, and Gluck's Orfeo are truly dominant roles in the sense that they are not required to compete with big powerful sopranos placed above them.

Female sexuality and desire in *Carmen* may only seem to fit conventions of gender-appropriate behavior that punish risk-takers and nonconformists. Micaëla, the "feminine" (and soprano) mediator, bears both maternal and patriarchal messages in the mother's letter, money, and kiss; Carmen, "messagère" of promiscuity, is the envoy of death. But Carmen is a resisting or "dissonant Other," notes Susan McClary, whose voice, "marked by chromatic excess," is more powerful and alluring than the men she dominates.[82] Her "object of desire is desire itself," says Nelly Furman.[83] Her voice is heard Sapphonically as defiant rupture and escape from patriarchal order. But, opera tradition insists, runaway female desire, Carmen's "rebel bird," must be captured, caged, crushed. While her voice may be dominant, the central role in the *narrative*, McClary reminds us, is not Carmen, but Don José: his story and fantasy "organizes the narrative" and ensures that the threat of female desire is contained.[84]

Second, *Carmen's* representation both of female desire as dominant and defiant, and of the cultural oppression of the sexual outsider, is *the* vocal and dramatic model for the operas of the lesbian composer Ethel Smyth (1858–1944), who, I believe, heard *Carmen* Sapphonically.

Smyth first heard *Carmen* performed in 1883 when she was a composition student in Leipzig and bought the full score to study. It became her favorite opera, perhaps for reasons that attracted her gay friend Tchaikovsky, who admired its "easy naturalism" in characters "whose feelings and experience I shared and understood."[85] The opera's theme of social and cultural oppression of an illegal, clandestine outsider who refuses fixed conventions of sexuality and gender and resists oppression resonates with gay and lesbian experience.[86] "As a Gypsy, there is no fixed place for Carmen," observes Catherine Clément. "At the moment of her death, [she] represents the one and only freedom to choose, decision, provocation. She is the image, foreseen and doomed, of a woman who refuses masculine yokes and who must pay for it with her life."[87]

That image of a feminist revolutionary who wants to be free of male desire, and free to love whomever she desires, came to be for Smyth, as, I believe, for Calvé and Fremstad, a Sapphonic figure and voice of rebellion and emancipation.

Smyth created the literary as well as musical narratives of her operas. She first conceived the story and characters, plotted the scenario from which she and her friend Harry Brewster collaboratively drafted a libretto, then reshaped the text as she composed to fit first her short vocal score, then the full orchestral score underlaid with dialogue, production notes, and cued performance directions. Moreover, Smyth shaped both sound and story to suit her own voice.

Her songs and opera parts for female voice fall predominantly in her own midmezzo range. Hers was not a professionally trained singing voice. "Real" singers thought her voice production "all wrong," she stated, but her main concern was to "make a pleasant noise, and to manage that every word should go straight home to my listeners—not a difficult thing to accomplish, if you mean what you say and *accompany yourself*."[88] In fact, she found her voice a great asset, using it to striking effect in making her music known to those who might produce it. To give the dramatic sense of a complete opera, she sang all the parts, including orchestral effects, to her own keyboard accompaniment.

Into her voice Smyth poured all the force and magnetism of her personality and musicianship. "The rare and exquisite quality and delicacy of her voice: the strange thrill and wail, the distinctive and distinct clear utterance...and the whirlwind of passion and feeling she evoked" seems to have fascinated friends, lovers, and professional musicians alike.[89] Some found her singing enigmatic, "the spirit of her strange, wild, suffering, striving heart, whose secrets none could fathom."[90] Others, for whom Smyth's secrets were an open book, heard not one voice but many: the contrapuntal sounds of "her true self...more startlingly revealed in her singing" than in her conversation or correspondence.[91]

In her songs, Smyth created Sapphonic space for the female singer-lover to voice lesbian desire. She admitted to using her own singing voice to "bribe" or lure women she loved with her music, and to addressing her beloved in the travesty voice of a lovesick pageboy.[92] Her music challenges an untrained voice, for it requires great strength and agility; even trained singers have complained of its technical risks. Productions of her first three operas were mostly under-rehearsed, poorly conceived, and ill-cast, factors which led Smyth to conduct her own work. In old age, in her memoir, she noted in all her theater experience only one triumph that gave her satisfaction: the Covent Garden premier of her second opera, *Der Wald*, in 1902, her London debut as an opera composer. Fremstad sang Iolanthe, Smyth's mezzo heroine, in her own London debut season.[93]

Der Wald was produced the following year at the New York Metropolitan Opera without Fremstad and with less success, the first, and, to this day, only opera by a woman composer produced there. Then in 1905 Calvé announced, "I *must* create the part of Thirza," the leading mezzo role in Smyth's new opera *Les Naufrageurs*, for a Covent Garden premier under André Messager and at Monte Carlo.[94] As plans for a production in French faltered, Calvé announced her retirement. The opera was translated into English as *The Wreckers* but first performed in Leipzig in 1906 as *Strandrecht.* Had Calvé intended Thirza to be her opera swan-song?

These events seem more mysterious to me than coincidental. My question is: what induced these internationally renowned divas at the peak of their careers to want to premier untried operas by a little-known composer—what is more, an English composer, a woman, a lesbian—when much new music, especially opera, failed professionally or was never performed? Consideration of fame or fortune seems irrelevant. Was it the quality or originality of the work? The composer's persistence? A personal connection?

I want to explore two possibilities. First, that these singers may have belonged as Smyth did to a homosocial and homosexual community of artists who performed one another's work. Second, that Calvé and Fremstad may have responded to Smyth's work as they had to *Carmen* and contemporary operas that broke with gendered conventions of women's social, sexual, and vocal categories, only more so. For here was a new woman-shaped and women-centered opera especially suited to their voices and a Sapphonic tradition of female difference and desire.

Smyth has a pivotal role in both that tradition and community. As a promising young music student of twenty-two, engaged in her first lesbian relationship, she had met through personal friendship with Clara Schumann the "master," Viardot. Twenty years later, if not at Covent Garden then through their mutual friend the Wagnerian diva and mezzo Anna von Mildenburg, Smyth met Fremstad. She was almost certainly introduced to Calvé by the Princess de Polignac (1865–1943), with whom Smyth was disastrously in love. The princess was behind the plan to have Messager produce *Les Naufrageurs* with Calvé in Monte Carlo or at the Théâtre de la Monnaie in Brussels, the venue for new French opera.[95]

The princess is central to my questions because she was central to a well-financed urban artistic community, a homosexual subculture in Paris that included expatriate Anglo-Americans, whose members actively promoted and performed one another's work. Born Winnaretta (Winnie) Singer, an American heiress, the princess was herself a cultivated pianist and painter, a lesbian married to a gay French composer, Prince Edmond de Polignac, whose niece Armande was also a composer. Their grand salon on rue Henri Martin, where mirrored windows reflected black and gold ceiling murals painted by Jose-Maria Sert of naked and reclining "Sapphic creatures voluptuously disporting themselves with monkeys and bacchic masks,"[96] was the *belle époque* scene of frequent concerts of both classical and new music generously commissioned or subsidized by the Polignacs from Fauré, Satie, Ravel, Debussy, Albeniz, Manuel de Falla, Reynaldo Hahn, Poulenc, Kurt Weill, and Stravinsky.[97]

In the 1890s, Oscar Wilde was a personal friend. Proust, his lover Lucien Daudet, Valéry, and Cocteau frequented the salon. So did artists, including Picasso, Juan Gris, Romaine Brooks (one of the princess's lovers) and John Singer Sargent, and dancers and musicians such as Ida Rubinstein, Wanda Landowska, Diaghilev, and members of the Ballet Russe. Isadora Duncan, onetime lover of Winnie's brother Paris Singer, danced for them in 1900. Lesbians in Winnie's inner circle included her lovers Olga de Meyer and Violet Trefusis, and writers Anna de Noailles, Augustine Bulteau, Vernon Lee, and Radclyffe Hall. Calvé certainly, Fremstad possibly, were part of this community, together with Smyth.

There can never be a question of competing with men but an everlasting one of creating something different…something yet unvoiced [that] lies at the bottom of the sea, where we are at home.[98]

—Ethel Smyth

During the decade 1896 to 1905 when Smyth composed *Der Wald* and *Les Naufrageurs*, what experiences, sounds, and stories that she heard or read may have suggested ways to express her vision of a "yet unvoiced" oceanic space of Sapphonic creativity and desire?

The subject of homosexuality and Sapphism continued to fascinate Smyth long after she came out to Brewster in correspondence in the early 1890s, and forms a continuous leitmotif in her conversations and correspondence with women. To friends in 1899 while "obsessed with *Der Wald*," she recited by heart the erotic Sapphic verses of Swinburne's *In Anactoria*. In 1902, as she planned *Les Naufrageurs*, she was absorbed simultaneously in Swinburne's passion for the sea in *Songs of the Springtides* (1880) and in an Italian criminology text that discussed "il terzo sesso" as a "perversion of the maternal instinct" in "old maids" devoted like herself "to dogs and politics."[99]

Smyth's memoirs illustrate not only her access and acceptance into aristocratic circles that sponsored her music but, more indirectly, her own proximity as a musician (and that of many of her upperclass friends and sponsors) to homosexual subcultures. In 1902, shortly before she joined the Polignacs' inner sanctum, and while awaiting in Berlin the premier of *Der Wald* as a guest of the German chancellor, Prince Bernhard von Bülow, and his wife, she twice met and dined with Kaiser Wilhelm II, and sang for his all-male company "banal songs" composed by Count Phillip Eulenberg, who accompanied her on the piano. No other women were present: "I suspect Madame [von] Bülow proposed me as a sort of man," Smyth said.[100] Within five years, both von Bülow and Eulenberg were subject to court trials in what became known as the Eulenberg Affair, a "stunning" scandal "in the history of the Second Reich...which turned upon the alleged homosexuality of the chancellor and of two distinguished members of the entourage of Kaiser Wilhelm II" (including the amateur composer Eulenberg), and which produced, according to James Steakley, the "same sort of 'ritual of public condemnation' that the Oscar Wilde trial had been for Victorian England in 1895."[101]

Another of the Kaiser's intimates, the Greek scholar Count Ulrich Wilamowitz-Moellendorff, who dined with Smyth after the Berlin performance of *Der Wald*, gave her a "new Sapphic fragment" he had translated, adding "that he considered Sappho the most maligned of women; that she really was a sort of high-school mistress, and that the famous 'passions' were simply cases of harmless response to the Schwärmerei of her pupils!" Smyth was otherwise convinced: "I dismissed this depressing view of 'burning Sappho' from my mind!"[102]

The historical fate met by Sappho and creative women troubled Smyth as she composed *Der Wald*. In April 1900, after the fiasco of her first opera *Fantasio*, her visit in Paris to the Irish-born composer Augusta Holmès (1847–1903) depressed her for its reminder of the obscurity to which the work of women composers, especially opera, was consigned.[103] The music of Holmès, like her own, evinced "by turns a charming tenderness, ardent passion, and masculine spirit."[104] Both women worked independently of the musical establishment; both wrote their own librettos. All of Holmès's operas (*Astarté*, *Lancelot du Lac*, and *Héro et Léandre*) were unperformed and unknown with the exception of *La montagne noire* (in four acts), produced at the Paris Opéra in February 1895. Smyth's efforts after their meeting to organize English performances for Holmès failed.[105] "I feel I must fight for *Der Wald* also," Smyth wrote, "because I want women to turn their minds to big and difficult jobs; not just to go on hugging the shore, afraid to put out to sea…[I]n my way I am an explorer who believes supremely in the advantages of this bit of pioneering."[106]

In Weimar in 1898, shortly before Smyth began the score of *Der Wald*, and while awaiting the premier of her first opera, *Fantasio*, she heard for the first time a performance of Gluck's *Orfeo* which marked "a milestone in my musical life": "I do not think I ever sobbed so unmanageably in public as then."[107]

Although her first three operas derive their motivic, structural, and instrumental techniques from German opera, especially Wagner, Smyth never wholly succumbed, as so many contemporary composers had, to Wagner's rapture with mystical eroticism.[108] Her music counterbalances a German romantic influence with the rugged dance rhythms and robust folksong melodies of her native English music and a French musical tradition of order, clarity, and (in opera) antisentimental realism. Her personal score collection contained operas by Bizet, Massenet, Berlioz, and Gounod alongside Mozart, Beethoven, and Wagner, and song collections by Fauré and Duparc as well as the German Lieder repertory.[109] Smyth shared an affinity with French culture and music, acquired in childhood from her Paris-born mother, with Harry Brewster and Vernon Lee, both born in Paris of part French parentage. In turn, Debussy and Fauré, whom she met through Winnie Polignac, admired both *The Wreckers* and her songs on French texts whose performance in Paris in 1908 Fauré helped organize.[110]

Smyth "wrangled" over Brewster's story idea for *Der Wald* on bicycle tours with him in Wales in 1895 and northern Italy in 1896. His scenario described

> a short and tragic story of passion, framed in the tranquility and everlastingness of Nature represented by the Forest and its Spirits. These Spirits or elemental forces are seen engaged in ritual observances. Unshackled by Time, they sing their own eternity, and the brevity of things human. A peasant girl, Röschen, is engaged to a young woodcutter, Heinrich. Iolanthe's horn is heard: merriment vanishes; terror-stricken the peasants fly. The lovers invoke the protection of the forest. Iolanthe is a woman of cruel instincts and unbridled passions, supposed to be a witch and dreaded with superstitious fear. She has complete sway over Rudolf, the liege lord of the country, whom she despises as a weakling. Struck by Heinrich's good looks she tries to detach him from his bride and make him enter into her service. Complaints and reproaches from Count Rudolf; anger and defiance on her

part. Her fascinations fail, however, to prevail over Heinrich's love for Röschen. He rejects [Iolanthe] and prefers love, which is deathless and mighty, to life which is weak and brief. Iolanthe gives the order and he is slain. The Spirits of the Wood take up their ritual.[111]

The score, begun in 1899, was completed in October 1902. The Berlin production (five performances) was a nightmare: while it was still in rehearsal the director collapsed and died, orchestral players rebelled at the changes and delays, and on the first night at the curtain a hostile claque booed and catcalled. Support gathered on subsequent evenings. Three months later, Fremstad and a "splendid cast" at Covent Garden gave Smyth "my only real blazing theatre triumph. I more or less trained all the principals myself, and of course the chorus."[112] Innovations by the producer, Francis Neilson, dispensed with footlights and proscenium lights throughout the drama. Neilson found the opera "strange and beautiful," and critic J. A. Fuller Maitland admired "a work of highly romantic character…by one who had mastered not only all the secrets of stage effect, but who understood how to make her climaxes impressive, and how to differentiate her characters."[113]

To a widowed female friend who objected that the opera made "illicit love-making" too "melodious and positive," Smyth defended: "[I]n fact…a highly moral little tale: a short poignant tragedy—an episode—the real story being the eternal march of Nature that enwraps human destiny and reeks nothing of the joys and sorrows of mortals, [not that] Iolanthe falls in love with the hero and has him killed because he would not meet her views."[114] But Iolanthe dominates the story. A younger friend, Maggie Ponsonby, amused Smyth by remarking that her heroine was "the type of woman who is all pearl necklace, bosoms, and rampant desires," but Maggie's mother heard Iolanthe's voice Sapphonically. Lady Mary Ponsonby, one of Smyth's great passions, told her that the opera, "from beginning to end, made me feel as I do when you are singing."[115]

The reviewer for *The New York Times* praised its performance at the Metropolitan Opera House on 11 March 1903, with the gendered term critics reserved for uppity women who risked the larger symphonic and opera forms: "The opera sounds the note of sincerity and resolute endeavor. [Smyth] uses the vocal and orchestral resources with masculine energy, and is not afraid of employing the most drastic means of modern expression."[116]

Even before her voyage to America, Smyth formed the idea for her third opera during a visit to Cornwall in October 1902, where she heard old-timers' strange tales of an intolerant, hypocritical religious community that once plundered passing ships after luring them on the rocks with false lights. She lay "on the cliffs, listening to the boom of the great Atlantic waves against those cruel rocks, and the wild treble cries of the seagulls."[117] In her memoir, she asks rhetorically: "Did I pick up down there a legend of two lovers who, by kindling secret beacons, endeavoured to counteract the savage policy of the community; the woman impelled by humanity, and perhaps hoping that her action might palliate her unfaithfulness to her husband, her lover because for her sake he was ready to take any risk; how they were caught in the act by the Wreckers' committee—a sort of secret court which was the sole authority they recognized—and condemned to die in one of those sea-invaded caverns?[118] Or did this story come to me in my sleep? I cannot say."[119] Could not? Would not? Was Smyth disingenuous?

During the Covent Garden season of *Der Wald*, and shortly before Smyth's Cornish journey, her friend Vernon Lee stayed with her. The first rough draft of the new libretto, *Les Naufrageurs* (hereafter *The Wreckers*) was finished in November, and Smyth began the score in the spring of 1903 on her return from New York.[120] Lee again visited her in England. At the time, Smyth was infatuated with Winnie Polignac, Lee with Augustine Bulteau, to whom Lee dedicated her newly published novel, *Penelope Brandling: A Tale of the Welsh Coast in the Eighteenth Century*.[121]

The story, setting, period, and heroine of Lee's novel are strikingly similar to Smyth's subsequent opera. A drunken, disgusting family of murderous wreckers lures ships to the Welsh shore and plunders them. A newly married couple, Sir Eustace and Penelope Brandling, returns from abroad to claim from the wreckers, his kin, the estate of St. Salvat as its rightful heirs. His wicked, lecherous uncle, Hubert, a preacher, having killed Eustace's older brother, conspires to imprison and poison husband and wife when they discover the wreckers' crimes. With Penelope's help, Eustace blows up the entire estate to obliterate all trace of the community, but both must then return to exile, where Penelope records this story in her diary for her grandchildren to read after her death.

Smyth has never mentioned Lee's novel. If she read it while composing her opera (I must assume she did), she would find in Penelope a model of Sapphonic courage and resistance. In Hubert's words, she is "a virago...a warlike lady" and "woman of spirit" (Lee: 174–5). Undeterred by what she considers weakness and paralysis of will in her husband, Penelope tackles Hubert alone: "I take it upon myself to judge and put you to death as a wrecker and a murderer," she says, and shoots him dead

Nor did Smyth acknowledge any musical influence on *The Wreckers* but the sounds of waves, wind, and seagulls. Jane Bernstein has traced Wagnerian influences in both operas: the forest setting and theme of salvation through death in *Der Wald*, and in *The Wreckers* her use of ballad-aria form and a close resemblance between the principal motif of her overture and the open-ing phrase in Wagner's overture to *Der fliegende Holländer*. Bernstein also finds that Smyth's "evocation of the sea and characterization of an isolated sea town" are "typical of an English opera" and, in turn, influenced Britten's opera *Peter Grimes* (1945).[122]

I suggest *Carmen* as the major vocal and dramatic influence on Smyth's representation of Iolanthe and Thirza, although Smyth both adapts and subverts that model. In *The Wreckers*, Thirza takes central position: the story is hers. Where Carmen joins an oppressed band of gypsy smugglers who are themselves outsiders, Thirza, who is twenty-two years old, is initially part of the dominant group of superstitious Cornish wreckers by virtue of her marriage to its leader and pastor, the fifty-five-year-old Pascoe. She is in love with Mark, a young fisherman who sets himself outside the community by lighting beacons to warn off the ships. For her adultery and betrayal, Thirza is doubly (sexually, socially) an outsider who must violently be cast out. Having wrecked the wreckers' livelihood, the lovers are judged and con-demned to drown in a cave that floods at high tide. As the community denounces her as "a vile priestess of dark evil," a "foreign" and "polluting" witch and whore, Thirza scornfully refuses to repent. Like Carmen, she curses, threatens, laughs in their faces. As death nears, she sings an exultant bridal song, her anticipated bliss first echoed, then inundated, by the wild rhythms of waves, wind, and sea, and the dark cave that is womb and tomb of her desire lit suddenly by sunlight streaming through its roof.

"To love is to die and newly-awaken," sings Thirza, and to make sense of her rapturous spiritual and sexual communion with death depends on how we read opera's "irrational romantic marriage between the erotic and the deathly" when voiced by a Sapphonic heroine.[123] And, indeed, on how Smyth read it. Marriage to death for Smyth's Thirza, as for Carmen, is not, like death in marriage, a necessary or arbitrary fate imposed by men, but a chosen act of feminist defiance. Like Carmen, Thirza is no passive sacrificial victim. She chooses her own death before others decide it for her. In an ecstasy of self-knowledge, death inscribes, then sets free, her sexuality.

Who or what is Thirza? Her name is associated with feminine discord, death, and the fetishized phallus.[124] She is a transvestic figure. Marjorie Garber discusses Byron's lament "To Thyrza" as "an act of poetic transsexu-alization in elegiac verses."[125] Hearing the echo of Thyrza's voice ("All that once was harmony/Is worse than discord to my heart"), the poet laments the death of John Edlestone, a choirboy when they met in Cambridge, and com-pares their homoerotic relationship to that of the biblical Jonathan and David. Smyth, too, *names* in her heroine an association with same-sex desire, not within the opera plot but to signify her own transvestic relationship to her "character"—an act of self-travesty that simultaneously travesties opera conventions of sexual disguise, ambiguity, and desire in powerful female roles. When deliciously unselfconscious, Smyth can be pure camp: as she completed the music to act 2 she sent off a telegram to Brewster that read, "Safely delivered of fine female child name Thirza Rampagia Smyth."[126]

Thirza is a strong dramatic mezzo. In duets with her lover her voice is generally pitched lower, as if to support his youthful tenor. Mark's similar vocal range does not exploit its full tenor possibilities, suggesting his immaturity or, since they are not yet lovers, dependence on the stronger woman. In Mark's first ballad-aria, for which he impersonates the voice of a lovesick woman, the minor-mode folksong melody and his gesture of flinging a flower in Thirza's window is camp Carmen. In her desire and vocal dominance, Thirza acts as Carmen's "rebel bird" when, fleeing marital authority, she tells Pascoe his "cage is empty" (act 2).

Another direct but inverted link with *Carmen* is provided in the "feminine" role and soprano voice of nineteen-year-old Avis, who, unlike the "good" Micaëla in *Carmen*, is destructive, jealous, manipulative, deceitful. She has believed herself loved by Mark, who underestimates and trivializes her desire for him. In a variety of revengeful postures, Avis first fights for Mark, then takes a younger rival (Jack, aged fifteen) and wrongly betrays Pascoe before finally denouncing Thirza. In act 1, her song "The Rat" is a violent adaptation of Carmen's *Chanson Bohème*, "Les tringles des sistres tin-taient," which begins act 3 in *Carmen*, with identical rhythm, tonality, and melodic phrases. Her taunt, "Scarce a man but has loved her—guard what's yours lest you lose it; take care lest you lose her," evokes Carmen's ironic habañera: "Love comes, it goes, and then returns; You think you hold it fast, it flees; You think you're free, it holds you fast."[127]

In act 1 of *The Wreckers*, a same-voice bivocal love scene between Avis and young Jack produces a Sapphonic effect because Jack is voiced by a mezzo-soprano. The two pairs of lovers (Thirza/Mark, Avis/Jack) have a different vocal effect from male-female couplings in traditional opera ensembles: their matched registers suggest mutual rather than disparate partnerships. Smyth's general tessitura is low-voiced—two tenor, two bass, one baritone, one soprano, two mezzo voices—an arrangement quite unlike the high female-dominated tessitura and texture in contemporary operas by Puccini and Strauss, for example, that represent the high voice as feminine dementia, hysteria, and excess. Smyth's Sapphonic voices, like her own, are unsentimental, powerful, and defiant in expressions of desire.

Iolanthe has that voice in *Der Wald*. She is proud, active, forceful, lustful. Smyth's description of her as "beautiful but terrible" recalls Micaëla's "elle est dangereuse, elle est belle" of Carmen in act 3, and Carmen's self-representation as "Never will Carmen give in; Free she was born, free she will die." The imperious huntress Iolanthe has something of Carmen's predatory carnal voluptuousness. Having tried to seduce Heinrich, she takes her revenge when he prefers Röschen and refuses to follow and serve her. Iolanthe orders her hunstmen to stab him, and poor innocent Röschen dies of grief. Like *The Wreckers, Der Wald* is a contest over female power, but Iolanthe is neither betrayed, as Thirza is, by a jealous female rival, nor, like Carmen, killed by the male victim of her desire. It is the weak who perish, not the woman men fear as a witch "who blights our maids, our youths with her devouring lust" (vocal score: 38). Leaving behind a trail of human destruction, with desire intact, if not humanly gratified, Iolanthe rides back into the forest whose eternal maternal spirits have protected and nourished her. Her mezzo voice of considerable dramatic power represents a conquering and unconquerable force of female desire.

Shortly before Smyth began *The Wreckers*, she visited a village in Calabria to observe a woman dance "seductively and with supreme rhythm" the rapid, accelerating measures of the tarantella, a Southern Italian folk dance. The frenzied dance that ends Smyth's first act is as emphatic and reckless as any in *Carmen*. Her dark cliff setting for *The Wreckers* is the same wild, perilous scene of *Carmen's* act 3. Caves; forests; rocky, barren shores in Smyth's operas may represent "the outlaw world of passion" that Nietzsche characterized in *Carmen* as contested sites of "mortal hatred" in the "war of the sexes" or, rather, according to Nelly Furman, a contest between polarities within each gender, between contradictory desires.[128] For Smyth's operas, as for the novels of Cather, Atherton, and Davenport, I prefer to think of these as Sapphonic sites of female power. Where convention may find a Don José, Pascoe, and Heinrich a male victim, each the cruel dupe of a woman who uses sex to entice and debase him, I hear a Carmen, Thirza, Iolanthe as a revolutionary feminist figure, each the Sapphonic voice of a woman's sexual rebellion and emancipation. No wonder a Fremstad, a Calvé, wanted to sing them.

Amour, amour, tu es l'éclair
Qui bondit comme un cris de joie.

Smyth was ill, sick with unrequited passion for Winnie Polignac, when she set these words to music for Thirza's first aria in *The Wreckers*.[129] Passion helped her to work, she said.[130] She thought this "one of the best things" she had done, except perhaps the orchestral prelude to act 2, "On the Cliffs of Cornwall," which she dedicated to Winnie.[131] But her joy in the opera was diminished by disastrous productions and a terrible press in Leipzig and Prague, and eclipsed by Brewster's death of cancer a few days after the London concert premier of acts 1 and 2. That performance, however, marks a further link in the Sapphonic continuum: Thirza was sung by the mezzo Blanche Marchesi, daughter of Matilde Marchesi who had trained Calvé.[132]

The Wreckers has never received the production, cast, and critical attention it deserves, although musicians agree it is Smyth's greatest achievement. Thomas Beecham, who conducted the first production in London on June 22, 1909, found it "one of the three or four English operas of real musical merit and vitality."[133] Bruno Walter, who met Smyth "carrying under her arm the score of her opera, clad in a nondescript baggy dress" when she called on Mahler in Vienna and sang all the vocal parts for Walter, conducted both the overture in 1909 and the full opera at Covent Garden in 1910. To Walter she was "a true composer...remarkable for the consuming fire of her soul."[134] Twenty years later he told how "I still feel the fascination of the scene of Thirza and Mark, the smell of the sea in your music to the final scene...the great passion in the musical language of your work."[135] Both men agreed the opera demands full professional treatment, skilled musicians, and gifted singers to do it justice. Smyth's Thirza still awaits her Calvé.

To find and fit her own creative and singing voice, Smyth took what was musically available to her both from a vocal tradition of a strong, flexible, wide-ranging, and risk-taking female voice, and from an opera tradition in which that voice represents unconventional, but powerful and seductive roles, images, and sites. Perhaps she also drew upon her experience as a lesbian, which told her there were musicians and listeners who would hear that voice as Sapphonic memory and desire. If that knowledge was largely hidden, shared only by a few singers, writers, and musical friends, Smyth could still be true to lesbian experience, yet use musical tradition and operatic convention as a way publicly to express her theme of the social and cultural oppression of homosexual desire and difference, and her lesbian vision of desire as "something yet unvoiced [that] lies at the bottom of the sea, where we are at home."[136]

Notes

Earlier parts of this essay were read at conferences in July 1991 on Feminist Theory and Music (University of Minnesota) and Music and Gender (King's College, University of London), and to my colleagues in the women's biography seminar at the New York University Institute for the Humanities, the Women's History Colloquium of Sarah Lawrence College, and the Gay and Lesbian Study Group at Columbia University. I thank these listeners and organizers, especially Lydia Hamessley, Sophie Watson, Nicola LeFanu, and Patrick Horrigan, for their Sapphonic responses. The voices of friends, especially Philip Brett, Suzanne G. Cusick, Joke Dame, Lawrence D. Mass, Susan McClary, and Suzanne Raitt, have inspired my own. I am particularly grateful to Wayne Koestenbaum, Sharon O'Brien, and Kate Stimpson for their own work, as well as generous suggestions and enthusiasm for mine.

1. Hélène Cixous, "Tancredi Continues" (1983), trans. and reprinted in *"Coming to Writing" and Other Essays*, ed. Deborah Jenson, with introductory essay by Susan Rubin Suleiman (Cambridge: Harvard University Press, 1991), 79.

2. "Voice" and "singing" in Don Randel, ed., *The New Harvard Dictionary of Music* (Cambridge: Harvard University Press, 1986): 926–7, 749–50.

3. "Lesbian continuum" is Adrienne Rich's term (1980) "Compulsory Heterosexuality and Lesbian Existence" in *Blood, Bread, and Poetry: Selected Prose 1979–1985* (New York: W. W. Norton, 1986), 23–75. Susan Gubar discusses women "coming to writing" through identification with Sappho in "Sapphistries," *Signs* 10, no. 1 (Autumn 1984): 43–62.

4. A Sappho poem warns, "If you are squeamish,/ Don't prod the beach rubble," but legend has it that after the Maenads dismembered Orpheus to avenge the Sirens whose vocal power and knowledge he had named his own, it was on Lesbos that his severed head, still singing, washed ashore. *Sappho; A New Translation* by Mary Barnard (Berkeley: University of California Press, 1958), 84. Joan de Jean raises mid-nineteenth-century French discussions of "Orphic life" (pederasty and "masculine loves") and Sappho as the female Orpheus in *Fictions of Sappho 1546–1937* (Chicago: University of Chicago Press, 1989), 220, 270.

5. Lesbian opera-loving readers of my essay say it voices what they have always only known intuitively. Trained singers ask: "How did you know? I *am* that voice!" Although I focus here on the trained opera voice, queer studies of pop vocalists also show Sapphonics at work: see Patricia Juliana Smith, "'You Don't Have to Say You Love Me': Dusty Springfield as White Soul Sister, Female Drag Queen, and Lesbian Diva," paper read at the fifth annual Lesbian and Gay Studies Conference, Rutgers University (November 1991), and Martha Mockus on k. d. lang in this volume.

6. "Un panier de framboises" in *HOW(ever)* 5/2 (January 1989): 3–5. Where Patrice Titterington translates "disperse moins" as lowering the voice, I understand dispersal as a breaking up and scattering about in particles.

7. Hector Berlioz, *Gluck and His Operas, with an account of their Relation to Musical Art (1915)* trans. Edwin Evans (reprint Westport, Conn.: Greenwood Press, 1973), 19–20, 14–15. Viardot reports how she "discovered three good ways of delivering the motif. The first time, sorrowful amazement, almost motionless. The second, choked with tears (the applause lasted two minutes, and they wanted an encore!!!), the third time, outbursts of despair. My poor Euridice remarked, as she arose, 'Mph! I thought that would last forever!'" in "Pauline Viardot-Garcia to Julius Rietz (Letters of Friendship)," trans. Theodore Baker, *Music Quarterly* 2 (1916): 44–6.

8.   Jean Chalon, *Portrait of a Seductress: The World of Natalie Barney*, trans. Carol Burko (New York: Crown, 1979), 76–7, 89.

9.   Louise Héritte-Viardot, *Memories and Adventures*, trans. E. S. Buchheim (1913), (reprint New York: Da Capo Press, 1978), 102–105 (emphasis mine).

10.   John Eliot Gardiner, "Hands Off 'Orfeo!'" and Tom Hammond, "'Orphée et Euridice': Gluck's final solution" and "A note on the aria di bravura 'L'espoir renaît dans mon âme'" in Patricia Howard, ed., *C. W. von Gluck: Orfeo*, Cambridge Opera Handbooks" (Cambridge: Cambridge University Press, 1981), 112–18, 105–11.

11.   Both Viardot (who sang both soprano and contralto roles in the same production of *Robert le Diable*) and her sister Maria Malibran (1803–1836) had this huge range. Nellie Melba, with a similar range, like Calvé was trained by Matilde Marchesi in vocal methods originated by Viardot's father Manuel Garcia and brother Manuel, the most famous voice technicians in Europe in the nineteenth century: Henry Pleasants, *The Great Singers from the Dawn of Opera to Our Own Time* (London: Gollancz, 1967), 85. The younger Manuel Garcia, inventor of Laryngoscopy, considered that voice register is produced "solely by the difference in the tension and the vibration of the vocal chords," not in the chest or throat. The other parts of the larynx influence only timbre: Appendix I in Louise Héritte-Viardot, *Memories and Adventures*, 257.

12.   Just how rare is it? Bernard Holland's recent review of the voice of Cecilia Bartoli echoes reports of Viardot and Calvé: "an important and rarely found phenomenon, an authentic coloratura mezzo-soprano darkly beautiful in sound, and able…to negotiate the vocal hazards of Mozart and Rossini arias." Bartoli's Sapphonics "turned her audience into quivering jelly. Nothing seems merely technical or calculated, though technique and calculation are behind a lot of what she does," *The New York Times* (22 August, 1992): C2.

13.   Paul Robinson, *Opera and Ideas: From Mozart to Strauss* (Ithaca: Cornell University Press, 1986), 174–77.

14.   Effects also exploited by black American lesbian blues singers Ma Rainey, Bessie Smith, and cross-dresser Gladys Bentley in Harlem in the 1920s.

15.   Henry Chorley, *Thirty Years' Musical Recollections* (London: Hurst and Blackett, 1862), quoted in Rupert Christiansen, *Prima Donna: A History* (New York: Viking, 1984), 79, 81.

16.   Shawe-Taylor thought Calvé's chest voice by comparison "luscious, dark, seductive, honeyed." Desmond Shawe-Taylor, "Emma Calvé, 1858–1942," in *Opera* 6 (1955), 220–23, reprinted, Harold Rosenthal, ed. *The Opera Bedside Book* (London: Gollancz, 1965), 63–68.

17.   Her fourth voice is heard on *Emma Calvé: Diva de la Belle Epoque* in songs by Gounod and an excerpt from *Carmen* recorded 1908, reissued by Fondation France Telecom (1990): MM–30365. Calvé's memoirs are excerpted in Georges Giraud, ed., *Emma Calvé*, (Paris: Millau, 1983). Sarah Vaughan, an American popular vocalist with the same range, also acquired a head voice falsetto.

18.   Isaac Nathan, *An essay on the History and Theory of Music, and on the Qualities, Capabilities and Management of the Human Voice* (London: Whittaker, 1823), 63. The term "musico" for the castrato was sometimes applied to a mezzo-soprano who specialized in male roles: on these voice types, see Christiansen, *Prima Donna*, 85, 358.

19.   Earlier gay studies of diva worship among opera queens, and camp impersonations (vocal voguings?) of vocal and sexual excess in the high female coloratura of bel canto singing, include Wayne Koestenbaum, "I Could Go On Singing: Diva Vocal Crisis," paper read at the fourth annual Lesbian and Gay Studies Conference, Harvard University (October

1990), and Lawrence D. Mass, "Homosexuality and Music II: A Conversation with George Heymont," in *Homosexuality as Behaviour and Identity: Dialogues of the Sexual Revolution*, vol. 2 (New York: Haworth Press, 1990), 55–77. Koestenbaum's new, brilliant book on queer listening is *The Queen's Throat: Opera, Homosexuality, and the Mystery of Desire* (New York: Poseidon Press, 1993).

20. Wayne Koestenbaum, "The Queen's Throat: (Homo)sexuality and the Art of Singing," in Diana Fuss, ed., *Inside/Out: Lesbian Theories, Gay Theories* (New York: Routledge, 1991), 205–34, reprinted in *The Queen's Throat*, 154–75.

21. The terms of a late nineteenth-century medicoscientific discourse that categorized the lesbian as neither male nor female but an ambiguously androgynous and immature "third" sex are applied in voice manuals to the castrato and prepubescent boy chorister, respectively.

22. Gilman links this voice to anti-Semitism as well: as the supposed speech of Jews, the breaking voice set Jews apart as separate and strange: Sander L. Gilman, "Strauss and the Pervert," in Arthur Groos and Roger Parker, eds., *Reading Opera*, (Princeton: Princeton University Press, 1988), 322–23, n.45.

23. Money, as quoted by Marjorie Garber, *Vested Interests: Cross Dressing & Cultural Anxiety* (New York: Routledge, 1992), 106. Also see Michel Poizat, *The Angel's Cry: Beyond the Pleasure Principle in Opera* (Ithaca, N.Y.: Cornell University Press, 1992).

24. Koestenbaum, "The Queen's Throat," 220.

25. cf. Maria Callas, who did not value it; who, after radical reconstruction of body and image, broke down and lost her voice. Koestenbaum, "The Callas Cult," in *The Queen's Throat*, 134–53.

26. Quoted as preface to Carl Van Vechten, *Interpretations* (New York: Alfred A. Knopf, 1920) (my translation), first published as *Interpreters and Interpretations* (New York: A.A. Knopf, 1912).

27. The Sapphonic voice is thus a metaphor for the inclusive role-playing entity proposed by Sue-Ellen Case, "Toward a Butch-Femme Aesthetic," in Lynda Hart ed., *Making a Spectacle: Essays on Contemporary Women's Theatre* (Ann Arbor: University of Michigan, 1989), 282–99.

28. "I no longer know whether my 'they' is masculine or feminine," says Cixous. "Listen. I say Tancredi, I'm not saying a woman; I could, but nothing is that simple. Listen: Rossini doesn't say that the hero, in order to be Tancredi, must be haunted by a woman's voice. He performs it." Cixous, "*Coming to Writing*," 80.

29. Rebecca Pope suggests Viardot's portrayal of Gluck's Orfeo inspired Eliot's verse drama, *Armgart* (1871), ironically a story of a great opera singer who refuses to abandon her career to marriage but loses her voice. See "The Diva Doesn't Die: George Eliot's *Armgart*," in Leslie C. Dunn and Nancy A. Jones, eds., *Embodied Voices: Female Vocality in Western Culture* (Cambridge: Cambridge University Press, forthcoming), and Susan Rutherford, "The Voice of Freedom: Images of the Prima Donna," in Vivien Gardner and Susan Rutherford, eds., *The New Woman and Her Sisters: Feminism and Theatre 1850–1914* (Ann Arbor: University of Michigan Press, 1992): 95–114.

30. George Sand, *Consuelo: A Romance of Venice* (1842, reprinted New York: Da Capo Press, 1979). Sand and Viardot were close friends, possibly lovers: Lillian Faderman, *Surpassing the Love of Men: Romantic Friendship and Love between Women from the Renaissance to the Present* (New York: William Morrow, 1981), 457, n7.

31. Mary Watkins Cushing, *The Rainbow Bridge* (1954, reprinted New York: Arno Press,

1977), 13, and Van Vechten, *Interpretations*, 16.

32. Sharon O'Brien, *Willa Cather: The Emerging Voice* (New York: Oxford University Press, 1987), 447. Lehmann's voice, travesty roles, and relationship with Fremstad also belong to Sapphonic legend. Ever disingenuous, Cushing repeats a rumor that the crisis that broke their relationship was Fremstad's "alleged romance" with Lehmann's husband, but insists there were no male lovers, "no scandals," in Fremstad's closet; Cushing, *The Rainbow Bridge*, 179.

33. Van Vechten, *Interpretations*, 11, 16.

34. Cather, *The Song of the Lark* (1915, reprint Boston: Houghton Mifflin, 1943), 236. Given Cather's ambivalence about her lesbian identity and "feminine friendships," and her identification of creativity with masculinity and her deviancy as male, her ideas on the female singing voice as a "natural," unsocialized force, rooted in the body, not dependent on a man, are problematic. Sharon O'Brien directs me to Cather's letters in the 1890s to Louise Pound, where she uses a "natural/unnatural" polarity in terms of voice, and see O'Brien, *Willa Cather*, 131, 134; and Eve Kosofsky Sedgwick, "Across Gender, Across Sexuality: Willa Cather and Others," *The South Atlantic Quarterly* 88, no. 1 (Winter 1989): 53–72.

35. Soprano Alma Gluck (1884–1938), who appeared with Fremstad at the New York Metropolitan Opera House from 1909 to 1912, was Davenport's mother; see Barry Paris, "Unconquerable Marcia Davenport," Profiles, *The New Yorker* (22 April 1991): 42–88; Gertrude Atherton, *Tower of Ivory: A Novel* (New York: Hurst, 1910); Cather, *The Song of the Lark*, preface and revisions by Cather, 16 July 1932; and Marcia Davenport, *Of Lena Geyer* (New York: Charles Scribner's Sons, 1936). Subsequent quotations are to these editions.

36. For added realism, a fictional Toscanini conducts Geyer's New York debut, a Mahler those of Kronberg and Styr. Grau's divas included Lehmann, Calvé, Nordica, Eames, Farrar, Melba, Tetrazzini, and Fremstad, who in 1905 was one of the Met's highest-paid singers, earning $1382 per single performance, at ten per month, when the average monthly income for a New York family was $850; Christiansen, *Prima Donna*, 184–8.

37. "Künstlerroman" as a novel of formation depicting the awakening and growth of a lesbian artist is discussed in Bonnie Zimmerman, "Amazon Expedition: The Lesbian Self," in *The Safe Sea of Women: Lesbian Fiction 1969–1989* (Boston: Beacon Press, 1990), 33–75.

38. Fremstad was adopted by a Swedish couple who migrated to St. Paul, Minnesota when she was twelve: see William Moran's brief biography concluding Cushing's *The Rainbow Bridge*.

39. In her preface to the revised edition of *The Song of the Lark*, Cather says Kronberg's story is the reverse of Oscar Wilde's *The Portrait of Dorian Grey*: "the harassed, susceptible human creature comes and goes, subject to colds, brokers, dressmakers, managers. But the free creature, who retains her youth and beauty and warm imagination, is kept shut up in the closet, along with the scores and wigs" (vi).

40. In lesbian fiction, gay artists who mediate between lesbian lovers and represent sexual experience but not a sexual threat include Jeremy Brockett in Radclyffe Hall, *The Well of Loneliness*, and Matthew O'Connor in Djuna Barnes, *Nightwood*. But as in many lesbian fictions, Davenport suppresses lesbian meaning in her novel by ending with a marriage of convenience between Geyer and an aged, widowed friend.

41. In a remarkable metaphor that turns the male gaze on itself, and inverts hunter into hunted/haunted, Archie calls this an attack of "buck-fever" comparable to elk hunting: "when a man's mind is so full of shooting that he forgets the gun in his hand and is

paralyzed when the target stares back at him" (Cather, *Song of the Lark*, 498–99).

42. Cushing describes a seven-year relationship with Fremstad as her companion, colleague, buffer, and junior partner as one of enchantment and willing enslavement; Cushing, *The Rainbow Bridge*, 69, 86, 111, 120.

43. Lilli Lehmann, *How to Sing*, trans. Richard Aldrich (1902, reprinted New York: Macmillan, 1960).

44. The quotation is by Willa Cather in James Woodress, *Willa Cather: A Literary Life* (Lincoln: University of Nebraska Press, 1987), 257.

45. Marjorie Garber discusses fetishism as "foundational to theater itself" and made possible in a theatrical space, in "Fetish Envy," chapter 5, *Vested Interests*, 118–27. See also Teresa de Lauretis, "Perverse Desire: The Lure of the Mannish Lesbian," in *Australian Feminist Studies* 13 (Autumn 1991): 15–26; and Elizabeth Grosz, "Lesbian Fetishism?" in *differences; A Journal of Feminist Cultural Studies* 3/2 (Summer 1991): 39–54.

46. In a similar argument, Sharon O'Brien considers narrator Nellie Birdseye's "acknowledged and unacknowledged investment in the subject is the story itself" in Cather's *My Mortal Enemy*; quoted in Richard Giannone, *Music in Willa Cather's Fiction* (Lincoln: University of Nebraska Press, 1968): 310.

47. For Cather, a woman's voice is an instrument or a medium of feeling and idea that communicates directly between creator and receiver: Giannone, *Music in Willa Cather's Fiction*, 7–8, 10.

48. Giannone, *Music in Willa Cather's Fiction*, 243, and see O'Brien, *Willa Cather*, 136.

49. Only when a young married man's desire threatens her career does an undefended Styr/Brünnhilde stage the death of desire by self-immolation. In a private midnight performance of *Götterdämmerung* staged for King Ludwig, Wagner's queer patron and Styr's never-seen admirer, she deliberately rides to her death in the blazing funeral pyre.

50. O'Brien's title is derived from Cather's idea that music (a "text without words") enters a realm beyond language to convey to a listener "the thing not named," in Willa Cather, *Not Under Forty* (New York: Alfred A. Knopf, 1936), 50; see O'Brien "'The Thing Not Named': Willa Cather as a Lesbian Writer," in Estelle B. Freedman, Barbara C. Gelpi, Susan L. Johnson, Kathleen M. Weston, eds., *The Lesbian Issue: Essays from Signs*, (Chicago: University of Chicago Press, 1985), 67–90. Gertrude Atherton, notable for her depictions of female sexual desire, suggests lesbian possibilities in the relationship between two women in *Perch of the Devil* (New York: Stokes, 1914); see Emily Wortis Leider, *California's Daughter: Gertrude Atherton and Her Times* (Stanford: Stanford University Press, 1991).

51. Kate O'Brien, *As Music and Splendour: A Novel* (London: Heinemann, 1958).

52. Joke Dame, "Unveiled Voices: Sexual Difference and the Castrato," in this volume.

53. Susan McClary's delicious queer phrase in *Feminine Endings: Music, Gender, and Sexuality*, (Minneapolis: University of Minnesota Press, 1991), 37. Philip Brett suggests the counter-tenor as a substitute for castrato can also be figured into the equation. Listeners might compare the fit: countertenor duets by Alfred Deller and John Whitworth in Purcell's ode, *Come All Ye Sons of Art* (1694; recorded L'Oiseau-Lyre 1958) or Catherine Gayer, soprano, and Brigitte Fassbënder, contralto, in *Il giardino di Amore* (ca. 1700; recorded DGG 1964), a serenade for two castrati by Alessandro Scarlatti and the vocal model for a duet between a fictional castrato (the hero Tonio in the soprano role of Adonis) and female contralto (the Contessa as Venus) in the living presence of Caffarelli (1710–1783), the most famous of all great castratos whom Bartolo refers to in the Lesson scene of

Rossini's opera *Il Barbiere di Siviglia*. The fiction is by Ann Rice, *Cry to Heaven* (New York: Alfred A. Knopf, 1982, reprint New York: Ballantine, 1991), see Afterword, 534. Rice consulted historical records, vocal methods, and medical experts; this portion of her novel was actually written to Scarlatti's music. Rice represents the "man playing a woman" as an illusion, "a complete lie" (370), a "defiance, knowing what others couldn't possibly know" (372–3), and erotic appropriation of the female voice: "It was as if he wanted the Contessa's voice, and she knew it. His voice was seducing her voice, not merely for its answers but for that moment when the two would come together in one song" (311).

54.　A vocal *and* visual drag, for example, by Arsace in Rossini's opera *Semiramide*, a solo female travesty voice of the female-as-man, the lost and found son who is in love with his/her mother. Octavian in *Der Rosenkavalier* and Cherubino in *The Marriage of Figaro* voice redoubled vocal drag as the female-as-man who cross-dresses as a woman who desires a woman.

55.　Viardot's handwritten cadenza to the aria "L'espoir renaît dans mon âme" is reproduced in Howard, *C. W. von Gluck*, 95.

56.　Conversation with Philip Brett. For a challenging discussion of castration and the "sonorous envelope of the maternal voice" in her reading of Julia Kristeva's texts "Stabat Mater" and "Motherhood According to Giovanni Bellini," see Kaja Silverman, (4) "The Fantasy of the Maternal Voice: Female Subjectivity and the Negative Oedipus Complex" in *The Acoustic Mirror: The Female Voice in Psychoanalysis and Cinema* (Bloomington and Indianapolis: Indiana University Press, 1988), 101–40.

57.　Willa Cather, *My Mortal Enemy* (1926, reprint New York: Vintage Classics, 1990).

58.　Giannone, *Music in Willa Cather's Fiction*, 180.

59.　Cather's article in *McClure's Magazine* as quoted in Christiansen, *Prima Donna*, 186.

60.　Herbert Lindenburger, *Opera, the Extravagant Art* (Ithaca: Cornell University Press, 1984), 191.

61.　Fremstad "loved" the novel, according to Edith Lewis, the woman who lived with Cather for forty years. See Edith Lewis, *Willa Cather Living: A Personal Record* (New York: Alfred A. Knopf, 1953), 92.

62.　Giannone: *Music in Willa Cather's Fiction*, 89.

63.　Ned Rorem, on the inadvisability of trying to make connections between homosexuality and music, in *The Later Diaries of Ned Rorem, 1961–1972* (San Francisco: North Point Press, 1983), 433.

64.　Mary Garden and Geraldine Farrar (another Sapphonic figure) together provide the composite portrait of Kitty Ayrshire in two stories by Willa Cather: "Scandal" and "The Gold Slipper." Diva Lillian Nordica inspired Cather's story "The Diamond Mine." While in lesbian contexts Garden is for me a Sapphonic figure, Wayne Koestenbaum tells me in conversation that she is equally the "quintessential diva adored by gay men, especially in camp contexts," a convergence in queer listening that would make a fascinating study. Farrar, who also studied voice with Lilli Lehmann, had an "appeal always as potent to girls as it was to men." Claques of besotted teenage girls "who screamed and waved flags at the stage door on Farrar nights were christened the Gerryflappers," see Christiansen, *Prima Donna*, 191–92, and Farrar's autobiography, *Such Sweet Compulsion* (New York: Greystone Press, 1938), 133, 216.

65.　Mary Garden and Louis Biancolli, *Mary Garden's Story* (New York: Simon & Schuster, 1951), 272, and Christiansen, *Prima Donna*, 277.

66. Pleasants, *The Great Singers*, 308.

67. Van Vechten, *Interpretations*, 72, 196, and Pleasants, *The Great Singers*, 312. Garden's voice in excerpts from *Thaïs* and *Le Jongleur* (recorded 1911–1912), and as Mélisande to Debussy's piano accompaniment, is heard on OASI Historical Recordings CD 7001.

68. Pleasants, *The Great Singers*, 358, and see Emma Calvé, *My Life*, trans. Rosamond Gilder (New York: D. Appleton, 1922).

69. Shaw, quoted by Pleasants, *The Great Singers*, 308, 303–7 and see Christiansen, *Prima Donna*, 272–4.

70. *Salome* was not again produced at the New York Metropolitan Opera until 1933. In 1907 Mary Garden also caused a sensation as Salome, performing her own dances at Oscar Hammerstein's rival Manhattan Opera House; Christiansen, *The Great Singers*, 186, 188.

71. Cather, quoted in Woodress, *Willa Cather*, 258; and see Cushing, *The Rainbow Bridge*, 56.

72. Cushing, *The Rainbow Bridge*, 54; see also Francis Neilson, *My Life in Two Worlds*, vol. 1 (1867–1915) (Appleton, Wis.: C. C. Nelson, 1952), 207–14.

73. Offenbach's contemporary satiric parodies of opéra comique include *Orfée aux enfers* (1858).

74. The following paragraphs are excerpted from "Vocal (S)exchange," my study in progress, where I also discuss the opera *Sappho* (1960) by Peggy Glanville-Hicks, who derived her libretto from the verse play by Lawrence Durrell (1950), the only opera on Sappho I have found composed by a lesbian. For a discussion of the Gautier and Daudet Sapphic fictions, see de Jean, *Fictions of Sappho*, 259–65.

75. Viardot's creation of powerful political roles as Norma, Valentine (*Les Huguenots*), and Fidès (*Le Prophète*) and travesty roles as Alceste and Leonore (Fidelio) also inspired Saint-Säens's creation of mezzo-voiced Dalila. In 1872, five years before *Samson et Dalila* premiered, Viardot sang Dalila for the composer in a private audition. Marilyn Horne records two arias from Gounod's *Sapho* on Editions Costallat (1985): MCE 75170.

76. Calvé recorded Fanny's aria, "Viens, m'ami," in 1919, reissued on Fondation Telcom CD: MN 30365.

77. See Austin B. Caswell, "*Ariane et Barbe Bleue*: A Feminist Opera?" paper given at the annual meeting of the American Musicological Society, Baltimore (November 1988). Terry Castle discusses Leblanc's lesbian *ménage* in her essay, "In Praise of Brigitte Fassbaender (A Musical Emanation)," forthcoming in *The Apparitional Lesbian: Female Homosexuality and Modern Culture* (New York: Columbia University Press, 1993). I am grateful to Terry for her dazzling discussion of "Sapphic diva-worship" and "homovocality."

78. William M. Curtin, ed., *The World and the Parish: Willa Cather's Articles and Reviews, 1893–1902*, (Lincoln: University of Nebraska Press, 1970) and quoted in Sharon O'Brien, *Willa Cather*, 136.

79. Faderman, *Surpassing the Love of Men*, 254, 263.

80. The vast repertory of operas set in foreign landscapes, cultures, and societies, along with issues of gender, race, class, and sexuality these operas raise, is an enticing field of inquiry for lesbian and feminist musicologists. See Marjorie Garber's chapter, "The Chic of Araby," a compelling discussion of the erotics of Western cultural appropriation of the Eastern Other and of cultural fantasies such as Wilde's *Salome* played out "in cross-dressing as well as in homo- and bisexual relations between East and West, European and Arab," that develop as Westerners "look East" for "role models and deliberate cultural masquerade" to a "place of liminality and change," a "site of transvestism as escape and rupture," in Garber, *Vested Interests*: 304–52. Also see Ralph P. Locke, "Constructing the

Oriental 'Other': Saint-Säens's *Samson et Dalila*" in *Cambridge Opera Journal* 3, no. 3: 261–302.

81. "Foreigners are necessary to assume the strangeness of a woman who is not really a woman," Catherine Clément says of the opera diva with the strange name (Callas, Caballe, Sontag, Malibran), the opera heroine (Carmen, Isolde, Butterfly) who is a foreigner even in her own "country," and the foreign language of opera itself. While Clément considers racism, imperialism, and patriarchal power in *Carmen*, it is ironic she ignores the huge influence on French operas, her own language and culture, of the feminist figure of Carmen: *Opera: Or the Undoing of Woman* (1979), trans. Betsy Wing (Minneapolis: University of Minnesota, 1988), 30, 58–59, 48–53.

82. McClary, *Feminine Endings*, 57.

83. Nelly Furman, "The Languages of Love in *Carmen*," in Arthur Groos and Roger Parker, eds., *Reading Opera* (Princeton: Princeton University Press, 1988), 176.

84. McClary, *Feminine Endings*, 58, 66.

85. Tchaikovsky, as quoted in Hamish Swanston, *In Defence of Opera* (London and New York: Penguin, 1978), 270.

86. Mérimée, childhood tutor of the Empress Eugénie, learned the story of Carmen from her Spanish mother. The empress was Smyth's friend, neighbor, and sponsor of her work, and possibly discussed with Smyth political and sexual overtones in the opera concerning the Second French Empire whose fall in 1870 brought about her exile in England. Among the Empress's many homosexual friends was the writer Lucien Daudet, Proust's lover and the son of Alphonse Daudet whose *Sapho* (1884) inspired Massenet's opera.

87. Clément, *Opera*, 48.

88. Ethel Smyth, *As Time Went On...* (London: Longman's, Green and Co., 1936), 129.

89. Maurice Baring, *The Puppet-Show of Memory* (Boston: Little, Brown, 1922), 139–40. Sargent's charcoal sketch of Smyth singing (the National Portrait Gallery, London) is discussed by Suzanne Raitt in "The Singers of Sargent: Mabel Batten, Elsie Swinton, Ethel Smyth," paper read at the conference on Music and Gender, King's College, University of London, in July 1991.

90. Sylvia Pankhurst, *The Suffragette Movement*, quoted in Christopher St. John, *Ethel Smyth: A Biography* (London: Longmans, 1959), 153.

91. St. John, *Ethel Smyth*, 78.

92. Smyth claimed that effect on Lady Mary Ponsonby, in *As Time Went On...*, 83–108. Her transvestic voice appears not only in her romantic lieder (op. 1 and 2) but also in large forms, e.g., the cantata *The Song of Love* (op. 8, 1888) for solo soprano and tenor, chorus, and orchestra, for which she created a text from the biblical Song of Songs that describes specifically female beauty, never male. For my study of Smyth's lesbian representations in music and memoir, see "Lesbian Fugue: Ethel Smyth's Contrapuntal Arts," in Ruth A. Solie, ed., *Musicology and Difference: Gender and Sexuality in Music Scholarship*, (Berkeley: University of California Press, 1993), 164–83.

93. *Der Wald* was first performed in Berlin on 9 April 1902, then in London at Covent Garden on 18 July 1902. Fremstad's first role in her London debut season was the mezzo Ortrud to Lillian Nordica's Elsa in Wagner's *Lohengrin*. At the time, Fremstad sang both mezzo and soprano roles (Fricka, Brangäne, Venus) in Wagner productions at Covent Garden, Munich, and the New York Metropolitan. Her New York debut in 1903 was Sieglinde in *Die Walküre*.

94. As reported by Smyth, *What Happened Next* (London: Longman's, Green & Co., 1940), 258. Calvé wrote Smyth (ca. 1906) suggesting contacts presumably to translate the opera libretto from French to German: undated manuscript in McMaster University Library, Hamilton, Ontario.

95. Smyth first met Messager in 1900; she reports he was most impressed with *Der Wald* in Smyth, *What Happened Next.* 174.

96. Arthur Gold and Robert Fizdale, *Misia: The Life of Misia Sert* (New York: William Morrow, 1981), 243.

97. Michael de Cossart, *The Food of Love: Princesse Edmond de Polignac (1865–1943) and Her Salon* (London: Hamish Hamilton, 1978).

98. Ethel M. Smyth, *Female Pipings in Eden* (London: Peter Davies, 1934), 53–56.

99. Smyth, *What Happened Next,* 126, 121. The Italian text was Guglielmo Ferrero and Cesare Lombrosa, *La Donna delinquente, la prostituta, e la donna normale,* published in English as *The Female Offender* (London: T. F. Unwin, 1895). On Swinburne's "In Anactoria" in *Poems and Ballads* (1866), in which Sappho complains to a fickle lover, see Faderman, *Surpassing the Love of Men,* 155, 459.

100. Ethel M. Smyth, *Streaks of Life,* (London: Longmans, Green, 1921), 209.

101. James D. Steakley, "Iconography of a Scandal; Political Cartoons and the Eulenburg Affair in Wilhelmine Germany," in Martin Bauml Duberman, Martha Vicinus, and George Chauncey, Jr., eds., *Hidden from History: Reclaiming the Gay and Lesbian Past* (New York: New American Library, 1989): 233–57.

102. Smyth, *What Happened Next,* 200. Wilamowitz-Moellendorff was antifeminist and his *Sappho und Simonides* (1913) promoted the fiction of a chaste Sappho "freed from the sin of lesbianism"; see de Jean, *Fictions of Sappho,* 207, 218–22, 307. In Paris, the celebration of Sappho by lesbian writers Natalie Barney and Renée Vivien as the poetic precursor of modern lesbian identity began at the time that Smyth's operas were first performed.

103. Smyth set Alfred de Musset's *Fantasio,* a play of transvestic rescue fantasies that encode his love affair with George Sand, as her second-choice libretto upon learning that Massenet had already begun an opera on *Thaïs,* the courtesan who converts to Christianity in the historical novel by Anatole France. I discuss this further in my forthcoming study of Smyth.

104. The quotation is in *Grove's Dictionary of Music and Musicians,* ed. Eric Blom (London: MacMillan, 1954), Fifth edition, vol. 4: "Holmès, Augusta," 329.

105. Smyth, *What Happened Next,* 210.

106. Sargent's charcoal drawing of Smyth (1901) in the National Portrait Gallery shows her singing "desperately exciting songs by Schubert and August Holmès"; Smyth, *What Happened Next,* 174.

107. The production was in Mannheim in October 1898: Smyth, *What Happened Next,* 100, 104.

108. Smyth claimed "I never was, nor am I now, a Wagnerite in the extreme sense of the word" in *As Time Went On...,* 62.

109. Ethel M. Smyth, *Inventory of Music* (1937) in the British Library, Add. Ms. 49196.

110. Smyth, *Songs* (1907) for mezzo voice and chamber ensemble include Odelette (Régnier), La Danse (Régnier), Chrysilla (Régnier), and Ode Anacréontique (Leconte de Lisle).

111. "Argument" by Harry Brewster, *Der Wald*, Music-Drama with Prologue and Epilogue in One Act by E. M. Smyth (London/Mainz/Paris: Schott, 1902).

112. Smyth, *What Happened Next*, 204–205.

113. Neilson protested for many years that the opera's libretto, scenario, and lighting, were entirely his invention: see *My Life in Two Worlds*, 207–14.

114. Smyth, *What Happened Next*, 164.

115. Mary Ponsonby to Smyth as quoted in Smyth, *What Happened Next*, 204.

116. Richard Aldrich, "Operatic Novelty at the Season's End," *The New York Times*, 15 March 1903: 25, cols. 5–6.

117. She represents this experience in the orchestral prelude "On the Cliffs of Cornwall," to act 2 of the opera.

118. The underwater cave in act 2 that floods at high tide replicates one Smyth visited many years before in the Scilly Isles.

119. Smyth, *What Happened Next*, 234–35.

120. Smyth worked quickly. On 31 May 1904 she had completed act 2 and on 13 December 1905 the third act and final score of *Les Naufrageurs*.

121. Published 1903 by Fisher Unwin in London.

122. Jane A. Bernstein, "'Shout, Shout, Up with Your Song!' Dame Ethel Smyth and the Changing Role of the British Woman Composer," in Jane Bowers and Judith Tick, eds., *Women Making Music: The Western Art Tradition, 1150–1950*, (Urbana: University of Illinois Press, 1986), 304–24. Bernstein notes that Donald Mitchell informed her that Britten did not know *The Wreckers* and the copy in the Britten-Pears library was a recent acquisition, a claim by Sir Peter Pears, as reported by Mitchell, I also have difficulty believing. The lesbian's opera, I suggest, may be the "beast" in Britten's closet. See Eve Kosofsky Sedgwick, "The Beast in the Closet: James and the Writing of Homosexual Panic," in Ruth Bernard Yeazell, ed., *Sex, Politics, and Science in the Nineteenth-Century Novel: Selected Papers from the English Institute, 1983–84* (Baltimore: Johns Hopkins University Press, 1986), 148–86.

123. Peter Conrad, *Romantic Opera and Literary Form* (Berkeley: University of California Press, 1988), 66.

124. Thyrza is also title and central character in a realistic London novel by George Gissing (1891). A thyrsus, or spear, of Dionysus was wreathed in ivy or vine and topped with a pinecone. Byron's poems to Thyrza are in *The Poetical Works of Lord Byron*, (London: Oxford University Press, 1959) 63–64. I find it otherwise an odd choice of name for an opera heroine because it is hard to pronounce in both French and German. "Th" in Smyth's own name presented a problem, for instance, when Brahms pronounced it Schmeiss and made a dirty joke about flies.

125. Garber, *Vested Interests*, 317 and 418, n. 30.

126. Smyth, *What Happened Next*, 253.

127. Smyth reports that the Empress Eugénie loved to sing "The Rat" and thought it the best in her opera. It intrigues me to imagine that its title and musical references to *Carmen* may encode a private lesbian reference to two Parisian bars, the "Rat Mort" and "Tambourin," bohemian cafés during the Second Empire reign of the empress and still frequented by lesbians in the 1880s. Reference to these bars is made by Michael Wilson,

"Gender and Transgression in Bohemian Montmartre," in Julia Epstein and Kristina Straub, eds., *Bodyguards: The Cultural Politics of Gender Ambiguity* (New York: Routledge, 1991), 210.

128. Nietzsche as quoted by Furman, "The Languages of Love in *Carmen*," 170.

129. Vocal score, act 1: 68.

130. Smyth, *What Happened Next*, 253.

131. Smyth, *What Happened Next*, 267.

132. Blanche Marchesi published a memoir, *Singer's Pilgrimage* (1923; New York: Da Capo Press, 1978).

133. Sir Thomas Beecham, *A Mingled Chime: An Autobiography* (New York: G. P. Putnam's Sons, 1943), 139.

134. Bruno Walter, *Theme and Variations; An Autobiography* (London: Hamish Hamilton, 1947), 169–70.

135. Bruno Walter to Smyth from California, 25 December 1939, reproduced in St. John, *Ethel Smyth*, 283–84.

136. In 1928, more than twenty years after *The Wreckers*, Radclyffe Hall published *The Well of Loneliness*, Virginia Woolf *Orlando*, and Djuna Barnes *The Ladies Almanack*. It is tempting to imagine, had these stories been available to Smyth in 1902, the operas she might have composed on Hall's lesbian underworld and dangerous wartime battlefield where lesbians could be gallant, patriotic, heroic like men; Woolf's gleeful fantasy of cross-gendered and cross-dressed masquerade rescued and redeemed by marriage; or Barnes's satiric wigging of Natalie Barney's Paris-Lesbos menagerie. Hall's story *Miss Ogilvy Finds Herself* (written in 1926 but not published until 1934) bears some resemblance to *The Wreckers*. Miss Ogilvy, an outcast lesbian misfit trapped in her inborn sexual identity, finds in a cave, just above the waterline, ancient stones and fragments that produce in her transvestic fantasies of herself as Amazon and tribal warrior, a young man, with a girl. Like Thirza, and unlike Cather's Thea Kronberg, she is found dead in the cave the next day. Miss Ogilvy represents an oppressive, tragic lesbian stereotype that Ethel Smyth refused in life and probably had no wish to replicate in art. At the time she composed her operas, and long afterward, few alternative imaginary or realistic literary representations of lesbian identity and experience existed.

4

ON A LESBIAN RELATIONSHIP WITH MUSIC
A Serious Effort Not to Think Straight

Suzanne G. Cusick

*H*O GRANDISSIMA PAURA.

Ecco'l fatto.

E sarebbe più facile dire'l mio tutto in italiano, una lingua che da molto è stata diventata per me come una lingua materna; cioè, la lingua più-che-materna, la lingua nel quale io vivo la mia vita più interiore, nel quale parlo col'io che esiste a priori dell'io musicista, l'io americana, l'io donna, anzi l'io lesbica. Sarebbe più facile in questa lingua che non è la mia perche qui, in questa lingua, non c'è l'illusione della naturale, della lingua "materna" e nativa che in verità è (già e sempre) la lingua dei padri; qui, in questa lingua, parlo della mia verità più originaria, cioè la mia verità di essere fuori sistema, sempre riconoscente di essere fuori sistema, e di esserne riconoscente prima che ho mai saputo di essere musicista, ó donna, ó lesbica; di esserla già e sempre quando non sono nessun'altra che questa.

I have great fear (I am very afraid. And they are not quite the same).

To speak publicly and truly about my own musicality (as private a part of me as my "sexuality"—and frightening to speak of for that, but more frightening still because it is more completely a part of me than that which the world calls "sex," being also the fabric of my public life).

To speak *not* from what Luisa Muraro calls the state of "faked being" (l'essere finta), whence the verisimilitude and credibility of one's topos and thesis are more important than truth, and are guaranteed by both topos and thesis coming from what has already been said, what can be verified by footnote.[1]

To speak...not just of the love that dare not speak its name...to say the word lesbian in a musicological crowd...to try to make sense of it there...

To speak of music differently...to look for a way to speak, to think, that which one doesn't ordinarily speak or think about music, about pleasure, about sex...

And it would be easier to say my say in Italian. It would be easier in that language that isn't mine because there, in that language, there is no illusion of the natural, native "mother tongue" (it would be thus easier for everyone to accept the not making sense that is the lingua franca of those who live outside the symbolic order; it would be thus easier, for everyone, to know that what I say is a translation, subject to infinite infinitesimal errors).

To say the word "lesbian" in a musicological crowd is to speak a foreign language, though at first it may not seem so.

To *have* great fear, to *be* very afraid...they are not quite the same.

To speak, then, a foreign language about that which has been the most passionate and the most passionately loved reality of my life—that is, music—

To try to speak both truly and helpfully

is a project of which I *have* great fear.

Ho grandissima paura.

Why am I talking about this?

The origin of this essay was in two moments of shock—a shock of non-recognition and one of recognition. I had sent copies of a book proposal on the impact of feminism on academic musical discourse to various people, soliciting their comments. The last copy I sent was to a colleague who is also lesbian. It was in writing a cover letter to her that I had my shock of non-recognition: to my amazement, to my horror, to my shame, I realized I had not only left out lesbians from the book proposal, I had not known I had left...I had not *known* I had left out myself, or a part of my self, from my own book. Desperate, supposing (as seemed logical and plausible to me then) that if anyone in the profession had worked out the apparent split between a lesbian identity and a professional one which I had just discovered in myself, she had done it, I asked for my colleague's help.

Her response brought the shock of recognition, as it *was* a shock of recognition. She hadn't got it worked out, either.

So if she hadn't worked it out, and I hadn't worked it out, and we were among the most likely people in the profession to be "out"...maybe no one had worked it out. In any case, I needed to work it out. I needed to understand what relationship, if any, I could suppose to exist between my being a lesbian and my being a musician, a musicologist.

This essay, then, is an assemblage of notes that constitute the less private parts of an interior conversation among the several selves I am, the several selves I have been as I have moved among languages, continents, and the various discursive acts that constitute the identities lesbian, musician, musicologist. I have no illusion or even hope that these notes constitute any grand unified theory of lesbian musicality—I only mean to further a conversation.

At first, I wanted to interrogate a perceived split within my self—I wanted to find the lesbian in the musicologist, or the musicologist in the lesbian. And I could find only the most banal of connections that were true for me. I had followed with interest conversations with and among other lesbians in the profession about whether there might be a lesbian aesthetic, that is, a preference for certain kinds of music that somehow reflected the patterns of lesbian desire or lesbian pleasure. I was forced to admit, finally, during one of those conversations, that the music under discussion (which I truly "love") seemed to me beautiful because it had to do with intensity of experience. For me, it was neither emotional nor sexual. I didn't say then, but I have noticed on reflection since, that for me it is about something more important *to me* than either emotion or sex as conventionally defined: it is about the transcendent joy of being alive, not dead, and aware of the difference.

The "I" who loves that work *seems* to me to be the "I" with whom I speak in Italian, she who exists a priori of the "I" musician, the "I" woman, the "I" lesbian, she whose two oldest memories are of being completely bewildered by the categories of the adult world, and of hearing music as the beginning of her dreams at night—a music which seemed palpable, shining, like silver air, a music through which one could pass out of the bewildering world and into reality. From the sweetness promised by that toddler dream to my work as an adult, I am in search of union with that music, and I am most alive when I find it. *That* union is more like the supposed thrill of sex, in the same proportion as, for me, the pleasure of sex with a woman is more 'like it' than anything I have experienced with a man. That is, the "I" who found neither emotions nor sex mirrored in the work proposed conversationally as consonant with lesbian aesthetics is the "I" described in Italian in my opening, she whose originating truth is an awareness of being outside the system (so outside it as even to be bewildered by the category of sex), outside a system that is not as "real" as music can be.

If these casual conversations about a lesbian aesthetic or a lesbian musicality were puzzling—and in some sense not true for me—I have come to

70 SUZANNE G. CUSICK

think my puzzlement was partly a response to a conversational failure to define terms, particularly terms as charged as "lesbian" and "sexuality", terms subject to alternative, intensely personal definitions when they are joined. (For surely one part of "lesbian"—either as an adjective or as a noun—consists in having, being, or acting out an alternative, intensely personal sexuality.) Perhaps more to the point, for me, was our conversational failure to interrogate the notion of identity itself, much less a "lesbian identity," which might then imply a "lesbian reception" of music's messages.

What do I mean when I say "lesbian" and use it as an adjective as I did in my title? What do I mean when I use "lesbian" as a noun, as when I wrote an old friend "I am a lesbian"? More troubling still, since "lesbian" is considered to be "a sexuality," what do I mean by "sexuality"? And more troubling still, does this or any other "sexuality" constitute so profound and pervasive a part of one's life that it might be an identity, inextricable from the "I" who listens, performs, or thinks about music? (And this is one reason I began in a foreign language, because as I have tried to think about these words they have become like words in a foreign language.) And, if sexuality is not an identity, what reasons might there be, nonetheless, for supposing that a person's sexuality and a person's musicality would be related? How might they relate? (And why should anyone care?)

Sexuality and Musicality: what am I talking about?

Suppose for a moment that sexuality isn't linked to reproduction—as it isn't anymore, as it never has been for the behaviors that have gotten some people called "homosexual"; then suppose that sexuality isn't necessarily linked to genital pleasure (as it isn't in the minds and practices of many American lesbians);[2] what, then, IS IT?

I propose this definition: it is a way of expressing and/or enacting relationships of intimacy through physical pleasure shared, accepted, or given.

What is "a sexuality," or, as more popularly phrased, a "sexual identity"? Given my working definition of sexuality itself, a "sexual identity" might be a person's position vis-à-vis the means of expressing and/or enacting relationships of intimacy through physical pleasure shared, accepted, or given. For some of us, it might be that the most intense and important way we express or enact identity through the circulation of physical pleasure is in musical activity, and that our "sexual identity" might be "musician" more than it is "lesbian," "gay," or "straight." Be that the case or not, one might expect a significant amount of bleed-through between a person's musicality and a person's sexuality as conventionally defined (that is, as the genitally focused enactment of intimacy through the circulation of pleasure). If music isn't sexuality, for most of us it is psychically right next door.[3]

If our musicalities and our sexualities are psychically next-door neighbors, how might we experience a cross-over between the two? It has seemed to me one might look for such cross-overs: (1) in choosing an intimacy/pleasure object, which one might do as a listener or a performer; (2) in establishing a relationship with an intimacy/pleasure object (or an intimacy/pleasure partner), which, again, one might do as either a listener or a performer; (3) in enacting that relationship publicly, as when our listening is transformed into teaching or criticism, or in public performances before audiences; and (4) in choosing to *be* a musician (if music is similar to sex, what does choosing music as a life's work mean? What do subordinate categories of that choice, like being in an art or an improvised tradition, or teaching but not performing, or doing musicology or composition, *mean?*).

Where might "lesbian sexuality" show up, in these places of potential cross-over between sexuality and musicality?

For a time, trying to puzzle out an answer to that question, I tried constructing a tandem musical/sexual autobiography, which was moderately interesting as an exercise in self-knowledge, but not so helpful in answering the question. One thing that intrigued me, however, was finding, as I reconstructed my own past, that the lesbian "I" seemed less consistently present than the "I" who was aware of being outside the system, she who sought and still seeks immersion in the shining sound that welcomes her into sleep and into a waking experience of great intensity she calls reality. The intellectual result of that realization was a questioning of what I meant by "lesbian."

"Being" a lesbian: what do I mean?

To answer, I must introduce an element of all relationships missing from the definition of sexuality I suggested above—power. All relationships are agreements about the distribution of power, agreements negotiated in varying degrees of intimacy. The *most* intimate are negotiated in large part through the circulation of pleasure. Sexuality, I would argue, is a practice which allows movement within a field defined by power, intimacy and pleasure—for the sake of conciseness I'd like to call it here the power/pleasure/intimacy triad.

The enacted structure of the power/pleasure/intimacy triad and the gender of the beloved are intertwined in what I mean by "lesbian."

Who do we usually mean by "lesbian"? Casually, we mean a woman who loves other women, and we usually mean to imply that her love is "sexually" expressed.

Do we mean, do we think, that when she loves a woman, she becomes a social man? Is every "lesbian" a butch when she loves, a femme when she is the beloved?[4]

When a lesbian loves a woman, does the power structure known as the gender system remain intact? With "woman" as less—worth less, power less—than "man"? So that her choice to love a woman effects her escape from *being* one?

Or is the whole relationship an escape (for all parties) from the power structure known as the gender system, that no one be in the position—worth less, power less—marked "woman," and no one be in the position—power full, worth full—marked "man"?

For me, the whole relationship is an escape.[5]

If the *whole* relationship is an escape from the power structure (a structure which serves the institutional interest of compulsory heterosexuality, which in turn serves the purpose of reproduction, among other things), why can't the "lesbian" escape it in a relationship with a man? Why does loving a woman trigger, or create, or enable this escape?

I *think* loving a woman triggers that escape more easily than loving a man (and trying to create an "escaped" relationship with him) because of how women are socialized, or, in more updated language, because of who the construct "woman" is: she is non-dominating; she has (we are told by psychoanalysts) porous ego boundaries; she is still connected to the Mother, and, by extension, to the rest of the social fabric, having achieved a less complete individuation in the Oedipal drama. She is non-power: to be in love with her is to be in love with, to be fascinated by, to be drawn to that which is non-power. With her, a self who is also non-power is more likely to create a relationship based on non-power—that is, a relationship in which a porous boundary exists at all moments between the she who seems to have the power and the she who doesn't, allowing for a flow of power in both directions. No one in the relationship has been formed to be the power figure, although all can play at it.[6]

Furthermore, because "women"—the people in this relationship—are worth less (power less) there are far fewer discursive and societal models for the relationships between women than there are for relationships which involve the power full and worth full men. (Women without men are, after all, unthinkable in the symbolic order of the phallic economy.)[7] The people in this relationship, by being constructed as "women," don't have to resist a model for their relationship that has anything like the coercive force of heterosexual marriage norms, both internalized and externally imposed, for heterosexual lovers. (Not that those norms aren't also internalized by lesbians, but once you're outside the heterosexual picture, there's so much "wrong with the picture" that it becomes relatively easier to just make up a new one.)[8]

"Being" a "lesbian" then…is a way of organizing the force field of power, pleasure, and intimacy that refuses the simple binary opposition male and female; that refuses the linking of those forces at their point of intersection with reproduction; that, therefore, refuses to play the game "phallic economy." Consequently, "lesbian sexuality" channels pleasure (and possibly the to me incomprehensible "desire" as Lacan defines it in the world of *l'essere finta*) much more diffusely than the phallic economy, admitting as sexual— that is, as valid currency in the exchange of pleasure that acts out or reinforces intimacy—pleasures and sites of pleasure beyond the usual ones. "Being" "lesbian" is a position which scrambles the usual components of "man" and "woman" (it is not about being a social man) and celebrates the scrambling. Implicit in this notion of scrambling the usual components of those categories is a notion of *playing* with them in a game in which everyone can play every position, everyone is expected to pay the closest possible attention to how everyone else is playing, and no one (if you play it well) accumulates the power of a social man. Consequently, no one accumulates the consolidated power we call "identity," because the pleasure of the game is living in a world free of fixed categories.

As I experience it, then, "lesbian" is not a noun. It is not a thing I always and everywhere *am*, as I am always and everywhere a human with graying hair. It is not an identity (and that's why I couldn't reconstruct "being a lesbian" at all the crucial junctures of my musical/sexual autobiography), but rather a way I prefer to behave, to organize my relationship to the world in a power/pleasure/intimacy triad.

And I think that as a way of organizing the power/pleasure/intimacy triad through various relational behaviors, *this* meaning of "lesbian" can be detected in my musicality. I therefore offer the notion that "a sexuality" is a way of structuring relationships as a fruitful way of thinking about all our sexualities as reflected in our relationships with music, and thus as ultimately constitutive of our musicalities.

But how? How do relationships in the power/pleasure/intimacy triad exist *with* music? Music is, after all, a thing, not a person, isn't it? And most of us form our intimate relationships with other *people*, don't we?[9]

If music might be for some of us, or for all of us sometimes, in the position sometimes called "significant other," then one might look for scrambling and shifting of roles with *it*, for funny power relationships with *it*, moments when *it* is the lover—that is, the active, pleasure-giving partner—and moments when *it* is the beloved—the partner who somehow receives pleasure or empowerment. And one might find oneself to be acting out all sorts of, well, positions and "sexual" behaviors with this "lover"/"beloved."

So...I have found it extremely fruitful to ask of *my* various relationships with music one of the two questions men (mostly) always want to ask about lesbians. No, not "what do they dooooo," but that other perennial...

"Who's on top?"

For most of my professional life I have acted out my relationship with music as a teacher (less consistently, I have been a performer, a scholar, a composer). Perhaps for the longevity of that acting out, perhaps because I haven't done it lately, it has been easiest for me to see "who's on top" when I like the way I teach—and the answer, when I have asked myself, has been so startling that I think it alone merits a public sharing of the question.

The answer is that I teach music as the lover, the active force which generates pleasure, which leads one body and soul into an alternate reality (definite traces of my toddler dreams), into intimacy. I ask my students to open themselves to the music they hear, to let music "do it" to them, to become more intensely aware (physically, emotionally, intellectually) of what's being done to them. I teach them to ask of the music, later, how it achieved that effect (and, in more advanced courses, I try to teach them to ask it why). These interrogations are designed, in effect, to increase the actual intimacy of my students' subsequent encounters with that music, or with any music, by increasing their knowledge of who it is, so to speak, who's been "on top," and by increasing their skill, through practice, in the art of being music's beloved. Former students confirm that this is exactly what I did for them.

Or what I did *to* them. For I have been horrified and interested to notice that the way I teach puts the listener flat on her back. Yes, rising to meet the offered caresses, and thus interacting in a way analogous to the way one can choose to accept "sexual" caresses or not. But on her back she is, even when she is a man: thus, I put my men students in an extremely uncomfortable position. If my notion that one's musicality is next door to one's sexuality is at all accurate, I am subverting their social construction as "men," all the while reinforcing the social construction of my women students as "women." The politics of that need some serious thought.[10]

But *why* do I teach that way? I have a lot of conscious reasons for having constructed such a strategy, including a passionate crusade to teach everyone I encounter to reconstruct their relationship to pleasure itself, which I think to be generally perverse in mainstream American culture. I am driven, always and everywhere, to get people to associate pleasure with joy instead of with danger and guilt. I try to teach my students to experience joy, the joy and sense of immersion in a reality beyond the bewildering "system" which music offered the toddler "I." I try to give them a version of my first love.

And I remember the first time I fell in love…staring up at a radio on top of the fridge, fascinated by the sound of a woman's voice coming from it…memorizing the song, somehow…*loving* it, racing to the kitchen whenever *it* was there, standing beneath it transfixed.

Then I lost it…it wasn't on the radio anymore, and eventually all I could remember of it was one line, so filled was my head with other songs (for that song began the spectacle of a toddler memorizing her college-age brother's record collection, singing grotesquely inappropriate words in chest voice like the women singers popular then, whenever my parents had company).

Years later, I found it again. I must have been eleven or twelve, for I was old enough to sit up for Guy Lombardo's New Year's Eve show, and thus to hear the retrospective of number one songs for the 1940s and 1950s. And there it was: 1951, "The Tennessee Waltz" (so I had been two when I fell in love).[11] I *still* loved it (although I was surprised to learn that the lyrics were sad). I had lost this song for years, and nothing—not even Mozart, not even Chopin, to whom music lessons had introduced me—matched its ability to extract a kind of passion from me, the passion to take it in, to know it, to make it part of my sound bank forever…I wanted to have it in my mind so I could replicate it with my body: love and desire, as the twelve-year-old "I" remembered and relived them from the two-year-old "I," became the desire to know the music as a means physically to *be* that music.[12]

That is still the way I love, when I love a piece of music. That way of loving defines the position from which I couldn't say, in the lesbian aesthetics conversation to which I alluded earlier, whether Barber's "Adagio for Strings" matched my sexuality or not. But it might be that Barber's "Adagio" allows me to listen and love from this (lesbian?) *position*, a permission not granted by all the music I hear.

I am certain that this is what I try to teach my students: the primal joys of fixation and mother-substitute love, and of immersion in something outside the solipsism of the individuated self. As a listening posture, this refreshes and renews me, gives me energy when I have none; reminds me I am alive, not dead; and enables me to return to the rest of the world that is the "not I" with the same intense attention, both sensual and cognitive. *Like good sex*, it is an experience that re-teaches me how to relate to the world, how to have the nerve to open myself to it.

Arguably, some kinds of music are aesthetically inappropriate for such an experience. The "pounding," "thrusting" gestures of Beethoven to which Susan McClary has thankfully drawn our attention,[13] or other gestures insistent, strident, or obvious...simply are not interesting enough to me to elicit the kind of attention I mean...don't give me the choice I cherish, which is to listen or not, to attend or not, to let the music "do it" to me (which the musics I love can only do if I have paid the most careful, intense, co-creative attention)...or not. Possibly, that is, there are musics which I dis-prefer because they upset a power equilibrium (my preference for which is reflected in my so-called "lesbian sexuality," the game where even the one who seems not to be on top has the power to deflect caresses, to decline the offer; indeed, where she who is not on top often directs the proceedings). Possibly for me there are musics to which I respond positively or negatively from the lesbian "I," as she continually reconstructs herself by her "sexual" behaviors. But that response is not exactly based on a direct correspondence among, say, Beethoven's insistent rhythms, their possible representation of male sexual thrusting, and my "rejection" of males as "sexual" partners. Nor is it based on a direct correspondence between my "woman's" body's supposedly diffused sexuality and the diffused "climaxes" of some musics. The chain of events in *my* "lesbian aesthetic" response, if it can be said to exist, leads to a preference for musics which invite extremely heightened, sensual, cognitive attention, musics which *invite* and allow me to participate or not as *I* choose, musics with which I experience a continuous circulation of power even when I let the music be "on top." Their representations of the traditionally defined "sexual" acts of traditionally defined genders is secondary to this larger issue of the power dynamic between music and me. For instance, Terry Riley's famously minimalist *In C*, hardly a representation of thrust, upsets the balance I seek as much as Beethoven's Fifth Symphony does.

So, when I teach, I teach my own listening posture, one which seeks to restore a primal reception of music through a listening strategy of extreme attentiveness. And I admit I teach attentiveness rather than analysis as a listening strategy for gender-laden ("sexuality"-laden?) reasons. For when I encourage students to receive music "on their backs," paying the closest of attention to what in the music gives them pleasure,[14] I am conscious of doing so to allow the music her own voice (and to allow the students theirs), *her* own wholeness of utterance, before analytical or cultural-historical interrogation.

In some way, I think, I identify the music as a(nother) woman. And because that means I also in some sense identify *with* her, I try to treat her analytically as I would be treated: as a subject who may have things to say that are totally different from what listeners expect to hear. By what feels like instinct, the strongest of instincts, I pass quickly over what *feel* like essentializing strategies (e.g., describing a work as an example of such and such a form, or Schenkerian analysis). I pass almost as quickly over discursively valued strategies (analysis of harmony, tonal structures) to less-valued, "sensual" features like texture and timbre. I feel a deep, deep reluctance to engage in what feels like the dismemberment of music's body into the categories "form," "melody," "rhythm," "harmony."[15] Because, I think, both the essentializing and the dismembering strategies *feel* akin to those violences as they are committed on the bodies and souls of real women, and because I am being serious when I say I love music, I cannot bear to do those things to a beloved. In some sense I love the music I teach as if it were a(nother) woman, a(nother) lesbian, and when I teach some ways of interrogating and thus knowing her in preference to other ways, I am again teaching a strange position to my students. (a gender position? a "sexual" position? certainly, a position in the power/pleasure/intimacy triad in which both musicality and sexuality negotiate).

Yet it is an active response—the joining of my body to the music in which "who's on top" keeps changing—which is truly my preferred response to music. That is, since the days of "The Tennessee Waltz," the moments wherein I have felt most fully alive, most fully myself, have been when I have *become* the music...when I have loved it in return...when, attending to its messages with ears, heart, and mind, I have used my own body to release those messages again into the air, for the pleasure of my own ears and mind, and of others' ears and minds. Which is what I experience myself do when, over and over again as an organist and choir director, I fall in love with new repertoire.

The *last* time I fell completely and hopelessly in love was Christmastime 1989, when I learned Bach's *Canonic Variations on "Vom Himmel hoch"* to play as a prelude on Christmas Eve. Specifically, I fell in love with the fourth variation.

What did I love? What *do* I love? Why have I, in enforced abstinence from organ-playing this year, physically longed for that variation? And what was my relationship with that which I so love when I played it that Christmas Eve—in terms of power, pleasure, intimacy, in terms of my relationship with the music, my relationship with my hearers?

I *love* hidden relationships, and I love revealing them to the attentive [!]. I *love*, about the fourth variation, the tension between the ostensible structure (the chorale tune in the pedal part, which the listener is conditioned to expect, to hear, to identify as important) and what is above it—a beautiful, passionate, uncanonic (literally) melody in the right hand that seems to exist on a completely different plane from the chorale, yet which includes bits of it in figuration, to be revealed or not depending on the performer's preference and skill. It seems like a tension between a social norm (conditioned by previous variations) and a very high degree of eccentricity, of hyperbolic (if playful) behavior. I *love* the right-hand melody and love its moment of fruition most of all, right before the chorale's moment of fruition, and I love the challenge of keeping it all together.

I love using my body to release the power of the uncanonic melody's climax, which to my ear occurs in the middle of the chorale melody's last phrase (its climax), the climaxes both simultaneous and not. I love using my body to enable the existence in the air of a model of independent intimacy. I love feeling like I'm on top, controlling with skilled hands the articulation of snippets of the chorale in the uncanonic melody, and I especially love the climax because it is at that moment that the music gets away from me, at that moment that *she* is on top in the sense that because of my hands' work *she* has all the power, and I am reduced to rapture by that power's release. I love using my brain and hands and feet to create for people I know (and in some cases love) the *possibility* that they might hear all the complex relationships which lead those melodies to their simultaneous but independent climaxes—even though I know from my own experience as a listener that a person cannot hear all the relationships at any one time.

Is there a lesbian, as I've defined her, in all this love? For me, yes: for when I play the fourth variation, a great deal of my pleasure derives from the jumbling of who's on top—am I playing "Vom Himmel hoch," or is she playing me? In all performances that give me joy, the answer is unclear—we are both on top, both on our backs, both wholly ourselves and wholly mingled with each other. Power circulates freely across porous boundaries; the categories player and played, lover and beloved, dissolve.[16]

This is dangerously close to public sex—in a Lutheran church yet. And in thinking about how very much what I *dooo* with "Vom Himmel hoch" is like what I *dooo* with my partner, I've come to a startling hypothesis about the relationship between musicality and sexuality.

What if they're NOT next-door neighbors of the soul, susceptible to sideways moves by which one's behavior in one house is repeated in the other (and both are places wherein we continually re-teach ourselves how to relate to a bewildering world)?

What if music IS sex?

If sex is free of the association with reproduction enforced by the so-called phallic economy (and it is, remember, exactly so for people called homosexual, as it has become in the last thirty years for people called heterosexual who practice contraception), if it is then *only* (only!) a means of negotiating power and intimacy through the circulation of pleasure, what's to prevent music from *being* sex, and thus an ancient, half-sanctioned form of escape from the constraints of the phallic economy?

Is that why we have so many intellectual barriers in place to prevent thinking about music as *like* sex, or as having the capacity to *represent* sexuality and gender? Is that why, in the Euro-American traditions anyway, we have such a history of anxiety about music's power "to ravish"?

Are all musicians sexual deviants, in that we *all* negotiate in the power/pleasure/intimacy triad in ways that are outside the phallic economy of compulsory/genital/reproductive sexuality? (Could that be why so many musicians are also deviants by more conventional definitions of sexuality and gender? That is, only fitful participants in institutionalized heterosexuality?)

What if hands are sex organs? *Mine are.*[17]

What if ears are sex organs? What if music-making is a form of sexuality in which (as in some other forms of sexuality) the sites of giving and receiving pleasure are separated?

If music IS sex, what on earth is going on in a concert hall during, say, a piano recital? When the pianist is on a raised stage, in a spotlight while we are in the dark...are we observers of a sexual act? Are we its object? Why, exactly, are we in the dark?

Does the...kinkiness of these questions account for the extremely rigid social codes surrounding concert decorum for all concerned?

Does it help account for the swooning over Liszt (in an 1840s construction of public group sex), over Elvis (in a 1950s construction of the same thing), over...Madonna...over, in the long-gone 1970s, Holly Near?

Arguably, *these* questions have nothing to do with a "lesbian relationship with music." But they are placed in the universe of thought at a point easily reached when your point of departure for thinking about either music or sex is an experience outside the phallic economy.

For me, the intuitions reflected in these questions have been around for a long time, and they do, in fact, weave together the lesbian "I," the musician "I," and even the musicologist "I" who, you may recall, was conspicuously absent from my Italian-language prologue.

But they are—this whole essay has been, I think—truly weird, truly counter-cultural. (And perhaps, after all, it *would* have been easier if I had said my say in a foreign language which, like the language of "lesbian" experience, some percentage of you would have directly understood.) This essay has been counter-cultural because I have not, except very briefly, addressed the texts of music, and addressing musical texts is still, these days, what we do. Even I do it, in my previous and continuing critical work on the "texts" of Francesca Caccini (with whom, of course, I try to have a lesbian relationship, amply spiced by that canonic musicological deviance, necrophilia).

Much as I love certain texts, though, texts are not all there is to musical experience. A focus on texts tends to trick us into staying in a power-over paradigm that is mighty close to the regime of compulsory heterosexuality. We are receivers, on our backs, or possibly we are voyeurs. We are people who say "yes" or "no," but not "how about it?"—people whose yes or no to music as perpetual lover may be said through critical or analytical strategies that respond to the power imbalance with symbolic violence to music's body (by mastery through dismemberment, for example). For our focus on texts, even in reception history, leaves only "composers" in the initiating position. And while a focus on texts is a perfectly reasonable position in which to have been placed by the technological availability of so many texts (at least in the overdeveloped world), it puts us at risk of forgetting that music (like sex, which it might *be*) is first of all something *we do*, we human beings, as a way of explaining, replicating, and reinforcing our relationship to the world, or our imagined notions of what possible relationships might exist. I suspect for all of us the originating joy of it comes from assuming more varied positions than we think we're allowed in regular life, positions that enable us to say yes or no, to immerse, to initiate, to have simultaneous but independent climaxes, to escape a system (maybe it was always the phallic economy) of bewilderingly fixed categories, to wallow in the circulation of pleasures that are beyond danger and culturally defined desires. Restoring that joy to ourselves—in our musics, our musicalities, our musicologies—may require of us all the foreignness of thinking that comes of not "thinking straight."

"Vi ringrazio per l'ascolto."[18]

Notes

An earlier version of this essay was presented at the Feminist Theory and Music conference in Minneapolis, June 1991. I am particularly grateful to Bridget Kelly Black, Lydia Hamessley, Margaret McFadden, Sandra Saari, and Elizabeth Wood for their helpful comments on this text, as well as for enduring the long and often vague conversational episodes that preceded its writing. Subsequent conversations with Marcia Citron, Joseph Dubiehl, Marian Guck, Roland Jordon, Fred Maus, Mitchell Morris, and Renato Rodolfo-Siosin have helped me focus certain parts of my argument. My thinking about the possible relationships between sexuality and musicality was initially sparked by Philip Brett's paper, "Musicality, Essentialism, and the Closet," presented at the fifty-sixth annual meeting of the American Musicological Society, Oakland 1990.

1. Luisa Muraro, *L'ordine simbolico della madre* (Rome: Editori Riuniti, 1991). The original version of this essay was created and circulated without footnotes, as it was intended as an effort to think from a place as far outside *l'essere finta* as I could get; indeed, it was drafted in the margins of newspapers and on the backs of envelopes during a month of commuting between Florence and Rome in the spring of 1991. I cannot pretend, however, that my thoughts were uninfluenced by years of reading. Intellectual honesty and kindness to readers obliges me, I think, to add footnotes—however ironic their addition is to the deliberate strangeness of my argument.

2. See Philip Blumenstein and Pepper Schwarz, *American Couples: Money, Work, Sex* (New York: William Morrow, 1983) and Boston Lesbian Psychology Collective, *Lesbian Psychologies* (Urbana: University of Illinois Press, 1987).

3. The intended audience for this thesis was a roomful of professional musicians: I do not presume to speculate about the relationship between musicality and sexuality for everyone, since there are some for whom music is simply irrelevant.

4. These questions, and much of the thinking behind this section of the essay, were conceived under the influence of Teresa de Lauretis, *Differenza e Indifferenza Sessuale: per l'elaborazione di un pensiero lesbico* (Florence: Estro Editrice, 1989); an earlier, English-language version of the essay is "Sexual Indifference and Lesbian Representation," *Theatre Journal* 40, no. 2 (May 1988): 155–77, reprinted in Sue-Ellen Case, ed., *Performing Feminisms: Feminist Critical Theory and Theatre* (Baltimore and London: Johns Hopkins University Press, 1990), 17–39.

5. De Lauretis makes a similar argument, as does Monique Wittig in *The Lesbian Body*, trans. David LeVay (New York: William Morrow, 1975) and "The Mark of Gender," *Feminist Issues* 5, no. 2 (1985): 71 (reprinted in Wittig, *The Straight Mind* [Boston: Beacon Press, 1992]); and Judith Butler in *Gender Trouble: Feminism and the Subversion of Identity* (London: Routledge, 1990).

6. This play at and with power positions and power figures is adduced to the real content of butch/femme and of lesbian sadomasochism. See particularly Sue-Ellen Case, "Toward a Butch/Femme Aesthetic" in Lynda Hart, ed., *Feminist Perspectives on Contemporary Women's Drama* (Ann Arbor: University of Michigan Press, 1991), 282–99.

7. I refer here to the explanation of gender identity and its irrevocable connection to language acquisition and use propounded by French psychoanalyst Jacques Lacan. In the "phallic economy," male subjectivity is constructed so that men always seek "the phallus" (symbolic power, substituting for the loss of the mother), while female subjectivity is constructed so that women are "the phallus." For a fuller introduction to Lacan's theory, see Juliet Mitchell and Jacqueline Rose, eds., *Feminine Sexuality: Jacques Lacan and the École Freudienne* (New York/London: W. W. Norton, 1985).

8. The sociological and psychological literature on American lesbians in this part of this century suggests that "lesbian" life is, these days, consciously intended as an escape from the power structure known as gender. There is overwhelming evidence that power sharing and power exchange (egalitarian relationships, free switching of "roles," sexually and otherwise, free choice among gendered activities like taking out the garbage, bringing up baby, etc.) are essential to positive experiences of "lesbian" life; even among couples who seem from the outside to be "into roles," their experience from within the relationship is

a constant shift of power. See Blumenstein and Schwarz, *American Couples*, and Boston Lesbian Psychology Collective, *Lesbian Psychologies*.

9. A few years ago I asked this question rhetorically of a music history class at Oberlin, as part of an exordium to the course that urged them to use music history as a means of knowing their beloved better—one of the duties, as it seemed to me, of a good lover. When I suggested that all of us were in that room because we *loved* and had our most intimate relationships with works of music and with instruments, I was rewarded with guilty smiles and nervous titters. I had struck a nerve of truth, and I have intermittently mused, ever since, on the notion of music as lover, or beloved.

10. At the time I first read this paper, I had not taught in three years and, as I remarked in a jocular aside, had no expectation of ever teaching again after saying such things as this in public. Three months later I *was* back in a classroom temporarily and found that it was possible to at least alternate the "positions" of my students. But my realization that the usual listening "position" in an introductory class (and in the texts written for them) was a gendered one was initially paralyzing, despite or because of twenty years' experience.

    Philip Brett has remarked to me that my notion of repositioning my students seems uncharacteristically "driven from on top"; surely I was re-imagining my role as well? Actually, I don't think I did re-imagine my role, which I still understood (understand) to be one of initiating the young into positions that will provide them pleasure.

11. Because a somewhat older colleague who read an early version of this essay heard Gene Autrey's 1940s rendition of the song in her mind's ear, I feel obliged to specify that it was with Patti Page's recording of "The Tennessee Waltz" that I fell in love.

12. When I fell in love with "The Tennessee Waltz," I was at the age when I ought to have been, by Freudian standards, negotiating a little girl's troubled individuation from her mother. As it happens, that year my mother disappeared from the household for eight weeks, her departure unexplained. While I'm not very convinced by Freudian interpretations of anything, I see that it is possible—if hilarious—to suppose that instead of constructing as a heterosexual by having a family romance with my father in this period (he, too, was absent most of my waking hours, visiting my mother in a hospital) I constructed as a lesbian musician by having the family romance with a pop song performed by a woman. It is also possible that music itself became a substitute mother and, eventually, therefore, a substitute lover for me. And I think it is true that the relationship I called love with that song was one in which I was the femme—the listening position I teach— one where ego boundaries were porous, one where knowledge was a way of maintaining the joy when the love was absent, one where immersion in pleasure triggered an intense experience that seemed more like reality than the ever-bewildering world.

13. Most notably in "Getting Down off the Beanstalk: The Presence of a Woman's Voice in Janika Vandervelde's *Genesis II*," in *Feminine Endings: Music, Gender, and Sexuality* (Minneapolis: University of Minnesota Press, 1991), 112–131. For a negative response to this aspect of McClary's essay see Pieter van den Toorn, "Politics, Feminism, and Contemporary Music Theory," *Journal of Musicology* 9, no. 3 (1991): 275–99, and Ruth Solie's reply "What Do Feminists Want? A Reply to Pieter van den Toorn" in the same journal, vol. 9, no. 4.

14. Marilyn Farwell might say I am teaching them to be lesbians; see her "Toward a Definition of the Lesbian Literary Imagination," *Signs* 14, no. 1 (1988): 100–118, reprinted in Micheline R. Malson, et. al., eds., *Feminist Theory in Practice and Process* (Chicago: University of Chicago Press, 1989), 210–20.

15. As I prepare this revised essay, I realize that my reluctance to engage in dismemberment had its origin in the offhand remark of an undergraduate teacher of mine, herself (I thought at the time) a lesbian as well as an ethnomusicologist. It was a reluctance that made me seem highly eccentric in graduate school.

16. A member of the adult choir I direct, for which I have composed several anthems over the years, recently pointed out to the group that all my pieces share the same "difficulty": it is difficult, she said, to keep straight who has the melody, because the texture is full of phrases wherein the melody, intact to the listener, weaves through two or more parts. The trick, she told newcomers, was to pay very close attention to the egalitarian sharing among the parts. I had not noticed this as a mannerism, though I had done it deliberately in one anthem for three sopranos that I conceived of as an image of women's relationship with each other. I now speculate that, unbeknownst to my choir, I have occasionally made musical lesbians of them all by requiring them to cope with a world where "who's on top" keeps changing. I am grateful to Joan Miller for the insight.

17. And what they are gifted at, fine motor control, I have trained myself to use in three ways that give me tremendous joy because they give pleasure to others: music, cooking (I'm vain about my knife technique, and about the fact that I can peel some fruits and vegetables without a knife so as to present them whole and wholly pleasurable), and sex. I use them in each case—I use my ability to control *myself* instead of controlling another—to produce sensual pleasure that conveys love by releasing the capacities of the touched. By earlier definition, then, they are "lesbian" hands because they give pleasure and power without necessarily taking either: they let the other, the touched, be powerful as a means of enacting their own power.

18. Literally "thank you all for listening." This is the standard sign-off at the end of a radio program on RAI, the national radio network of Italy.

5

A CONVERSATION WITH NED ROREM

Lawrence D. Mass

N ED ROREM, THE PULITZER PRIZE AND Grammy Award-winning composer and author of twelve books, including *The Paris Diary* and *The Nantucket Diary*, was one of the first and has remained the best-known of openly homosexual figures in the world of music. His most recent book is *Settling the Score: Essays on Music.*[1] (Harcourt Brace Jovanovich, 1988). The following conversation, which focuses on opera and homosexuality, began in Rorem's living room in New York City on February 15, 1988, and was completed by correspondence in mid-1989. Entitled "Homosexuality and Music III" (following conversations on homosexuality and music with Philip Brett and George Heymont), it was published in my *Homosexuality as Behavior and Identity: Dialogues of the Sexual Revolution, Volume II.*[2] A specially abridged version appeared in *Opera Monthly.*[3]

My dialectic with Ned, rich and frustrating, was inevitably about group bonding and identity. Ned had often made the point—in interviews, in his diaries, and in conversations and correspondence with me—that being homosexual was no more interesting or pertinent, no more worthy of comment or analysis, than being heterosexual. In *The Nantucket Diary*, his engagement of our debate revealed earnest struggle and courage as well as generational differences:

> The so likable, and to an extent intelligent, Larry Mass, unable to see the forest for the trees, keeps writing me about what he feels to be the responsibility of the gay composer. Yes, at this point I am indeed attracted by the thought of a "gay libretto" (whatever that might be), but I'm more strongly drawn to a pacifist libretto. I am as much a Quaker as a gay, and man's inhumanity and identity and poetry are expressed as much through common conflict of our fatal globe as through sexual conflict. Perhaps an opera

on a debarred hero? Oscar Wilde? Even Alexander the Great?…

Larry Mass responds docilely to my ultimatum about discontinuing our, to me, fruitless exchange on gay music, with: "On Thursday Arnie and I are going to see [sic] the NYC Gay Men's Chorus, which will feature music by Barber, Bernstein, Copland, Gershwin, Porter, and Rorem. Nowhere, not in the program notes, certainly not in the mainstream press, but probably not even in the gay press or in Ned Rorem's diaries, however, will one read that all of these composers were/are homosexual, or any analysis of what that might mean."

Larry can't stop. Perhaps pink triangles could be placed by appropriate names in the program (although I never knew that Gershwin was homosexual). Doesn't Larry worry about Jewish composers? What has Bernstein's and Copland's (and, yes, Gershwin's) Jewishness to do with their music?…What would a program note say about, for example, Poulenc? "Poulenc, rumored to be gay (although he sired a daughter upon whom he doted), wrote his mass in…" Or Copland? "Copland, rumored to be gay, was also Jewish, but wrote goyish music all his life, being the first to celebrate cowboys." To dignify Larry's obsessions here is sadistic. Maybe I'll eat my words one day.[4]

The answer to Ned's first question is a resounding affirmative. Stimulated by my evolving awareness of sexual identity, I naturally have pondered the issue of the Jewishness of Jewish composers. What I've discovered, moreover, is that it is almost as closeted as the sexuality of homosexual composers, and in similar ways. The greatest culpability for this, I believe, rests with Richard Wagner, the composer whom the lovers of European classical music relish finding excuses to adore. Owing to Wagner, principally, and the racist and nationalist attitudes everyone knows he propounded—most notoriously in his anti-Semitic tract, *Jewry in Music,* among many other political writings, and metaphorically in his *Nibelung* tetralogy and *Die Meistersinger,* among other operas—the earnest desire was born after World War II to minimize, if not completely repress, awareness of the Wagner problem, a movement that was central to the greater process of attempting to establish nonpolitical status for music in a world of post-Holocaust chaos, wherein any significance that might be granted to the Jewishness of Jewish composers would be effaced. For an example of the internalization of the anti-Semitism resulting from this, one has only to turn to Eric Gordon's biography of Marc Blitzstein to reveal a case both combined with and paralleling internalized homophobia. "Blitzstein rarely thought about his Jewishness," Gordon observes, "and took no pains to explore Jewish themes in his work. He knew almost nothing of Jewish history…"[5] "Rather like Ned Rorem's frequent assertions," I concluded in my review of Gordon's book, "ongoing today, that homosexuality has nothing to do with art and music, Blitzstein's rare observations about Judaism and music were negative and defensive…"[6] As for Ned's second question—what would programs say about the gayness or reputed gayness of composers such as Copland and Poulenc?—if you take out the facetiousness, what he wrote isn't a bad start (though, "true to form," as my life partner Arnie Kantrowitz observed after reading these *Nantucket Diary* comments, "Rorem doesn't know there *were* Jewish cowboys"). I not only agree with Ned's (devil's advocate?) point about the pertinence of Copland's Jewishness to his art, but I suspect that, as with Blitzstein, it probably cannot be disentangled from the pertinence of this important American composer's homosexuality.

Since some degree of ambiguity is central to the nature of much, if not all, art, and because of the multiplicity and complexity of variables involved in its creation and appreciation, questions of the relationships of art to politics and identity, like those of the relationships between behavior and identity, will never be answerable absolutely. But it is important to continue the dialectic, a process that is as integral to the vitality of art as art is to vitality. In the interview that follows, Ned Rorem again demonstrates his formidable gift for insight and debate, even with regard to scores that, in a more progressive and knowledgeable era of gay liberation, we may believe are being permanently resettled.

Lawrence Mass: Where do you think you stand as an opera composer today?

Ned Rorem: Can one ever know one's own standing? We are not given to "see oursels as ithers see us." All I can provide is facts rather than opinions.

I've composed seven operas, each of them published and available. The first, *A Childhood Miracle*, in 1951, was based on a Nathaniel Hawthorne text and was a collaboration with my friend [*Village Voice* film critic] Elliot Stein. It runs approximately thirty-five minutes and is a virtuosic turn for thirteen instruments and six singers. It was first done in 1952 and later televised in 1956 in Philadelphia with Curtis undergraduates. An adolescent Benita Valente starred, and a boy of fifteen named Jaime Laredo was concertmaster. Another Curtis student, Plato Karayannis (now head of the Dallas Opera), directed. Then I did a second one-acter affair called *The Robbers*, based on a Chaucer tale and using my own libretto. Marc Blitzstein drastically revised the rather arch text. In 1965 I wrote *Miss Julie*, my only "full-length" opera, though I've never quite known what this term means (isn't a short work full-length?) other than a full-evening's opera. My cowriter was Kenward Elmslie, and the piece was glamorously though unsuccessfully produced by the New York City Opera. Next came *Bertha* and *Three Sisters Who Are Not Sisters* in 1968, both on commission (unpaid) from the Met Opera Studio. The librettos were by Kenneth Koch and Gertrude Stein. In those days, I was still young enough to do things because I liked to do them. Later came *Fables*, five operas in a grand total of twenty-two minutes, based on Marianne Moore's glittering translations of La Fontaine. In 1965 there was yet another opera, *Hearing*, originally a song cycle on poems of Kenneth Koch, which Jim Holmes, many years later, reworked into a scenario which I orchestrated for an unusual combination of nine instruments.

So, of my completed operas, six of the seven are brief, and they all saw the light between 1951 and 1968. It's been twenty years since I've written a new opera. There are still four that are half done—one based on *The Suicide Club* of Robert Louis Stevenson; another on *The Matron of Ephesus* from a tale in Petronius; a student work in 1946 drawn from Paul Goodman's play, *Cain and Abel*; and, in 1962, to Jascha Kessler's libretto, I all but completed and even partially orchestrated *The Anniversary* for the City Opera before we scrapped it in favor of *Miss Julie*. For completeness, let's include a pop musical called *The Ticklish Acrobat* written in 1957 with Elmslie, but never produced; and a seven-minute *scena* I composed just last spring on Cocteau's *Anna La Bonne*. Which brings the wavering total to thirteen, most of them, to some extent, on books of my choice, without any coercion.

I know that you're interested in finding relationships between composers and their choice of librettos, and there have to be such relationships, but I've never really thought much about that.

As to where I stand…I would love to write another (and I use the term opera *faute de mieux*)…another dramatic piece for singers before I die. Not a cantata, but a staged affair. Whenever I get around opera people, as in Santa Fe or like [philanthropist and leading opera patron] Robert Tobin, who's contributed lavishly to the Met, and the conversation turns to "What shall Ned do?" I get enthusiastic, but it's dangerous to get too enthusiastic about an opera unless you're going to be commissioned. Because unasked-for operas never get done.

Mass: Several years ago you told me that there was a possibility of a commission from the Santa Fe Opera.

Rorem: I did talk to John Crosby [director of the Santa Fe Opera] at some length in 1985, and he said, "Write me an outline." Robert Tobin was anxious to subsidize it if he, Robert, could also have a say about the subject. If I were them, I'd want to have that say, because more than any other musical format, opera is a collaborative venture. But I'm not very good at collaborating.

Mass: In *The Nantucket Diary* you discuss some of the subjects you've considered for a new opera. You then go on to say, "Probably I'll settle with JH [musician and writer James Holmes, who is also Rorem's life partner] on a sort of 'Life of Whitman,' or 'Aspects of Walt,' rather like *The Mother of Us All.*

Rorem: Jim [Holmes] and I were extremely enthusiastic, but Robert Tobin felt that Whitman was out of date. Tobin was upset by the AIDS crisis and felt we needed to do something more "timely." What does that mean? Is *Oedipus Rex* timely?

Mass: You say that Tobin was upset by the AIDS crisis. Did he want you to do something about AIDS? Did he have a specific suggestion for a libretto?

Rorem: What he wanted was that it *not* be about Whitman.

Mass: As I recall, around 1985, when you first told me about the possible commission from Santa Fe, you were considering a wide range of subjects, including *Oedipus*. In fact, you asked me if I had any ideas for operas with gay themes. I suggested two possibilities: Mishima's *Confessions of a Mask* and the story of Ganymede. You read *Confessions*, but decided it wasn't right because, among other reasons, it wasn't sufficiently "mythic." Obviously, that was not the reason for rejecting Ganymede, but I don't remember what the reason was. In *The Nantucket Diary* you imply that you also considered *Kiss of the Spider Woman* and an unspecified collaboration with William M. Hoffman. Clearly, the possibility of doing an opera with a gay theme has been an issue you've grappled with.

Has anyone ever written an opera about Walt Whitman?

Rorem: I don't think so. [Theatre producer, director, and designer] John Wulp wanted me to do an opera on the life of Henry James. I read all five of the Leon Edel books with mixed feelings. I worship James, but operas on the lives of great men are flirting with danger. Like that movie on the life of Billie Holliday using another singer. The greatness was in the *oeuvre*, not in the life.

Mass: You say that you and Jim were extremely enthusiastic about the idea of doing an opera about Whitman. Have you and/or Jim done any work yet on such a project?

Rorem: No, for the simple reason that I haven't pushed it. If I really wanted to do this opera, if I were ready, I could probably arrange to get a commission. Maybe there's something in me that refrains. Most opera composers always have a new opera up their sleeve. I don't. But I do have enough other work contracted for during the next few years to keep me from brooding too much about an opera.

Mass: In your essay on Joe Orton[7] (from *The Advocate*, June 9, 1987), you say that you would love to have had an opera libretto from him. In the absence of a specially conceived libretto, would you, if you had the time, consider setting one of his farces, such as *Entertaining Mr. Sloane* or *What the Butler Saw?*

Rorem: Orton's plays are already very musical, like Edward Albee's, oozing with echoes, rhythms, and colors that are so exact in themselves, and with wit so pungent and dependent on time, music could only slow them down. As opposed, say, to Tennessee Williams. The difference between Albee and Williams is that Albee's theater is music already. [Scored] music cannot add to it. It would only detract from the icy aptness of his clipped phrases; whereas Tennessee's writing is all rhapsodic. It's about music, but it is not music in itself, which is why Tennessee's plays lend themselves so much more gracefully to opera. I worked with Tennessee on two occasions (providing incidental background music to *Suddenly Last Summer* and to *The Milk Train*). But I wouldn't consider turning any of his plays into an opera now. They don't hold up with the passing of time. They embarrass me.

I read everything that has been published of Joe Orton's in preparation for that essay, but song didn't come into it. When I reread Jane Bowles's *In a Summer House* every five years, I think maybe I should do that. But the last act deteriorates. It's a noble failure. I've also considered Colette's *Chéri*, which would have been ideal for Poulenc. But whenever I reconsider it for myself, it becomes more and more remote.

It's easy to know what you don't want to do. In the abstract, I know what I do want to do. Something about myself. I'd need to be inside of the main male or female character if I'm going to live two years with those damn people. Something of Mishima, yes, might work, but not Ganymede, since I'm not interested in children. There's a lot of me in Chéri, and in Leah, his mistress, but the story is dated. Of course, all art dates from the moment it's penned. Beethoven and Stravinsky date well. Tennessee Williams doesn't. Colette dates wonderfully, but *Chéri* isn't apropos any longer.

Mass: We were talking about Orton. Charles Ludlum is an artist whose work you've said you believe in as much as Orton's Did any of his works present themselves to you as possibilities for opera?

Rorem: I haven't seen much of his work. I seldom go to the theater anymore because it's dull and expensive. I go to movies. Ludlum's plays aren't all that suitable for singing for the same reasons that Orton's aren't. They're ironic and crisp and extremely dependent on words and on timing. Wit in opera is not the same as wit in plays. Nobody's going to understand the words anyway.

There's more potential with film. Like every self-respecting American, I was raised on movies. *The Umbrellas of Cherbourg* bowled me over. That was twenty-five years ago, but it's still the sole opera originally conceived for the movies. In all of its corny glory it truly works. Since then nobody has tried anything else new with opera and film. It's an open field. There are, of course, the television and screen adaptations of the standard repertoire, and many of these come off well. I got a lot more out of the TV presentation of *Lulu*, for example, than I ever did from seeing it on the stage. Interestingly, George Perle, the world's foremost Berg scholar, told me he really understood *Lulu* when he saw it on the tube, and he adored the subtitles.

Mass: Are you saying that if you were to do a new opera you'd like to conceive it for the cinema?

Rorem: Yes. If I had an idea. I'd want to work with a director like Antonioni, for example, not a director who knows about music so much as one who knows about film.

Mass: Is Antonioni still doing films? (Is he still alive?) In *The Nantucket Diary* you discuss your work with such famous directors as Zeffirelli. But there are a number of leading directors you don't mention, like Visconti, Ponnelle, Caldwell, Felsenstein, Wieland Wagner, or Chéreau. Any comments?

Rorem: In 1962 Zeffirelli had never directed anything in America. That's when the Strasbergs reigned supreme. Zeffirelli thought he'd like to begin big, so he hired Susan Strasberg, the world's least talented actress, to take the role of Marguerite Gautier in *The Lady of the Camelias*, adapted by, among others, Terrence McNally. I wrote the score, working every day for a month with Zeffirelli. They put it on as a Broadway play. I wrote about forty minutes worth of music for four or five instruments filtered through an echo chamber. Romantic, Chopinesque, Frenchish, decadent. It was a horrible experience. Collaborations always are. It lasted four performances. I didn't personally care for Zeffirelli. His vain gloriousness was oppressive.

We were all raised on Visconti's films. When I lived in Rome in 1954–55, he was sort of a god. I met him once or twice at Bill Weaver's. That's in the days when I never knew what to say to idols, so I'd get drunk. I was very impressed. Late one night we all went to a nightclub with Massimo Girotti. Remember him from *Teorema* (which, incidentally, is going to be made into an opera by Michael Torke)? Remember that last scene, when Girotti, virile head of the family, ends up sneaking in and out of a men's room in a Milan bus terminal? Very, very sad. When you recall that in *Reflections of a Golden Eye*, Brando had taken a homosexual role similar to Girotti's in *Teorema*, and then recall these two old icons in their scene together in *Last Tango in Paris*, it was something very special.

I saw the Callas-Visconti *Sonnambula* at La Scala that Lenny Bernstein conducted. Visconti, like all Italians, knew what opera was, and he knew how to cope with Callas. But I once overheard her talking to someone at the little café next to La Scala (she was toying with fresh strawberries in mid-February) about how he was on the right track but got off somehow. "Era sulla buona strada," said she in her accented Italian. I heard Callas many times. Now, I don't worship divas, but Callas represents one of the two or three greatest experiences I've ever had in any theater. The others were Mary Wigman, the dancer, when I was in third grade, about 1932, the early Martha Graham, Billie Holiday, Nazimova in Ibsen, Edith Piaf. All female, needless to say. There are no male equivalents, Whitman notwithstanding. Theater is artifice and artifice is feminine.

I've never seen a Felsenstein production, but I've seen many of Caldwell's things, and so many of my friends have worked with her and just adore her. Let's see. I saw the *Lulu* at BAM [Brooklyn Academy of Music]. She may be a bit on the gimmicky side. Ponnelle?

Mass: I don't think gay men are more involved with divas than divos because "artifice is feminine." I think the reason gay men's stage and screen idols have been predominantly female has mostly to do with our stronger identification with women. (We identify more with Judy Garland and Maria Callas than with Frank Sinatra or Elvis Presley.) For gay men in our time, this identification is a lot more easily expressed than sexual attraction, whereas the opposite is grossly true of heterosexual women. If there were no homophobia, maybe gay men would be more prominent among the fans of the Sinatras and Presleys. Conversely, if our operas, movies, and songs were less patriarchal (conceived, written, and directed by men), maybe women would be more prominent among the most ardent fans of the likes of Garland and Callas. [These issues are explored in Catherine Clément's *Opera, or the Undoing of Women.*—L.M.]

Ponnelle's the one who did the recent *Manon* at the Met. You know, the one where Manon ends up in a pile of garbage.

Rorem: The trouble with all of those directors: they're trying to breathe life into dead horses. Why doesn't Chéreau coerce his friend Boulez into writing an opera instead of doing the Ring? They spend their energies on masterpieces that have long since proved themselves. They're not taking any real chances. The important thing is new music. It always was until our century. Now all we do is these eternal revivals. The so-called "alternative versions" of the Ring or Manon or whatever, say, Frank Corsaro touches, all deal with updating, so that today's public will find it relevant. They update the costumes, sets, direction, viewpoint—everything except the music. But why not the music too? Why not add a "beat," as someone once did to Bach, adding tom-toms to *The Well-Tempered Clavier*? Because then it would be a truly new opera. Well then, just commission new operas instead of sprinkling bitter sugar—expensive sugar!—on old chestnuts?

Mass: On this extremely important point, I've heard you say that concert music and opera, as we present and appreciate them here in the U.S., are the only major art forms whose art is almost exclusively of the past. Would you care to say more about this?

Rorem: Movies didn't exist before our century, so they're by definition new. At the theater, nine out of ten plays are by living playwrights. Such plays of the recent past as those of Inge or Williams or O'Neill are called revivals. (Imagine calling a Beethoven symphony a revival, since Beethoven is the rule, not the exception.) The book reviews we read in *The New York Times* are virtually all about vital, breathing authors. The exhibitions in the galleries are nearly all by vital, breathing painters. (Only in the museums is there emphasis on the past.) This is true of every art except music, where the present is anachronistic and the past is sovereign. For most people, the serious living composer isn't even a despised minority. He doesn't exist enough to be despised. The vitality of contemporary music is something that even cultured nonintellectuals mostly aren't aware of. And I'm afraid that's true of people like Ponnelle and Chéreau too.

Mass: But it's not just the directors. Who shares the responsibility for the mortuarial state of opera today? Is it our critics? Our audiences?

Rorem: It's our managers. There are more gifted young composers around today than there ever were, but there's no outlet for them. No big orchestra will touch them. No opera company or recording company or publisher cares about them. So they are going to have to find their own way as creative artists, just as they will be forced to concoct new sexual rules since the advent of AIDS. They're going to have to do what Britten did in Aldeburgh or Peter Maxwell Davies in Scotland—start their own little groups. Management has a lot to do with it. Impresarios are in it for the dough and they lie when they say they're not.

Mass: Herbert Breslin is in it more for the money than the art? I don't believe it!

Rorem: To think that the great Jennie Tourel was required by her manager to go out on those tours in the sticks and sing "My Hero" from *The Chocolate Soldier*, in the face of her nuanced repertoire in eleven languages! And the condescension that her managers forced her into, of singing music that she didn't sing very well simply to pay the bills. Money shouldn't be what dictates. Beverly Sills shouldn't have to say, "I can't afford to take the chance." In every era but ours, one could afford to take the chance. Now, it's difficult if Pavarotti can make $100,000 for one concert—three times the amount a composer gets to write a whole opera. Conversely, it's difficult for a manager to ask a Pavarotti to sing a recital of contemporary American songs, or even one such song.

The legitimization of pop music with its huge public has thrown a monkey wrench into the situation. With that kind of potential for making money, why would managers want to do anything else? William Parker, for example, the best recitalist in America, has exactly zero recitals lined up for the next year. His singing engagements are mainly for foreign-language operas. There isn't one singer in America today who can earn a living fundamentally as a recitalist. In Europe, the few who can, like Ameling, Souzay, and Fischer-Dieskau, are all over the hill. As a result, the whole sense of how to shape a song is fading. There's no public for it, and that's management's fault. I don't know many managers personally. I don't have much to do with them because they have so little to do with living composers. I sometimes meet them at parties and never fail to say what I think. What have I to lose? With rare exceptions, they are unconcerned with contemporary American music. Yes, Matthew Epstein says he is. Tommy Thompson (who was Donald

Gramm's manager) has been terrific. On the whole, though, they don't want their string quartets even playing Bartók, much less Elliott Carter, if it's going to scare away the women's club in Podunk. The dishonesty lies in their saying, "I want such and such singer to sing this, but the audience doesn't." Now, audiences will take what they get, if it's given to them right.

American singers are the only singers who don't sing first and foremost in their native language. They learn to sing badly in every language except their own, and on the rare occasions that they approach their own, it's by rolling their r's and doing all kinds of Europeanistic things that have nothing to do with English. Imagine a young French singer specializing in every repertoire except French! When American singers understand what they're singing about, they're terribly embarrassed. The great poetry in English is not really part of the tradition of American song. If you do get a small audience of 300 in a small theater for a recital of songs based on poems by Emily Dickinson or Elizabeth Bishop or John Ashbery, that can be a very heady experience. Managers would like to discourage this, because they don't want audiences of 300. They want 300 million. They're size queens.

Mass: Hmmm…I never thought of Cynthia Robbins as a size queen before. And what about our critics? Do you think they could have more influence on this situation?

Rorem: Most of them have their hearts in the right place. But take Andrew Porter, who is arguably the most read critic in the country. He just doesn't have that much influence, judging from all the suggestions he makes that are never taken.

Mass: Somewhere in the new *Diary* you note that John Rockwell wrote his annual piece urging the New York City Opera or the Met to do *The Mother of Us All* or *Four Saints in Three Acts*. And you ask, why doesn't he ask the managers directly?

Rorem: Critics write these things, but nobody listens. Occasionally, a performer might become interested in a piece the critic has mentioned, but that's about it. Critics can stifle or even break a performer's career if it hasn't already gotten off the ground. But they can't really launch a young composer, or do much damage to an old one.

Mass: One more thought about management. Any observations about Terry McEwen? [McEwen had just announced his retirement, for reasons of health, from the position of director of the San Francisco Opera.]

Rorem: None, except that he's an old friend. His tastes are specific. He once said to me, "I'm not a music lover, I'm an opera lover." [As director of the San Francisco Opera], he couldn't have been more reactionary.

Mass: Yes. During his tenure there was no emphasis on new works.

Rorem: Yet he did commission, of all people, Hugo Weisgall, who writes very knotty music. When people like Terry finally decide to do their good deed, they'll be damned if they'll call on someone "accessible," like Carlyle Floyd or Tom Pasatieri.

Mass: Terry McEwen is widely known in the gay community to be gay, though he has never been openly so in interviews. Respecting that opera was McEwen's business and that he was a professional, I think it says something about the minority status of gay people in the music world that he was the officially closeted homosexual director of the opera company of the city with the world's largest (proportionately) and most politically progressive gay community and audience during the era of gay liberation and the AIDS crisis. For New York, I think similar observations could be made about such leading musical figures as Stephen Sondheim.

We touched on McEwen's tenure as director of the SFO and the issue of new commissions. To some extent, we've been exploring the status of opera in America. How would you contrast the place of opera in America with that in Europe? [The reason for the abrupt transition from discussion of McEwen and Sondheim to the question about contrasting the place of opera in America with that in Europe is that Rorem refused to comment on the homosexuality of living, closeted figures in the music world. As he says later in this interview, "I will not, and neither will Lou Harrison, compromise my friends, especially those of an older generation (those happy few!) who have their own perfectly decent set of standards. If I've done so in the past, I regret it." On this account, I was obliged to make a statement out of what had been a question ("How do you feel about…?"), and move on to the next topic. In a recent telephone conversation, incidentally, Lou Harrison, with whom I've been in contact in efforts to set up an interview, tentatively confirmed Rorem's statement that he (Harrison) would not out someone who wasn't overtly involved in homophobic or fascistic endeavors and who didn't wish to be publicly identified as gay or lesbian—L. M.]

Rorem: Almost without exception, opera in Europe has been written by what we call experimental composers, from Monteverdi through Wagner to Nono and Berg, by chromatic composers, composers breaking or inventing the mold, starting new musical as well as theatrical systems. One of the reasons this has been so is the subject matter, which in Europe has always been rather short on humor and high on horror. Murder, incest, rape, you name it, from *Poppea* to *Lulu.* Except for Mozart—and Mozart was not necessarily, fundamentally an opera composer—I think this obtains. The Europeans were fundamentally opera composers—experimental, nondiatonic.

The reverse obtains in American. We don't have much of a history of opera, but what we do have is by plain diatonic composers. The operas that have lasted are the two operas by Virgil Thomson, which are possibly the best by an American, maybe Deems Taylor's two operas, Aaron Copland's one, Barber's two, the several by Douglas Moore, Blitzstein, Menotti. All of this is music with no accidentals. White-key music, as we say.

Look at the operas in this country that work. They aren't by Elliott Carter or John Cage. They're by Philip Glass and John Adams, and it's all nonmodulatory, super-simple music.

Doesn't this reflect a difference in the psychology of Europe and America? Is that why jazz is an American rather than a European thing and why a lot of our opera, like Gershwin's *Porgy and Bess*, stems from that kind of music? It's something to think about. Our opera themes aren't psychotic themes.

Mass: What about *Lizzie Borden*?

Rorem: But *Lizzie Borden* was never a hit. I'm talking about our most successful operas.

We don't even have a failed opera by, say, Milton Babbitt. We do have madness, however, in the tradition of Martha Graham. There is no new music being written for so-called modern dance today, but there used to be. For every new score that's used, now, fifty are based on preexisting music. Except for Martha Graham, who's deliciously psychotic. She once commissioned a hundred different composers. But them days is gone forever.

Mass: On the subject of utilizing preexisting music, I want to ask you something about your hypothetical Whitman opera. You've set a lot of Whitman to music already. How would those compositions that you've already created figure in with the new one?

Rorem: It's always tempting in a case of this sort to want to cheat, to reuse something you've already composed. Yes, I have set a lot of Whitman to music. I've found, though, that when you cheat in that way, it never works. I might be able to use a tune or two, but I doubt that I could take intact a song written thirty years ago and put it into the opera. Unless the opera were a mere garland of songs and were in a sense my biography as well as Whitman's. But there's a difference in kind between a song and an aria, between something that's sung in a theater and on a recital stage. There's a difference in scope and intimacy.

For example, Whitman wrote the following:

> Stranger, if you passing meet me and desire to speak to me, why should
> you not speak to me?
> And why should I not speak to you?

(The answer to the poem's questions, by the way, is: because you might get a sock in the jaw.)

I set that to music for piano and voice. It takes the same time to sing it as to say it. Now if I were to rethink that and put it into an opera, it would need some sort of introduction and postlude, something to get the piece onstage and off. Would I use the same music? Maybe not.

Mass: Are there many examples of composers who take the text and rework it with lots of different versions?

Rorem: Usually opera composers are not song composers. For example, Verdi and Menotti aren't known for their songs, and Schubert and Fauré aren't known for their operas. There are exceptions, like Virgil Thomson and Britten and Poulenc.

Mass: And Richard Strauss.

Rorem: Yes, but for every exception…People always use to say, "Ned, you write such great songs, you were born to write an opera." It doesn't necessarily follow. Song is a self-contained experience of two or three minutes. It's a distillation. A song is conceived on preexisting poetry that is unaltered, or should be unaltered. Operas are based on prose that often can't stand alone. When they try to write operas, song composers write visual song cycles and then cross their fingers. Opera composers are more involved with dramatic thrust. It must be worth watching as well as hearing. Arguably, Wagner fails. But Menotti, who is no Wagner, does not write boring operas…at his best.

Mass: Did you see *La loca* or *Goya*?

Rorem: Before I saw *Goya*, I read the frightful reviews and sent a letter of condolence to Menotti, who is an old acquaintance and who was my teacher when I was a nineteen-year-old at Curtis. About ten or twelve years ago I wrote an essay in his defense, against Henahan who had given him short shrift in a way that seemed undeserved. Henahan smirked about Menotti's moving to Scotland, more or less saying good riddance and isn't it silly that Menotti should take himself seriously. Well, I don't think that's very nice or right since Menotti, whatever he may be "worth" in retrospect, single-handedly put opera on the map in America.

Anyway, when he got my letter about the reviews of *Goya*, he phoned in tears, saying, "Oh, Ned, you're the only one who understands!" in that Italian way, and, "Let's get together soon," etc. Then I saw *Goya* on the television, and, well, I should never have sent that letter. The Menotti situation is a sad one. *The Medium* and *The Consul* are unflawed in their own way. His music is corn, but it's inspired corn. Like Tennessee Williams. After those early plays, everything went downhill. *Goya* missed the boat at every turn. Domingo was valiant to learn that thing by heart.

Years ago, around 1946, Menotti said in my presence that he would like to write a homosexual opera. One didn't say gay in those days. He wanted to do something on Proust, which, God knows, would certainly tempt me. But it can't be done. Like Kafka. It's too personal.

Mass: If you were to write a new opera, would you write it with a specific singer in mind (e.g., the way Menotti wrote *La loca* for Sills and *Goya* for Domingo, or as Barber wrote *Antony and Cleopatra* for Price)?

Rorem: It's hard to explain why the least difficult aspect of writing an opera is the music and the most difficult is finding a proper book and honing it into singable shape. What you're asking about is really one of the last considerations. To come up with a good idea about Whitman is simply the tip of the iceberg. You get the idea but *then* what? Sometimes a perfect preexisting text falls in a composer's lap. Lee Hoiby took *Summer and Smoke* and used it intact, after Lanford Wilson dolled it up a little. Barber did the same with *Antony and Cleopatra*. These operas are literally the play. *Les Dialogues de Carmélites* is exactly the Bernanos film script plus a few set numbers from Catholic liturgy. If the right property existed now and didn't need to have much done to it, and it were in public domain, I'd grab it, whether it was old or new.

In the case of Walt Whitman, the work would need a point of view, which I still don't have. Once you get the point of view, the work should let him speak for himself through his own words, while trying also to be a biography.

As for a specific singer, I would coldly decide the role's going to be this or that kind of voice. Sometimes it's interesting to go against typecasting. It'd be interesting to do Whitman as a black countertenor.

Mass: My first thought was that this would have been the perfect vehicle for the late Donald Gramm.

Rorem: But Donald's dead now. He was the most intelligent and persuasive male singer we've ever known. I would have entrusted the role to him, but that's now idle conjecture.

Mass: In *The Nantucket Diary*, you repeat a question someone asked you about which singers do you admire. You then go on to list a number of wonderful American singers, many underappreciated, about whom you say wonderful and interesting things. There were several prominent ones you didn't mention. Teresa Stratas, for instance.

Rorem: Don't forget that a lot of the diary entries you're talking about were written years ago. Well-known singers change quickly.

Fifteen years ago I was a different person and the singing situation was different. I was the sole composer in the U.S.A. one thought about when American song was mentioned. That's not the case today. I'm not complaining, simply stating a statistic. They sing songs by Bolcom now and they still sing Barber a lot, but they don't sing my songs much, which makes me wistful.

Stratas? I've seen her in *Lulu*, in *Mahagonny*, and in the movie of *Traviata*. I don't care for her record of Kurt Weill; it's too slick and Slavic, but she's otherwise pretty interesting, though no more so than Migenes-Johnson.

Mass: Did you see/hear her Mélisande?

Rorem: Yes, years ago, and I liked it. It was too slow, but that was Levine's fault. I heard Von Stade do it on the radio the other day and I like her, too. Cool and mature. *Pelléas et Mélisande* is my favorite opera. Of course, Pelléas and Mélisande are really silly children. Bruce-Michael Gelbert recently quoted me for having once used that naughty word "gay" to describe Pelléas on the grounds of the text. There *was* something up between him and

Marcéllus, whom he never gets to see again. But it's another one of those cryptic, dangling themes that's introduced by Maeterlinck, dropped, and never resumed. So Pelléas decides he's in love with Mélisande, but I think he's telling the truth when he says they've never sinned together. They were just pals.

Von Stade lent an unusual dimension to Mélisande, probably because of the darker sound of her mezzo, but also because of her less babyish (babyish the way Bidu Sayão used to do it) point of view…Mélisande is the escaped last wife of Bluebeard, or so Mary Garden used to contend, justifying her crazed performance.

Mass: I remember when I read Mary Garden's biography I got the very strong impression that Garden had fallen in love with Lily Debussy.

Rorem: Why not?

Mass: In *The Nantucket Diary* you say that "the most valuable composers are apolitical and aristocratic (Wagner, Ravel, Stravinsky), or bourgeois and bearish and pseudopolitical (Bach, Beethoven, Debussy), or just straightfor-wardly religious members of the status quo, like all those before the Industrial Revolution." Please elaborate.

Rorem: Art can make political statements, but it cannot have political effect. Art is not moral, it is something else. It cannot change us, but it *can* reinforce our convictions and help us get through life. If I were able to make a political statement as an artist, I would. If I were able to write a song that could make people march away from war, I would. The way to stop wars is not to fight them. Art is created in leisure, not in the heat of battle. Art won't make a Democrat out of a Republican and it won't make a peacenik out of a warmonger, as the Nazis, who were very sensitive to music, have proved. And it won't make a nice person out of a bad person, as Wagner, who was a great genius and misguided rascal, has also proved.

I've written only one "political" piece, which is "War Scenes," drawn from Whitman's Civil War diary, but that could just as easily have been about the Trojan or the Viet Nam war. It's about the horror of war in general. I'm moved by Britten's *War Requiem*. Who isn't? It's political yet enduring; but, again, he's using timeless words rather than timely ones.

Mass: You're acknowledging that something timely can be just as timeless as something ancient or mythic, but you're skeptical about the prospects for anything very topical enduring as art. "Imagine *As Is* as an opera!" you once quipped. Hence your skepticism about doing a "gay" opera. Perhaps that's why, up until your current setting of one of Paul Monette's *Elegies for Rog* for the New York City Gay Men's Chorus, you had never scored anything with explicitly gay or other "political" content. I think it's sad that the only conceivable contribution of the Santa Fe Opera (the management of which has always had gay people in its highest ranks) to the AIDS crisis ended up being Penderecki's *The Black Mask* (based on Nazi collaborationist Gerhard Hauptmann's racist 1929 soap opera about the second wave of the black death in seventeenth-century Europe). Why couldn't a new opera about real people of our time (but no more than the extent to which *Figaro* and *Lulu* are explicitly of their times) have made just as strong a bid for artistic propriety?

[At its premiere in San Francisco in May 1989, *Least of My Children* by Donald Briggs and Loren Linnard became the first opera to deal explicitly with the AIDS epidemic, and there are several operas-in-progress that are about AIDS, including one based on a text by Sarah Schulman commissioned by the Houston Grand Opera.—L.M.]

Did you see *Malcolm X*?

Rorem: Yes. In a Philadelphia tryout. I certainly wasn't against it in principle. Malcolm X was a powerful figure, a hero, but also an abstraction. You can humanize a hero, but not until enough time has passed for the hero to become a symbol, an invention, like Julius Caesar or Henry VIII. Real live heroes don't go into the street singing.

Mass: Had enough time elapsed, according to your criteria, for this to work? That is, was *Malcolm X* a success, and, if not, was it because it was "too political" or "too timely"?

Rorem: No. The main problem was that it was unbalanced. The whole first section was completely improvisatory and fell flat. But as a tragedy it worked.

Mass: What about *Mahagonny*?

Rorem: Brecht was a political man and a less important artist than Kurt Weill. Weill succeeds in spite of his propaganda content rather than because of it. Music, insofar as it's propagandistic, can never persuade. Insofar as it veers from propaganda, it can work. *Malcolm X* became a tragedy about a hero, but Malcolm X himself is too remote now for even me to quite remember. A speech *by* Malcolm X is far more jarring than an aria *about* him.

Mass: But in addition to the general human interest in Malcolm X as a tragic human being, the hero's main concern, racism, *is* timely, just as the fate of capitalism, the principal subject of *Mahagonny*, remains timely. So *Malcolm X* and *Mahagonny* are political, rather the way *Figaro* was. *Figaro* was literally revolutionary in its views of contemporary class relations, and it dealt with everyday people and everyday life in contemporary Europe and was based on a play by a living playwright. It incited people to riots. What you're saying is that the long-range value of, say, *Figaro* transcends the class struggle in France that stimulated and permeates it. Everyone can agree with that. What I'm emphasizing, though, is that some great, timeless works like *Figaro* were originally as topical as some of the contemporary works—operas about Viet Nam, racism, sexism, homophobia and AIDS—you're so certain would be too propagandist, too timely, to endure.

But even when an artist's themes are ancient and mythic and don't appear to be political, they often are, as in the case of Wagner. I was thus intrigued by your generalization that Wagner was apolitical.

Rorem: The Wagner case is a healthy example, like that of Rock Hudson dying of AIDS. Hudson showed that even a national idol can have AIDS. Wagner showed that a great artist can also be a son-of-a-bitch, even wicked. It's necessary to demythologize the Hollywoodian notion of artists as "good people." I'm always moved when strangers tell me what a good person I must be, because I'm not. If they knew the real me!

Mass: Some writers characterize *Lulu* as a "feminist opera." Are they bad?

Rorem: Bad? The use of words like homosexual, negro, black, gay, depends on how old you are, what part of the country you're from, and to the class of people you hang out with. The word feminist didn't exist during the 1930s when Berg wrote *Lulu*, at least not with the same resonance as today. Negro was a noble word when I was a kid, in an extremely radical milieu. Now that word is banned and we're supposed to say black, which used to be a "wrong" word. Well, Paris is worth a mass, so I say gay now and black too, though I never used to. Like friends who change their names when they become famous. Sooner or later you get the hang of it.

Mass: Do you think gay liberationists like myself are misguided in regarding the Countess of Geschwitz, the first explicitly lesbian and homosexual and feminist character to enter the international repertoire, as a source of gay and feminist pride? Or is she no more interesting or pertinent to gay or feminist history or to the so-called heritage I'm claiming of gay people and women in music and opera than, say, Mohammed, "Der Kleine Neger" in *Der Rosenkavalier*, is to the musical heritage of black people?

Rorem: You've criticized me for talking about groups of people, like Jews, as though they weren't individuals. But you are included to talk about gay people as a group. I'm willing to talk about gay people as a group if it helps the situation. I don't think that homosexuality is a very interesting subject, *except* politically, just as heterosexuality is not a very interesting subject. As you well know, homosexuals are just as boring as heterosexuals. Homosexuality is interesting only insofar as homosexuals are a persecuted minority. (Of course, that's pretty interesting.)

We can make the past what we want to make of it. We can put motivations into Berg's works, and we might even be correct on one level, although he may have been quite unaware of what we think he was thinking. One can write doctorates about *Lulu* until the cows come home. The Countess can be interpreted in many different ways, unsympathetically as well as sympathetically. Finally, she is only what the music tells us she is.

Mass: You must think, then, that I am likewise misguided in expecting our music critics to have said something about why the Countess might be especially interesting to today's opera-going public, with its large numbers of gay and lesbian persons, during this era of gay liberation struggles and AIDS. Incidentally, George Perle, who has characterized lesbian sex as "naughty," wrote me that he knows of no criticism, neither at the time of the writing and premiere of *Lulu* nor today, that engaged this question, period. I don't think he sees the pertinence of the Countess to today's audience and to our time as any more worthy of comment than you or Peter G. Davis do.

Rorem: George was being naughty himself to have used such a characterization. Of course, all sex is naughty, which is why it's fun. Now, when you say critics, you're talking about nongay as well as gay critics. I recently read Ed Sikov's comments about [Christopher] Lehmann-Haupt's review of the Oscar Wilde book [by Richard Ellman] in the *Native*. Sometimes people point out homophobia where I don't see it, but in this case I did.

I was interviewed recently by somebody in Philadelphia for a straight magazine. In the galleys, the interviewer said something about "cheery" homosexuals. I wrote him back that I thought it was homophobic to stereotype a bunch of people as "cheery." He changed the reference, but reluctantly. By the same token, I'm not looking for homophobia all the time.

Lehmann-Haupt would doubtless deny that he's homophobic, while being more careful in the future.

Mass: Like your good friend, John Simon, who graduated from his interview with you, in which his homophobia is the principal subject addressed, to become the film critic for William F. Buckley's *National Review*? Lehmann-Haupt has been homophobic many times in the past, and there have been repeated complaints in the gay press. I myself have written him letters.

Rorem: Did he ever respond?

Mass: No.

Rorem: The disappointing thing is that someone like Norman Mailer, who's smart and, I gather, rather well read, is homophobic. It would be so much more interesting if he weren't. Most of our star heterosexual writers are inadvertently homophobic—Styron, Updike, Mary McCarthy...But going back to the question of critics, I think you're asking them to discuss something that's not pertinent in a review. It might be in a Sunday article.

Mass: In a little review in *The New York Times* of *Albert Herring*, Donal Henahan, of all people, suggested that perhaps Britten identified with the character as a homosexual and that it's possible to see the opera as a kind of "coming out" story. *That's* the kind of *timely*, pertinent observation about something of interest to lesbian and gay persons that we almost never get in mainstream music writing, even when the critic is gay.

Rorem: But Henahan's point had to do directly with Britten and the opera. With *Lulu*, you're asking critics to talk about social issues in their performance reviews.

Mass: When the social issues are pertinent and interesting, yes, that's precisely what I'm asking them to do!

When the Waldheim affair broke, *The New York Times* published several op-ed pieces (by Anthony Lewis and others) urging James Levine to cancel his performances in Vienna and Salzburg, the way Toscanini did in protests to the Nazis and Fascists. Not only didn't Levine cancel his performances, he never publicly responded to these challenges. Was he wrong?

Rorem: During the Second World War, I was almost a conscientious objector because my mother wanted me to be. But at the army exam, I arranged to get rejected, not as a CO, but as a 4E, on the basis on nearsightedness and flat feet. A year later I again had to go through that same sordid business of the induction exam, so I got a letter from my psychoanalyst, who explained that I was "not sufficiently mature" to be in the army. (The army, as we know, is made up only of mature people!) I felt, and my parents agreed, that since the army is immoral, why be "moral" about staying out of it? I didn't want to be a conscientious objector. My sister's husband was a conscientious objector, and it was hideous. I'm not of that fiber. I have music to write. I don't like to throw stones…During the 1950s when I was living in Europe, and people talked about the cold war and collaborationists—did you know that so-and-so went to bed with German soldiers during the occupation?—I kept my mouth shut and listened. Who am I to say what they should or should not have done, since I was not in their place? Nobody has asked me to go to Austria. If I had been asked to go to Austria and my friends had asked me not to, I would certainly have thought about it. If I were Jewish, I don't know what I would do. I know people who have gone to South Africa. Will Parker, for example, gave recitals there but told his friends to keep quiet about it. Edward Albee, meanwhile, refused to allow his plays to be done there, which is sort of pretentious. It doesn't accomplish anything, unless it gets a lot of publicity. I can't presume to speak for James Levine. But Lenny Bernstein conducts in Vienna, and he's not exactly a fascist.

Mass: In *The Nantucket Diary* you quip that you are a "gay pacifist," as opposed to being a gay activist. Actually, you're not the only prominent composer who is known to be both homosexual and pacifist. Britten and Tippett are two others. Do you know of any straight composers who are similarly, outspokenly pacifist?

Rorem: Sexual orientation and pacifism are not related, certainly not in my case. I was born a pacifist and raised by convinced Quaker parents, both of them ardent heterosexuals. Britten, on the other hand, came to his pacifism by conviction. Probably, the same 10 percent of pacifists are homosexual as the 10 percent of taxidermists or horse racers are. I don't think there are any real generalities that can be made here. It has never occurred to me that homosexuality and pacifism have anything to do with each other. Pacifism is far rarer than homosexuality and, unlike homosexuality, pacifism has to do with intelligence. Pacifism used to be a dirty word. It's become less so since the 1960s. Also, with regard to your quoting of me, the opposite of pacifist is not activist. Pacifist has to do with peace, not with passivity. So it's a false play on words.

Mass: In your essay on "Women in Music" in *Setting the Tone*, you ask the question, "Why have there been so few women composers?" If you've given the answer somewhere, I've missed it. Beyond your belief that art is ineffable and follows no rules, do you have a theory?

Rorem: They've all been discriminated against. It's that simple. There are more women poets because there's less "manual" labor, less dirty work, involved in being a poet than in being a composer. It's hard to raise children and still spend twelve hours a day orchestrating.

But all composers are discriminated against. I don't think female composers today are any worse off than male. If I had to name twelve living composers who interest me, four or five would be women: Thea Musgrave, Betsy Jolas, Barbara Kolb, Louise Talma, Miriam Gideon...

Mass: You've pointed out that I speak about gay people as a group. I do, to some extent, even though that group, like all groups, is unquestionably made up of a wide diversity of individuals. But as you've also acknowledged, most of my generalizations about gay people are affirmatively defensive of gay people as a minority. Your observations about Jews, by contrast, are often negative stereotypes about the entirety of a people. You once asked me if I thought you were anti-Semitic. I said then that I didn't think you were. I'd like to continue to believe that you're not anti-Jewish, Ned—and I know that many of your best friends and at least one of your principal patrons are Jewish—but a number of entries in *The Nantucket Diary* challenge that belief.

For example, the last entry of 1973 concludes as follows: "I've never read *The Diary of Anne Frank* ([Meyer] Levin's book [*The Obsession*] concerns her rape by those presumed monsters who denied him use of his own theater adaptation), but while hearing him kvetch one wonders if [Otto] Frank did not himself author that diary. Could such a document—an intact work of art—have just been left like that? And many a brokenhearted poet has keen financial instincts."

Now, how is this different from the sick jokes that were circulating about Marilyn Klinghoffer conspiring with the terrorists aboard the Achille Lauro to murder her husband so she could collect the insurance money? In any case, hasn't the authenticity of *The Diary of Anne Frank* already been proved beyond a reasonable doubt?

Rorem: You're making a comparison that I didn't make. I don't know the Achille Lauro details. Nor do I see anti-Semitism in what I wrote. I *do* believe there's too much objective distancing in the Anne Frank book to convince me that she wrote it, such as after-the-fact generalities about the Holocaust that she couldn't have known both because of her age and when she lived. In any case, why is it anti-Semitic to believe this? Or am I obtuse?

Mass: In transcribing your remarks here, I've capitalized Holocaust, mindful of your observation in *The Nantucket Diary* that you're tired of hearing about the six million. From now on, you want to hear about the 20 million or not at all.

We touched on the subject of sick jokes. On page 407 you state categorically that "Jews did invent the sick joke." Certainly, it's legitimate to talk about Jewish humor, as you do in several places, but Ned, is there any real basis for this allegation? I mean, is it something you could prove, or even develop a consensus on?

Rorem: I was quoting Paul Goodman, who was Jewish. I should have credited him. By sick joke he meant the joke of despair—when all is so hopeless there's nothing left but laughter. He even wrote a play about it, *Jonah*, which Jack Beeson (a gentile) made into an opera.

Mass: That's what seems so fascinating and contradictory about you, Ned— your willingness, habitual and often zealous, to generalize about every group one could think of *except* homosexuals.

Rorem: That's mostly because when they themselves generalize, they get ungrammatical [laughter]. Every time I pick up the *Native*, I read something like "gay people don't like lavender but we do like gin." It should always be "We gay people don't like lavender, but..." etc. In their zeal not to be thought of as standing apart from their brothers and sisters, they forget to scan their written phrases. Even Ed White should know better.

Mass: Let me ask you about one more of these statements. On page 412 of *The Nantucket Diary* you say, "Jews, more than Catholics or American WASPS, seem to feel a loathing for homosexuality." In view of the exhaustive history of Catholic and Puritanical tortures, witch burnings, and other Inquisitional persecutions of homosexuals (which has no counterpart in Jewish history, whatever the Old Testament prejudices and whatever the prejudices of Jewish fundamentalists and neoconservatives), and especially with regard to the current positions and statements of the Catholic church, is this statement really tenable?

Rorem: My understanding of Jewish upbringing is that the notion of homosexuality is offensive biblically to Jews, whereas it doesn't even arise in the New Testament, much less in the Koran.

Mass: I often wish you would tell us more about the gay lives of many of the important people you discuss, especially those who are still officially in the closet. The reason I wish you would do so is that it's in the interests of clarity as well as truth. Here's an example of what I mean. On page 196 of *The Nantucket Diary*, you note that you attended a recital by Eleanor Steber at the Waldorf Hotel, where you ran into socialite musicologist Joseph Machlis, who whispered to you: "It's like running into your best friend at a whorehouse." Now, that's very funny. But it's a lot funnier knowing that both of you are gay. Since Joe is still in the closet, however, this part of the humor (and the psychology it exposes) is lost on the vast majority of readers. By the way, in *The Nantucket Diary*, you mention a documentary for television about gay composer Charles Griffes. It was to be produced or directed by Roger Englander and hosted by you. Do you know if it dealt with (or was to have dealt with) the composer's homosexuality?

Rorem: As narrator, I wrote my own script from this documentary. Naturally, I mentioned Griffes's policeman boyfriend, but CBS cut the reference.

Mass: Generally speaking, do you think your being gay has had any impact on your progress as a musician and writer?

Rorem: I don't know. You've pointed out that I've written pieces on Sappho and Whitman and Stein, but Whitman is the most used poet, internationally, by composers. In Japan his words are set to music, and by heterosexuals—Kurt Weill and Hindemith and Roger Sessions—right and left. It's not his homosexuality but his universality that has made him beloved throughout the globe. The first Whitman I used was in 1946, a pacifist poem, but also quite homophilic. I used Sappho the same year for choruses, but Sappho and Gertrude Stein are not exactly unknown and their publics are not queer publics, except for the classical 10 percent. Also you overlook the fact that if I've done these three, I've done approximately 150 other poets, 90 percent of whom are, or were, straight, though some were drunks. Roethke for example. These issues don't arise when I'm composing—except, maybe, with the

Calamus poems and *The Whitman Cantata*, which were made for special occasions. I will sometimes, because of the commissioner, use something that's a bit gayer than something else, most recently the setting of Paul Monette's excruciating AIDS elegy for the Gay Men's Chorus. But on the whole, I set whatever speaks to my condition, of love or hate or hunger. Too many nongay American bards have uttered universal feelings that strike home—Wallace Stevens, William Carlos Williams, Robert Frost, and so on—for me to restrict myself. Music cannot be defined as having any sexuality, although words, especially the prose of a libretto, can.

Mass: Ned, with all due respect, may I suggest that what you can't see is how negatively defensive you are, like most homosexual artists of earlier generations, but in striking contrast to your colleague Lou Harrison. You're saying, yes, such and such person may be homosexual, but that has no meaning or importance, except for the fact that we are a persecuted minority. Bill Hoffman is similarly defensive about being called a gay writer. By contrast, Toni Morrison is proud to be thought of as a black writer, just as Isaac Bashevis Singer is glad to be called a Jewish writer. Morrison sees clearly that being a black writer does not mean that she's not also a woman writer and an American writer and a great writer. It's the same with Lou Harrison. Being gay is something affirmative. He's proud to be a gay composer and interested in talking about what that might mean. He doesn't feel threatened that this means he won't be thought of as an American composer who is also great and timeless and universal. Am I being bad again?

Rorem: You say I'm defensively negative, but how can I win when you're making the rules? I'm not defensive. I'm simply defending myself. I will not, and neither will Lou Harrison, compromise my friends, especially those of an older generation (those happy few!) who have their own set of perfectly decent standards. If I've done so in the past, I regret it.

Mass: The standards of older generations of closeted gay composers may have been decent and sympathetic twenty, even ten, years ago, but they're not now. They obscure the truth and abet homophobia. You keep saying that artists and composers are more discriminated against in our society than gay people. Ned, are artists routinely, daily, mugged, maimed, and murdered for being artists the way homosexuals are for being homosexual?

Rorem: Jim has told me I must stop going around saying that. What I should say is that I have suffered less for being homosexual than for being an artist.

I did suffer to some extent during childhood, when I was called a sissy, but my primary identity is as a musician. I do what I do best. I could never do what you and Larry Kramer and Andrew Humm are so nobly doing.

Mass: But that's what's so funny about you. You do! As Bruce-Michael Gelbert recently suggested, you're like Katherine Hepburn, a living champion of women and feminist goals who vigorously denies having anything to do with women's liberation.

Rorem: I think Gelbert's constant chiropractic bending of anything toward gaiety is at once touching and burlesque. It distracts from the business at hand: his often perceptive, often caring, criticism of music.

Mass: I have the opposite reaction to Bruce-Michael. I think he communicates gay perspectives that are legitimate for the audience he's writing for (and often for a more general readership), and that he does so naturally, richly, and professionally, without eschewing the caring, objective criticism of music that may or may not be of overriding interest.
 You refer to Parker Tyler in your writing. Tyler wrote about homosexuality and movies. Did it ever occur to you, in the course of your friendship with him, that someone might write about homosexuality and music?

Rorem: Parker didn't write about gay people in movies. He wrote about gay movies. Yes, somebody could write about gay music, but they'd have to be able to define it first. A movie is definable. Music is not. You're comparing genres that aren't comparable. Still, I'm not saying it can't or shouldn't be done.

Mass: I think the following statement by another very outspoken gay American artist might well apply to you: "Do I contradict myself? Very well then I contradict myself. I am large. I contain multitudes." Am I wrong?

Rorem: Of all the silly statements Whitman ever made, that's the most irresponsible. Even poets should not give themselves a loophole by saying they are so complicated that they think all sorts of different things. Of course, they do...But the contradictions need to be organized and then frozen into art. For people to use their complexity as an excuse for laxity is too easy an out. I don't approve of it, not for Walt Whitman, not for me nor anyone else. In the guise of being contradictory, evil things can happen.

Notes

1. Rorem, Ned, *Settling the Score: Essays on Music* (San Diego, New York, London: Harcourt Brace Jovanovich, 1988).

2. Mass, Lawrence D., *Homosexuality as Behavior and Identity: Dialogues of the Sexual Revolution* (Binghampton, NY: Harrington Park Press, 1990), II, 78–104.

3. Mass, Lawrence D., "Ned Rorem," *Opera Monthly* 2, no. 10 (February 1990): 4–13.

4   Rorem, Ned, *The Nantucket Diary of Ned Rorem: 1973–1985* (San Francisco: North Point Press, 1987), 576, 578.

5. Gordon, Eric, *Mark the Music: The Life and Work of Mark Blitzstein* (New York: St. Martin's Press, 1989) 506.

6. Mass, Lawrence D., "Mark the Music," *Journal of Homosexuality* 21, no. 3 (1991): 134.

7. Rorem, Ned, "Beyond Despair: Joe Orton Revisited," *The Advocate* (9 June 1987): 126–27.

Part Two

CHRONICLES

HENRY LAWES'S SETTING OF KATHERINE PHILIPS'S FRIENDSHIP POETRY IN HIS
Second Book of Ayres and Dialogues, 1655
A Musical Misreading?

Lydia Hamessley

But as the morning sun to drooping flowers,
As weary travellers a shade do find,
As to the parched violet evening showers;
Such is from thee to me a look that's kind.

But when that look is drest in words, tis like
The mystic pow'r of music's unison;
Which when the finger doth one viol strike,
The other's string heaves to reflection.

To My Lucasia, in Defence of Declared Friendship
—Katherine Philips (1631–1664)[1]

THROUGHOUT THE HISTORIES OF MUSIC Henry Lawes has been viewed as a composer who was quite skilled at setting the poetic texts of numerous Cavalier writers, among them Herrick, Carew, Suckling, Lovelace, Waller, and Milton.[2] Many of these poets wrote praises to him detailing his skill and offering their gratitude for the way he elevated and, in a sense, completed their poetry with his music. Katherine Philips, another of Lawes's contemporaries, was among the many poets impressed with him. Her poem of praise to Lawes was printed in the opening pages of his *Second Book of Ayres and Dialogues* of 1655, and it pays homage to his ability to uplift the poetic text through music.[3] She writes:

> Nature which is the vast Creation's Soule,
> The Art of Heav'n the Order of this Frame,
> Is only Musick in another Name: . . .
> Thou dost above the *Poets* Prayses live,
> Who fetch from Thee th' Eternity they give;
> And as true *Reason* triumph's over Sense,
> Yet is subjected to *Intelligence*;
> So *Poets* on the lower World look down,
> But *Lawes* on them, his height is all his own:
> For (like Divinity it selfe) his Lyre
> Reward's the wit it did at first inspire:
> And thus by double right Poets allow
> Their and His Lawrells to adorn his brow.

Philips's connection with Lawes, however, goes far beyond her commendatory poem. Indeed, one poem by Philips was set to music for this collection, and her circle of friends played a significant role in Lawes's *Second Book of Ayres*, a fact which has been brought forward by literary historians and musicologists alike.[4] What has not been considered by scholars, however, is the way in which the Philips/Lawes artistic collaboration operated, and if Lawes in fact did for Philips's poetry what so many other poets claimed he did for theirs. Also, since Philips's work is at least woman-identified, if not actually lesbian, several theoretically interesting questions arise. How is Philips's lesbian stance delineated in her poetry? What was the seventeenth-century's understanding of female friendship and love, the subject of most of Philips's poetry? And finally, how did Lawes set her verses, and did his musical response project, mask, or suppress the lesbian voice?

Philips's poetry is usually viewed as a minor contribution to the storehouse of seventeenth-century verse. Her writing is lyric and is informed by the literary conventions of French *préciosité*, the Metaphysical poets (in particular John Donne), and the neoclassical and pastoral rhetoric of the Cavalier poets.[5] She wrote political poetry, poems of praise, elegies, and meditative verses. But her best poetry, by far, is that which chronicles her passionate relationships with women.[6] To express her intensely passionate and erotic feelings for the women in her life, Philips used literary conventions usually employed by male poets to address their female lovers: "the courtly love address to the beloved and her response, the idealized pattern of Platonic same-sex friend-ship, and the hermaphrodite perfection of the beloved who incorporates the best of both sexes."[7] But Philips also "challenge[s] the conventional male/female structure of a conquest poem," and "create[s] a woman's voice that can be simultaneously submissive and aggressive."[8]

In her poetry she assigned pseudoclassical names to her friends; she herself took the name Orinda. The majority of this verse is directed to two women in particular. The first is Mary Aubrey, whom Philips dubbed Rosania. Philips's verses to Rosania followed the course of their five-year relationship. Of their first days of happiness she wrote, "Soul of my soul, my Joy, my Crown, my Friend, /…How happy are we now, whose souls are grown, / By an incomparable mixture, one."[9] As Rosania's affection cooled, Philips declared, "Divided rivers lose their name; / And so our too unequal flame / Parted, will Passion be in me, / And an indifference in thee."[10] And when Rosania married in a private ceremony in 1652, Philips recorded her heartbreak with the words: "Yet I'll adore the author of my death, / And kiss the hand that robs me of my breath."[11]

Happily, though, as her relationship with Rosania diminished, Philips met Anne Owen in 1651. Anne, or Lucasia as she was called by Philips, was the object of her affection and poetry for eleven years, until she too married and the friendship withered. Typical of Philips's lines to Lucasia are these:

> I did not live until this time
> Crown'd my felicity,
> When I could say without a crime,
> I am not thine, but Thee.…

> For as a watch by art is wound
> To motion, such was mine:
> But never had Orinda found
> A soul till she found thine.[12]

In this poem Philips demonstrates her use of standard literary conven-tions: the elaborate analogy of the watch is a conceit typical of Donne. Yet, while taking Donne's erotic poetry as her model, Philips "channels a passionate emotional intensity into acceptable metaphysical images and argument,"[13] and she reshapes these conventions to suit her own intent. A striking example is found in one of her best-known poems, "To my Lucasia, in Defence of Declared Friendship."

Although we know we love, yet while our soule
Is thus imprison'd by the flesh we wear,
There's no way left that bondage to controul,
But to convey transactions through the Eare.

Nay, though we read our passions in the Ey,
It will obleige and please to tell them too:
Such joys as these by motion multiply,
Were't but to find that our soul told us true.

Believe not then, that being now secure
Of either's ear, we have no more to doe:
The Sphaeres themselves by motion do endure,
And they move on by Circulation too.

And as a River, when it once has pay'd
The tribute which it to the Ocean ow's,
Stops not, but turns, and having curl'd and play'd
On its own waves, the shore it overflows:

So the soul's motion does not end in bliss,
But on her self she scatters and dilates,
And on the Object doubles, till by this
She finds new Joys, which that reflux creates.[14]

The metaphysical images in this poem are typical "of the male discourse of metaphysical passion for women." But Philips adds her own images, in particular the "female and subliminally erotic analogy of a river's flow, which captures the rhythms of female sexual passion."[15]

In other poems, Philips reveals significant differences between her erotic relationships and those of which Donne wrote. In order to delineate an egalitarian relationship, as opposed to a hierarchical one, she reworks the conventions of metaphysical love poetry. In "The Canonization" Donne writes that he and his lady "prove / Mysterious by this love," while in "Friendship's Mystery, to My Dearest Lucasia," Philips and Lucasia "prove / There's a Religion in our Love." Even more striking is the difference Philips makes when she reworks Donne's poem "The Sun Rising" in which Donne declares that "She is all States, all Princes, I, / Nothing else is." By contrast, Philips imagines an equality between herself and Lucasia, as in the line "all our Titles [are] shuffled so, / Both Princes, and both Subjects too."[16]

It is to this passionate poetry of Philips that Henry Lawes seems to have been drawn. How did Lawes respond to Philips's poetry when faced with her particular use of conventional language? Did he reflect the unique way she recast familiar metaphysical images—including the implicit lesbian erotic elements? He set three of her poems to music, but only his setting of "Friendship's Mystery, to My Dearest Lucasia" is extant (see text in appendix A).[17] Lawes included his setting of this poem in his *Second Book of Ayres,* and he retitled the poem "Mutuall Affection Between Orinda and Lucasia."

The piece falls into the category of "tuneful song" or ballad, as opposed to declamatory song,[18] and like many of Lawes's tuneful songs, this piece is in triple meter and is strophic (see example 1). Ian Spink has demonstrated that songs set in this strictly metrical and strophic manner usually fail to bridge the points of enjambment satisfactorily, bringing about a musical halt where the literary motion is at its greatest.[19] The intense metaphysical language of "Friendship's Mystery" suffers from this phenomenon. Each stanza consists of five lines that are linked by the rhyme scheme in a 3 + 2 arrangement. However, this formal structure is not reflected in the semantic arrangement of every stanza: according to the meaning of the text, the first stanza is 3 + 2 while the second stanza is clearly 2 + 3. It is no surprise that Lawes chooses a 3 + 2 musical form, reflecting the rhyme scheme as well as the meaning of the first verse, since strophic settings typically take their

Mutual affection between *Orinda* and *Lucatia*

Mr. *Hen. Lawes.*

For though we were design'd t'agree,
That Fate no liberty destroys,
But our Election is as free
As Angels, who with greedy choice
Are yet determin'd to their joys.

We court our own captivity,
Then Thrones more great and innocent,
'Twere banishment to be set free,
When we wear fetters, whose intent
Not bondage is, but ornament.

Our hearts are doubled by their loss,
Here mixture is addition grown,
We both difuse, and both ingross,
And we whose minds are so much one,
Never, yet ever are alone.

Divided joys are tedious found,
And griefs united easier grow,
We are our selves but by rebound,
And all our titles shuffl'd so,
Both Princes, and both Subjects too.

Example 1

musical cue from the first stanza. The result, of course, is that the sense of the text of some stanzas is maintained, while at other times it is interrupted, in this case, by the placement of the strong cadence after line three. For instance, in the first stanza, the lines "That miracles men's faith do move / By wonder and by prodigie" are joined by the forward motion brought about by the first-inversion pause on the word *move*. By not grounding the poetry at that juncture on the expected cadence, a root-position D major triad, Lawes propels and extends the music through to the rhetorically stronger point made in the line, "By wonder and by prodigie." Similarly, Lawes calls on the first-inversion triad at the cadence that ends the line, "To the fierce angry world let's prove." Again the musical line cannot halt completely but must move forward through the last line of the stanza. Nevertheless, the limitations of this strophic setting become apparent in the second stanza. Here the first-inversion cadence coincides with the line that completes the first thought of the stanza, "That Fate no liberty destroys." The stronger root-position cadence that occurs at the end of the third line, "But our Election is as free," interrupts the obvious enjambment between the third and fourth lines which should be understood as "But our Election is as free/As Angels'…"[20]

Lawes's harmonic procedures are also significant in reading this piece. Through parallel first-inversion triads and cadences in first inversion, Lawes articulates a gentle, almost tentative, feeling in this song.[21] Thus the text is delineated without force, determination, or strong goal orientation, with the exception of the one strong cadence at the end of line three in each stanza. Such a song, imbued with diffusive cadences and sweet parallel thirds and sixths, is aptly described as elegant and refined. As is typical of this type of setting, the meaning of the words take a secondary position to the music, which, in this case, gracefully glides over them. The question remains though, did Lawes capture the sense of these words with his music?

Philip Brett points out that such procedures have a long history in English song. In his study on text-setting in William Byrd's songs, Brett suggests that strophic settings are expressive of the form of a poem rather than of its meaning, and that they are perhaps better solutions for setting texts containing moral statements than a madrigalian treatment, which "tends to reduce verse to a prose reading," or a declamatory setting, which masks the formal structure of the poem and emphasizes meaning. Thus, in his treatment of Philips's text, Lawes recalls a musical tradition that Brett refers to as "non-representational."[22]

However, it can also be argued that poetry such as "Friendship's Mystery" is better suited to a declamatory setting. Spink suggests that "…metaphysical verse tends to be unmusical. The language of philosophy, theology, or science is not suited to music, and thus the elaboration of a conceit is nothing more than misplaced ingenuity in a song, for music is a language of the emotions, not of verbal ideas." Furthermore, Lawes's solution to this challenge was often to set such metaphysical verses to declamatory, through-composed music.[23]

Clearly, Lawes had a choice in setting "Friendship's Mystery"; he could have used a setting that emphasized either the form (a strophic setting) or the meaning (a declamatory one). That he chose a strophic setting reveals his privileging of form and his elision of meaning, in this case the love between women. The strophic setting is especially striking since Philips's poem is clearly more complicated both in content and in structure than some that Lawes gives a declamatory, through-composed setting.[24] One such poem and its musical setting is of particular interest at this point because it, like "Friendship's Mystery," is addressed to Lucasia, and included in the *Second Book of Ayres and Dialogues*, but it is by a male poet.

"No Reprieve," as Lawes titled it, was written by John Berkenhead, a friend of Philips and Lucasia (see the complete text in appendix B). According to Berkenhead's biographer, the poem is "a conventional persuasive to an unwilling mistress. [It] is distastefully melodramatic, and exhibits the masochistic self-pity of the Platonic lover at its worst. One is not sorry when 'Charon's boat' heaves in sight to carry off the expiring swain to the accompaniment of an execrable refrain."[25] The poem consists of four stanzas separated by the refrain, "Alas, undone to Fate, I bow my head / Ready to die, now die, and now, now, now am dead."[26] Lawes sets these stanzas in a declamatory style that is through-composed, except for the triple-meter refrain that returns throughout the piece unchanged. His mastery of text-setting is evident throughout the song. In the third stanza he captures the gasping of the soul with a well-placed minor sixth, and a few notes later he depicts Nature's vain striving through chromatic motion and unexpected harmonic twists (see example 2). Surely such a poem, much less abstract in its imagery than Philips's and with very little enjambment, is ripe for a strophic setting. To follow the line of thinking Spink suggests, one would expect the Berkenhead poem to have a more "musical," i.e., metrical, strophic, setting since it is a poem of emotions. Philips's metaphysical verses, replete with conceits, philosophy, and science (alchemy), would seem more suitable for a declamatory setting.

What can we make of the difference in the settings of these two poems? One might suggest that the difference is a purely practical one. Willetts has written that "tuneful songs" were intended for his pupils, "most of whom would not have had the vocal ability or dramatic gifts necessary for the per-

No Reprieve

Example 2

see how cold, how pale and gasp-ing my Soule lies, which Na-ture strives in vain to hold;

whilst wing'd with sighs a-way it flies. A-las! un-done to Fate, I bow my head rea-dy to die; now

die, and now now now am dead. See see al-rea-dy Cha-ron's boat, who grim-ly asks, Why

all this stay? Hark how the fa-tal Sis-ters shout! and now they call a-way a-way. A-las! un-done to Fate,

I bow my head, rea-dy to die, now die, and now now now am dead.

Mr. *Hen. Lawes.*

Example 2, continued

formance of monodies or even serious songs," and Lawes was dependent on his private teaching late in his life after he lost his position at court following the Civil War.[27] Although it seems somewhat unlikely, perhaps Philips's poem was to be sung by a particular performer who was less accomplished than the intended performer of Berkenhead's piece.

As must be clear by now, I am arguing that these very different settings reveal the way not only Lawes, but the seventeenth century in general, might have received and interpreted these two poems. Verses such as Berkenhead's are common throughout this period, so the theme is well known: a male lover is thwarted by a cruel woman who will have no pity on him. Some are full of hateful revenge, others full of masochistic suffering, but all play out an accepted script for love relationships between men and women. Lawes's setting of this poetry is likewise full of conventions. He matches the dramatic, even extreme, language Berkenhead uses by setting it in a declamatory style and articulating such standard musical conventions as the descending sixth for gasping and the tritone and chromatic descending line for the inexorable dying of the refrain.[28] In short, the musical language that Lawes speaks in this setting is also an accepted script or set of musical procedures for a man to declare his love for his female lover.

While Berkenhead's poetry is typical of, if inferior to, much seventeenth-century verse, Philips's poetry is radically different. She wrote about same-sex friendship and love by appropriating a male, heterosexual poetic discourse and nonetheless stated her ideas passionately, erotically, and with determination.[29] That Lawes's setting does not support or articulate Philips's resolve and daring is not surprising. He was setting the familiar metaphysical language of love, but the participants in such a text were not typical. Philips may have been speaking in a conventional literary style that made her ideas more acceptable, but she was nevertheless a woman, and thus not really to be taken too seriously, particularly in matters of friendship and love. So in order to account for the discrepancy between the two settings and the reasons for the choices Lawes made, we must analyze his treatment of Philips's verses in light of the seventeenth century's beliefs about both friendship and love between women.

The notion of women as participants in friendship is a concept virtually unheard-of in the seventeenth century. Montaigne suggests that female friendships were weak since women were not "endued [endowed] with firmness of mind to endure the constraint of so hard and durable a knot." It was further believed that women could not participate in the Greek tradition of classical friendship because they lacked "the passion, sense of individuality, and presence of a common world and worldliness that make friendship possible." Women's supposed incapacity for thought was another obstacle.[30]

Philips must have come up against this belief with some regularity since she argues against it in her poem "A Friend" (see text in appendix C):

> If souls no sexes have, for men t'exclude
> Woman from Friendship's vast capacity,
> Is a design injurious or rude,
> Only maintain'd by partial tyranny.
> Love is allow'd to us and Innocence,
> And noblest friendships do proceed from thence.[31]

A number of writings from the seventeenth century reveal the strong opinions that Philips was trying to counter. In his essay on friendship written for Philips, Jeremy Taylor writes,

> [Y]ou may see how much I differ from the morosity of those cynics, who would not admit your sex into the communities of a noble friendship. I believe some wives have been the best friends in the world...[32]

Nowhere in the essay does Taylor ever consider the possibility of friendship between women; he seems only concerned with possible friendships between men and those between husband and wife. After a short discussion about women as friends he concludes:

> I cannot say that women are capable of those excellencies by which men can oblige the world; and therefore a female friend in some cases is not so good a councellor as a wise man, and cannot so well defend my honour, nor dispose of reliefs and assistances if she be under the power of another. ...A man is the best friend in trouble, but a woman may be equal to him in the days of joy: a woman can as well increase our comforts, but cannot so well lessen our sorrows....virtuous women are the beauties of society and the prettinesses of friendship.[33]

Edmund Waller, the Cavalier poet and author of such memorable verses as "Go Lovely Rose," set out his ideas on female friendship in his poem, "On the Friendship Betwixt Two Ladies" (see the complete text in appendix D).[34] As the first stanza clearly demonstrates, Waller considers female friendship only insofar as it affects male desire. Lillian Faderman explains:

> ...[Waller] decides that their ostensible love for each other is only cunning; they display their passion for male benefit in order to "control" men's love. They are like debtors who, not wanting to pay a debt (give themselves up to a man), avoid the law by signing away all their property (their store of love) to a friend. The debtor and the friend understand, of course, that

the gesture is only a pretense. Waller implies that romantic friendship is charming to observe but has little substance, and it would not exist at all if women did not desire a playful tool with which to tease their male lovers.[35]

Certainly this opinion of female friendship was pervasive, and it seems reasonable to suggest that this seventeenth-century view of female friendship was brought to bear in Lawes's setting of "Friendship's Mystery."

As for love between women, there were literary conventions for representing it, but they diffuse and control the potential threat of lesbianism.[36] In his study of the poetry of Andrew Marvell, John Milton, and John Donne that depicts lesbians, James Holstun identifies two poetic techniques, periodization and mirroring, that "simultaneously acknowledge and master lesbian sexuality."[37] Through periodization, "in each [poem] lesbian sexuality becomes a phenomenon of the past which can be discussed only in retrospect."[38] This technique is obvious in Donne's poem, "Sapho to Philaenis," in which Donne "turns the love of gay women into little more than a classical allusion." By distancing discussions of love between women through the invocation of Sappho, poets could control the expressions of lesbian love. "We need only imagine the radical effect of anglicizing the poem—say, as 'Joan to Julia,'" to appreciate the effect of periodization.[39]

While Philips herself used pseudoclassical names, she also used the real name of her beloved at times. Further, her poetry was circulated within a small circle where it was taken to be autobiographical and of the present moment. The names might be understood to be protective and indicative of a special circle of friends, but they do not bring about the kind of historical and personal distancing found in Donne's poetry.

Periodization was also used to "protect" Philips's reputation. When her poetry was collected and published in 1667, three years after her death, she was dubbed "The English Sappho" in the book's preface, and several poets wrote verses in praise of Philips using this same sobriquet. However, this comparison itself was problematic, for although Sappho's poems were considered the pinnacle of literary achievement in lyric poetry by a woman, seventeenth-century poets believed her subject matter to be highly suspect.[40] To downplay the sexual implications of the comparison, many writers insisted that Philips's moral virtues far surpassed Sappho's. Abraham Cowley, for example:

> They talk of Sappho, but, alas! the shame
> Ill Manners soil the lustre of her fame.
> Orinda's inward Vertue is so bright,
> That, like a Lantern's fair enclosed light,

It through the Paper shines where she doth write.[41]

The strategy of periodization is clearly in evidence in verse such as this. While Philips is meant to gain by comparison to the ancient Sappho (equal in skill, superior in virtue), the lesbian character of her poetry is virtually erased.

Lesbian sexuality was also diffused in Donne's poetry through the image of Sappho imagining her lover's body as she gazes at her own reflection in a mirror. Donne thus turns lesbian desire into "autoerotic" desire:[42]

> My two lips, eyes, thighs, differ from thy two,
> But so, as thine from one another do;
> And, oh, no more; the likeness being such,
> Why should they not alike in all parts touch?
> Hand to strange hand, lip to lip none denies;
> Why should they breast to breast, or thighs to thighs?
> Likeness begets such strange self flattery,
> That touching myself, all seems done to thee.
> Myself I embrace, and mine own hands I kiss,
> And amorously thank myself for this.
> Me, in my glass, I call thee; but alas,
> When I would kiss, tears dim mine eyes, and glass.[43]

In many ways, *mutuality* defined this lesbian sensibility. But, for Donne, spiritual and physical love was hierarchical—remember the lines mentioned earlier from "The Canonization": "She is all States, and all Princes, I, / Nothing else is." Since lesbian love according to Donne is symmetrical and autoerotic, a love between two equal persons, lesbian sexuality could not possibly participate in Donne's metaphor of political and erotic domination.[44]

Philips herself reworked this idea in the fifth stanza of "Friendship's Mystery," and the concept of mutuality fills the entire poem, including the last stanza, which was not set by Lawes. Thus, one might argue that Philips also participated in this mirroring device. However, her concept of mutuality differs from Donne's. Philips often describes her relationship with Lucasia or Rosania as one in which they possess "twin-souls." For Philips, the phenomenon is not so much one of mirroring, but of joining or entwining. She and her beloved are alike, not because they reflect one another's image, but because they share one soul and metaphorically inhabit one another's body. The joining is so complete at times that they lose a sense of individual identity, and through what Celia Easton calls "a fluidity of roles, she [Philips] dismantles the power relations of erotic expression."[45] Several excerpts from her poetry demonstrate the difference between Philips's and Donne's notions of mutuality and mirroring:[46]

> Our chang'd and mingled souls are grown
> To such acquaintance now,
> That if each would resume their own,
> Alas! we know not how.
> We have each other so engrost,
> That each is in the union lost.
>
> Thus our twin-souls in one shall grow,
> And teach the World new love...[47]
>
> The Compasses that stand above,
> Express this great immortal Love;
> For friends, like them, can prove this true,
> They are, and yet they are not, two.[48]
>
> Your own destruction gives you now Content:
> For our twin-spirits did so long agree,
> You must undo yourself to ruin me.
> And, like some frantic Goddess, you're inclin'd
> To raze the temple where you are enshrin'd.[49]
>
> O may good Heav'n but so much virtue lend,
> To make me fit to be Lucasia's Friend!
> But I'll forsake myself, and seek a new
> Self in her breast that's far more rich and true.[50]

Beyond periodization and mirroring, Elizabeth D. Harvey suggests that in "Sapho and Philaenis," Donne also "domesticates" the lesbian "image of the self, a process that is mediated both by ventriloquism and by voyeurism."[51] Again, Philips does not call on these devices; she is speaking in her own voice, based on what we know of her relationships with these women.[52] Philips writes realistically of the women in her life and her relationships with them; she refers to specific events they have shared, their disagreements, and her own feelings of joy, rejection, or loss. Her emotional goal in her poetry is to make an impact on her beloved. She writes verses that in effect are seductive, and she often implores her friend to speak of their love. In times of trouble, Philips expresses her disappointment, anger, or loss, often in the hope that the relationship will improve. Furthermore, her longing for her lovers never results in an objectifying gaze, while in Donne's poetry, the "dislocation of voice reveals both the ventriloquist and the voyeur, the first producing speech that appears to emanate from a source other than the real speaker, and the other deriving pleasure from a looking that requires no participation."[53]

I would argue that Lawes's setting of "Friendship's Mystery" is part of the set of techniques outlined above that aim to control lesbian sexuality. By setting Philips's words to music, Lawes inescapably blurs the authorial voice and thus rewrites the relationship as he wishes to view it. As we have already seen, his setting invokes no possibility of power or erotic strength. Further, it must be remembered that he retitled her poem "Mutuall Affection Between Orinda and Lucasia." While Philips certainly played into his hands by using classical names for herself and her friends, she still gave the poem the title "Friendship's Mystery, To My Dearest Lucasia." Her emphasis is upon the mystery of their union, not the mere fact of its mutuality. His voyeuristic stance is emphasized by the strophic setting of "Friendship's Mystery," one that privileges structure over content and relieves the composer of his own "subjective responses."[54] Thus, Lawes was able to remain detached from the emotional level of Philips's verse, delighting instead in the form of her verse.

In contemplating the connection between Lawes and Philips it is clear that Lawes was aware of her relationships with Lucasia and Rosania. He set a number of her poems to these women, and he was intimately connected with her circle of friends. Furthermore, Philips must have approved of Lawes's musical expression of the "Mutuall Affection Between Orinda and Lucasia" in light of the commendatory poem she addressed to him, as well as other compliments she is known to have paid him.[55] Yet despite his proximity to Philips, it is also clear that Lawes did not come close to expressing the depth of feeling and strength of commitment that she avows in her poetry. This situation may be due to his own lack of understanding of what Philips's relationships meant to her, given the social conventions at the time. Or perhaps he felt a need to resolve the tension between Philips's strong language and the currently accepted notion of what female friendship and love between women entailed. In any case, for Philips, in 1655, her relationship with Lucasia was primary; it was her emotional lifeline, and it was adorned, but neither understood nor expressed, by Henry Lawes's music in the *Second Book of Ayres and Dialogues.*

Instead of matching Philips's impassioned argument with a strong musical discourse, Lawes seems to match the seventeenth-century view of female friendship with his elegant setting. In this song her verses are adorned with music that embodies refinement, charm, tentativeness, and gentleness. Nevertheless, her words are those of action, of articulating an elaborate, intellectual, and emotional philosophy of friendship. But Lawes wrote music to charm, not to move to action. In short, Philips's appropriation of a male poetic discourse is not articulated musically. If Lawes had set her poem to a musical discourse reserved for passion between men and women, he would have given her words the kind of power not in currency for either friendship or love between women. With this setting he instead represented musically what seventeenth-century men imagined female friendship and love to be.

Aside from what these facts and speculations tell us about Lawes's working relationship with Philips and his manner of setting her poetry, the issues I have explored raise questions that I believe are pertinent to any number of other situations. Whenever a composer sets a text, she or he is performing an act of interpretation, and we hear the text from that new perspective. It seems crucial that we take time to examine the social conventions that affect the way a composer might choose to interpret a text, especially when the texts of women are interpreted by men, or vice versa. By posing these questions, we open the possibility of learning more about the lives and beliefs of composers we have come to know so well. And just as exciting, we can begin to learn about the many people whose names and lives remain unknown to us, even though we may already know their words through someone else's music.

Appendix A

Friendship's Mystery, To My Dearest Lucasia[56]

> Come, my Lucasia, since we see
> That miracles men's faith do move,
> By wonder and by prodigy
> To the dull angry world let's prove
> There's a religion in our Love.
>
> For though we were design'd t'agree,
> That Fate no liberty destroys,
> But our Election is as free
> As Angels', who with greedy choice
> Are yet determin'd to their joys
>
> Our hearts are doubled by the loss,
> Here mixture is addition grown;
> We both diffuse, and both ingross:
> And we whose minds are so much one,
> Never, yet ever are alone.

We court our own captivity
Than thrones more great and innocent:
Twere banishment to be set free,
Since we wear fetters whose intent
Not bondage is but ornament.

Divided joys are tedious found,
And griefs united easier grow:
We are ourselves but by rebound,
And all our titles shuffled so,
Both Princes, and both subjects too.

Our hearts are mutual victims laid,
While they (such power in Friendship lies)
Are Altars, Priests, and Off'rings made:
And each heart which thus kindly dies,
Grows deathless bỳ the sacrifice.

Appendix B

No Reprieve[57]

Now, now Lucatia, now make haste,
If thou wilt see how strong thou art,
There needs but one frown more to waste
The whole remainder of my heart.
    Alas undone, to Fate I bow my head
    Ready to die, now die, and now now now am dead.

You looke to have an age of tryal
Ere you a Lover will repay,
But my state brooks no more deniall;
I cannot this one minute stay.
    Alas undone, to Fate I bow my head
    Ready to die, now die, and now now now am dead.

Look in my wound and see how cold,
How pale and gasping my Soule lies,
Which nature strives in vain to hold,
Whil'st wing'd with sighs away it flies.
    Alas undone, to Fate I bow my head
    Ready to die, now die, and now now now am dead.

See, see already Charon's boat,
Who grimly asks why all this stay?
Hark how the fatal sisters shout,
And now they call, away, away,
 Alas undone, to Fate I bow my head
 Ready to die, now die, and now now now am dead.

Appendix C

A Friend[58]

The chiefest thing in friends is Sympathy:
There is a secret that doth friendship guide,
Which makes two souls before they know agree,
Who by a thousand mixtures are allied,
And chang'd and lost, so that it is not known
Within which breast doth now reside their own.

Thick waters show no images of things:
Friends are each other's mirrors, and should be
Clearer than crystal or the mountain springs,
And free from clouds, design or flattery.
For vulgar souls no part of Friendship share:
Poets and friends are born to what they are.

Absence doth not from Friendship's right excuse:
Them who preserve each other's heart and fame,
Parting can ne'er divide, it may diffuse;
As a far stretch'd-out river's still the same.
Though presence help'd then at the first to greet,
Their souls know now without those aids to meet.

Appendix D

On the Friendship Betwixt Two Ladies[59]

Tell me, lovely, loving pair!
Why so kind, and so severe?
Why so careless of our care,
Only to yourselves so dear?

By this cunning change of hearts,
You the power of love control;
While the boy's deluded darts
Can arrive at neither soul.

For in vain to either breast
Still beguiled love does come,
Where he finds a foreign guest,
Neither of your hearts at home.

Debtors thus with like design,
When they never mean to pay,
That they may the law decline,
To some friend make all away.

Not the silver doves that fly,
Yoked in Cytherea's car;
Not the wings that lift so high,
And convey her son so far;

Are so lovely, sweet, and fair,
Or do more ennoble love;
Are so choicely matched a pair,
Or with more consent to move.

Appendix E

Content, To My Dearest Lucasia[60]

Then, my Lucasia, we who have
Whatever Love can give or crave;
Who can with pitying scorn survey
The trifles which the most betray;
With innocence and perfect friendship fir'd
Be Virtue join'd, and by our choice retir'd.

Whose mirrors are the crystal brooks,
Or else each other's hearts and looks;
Who cannot wish for other things
Than privacy and friendship brings:
Whose thoughts and persons chang'd and mixt are one,
Enjoy Content, or else the World hath none.

Notes

A shortened version of this article was read at the national meeting of the American Musicological Society, Chicago, 1991 and at the Feminist Theory in Music Conference, Minneapolis, Minnesota, 1991. I would like to thank Nancy Sorkin Rabinowitz and Katherine Rohrer for their helpful suggestions.

1. Quoted in George Saintsbury, *Minor Poets of the Caroline Period,* 3 vols. (Oxford: Clarendon, 1905), I: 555. This is a reprint of Katherine Philips, *Poems* (London: J. M. for H. Herringman, 1667). All quotations of Philips's poetry are taken from this source unless otherwise noted.

2. See Willa McClung Evans, *Henry Lawes, Musician and Friend of Poets* (New York: Modern Language Association, 1941; reprint, New York, 1966), R. J. McGrady, "Henry Lawes and the Concept of 'Just Note and Accent,'" *Music and Letters* 50 (1969): 86–102, and Wilfrid Mellers, "Henry Lawes and the Caroline Ayre," in his *Harmonious Meeting: A Study of Music, Poetry and Theatre in England, 1600–1900* (London: Dobson, 1965), 107–17. Milton's sonnet first appeared in print in Henry Lawes and William Lawes, *Choice Psalms* (London: James Young, 1648); see Evans, *Henry Lawes,* 181 for a facsimile. A modern edition of the poem is in John Milton, *Complete Poems and Major Prose,* ed. Merritt Y. Hughes (New York: Odyssey, 1957), 144. For critical analyses of the poem see Audrey Davidson, "Milton on the Music of Henry Lawes," *Milton Newsletter* 2, no. 2 (1968): 19–23 (also printed as "Milton's Encomiastic Sonnet to Henry Lawes," in her *Substance and Manner: Studies in Music and the Other Arts,* [St. Paul: Hiawatha, 1977]: 13–20); Nan Cooke Carpenter, "Milton and Music: Henry Lawes, Dante, and Casella," *English Literary Renaissance* 2 (1972): 237–42.

3. "To Mr. Henry Lawes," Saintsbury, *Minor Poets,* I: 518–19.

4. Philips's circle of friends included a number of people who appear in Henry Lawes's *Second Book of Ayres and Dialogues* (London: T. Harper, 1655). Lawes dedicated the book to Lady Dering, a student of his. Lady Dering also composed the music for three songs that Lawes included in his collection. The poetry for these songs was written by her husband, Sir Edward. Lady Dering was a school friend of Philips's, and both she and her husband received poetic tributes from Philips. Two other friends of Philips's, Francis Finch and John Berkenhead, also provided poetry for several of the songs that Lawes set in the collection and were the recipients of poems by Philips. Sir Edward, Finch, Berkenhead, and Philips wrote commendatory verses to Lawes for the preface of the

book. *The Second Book of Ayres* was not the first time these poets had come together. In 1651, these men decided to publish a collection of the late William Cartwright's poetry. They each wrote a poem in Cartwright's memory and asked Philips to do the same. (Evidently, by age twenty Philips's talent as a poet was well known; her poetry was circulating in manuscript form well before her poem to Cartwright appeared.) From this evidence it may seem that Philips was included in Lawes's collection only through their mutual acquaintances, particularly since there is no record of an actual meeting between Lawes and Philips. However, it is probable that Philips attended one of the many private concerts Lawes held at his home in London. Lady Dering, as well as other friends of hers, are known to have attended these evening concerts. Although we can not be certain that Philips was ever present at these events, it is nonetheless likely that Lawes knew her personally. See Allan Pritchard and Patrick Thomas, "Orinda, Vaughan and Watkyns: Anglo-Welsh Literary Relationships During the Interregnum," *The Anglo-Welsh Review* 62 (1976): 96–102. For biographies of Philips, see Philip Webster Souers, *The Matchless Orinda*, Harvard Studies in English 5 (Cambridge, Mass.: Harvard University Press, 1931); Lucy Brashear, "The Forgotten Legacy of the 'Matchless Orinda,'" *The Anglo-Welsh Review* 65 (1979): 68–76.

5. However, her poetry differs from much Cavalier verse in significant ways. In his "Introduction to Henry Lawes," (*Music and Letters* 4 [1951]: 217–25 and 328–44), Eric Ford Hart suggests that "Cavalier poets were…flippant…because in their poetry they ignored the realities of the age in which they were living, and confined their attention to purely personal matters, the most important of which was love," (223). Whether or not one agrees with Hart's assessment, Philips was certainly not typical in this regard.

6. See Claudia A. Limbert, "Woman to Woman: The Female Friendship Poems of Katherine Philips," Volumes 1–3, *Dissertation Abstracts International* 49, no. 6 (Ann Arbor: University Microfilms, 1988): 1463A–64A.

7. Arlene Stiebel, "Not Since Sappho: The Erotic in Poems of Katherine Philips and Aphra Behn," *Journal of Homosexuality* 23, nos. 1/2 (1992): 161–78. I would like to thank Stiebel for providing me with a copy of her article before its publication. For further discussion of Philips's use of literary conventions see Harriette Andreadis, "The Sapphic-Platonics of Katherine Philips," *Signs: Journal of Women in Culture and Society* 15 (1989): 34–60, especially 39.

8. Celia A. Easton, "Excusing the Breach of Nature's Laws: The Discourse of Denial and Disguise in Katherine Philips' Friendship Poetry," *Restoration: Studies in English Literary Culture*, vol. 14 1660–1700 (Knoxville: University of Tennessee, 1990): 4. Easton, Stiebel, and Andreadis all advance, although each somewhat differently, a lesbian interpretation of Philips's poetry. They also address the issue of the problematic term "lesbian" and argue convincingly for its use.

9. "To Mrs. Mary Aubrey," Saintsbury, *Minor Poets*, I: 548–49.

10. "To Rosania, now Mrs. Montague, being with her," Saintsbury, *Minor Poets*, I: 540–41.

11. "Injuria Amicitiae," Saintsbury, *Minor Poets*, I: 538–39.

12. "To my Excellent Lucasia, on our Friendship," Saintsbury, *Minor Poets*, I: 537–38.

13. Andreadis, "Sapphic-Platonics," 40.

14. "To my Lucasia, in defence of declared friendship," Saintsbury, *Minor Poets*, 554–56.

15. Andreadis, "Sapphic-Platonics," 40.

16. Elizabeth H. Hageman, "The Matchless Orinda: Katherine Philips," in Katharina M. Wilson, ed., *Women Writers of the Renaissance and Reformation* (Athens, Ga.: University

of Georgia Press, 1987), 572–73.

17. Lawes set "To Mrs. M. A. upon Absence," and "A Dialogue of Absence twixt Lucasia and Orinda," Saintsbury, *Minor Poets*, 548 and 522 respectively.

18. These categories are outlined by Ian Spink in *English Song: Dowland to Purcell* (New York: Charles Scribner's Sons, 1974), 89–93. See also Hart, "Introduction to Henry Lawes," 333–34.

19. "A long note at the end of a line in a tuneful song will naturally fail to be entirely satisfactory where there is an enjambment, since it will hold up what (from the literary point of view) ought to run on," Ian Spink, *English Song*, 88–89. Willetts describes these tuneful songs: "[They are] often composed in triple time, with no pretension to depth of feeling and no particular attention to the word-setting. A light catchy tune repeated for each stanza is the aim. These strophic settings suffer from the inescapable defect of their structure: few poems are absolutely regular in metric construction, thus a melody which fits one verse will probably distort a word or so in another." Pamela J. Willetts, *The Henry Lawes Manuscript* (London: Trustees of the British Museum, 1969), 4.

20. I would like to thank John O'Neill for his thoughts on enjambment and verse structure in "Friendship's Mystery."

21. I would like to thank Susan McClary who shared her understanding of these harmonic procedures with me. DonnaMae Gustafson also shared her impressions with me to my benefit. I am grateful to Phil Rukavina and Lisa Carney for learning and performing for me the two pieces discussed here.

22. Philip Brett, "Word-Setting in the Songs of Byrd," *Proceedings of the Royal Musical Association* 98 (1971/72): 47–64. See pages 52–55 in particular.

23. Spink, *English Song*, 79–83. Spink discusses Lawes setting of Carew's "To an inconstant Mistris" ("When thou, poore excommunicate / From all the joyes of love, shalt see").

24. See Ian Spink, *English Song*, 79–83 for an analysis of a similarly complex poem set in a declamatory, through-composed fashion by Lawes.

25. Peter William Thomas, *Sir John Berkenhead, 1617–1679: A Royalist Career in Politics and Polemics* (Oxford: Clarendon Press, 1969), 188–89.

26. This text recalls the Elizabethan choirboy plays that included laments focused on the repetition of words such as *I die, alas,* etc. Such texts were so pervasive that Shakespeare parodied them in the last act of *A Midsummer Night's Dream* with the death songs of Pyramus and Thisbe. For further information see G. E. P. Arkwright, "Elizabethan Choirboy Plays and Their Music," *Proceedings of the Royal Musical Association* 40 (1913/14): 117–38. See also Philip Brett's remarks in his edition of choirboy laments in *Consort Songs*, Musica Britannica, vol. 22 (London: Stainer and Bell, 1967), xvi.

27. Willetts, *The Henry Lawes Manuscript*, 5.

28. These musical gestures are also not unlike those of the Elizabethan choirboy laments. See Philip Brett, *Consort Songs*, for modern editions of several laments.

29. Andreadis, "Sapphic-Platonics," 42–43.

30. Janice Raymond, *A Passion for Friends: Toward a Philosophy of Female Affection* (London: The Women's Press, 1986), 224.

31. "A Friend," Saintsbury, *Minor Poets*, I: 561–63.

32. Jeremy Taylor, "A Discourse of the Nature, Offices, of Friendship and Measures, With Rules of Conducting It, In a Letter to the Most Ingenious and Excellent M. K. P.," 1657,

in Reginald Heber, ed., *The Whole Works of Jeremy Taylor*, vol. 11 (London: Ogle, Duncan and Co., 1822), 330. See also Hageman, "The Matchless Orinda," 574.

33. Taylor, "Discourse," 330–31.

34. Edmund Waller, *The Poems of Edmund Waller*, ed. George Thorn Drury (London: Routledge, 1893), 60–61.

35. Lillian Faderman, *Surpassing the Love of Men: Romantic Friendship and Love between Women from the Renaissance to the Present* (New York: William Morrow and Company, 1981), 72. It is interesting to note that Katherine Philips disliked Waller. See *Letters from Orinda to Poliarchus*, (2d ed., London: printed for B. Lintot, 1729), 189–90.

36. It seems that it was only after Katherine Philips that women began explicitly to write poetry about lesbian relationships. Most notable among the later poets was Aphra Behn. See her poem "To the Fair Clarinda, Who Made Love to Me, Imagined More than Woman," in Sandra M. Gilbert and Susan Gubar, eds., *The Norton Anthology of Literature by Women: The Tradition in English* (New York: Norton, 1985), 94. For an examination of women who took Philips's poetry as a model for their own poetry about female friendship see Marilyn L. Williamson, "Orinda and Her Daughters," *Raising Their Voices: British Women Writers, 1650–1750* (Detroit: Wayne State University Press, 1990), 64–133. An example of this poetry can be seen in the work of Anne Finch, Countess of Winchilsea. Her dialogue "Friendship between Ephelia and Ardelia" is obviously indebted to Philips. It is available in Dale Spender and Janet Todd, eds., *Anthology of British Women Writers* (London: Pandora Press, 1989), 156–57. For other anthologies see Moira Ferguson, ed., *First Feminists: British Women Writers 1578–1799* (Bloomington: Indiana University Press, 1985); Mary R. Mahl and Helene Koon, eds., *The Female Spectator: English Women Writers Before 1800* (Bloomington: Indiana University Press, 1977); Angeline Goreau, ed., *The Whole Duty of a Woman: Female Writers in Seventeenth-Century England* (Garden City, New Jersey: Dial Press, 1985); Germaine Greer, et al., eds., *Kissing the Rod: An Anthology of Seventeenth-Century Women's Verse* (New York: Farrar Straus Giroux, 1989).

37. James Holstun, " 'Will You Rent Our Ancient Love Asunder?': Lesbian Elegy in Donne, Marvell, and Milton," *E.L.H.* 54, no. 4 (1987): 835–67.

38. Holstun, "Will You Rent Our Ancient Love," 837.

39. Holstun, "Will You Rent Our Ancient Love," 845–46.

40. Andreadis, "Sapphic-Platonics," 51. For a consideration of the ways the figure of Sappho was defined, redefined, and used throughout French literary history see Joan DeJean, *Fictions of Sappho, 1546–1937* (Chicago: University of Chicago Press, 1989).

41. Quoted in Andreadis, "Sapphic-Platonics," 52.

42. Holstun, "Will You Rent Our Ancient Love," 843.

43. John Donne, "Sapho and Philaenis," lines 45–56, quoted in Elizabeth D. Harvey, "Ventriloquizing Sappho: Ovid, Donne, and the Erotics of the Feminine Voice," *Criticism* 31, no. 2 (1989): 127.

44. Holstun, "Will You Rent Our Ancient Love," 840.

45. Easton, "Excusing the Breach of Nature's Laws," 5.

46. For further examples, see excerpts from her poetry in appendix E.

47. "To Mrs. M. A. at parting," Saintsbury, *Minor Poets*, I: 550–51.

48. "Friendship in Emblem, or the Seal. To my dearest Lucasia," Saintsbury, *Minor Poets*, I: 529.

49. "Injuria Amicitiae," Saintsbury, *Minor Poets*, I: 538–39.

50. "To my Lucasia," Saintsbury, *Minor Poets*, I: 541.

51. Harvey, "Ventriloquizing Sappho," 126.

52. For a compelling discussion of the "tension of repression" between Philips's voice and Orinda's, see Easton, "Excusing the Breach of Nature's Laws."

53. Easton, "Excusing the Breach of Nature's Laws," 129.

54. Brett, "Word-Setting in the Songs of Byrd," 54.

55. Souers, *The Matchless Orinda*, 181.

56. Saintsbury, *Minor Poets*, 520.

57. John Berkenhead, quoted in Souers, *The Matchless Orinda*, 66.

58. Saintsbury, *Minor Poets*, 561–63.

59. Waller, *The Poems of Edmund Waller*, 60–61.

60. Saintsbury, *Minor Poets*, 520–22.

7

UNVEILED VOICES
Sexual Difference and the Castrato

Joke Dame

The phallus can play its role only when veiled.

—Jacques Lacan

*A*LONG TIME AGO, when I was first confronted with a high male voice—a countertenor, probably Alfred Deller—I did not recognize it as a man's voice. As far as I knew, vocal tones above a certain frequency were women's voices. There were basses and tenors and these were men. Women, and children, were altos and sopranos. When I heard the counter-tenor, or male alto, I was at a loss. Gender confusion tends to make one nervous.

Nowadays, no one is so easily confused on hearing a countertenor—male altos have once again become so widely known that we have learned to distinguish them from female altos. But in the case of male sopranos or sopranists, as they call themselves, the confusion continues unabated. What is a sopranist? A castrato? An extremely high falsetto voice? A fraud, for is he a man at all?[1]

Even in our time the need to categorize a voice according to gender, to assign a sex to the voice, has not ceased. And one can sympathize with the shock experienced by Sarrasine, the sculptor in Balzac's novella, when he discovers that his great love and ideal of female beauty, the singer Zambinella, is not a woman, but a man—or in his own words, "a nothing," for Zambinella is a castrato. The only difference is that today Sarrasine's horror is replaced by a certain excitement.

Voice and gender. Does the voice have a gender? One is inclined to say that it does. After all, in most cases we do hear correctly whether a voice comes from a female or a male body. Nonetheless, pop music provides crafty examples of gender-disguised singing. Equally in Western art music and non-Western music there are examples that might give rise to doubts as to the "genderedness" of the voice.

I would like to discuss the question of voice and gender in terms of the castrato, a special figure in the history of Western classical singing. I take as a starting point a notion of sexual difference central to recent feminist theory: that gender is constructed, and femininity and masculinity are neither natural nor unalterable, but rather socioculturally and historically determined categories, and therefore subject to change. One of the consequences of the theory of gender as construction is that gender—normally regarded as an extrastylistic attribute—can be thought of as a matter of choice, hence of stylistic variation. Thus it can be argued that voice categories (soprano, alto, and so on) are not sexually fixed categories but prone to choice as well. Both the denaturalization of sexual difference and the denaturalization of voice difference make it in their own ways possible to sever the link between sex, voice pitch, and timbre. From this point of view, and on the basis of descriptions in musicological discourse, I examine the castrato's singing voice, ending with a reflection on the casting of castrato parts in modern revivals of baroque opera, whereby gender and voice is put into action as a stylistic option, as choice.

The phenomenon of the voice is a recurring theme in the oeuvre of Roland Barthes. His focus on the physicality of the voice, his preference for what he calls "the grain of the voice," have become well known. He often mentions the voice in relation to gender and sexuality. When he speaks of sexual difference his aim is always to neutralize the binary opposition male-female at the biological level, in order to escape from a fatalistic essentialism of the sexes. In *Roland Barthes by Roland Barthes* he writes:

> The opposition of the sexes must not be a law of Nature, therefore, the confrontations and paradigms must be dissolved, both the meanings and the sexes must be pluralized...[2]

Barthes's dream of plurality, whereby borders are crossed to discover a veritable playground of textual and sexual possibilities, can be found in almost all of his works. One of its implications is that we must speak of homosexualities in the plural instead of the singular.[3] We find the most elaborate example of the transgression of sexual difference, however, in *S/Z*, his analysis of Balzac's novella *Sarrasine*.[4]

Barthes shows cunningly and persistently that the characters in the novella cannot usefully be classified according to their biological sex, and that they should instead be divided into the categories active, or castrating, and passive, or castrated. Having the phallus, or being the phallus, not having the phallus, or not being the phallus, are all positions that can be taken by both men and women. Barthes's purpose is to disconnect the stereotyped linkages man-active-phallic and woman-passive-castrated, and in his reading of Balzac's novella it is the castrato Zambinella with whom the process of disconnection starts. In Barthes's vocabulary, the castrato is either the neuter, a negative qualification, as neither man nor woman; or he is positively qualified as a composite, as both man and woman, in fact as androgyne. As a neutral or composite center in the middle of polar extremes—that is, on the one hand, the active, castrating Mme de Lanty, and, on the other, the passive, castrated sculptor Sarrasine—he, Zambinella, as Barthes says, "is the blind and mobile flaw in this system; he moves back and forth between active and passive: castrated, he castrates…"[5]

In her article "Dreaming Dissymmetry: Barthes, Foucault, and Sexual Difference," Naomi Schor points out that denaturalization of difference does, of course, make sense:

> Feminists have long sought to break down the assignation of fixed sexual roles to biological men and women and claimed for women but also for men the possibility of oscillating between activity and passivity….[6]

There is a catch, however, according to Schor, because Barthes's disconnection is illusory. His definition of masculinity, although not necessarily tied to a male body, is based on the traditional view of masculinity. And in the same way, Barthes's femininity, in whatever body it appears, does not escape the clichéd view of women. Schor argues that in describing Mme de Lanty as "endowed with all the hallucinatory attributes of the Father: power, fascination, instituting authority, terror, power to castrate," Barthes still classifies her as a woman, only with reversed features. As a result, "she has been reclassified," according to Schor, "as that most fearsome of female monsters: the castrating woman, the phallic mother with all her terrifying attributes of superpower."[7]

In Schor's opinion, there are two reasons why Barthes's strategy is essentially reactionary:

first because it lends credence to a phantasmatic construct of maternal superpower, second because it is merely a reversal, which leaves standing what Barthes was to call some years later the "binary prison" of sexual classification.[8]

Such a reversal becomes counterproductive: it undermines Barthes's actual intention for a plurality of the sexes, freed from any typology. Schor concludes that we should be on our guard when attempts are made to undermine sexual classification, because

> [d]enied sexual difference shades into sexual indifference and, following the same slippery path, into a paradoxical reinscription of the very differences the strategy was designed to denaturalize.[9]

She considers Barthes's fascination for the figure of the castrato as a "neuter" as a refusal to deal with the question of sexual difference in a serious manner. In addition she quotes Jane Gallop, who characterizes the wish to escape sexual difference as "just another mode of denying women."[10]

Schor's and Gallop's discourses are both part of the feminist debate on the classical view on the androgyne. Here, male interest in the androgyne has been unmasked as a strategy of annexation, as a one-sided appropriation of the female by men. For only male subjects can enrich and complete themselves by adopting female properties. As soon as women show male characteristics they are, in dominant male discourse, immediately classified negatively, that is, as castrating women and phallic mothers. This is true even of Barthes, as we have seen in his description of Mme de Lanty.

So far this discussion about sexual difference and the castrato has only referred to his physical appearance, whereas the very reason for his existence—his voice, more precisely his singing voice—has not been questioned. And this makes sense: Zambinella is a literary figure and no more than a few lines are devoted to his voice. These lines, in which Barthes puts forward some remarkable views on the voice of the castrato, are nonetheless extremely significant. I would therefore like to draw the voice itself, and musicological research on the historical castrato, into the discussion.

How do musicologists describe the castrato? It is striking that they all use terms like androgyny, hermaphroditism, and sexual ambiguity, for images that correspond with the common image of the castrato, for instance, in literature. Their discourse also conveys the idea of the neuter, the suggestion of "the empty spot," "the void" upon which all sorts of fantasies can be projected. As musicologist Dorothy Keyser says in an extraordinary article on the castrato:

> To baroque society they appear to have been perceived as blank canvases on which either sexual role could be projected, in real life as on the stage. …In a society that prized virility in its men and fertility in its women, the ambiguous figure of the castrato was endlessly fascinating.[11]

Some musicologists stress femininity rather than ambiguity in their descriptions of the castrati as "feminine men," "perfect nymphs," "more beautiful than women themselves." Others report their extreme weakness, as John Rosselli mentions from early sources: "Castrati tended to have weak eyes and a weak pulse, lacked fortitude and strength of mind, and had difficulties in pronouncing the letter R."[12] Ultimately the castrato is effectively excluded from the category of humanity at all. He is called "angelic," "mechanical," "constructed," "artificial," "a singing machine." In the words of Paul Henry Lang: "The castrato had neither sex nor natural personality; he was an instrument of prodigious versatility and perfection, but still a musical instrument and not a living character."[13] Ambiguous, feminine, weak, or nonhuman—these are the terms musicologists use when describing the castrati of bygone days. But as soon as the voice of the castrato enters the descriptions, a more complex image arises, and a fresh element can be detected in scholarly discourse. So long as pitch is the exclusive subject of discussion, again the "unreal and artificial character of the voice," the "ambiguous," "sexless," and "angelical" are stressed. However, there is more to a voice than merely pitch. The tension of vocal chords, larynx, and pharynx—that is, the physical effort involved in producing a tone—is just as characteristic. The same is true for resonance cavities.[14] In other words, what you hear is not simply a certain pitch, you also hear a body. As Barthes would say: you especially hear a body.

This explains why the voice of a castrato, despite a comparable range to either the female soprano or contralto, was not perceived as a woman's voice. Earwitness accounts—some of which are quite recent, for castrati existed up until this very century—discerned significant differences. As musicologist Kurt Pietschmann states:

> The voice…combined the timbre and range of boys voices—soprano and alto—with male lung capacity and chest resonance…Amongst their excellent features are a wide range…and the fact that their voices lasted longer than women's voices. Because their larynxes remained supple, some of them could perform up into their seventies.[15]

The voice of the castrato is depicted as powerful and strong; it penetrates the accompaniment, it rises above all instruments. It is hard, dry, with an enormous range and a remarkable loudness. The voice is piercing like a trumpet, can handle large intervals, has tremendous staying power, and, in some cases, can produce coloratura "*mit der Brust gestossen*" (belted out with the chest). In short, the castrato voice has an "unusual vocal power and range." As castrato expert Franz Haböck suggests, "no one could surpass the castrato in force, flexibility, penetrating quality, and fullness of voice and breath control."[16] With these terms of power, force, persistence, and the piercing quality of the voice, a totally different image of the castrato is evoked than the one that emerges from descriptions of the castrato as a person. And it is not only the sound descriptions that have contributed to this alternative image. Myths of castrato achievements convey this same image of power. Some castrati were able to gather large fortunes through their singing—which is also true for Balzac's Zambinella. The Neapolitan castrato Farinelli is said to have cured the depression of Phillip V of Spain through his magnificent voice.

In other words, when musicologists describe the features of the castrato's voice, the qualifications they deem appropriate are male connoted. As a result it seems justifiable to regard the voice of the castrato as a male voice, a high male voice to be precise: a male treble, or a male alto. A closer look at the various descriptions seems to suggest that the castrato's virility, the phallus, has been displaced into his voice.

Under the heading "The Voice" in *S/Z*, Barthes refers to this phenomenon of displacement and the phallic character of the castrato voice:

> Italian music...connotes a "sensual" art, an art of the voice. An erotic substance, the Italian voice was produced *a contrario* (according to a strictly symbolic inversion) by singers without sex: this inversion is *logical*, as though, by selective hypertrophy, sexual density were obliged to abandon the rest of the body and lodge in the throat, thereby draining the organism of all that *connects* it. Thus, emitted by a castrated body, a wildly erotic frenzy is returned to that body: the star castrati are cheered by hysterical audiences, women fall in love with them.[17]

One comes across this phallic, virile capacity of the castrato's voice in Balzac's tale *Sarrasine*. Of course, it is the writer who provides the castrato Zambinella with his voice, but the correspondence between the phallic capacity of Zambinella's voice and that of the historical castrato is obvious, and has been underlined, as we have seen, by Barthes in *S/Z*. The fragment in which the sculptor Sarrasine hears Zambinella's singing voice for the first time is summarized by Barthes as follows:

> [Sarrasine] enters a theater by chance, by chance he is seated near the stage; the sensual music, the beauty of the prima donna and her voice fill him with desire; because of his proximity to the stage, he hallucinates, imagines he is possessing La Zambinella; penetrated by the artist's voice, he achieves orgasm; after which, drained, sad, he leaves, sits down and muses: this was his first ejaculation...[18]

"Penetrated by the artist's voice, he achieves orgasm." One should not forget, this is Barthes's reading; obviously Balzac uses different words. However, the point is neither Barthes's interpretation nor whether he is "right" or "wrong." The point is how he reads the characters along the lines of sexual difference. He characterizes both positions, Sarrasine's and Zambinella's, in one and the same phrase:

> The voice is described by its power of penetration, insinuation, flow; but here it is the man who is penetrated; like Endymion "receiving" the light of his beloved, he is visited by an active emanation of femininity, by a subtle force which "attacks" him, seizes him, and fixes him in a situation of passivity.[19]

What does this mean? Barthes describes an immaculate symmetrical reversal: an active woman penetrates a passive man. In his voice Zambinella is portrayed as active, virile, and phallic. For Barthes, in order to get at the intended disconnection, Zambinella cannot be male. Even the so-called neutrality of the castrato does not provide the necessary counterbalance. Barthes reads Zambinella, at least in this fragment, through the eyes of Sarrasine; that is to say, as a woman.

On the other hand, according to Barthes, the male subject Sarrasine has been placed in the female position: passive, overwhelmed, and overpowered. Thus the fragment anticipates his death—his castration, as Barthes puts it—at the end of the tale.

However, in the same excerpt Balzac reveals more about the sculptor. Apart from the passive feminine features observed by Barthes, Balzac provides Sarrasine with some other characteristics:

> Sarrasine wanted to leap onto the stage and take possession of this woman. ...Moreover, the distance between himself and La Zambinella had ceased to exist, he possessed her, his eyes were riveted upon her, he took her for

his own. An almost diabolical power enabled him to feel the breath of this voice, to smell the scented powder covering her hair, to see the planes of her face, to count the blue veins shadowing her satin skin.[20]

As a partner for the active Zambinella we find a similarly active Sarrasine in the traditional sequence man-male-active-phallic. But this Sarrasine is ignored by Barthes.

In short, Barthes reads the characters in this excerpt of Balzac's story solely with reversed traditional features. The male subject Sarrasine is female in his passivity; for him to be active and phallic, the castrato Zambinella must be a woman. What Barthes does not read is the confrontation between two traditional male subjects, both masculine, both active and phallic. Against "better judgment" and despite Balzac's revealing language, Barthes seems firstly to cover up Sarrasine's masculinity in this fragment, and secondly, just like Sarrasine himself, to close his eyes to the *man* in the castrato.

However, Barthes's focus as a reader does not coincide with Sarrasine's, and, like any other reader, he knows perfectly well that Zambinella is not a woman. In an earlier article about *Sarrasine*, Barthes says: "It is not difficult to show that Sarrasine loves in Zambinella the castrato himself." He can say this partly on the basis of Sarrasine's persistent declarations of love for exactly that which makes Zambinella a castrato: "Oh, soft, frail creature, how could you be otherwise?"[21]

Here Barthes brings in his argument for the neutrality of Zambinella. Whereas earlier the female in the castrato was stressed in order to compensate for, or "neutralize," his explicitly masculine behavior, now it is the neuter that counterbalances the traditional female properties. In this way, the blending of the sexes remains a constant in the castrato. However, with the neuter, Barthes once again obscures the male in Zambinella. It seems as if Barthes cannot even consider Sarrasine to be in love with weakness and frailty *in a man*.

Yet this is exactly what seems to be the case in Balzac's novella. Sarrasine voices his aversion for both weakness and strength in women. He says to Zambinella: "This extreme weakness, which I would find hideous in any other woman, which would displease me and whose slightest indication would be almost enough to choke my love, pleases me and charms me in you…" Later he says: "I think I would detest a strong woman, a Sappho, a courageous creature full of energy and passion."[22] One thing is obvious: Sarrasine feels repulsion for every woman. It is not until he sees Zambinella, a man disguised as a woman, that Sarrasine has his first passionate experience (and the masquerade probably serves to postpone the recognition of his homosexual feelings). Moreover, Sarrasine indicates in all sorts of ways that he is interested in women only from an artistic point of view: "This was more than a woman, this was a masterpiece!"[23] Sarrasine is clearly not sexually attracted to women at all, and the intense passion he feels for the castrato Zambinella must be seen as an intense passion for the man Zambinella.

What conclusions can be drawn from this? First, Barthes's interpretation does indeed show the danger of the denial of women, as Gallop described. The female in a positive way can only exist in a male subject and in male appropriation of the female. Second, and this is even more striking, Barthes's neutrality strategy denies the man in the castrato. By that, a homosexual reading, certainly a mode of Barthesian *jouissance*, is precluded and even made impossible.

Homosexuality not only influences the construction and interpretation of literary figures like Zambinella. The historical castrato induced a similarly sublimated homoerotics in opera. After all, it was unusual for the male leading part to be sung by anyone but a castrato. These parts always depicted rulers, like Caesar, Xerxes, or Nero. Neither was it uncommon for his beloved, a female part, also to be performed by a castrato. Thus the audience in the seventeenth and eighteenth centuries, who did not, as we do, automatically associate high-pitched voices with women only, were confronted with men who sang their love for each other in similar registers, regardless of the gender ascribed to them by the libretto. In this way some baroque operas gave rise to what might be called aural homosexuality—a kind of Barthesian *jouissance de l'écoute*.

At least one earwitness was susceptible to this, albeit unconsciously. It was Goethe who wondered, in all his pre-Freudian naïveté, why these men in women's parts excited him so much. His explanation is conveniently aesthetic and harmless:

> I reflected on the reason why these singers pleased me so greatly, and I think I have found it. In these representations, the concept of imitation and of art was invariably more strongly felt, and through their able performance a sort of conscious illusion was produced.[24]

The famous Casanova was equally sensitive to this homoerotic play when, in one of his diaries, he described an evening at the opera house, where the leading female part was performed by a castrato:

> In a well-made corset, he had the waist of a nymph, and, what was almost incredible, his breast was in no way inferior, either in form or in beauty, to any woman's…to resist the temptation, or not to feel it, one would have had to be cold and earthbound as a German. When he walked about the stage during the *ritornello* of the aria he was to sing, his step was majestic and at the same time voluptuous; and when he favored the boxes with his glances, the tender and modest rolling of his black eyes brought a ravishment to the heart. It was obvious that he hoped to inspire the love of those who liked him as a man, and probably would not have done so as a woman.

Casanova adds:

> Rome the holy city, which in this way forces every man to become a pederast, will not admit it, nor believe in the effects of an illusion which it does its best to arouse.[25]

We can suppose that, on some deeper level of consciousness, most listeners experienced the castrato as a *man* with a high *male* voice. Precisely this aspect posits a real problem for the performance of seventeenth- and early eighteenth-century operas (opera seria) today. Who is to perform the role of the castrato in modern revivals? A sopranist would be the most obvious answer, although not a very practicable one. There are too few of these trained male sopranos today. Nevertheless, a prominent expert in early music seriously proposed to hunt down these natural "castrati" to use in the period performances of baroque operas.[26]

Three realistic options remain, which I will examine in the light of Monteverdi's opera *L'incoronazione di Poppea* (Venice 1643). For the various casting possibilities of this opera, the guideline is not the notion of "authenticity" in the sense of the true reconstruction of the composer's original intent,[27] but rather, in the words of Philip Brett, a kind of "understanding" which is "bound up with…the acknowledgement of our own difference. And that acknowledgement entails a recognition of our own temporary need."[28]

In his essay "Text, Context, and the Early Music Editor" Brett argues strongly for focusing on the singers of a period performance instead of considering composers' intentions. Quoting Reinhard Strohm's essay "Towards an understanding of *opera seria*," Brett states:

> "What is to us the 'work,'" [Strohm] writes, "was 250 years ago only the 'production,'" and that was dominated to such an extent by singers that, as reconstruction, "a revival of an opera seria today should really concentrate less on what Handel or Hasse wrote than on what Senesino or Farinelli did with the chief role." And if we had a Senesino, "it might not matter so

much that some of his arias were by Harnoncourt and not Handel. In fact they could even be by Penderecki."[29]

Although Brett is obviously concerned with the aria-centered *opera seria*, I would like to borrow this view for seventeenth-century (Venetian) opera as well.

In the first option, both the lower and higher castrato parts, the alto and soprano, are sung by countertenors. This is far from ideal, since the sound of the countertenor's falsetto differs in many ways from the sound of the castrato voice, at least according to descriptions of the period. The falsetto voice is softer, less penetrating, less piercing, and less powerful. For these reasons, countertenors were mainly used in church music during the baroque period, and rarely in operas. Besides, this option might leave the soprano parts unaccounted for, as there are too few countertenors with the exceptionally high range of the soprano.

The second option is to use women in the castrato roles. The advantage is that this provides a solution for both soprano and alto parts. There is also a difference in sound in this case. Still more blatantly obvious, however, is the difference in gender. For some musicologists, opera directors, and producers, this has proved to be insurmountable. So long as the castrato role is a female part there is, of course, no problem. Take for instance Euridice in Monteverdi's opera *L'Orfeo*. This part was sung by a castrato at its premiere in 1607.[30] That a female soprano should sing the part in the subsequent revivals presents no problem whatsoever. However, the person of Nero in *L'incoronazione di Poppea* is highly problematic. Both Nero's part and that of his beloved Poppea are composed for sopranos. It is quite likely that both roles were sung by castrati. In his struggle against cross-sexual casting in modern revivals, the musicologist Paul Henry Lang argues: "The contrast between men and women is vital, there can be no drama without it."[31] While this view may be shared by some people in our day and age, in the baroque period people thought differently. In early opera, voices were chosen for their beauty, their potential, their virtuousity, and not for their gender. I would even go so far as to suppose, though it is difficult to prove, that voices were cast on similarity in timbre. Two castrati in the leading parts, or two women, might have been preferable to the combination of a man's and a woman's voice.[32] Apart from the homoerotic *jouissance de l'écoute* that consciously or unconsciously entered into it, the main reason for equal-gendered casting might have been a musical one: equal voices, or rather equal timbres, provide different results in, for instance, love duets than do contrasting timbres.[33] I will come back to this later.

The third option has drastic musical consequences. The male soprano part can be transposed to bring the part within the range of the regular tenor. This involves a lowering of the pitch by an octave. According to the proponents of this third option, the advantage is that the dramatic tension of the man-woman opposition can still be maintained. All male soprano parts will be transposed, while the female soprano parts remain unchanged. Unlike the audience in baroque society, we can no longer accept male heroes with soprano voices and old women with tenor voices, according to Lang. He argues: "Once we have established inseparable union of voice timbre and sex there is no turning back…"[34] However, the musical drawbacks of this operation are huge. In duets the intervals are greatly enlarged. Thirds become sixths and even tenths. Because of the distance between the voices, melodies twirling around each other are no longer audible as such. Certain effects like echo, unison, melodic intertwining will be lost. For precisely these effects, many of the important duets in early opera were written. This can be illustrated by an example from Monteverdi's *L'incoronazione*: Nero and Poppea's duet from the third act, scene 5. As sung by regular tenor and soprano, the two voices do not actually touch one another. The natural octave interval keeps their voices apart. However, the performance by two sopranos immediately reveals different intentions. The dissonances are very close and cause frictional moments of an almost physical nature. In the cadential notes, a unison, the lovers literally merge into each other and fuse into the prime. How different from the tenor and the soprano, where the octave interval remains as an unbridgeable gap between them.

Sometimes an intended gap between characters dissolves through octave transposition. The singing parts of the two nurses, Arnalta and Nutrice, are written in the tenor and countertenor/alto range, and both parts are quite often performed by men (although Nutrice may be performed by a woman's low voice). It is important to know that, unlike in romantic opera, the tenor part in baroque opera was seldom a heroic part. Octave transposition makes the logical voice distance between the old women and the young hero disappear so that Nero descends vocally to the same level as the nurses.

Finally I would like to point out a remarkable timbre effect that occurs in option two, where the leading roles are sung by two sopranos.[35] Whereas in the dialogues Nero and Poppea are clearly discernable—Nero with a twentieth-century gendered voice, that is to say, dark in timbre, and Poppea light and silvery—in the duets their voices start to sound alike. The tone colors of the two sopranos assimilate, even to the extent that it becomes difficult, at times even impossible, to tell them apart. And that is in keeping with the music. Both duets are composed in such a way that Nero and Poppea sing the highest parts alternately. In other words, as one in their melodic lines, as one in timbre, color, and pitch, and with the bodily dissonances of the seconds resolving in the unison, they symbolize perfect love. What will survive of this unity if the duet is sung by a soprano and a tenor, with the unbridgeable octave interval and the inevitable difference of tone color? The casting of women in the leading parts is the contemporary counterpart of the historical baroque performance where the homoerotics of the castrati have been displaced by lesbian erotics. Those who are deaf to this, can stay deaf. Though male voyeurism has rarely objected to lesbianism in art, for my part I consider this lesbian representation in modern revivals of baroque operas a present from history, a history that has rendered the authentic casting of castrati impossible, probably for good.

Notes

My thanks are due to Philip Brett, Mieke Taat, and Elizabeth Wood for their helpful comments on earlier versions of this essay.

1. The categories *soprano* and *alto* are in this respect fairly unspecific, since both voice types are found among women and children as well as men, although the latter is a rather unfamiliar phenomenon.

    Two kinds of male sopranos are discernable. Firstly, the so-called *sopranists,* who keep their "natural" high voices (either caused by an exceptionally high countertenor voice, or the result of a physical defect). There are, and have been, very few of these natural male sopranos, who cultivate their high tessitura. Secondly, there used to be the *castrati,* whose vocal chords and larynxes were prevented from thickening and growing as a result of deliberate surgery, which had to take place before puberty. This practice existed exclusively for the benefit of the art of singing and had its peak in the seventeenth and eighteenth centuries. Nonetheless, the last castrato performed up to the beginning of this century.

    There are also two kinds of male altos. The so-called *countertenors* develop the highest natural registers of their voices, their falsetto (some of them, though very few, up to the mezzo-soprano's and even soprano's register). Some experts distinguish between the male alto (a bass or baritone who sings falsetto) and the countertenor (with a natural high—not falsetto—voice). Others reject this distinction, claiming that both the countertenor and the male alto use their falsetto range. In this view—which I share—the two designations are synonymous. The second category of male altos existed among the castrati. Handel, especially in his operas, wrote many parts for alto castrati.

2. Roland Barthes, *Roland Barthes by Roland Barthes* (New York: Hill and Wang, 1977), 69. Trans. Richard Howard from *Roland Barthes par Roland Barthes* (Paris: Editions du Seuil, 1975). See also Naomi Schor, "Dreaming Dissymmetry: Barthes, Foucault, and Sexual Difference," in Alice Jardine and Paul Smith, eds., *Men in Feminism,* (New York/London:

Methuen, 1987), 100.

3. Barthes, *Roland Barthes by Roland Barthes*, 69.

4. Roland Barthes, *S/Z* (New York: Noonday Press, 1988). Trans. Richard Miller, from *S/Z* (Paris: Editions du Seuil, 1970). Sexual difference is not the main theme in this book. In *S/Z* Barthes develops his famous theory on the "readerly" (*lisible*) and the "writerly" (*scriptible*) text.

5. Barthes, *S/Z*, 36.

6. Schor, "Dreaming Dissymmetry," 102.

7. Schor, "Dreaming Dissymmetry," 102.

8. Schor, "Dreaming Dissymmetry," 102.

9. Schor, "Dreaming Dissymmetry," 100.

10. Schor, "Dreaming Dissymmetry," 100.

11. Dorothy Keyser, "Cross-Sexual Casting in Baroque Opera: Musical and Theatrical Conventions," *Opera Quarterly* 5/4 (1987/88): 49–50.

12. John Rosselli, "The Castrati as a Professional Group and a Social Phenomenon, 1550–1850," *Acta Musicologica* 60 (1988): 145.

13. Paul Henry Lang, *George Frideric Handel* (New York: W. W. Norton, 1966), 170.

14. An example will clarify matters. Male and female altos have roughly the same tessitura. In the case of men this area is at the top of their voices, they sing (mostly, and at least for the higher notes) in their falsetto register. The strain upon vocal chords, larynx, and pharynx is intense; resonating cavities are mainly those in the head. With women altos things are different. The lowest part of their voices is developed, throat tension is moderate, and the main resonators are in the chest. In other words, pitch alone does not make a voice; voice tension and resonating cavities determine a voice as well.

15. Kurt R. Pietschmann, "Händels 'Kastrat' heute. Zur Problematik der Besetzungspraxis bei Händel," *Opernwelt* 9 (1986): 9.

16. Franz Haböck, *Die Kastraten und ihre Gesangkunst* (Berlin/Leipzig: Deutsche Verlags Anstalt Stuttgart, 1927), 135.

17. Barthes, *S/Z*, 109.

18. Barthes, *S/Z*, 119.

19. Barthes, *S/Z*, 118.

20. Barthes, *S/Z*, 116–17.

21. Roland Barthes, "Masculin, Féminin, Neutre," in Jean Pouillon and Pierre Maranda, eds., *Echanges et Communications II* (The Hague/Paris: Mouton, 1970): 903 n6.

22. Barthes, *S/Z*, 248–49.

23. Barthes, *S/Z*, 238.

24. Cited in Angus Heriot, *The Castrati in Opera* (London: Da Capo Press, 1975), 26. (Reprint of the 1956 ed.)

25. Heriot, *The Castrati in Opera*, 54–55.

26. Peter Giles, *The Counter Tenor* (London: Frederick Muller, 1982), 75. (Unfortunately, the name of this expert is not given.) As one of the possible ways of becoming a "natural castrato" Giles mentions "diseases, such as mumps, at the correct age" that "cause the hormones necessary for normal sexual development to be suppressed" (75). Although in

our day this problem is easily remedied by hormone treatment, some of these "castrati," like the French singer Rophée, cherish their ambivalent sex and refuse to have their voices lowered down to the male register by the injection of hormones. Rophée speaks of himself in the feminine:

> It sometimes happens that juveniles have hormonal insufficiencies. But medicine has made progress. They have to be taken care of, nowadays, their virility should be safeguarded. I myself, I did not want to be treated, for I have a feminine character. *Je suis heureuse ainsi.*

See Jean Vermeil, "Les nouveaux castrats," *Diapason* 285 (July/August 1983): 34, [my translation].

27. For an interesting discussion of authenticity see Nicholas Kenyon, ed., *Authenticity in Early Music,* (Oxford/New York: Oxford University Press, 1988).

28 Philip Brett, "Text, Context, and the Early Music Editor," in Kenyon, *Authenticity in Early Music,* 114.

29. Philip Brett, "Text, Context, and the Early Music Editor," 107, quoting Reinhard Strohm, *Essays on Handel and Italian Opera* (Cambridge: Cambridge University Press, 1985), 94–98.

30. Iain Fenlon, "Monteverdi's Mantuan 'Orfeo': Some New Documentation," *Early Music* 12 (1984): 163–72.

31. Lang, *George Frideric Handel,* 173. See also Pietschmann, "Händels 'Kastrat' heute," 9–10. In this report of the second "Internationale Händel-Akademie Karlsruhe," Wolfgang Kersten is paraphrased arguing that in modern revivals of Handel operas (from 1952 to 1979 in Halle) the main goal was to reach a large audience. So " 'psychological naturalness' was meant to make it easier to empathize with the emotions. ...For this reason the casting of castrati parts with female singers should be rejected: it jeopardizes the partner tensions" (Pietschmann, 9, my translation). Taking the opposite view in this debate on women in male castrato roles, Handel scholar Winton Dean argues strongly in favor of women in his final chapter "Modern Revivals" of *Handel and the Opera Seria* (London: Oxford University Press, 1970), 200–214.

32. There is some evidence for this: Dorothy Keyser, for instance, mentions in her article "Cross-Sexual Casting in Baroque Opera," the (Mantua, 1607) performance of Monteverdi's *L'Orfeo,* with an all-male cast: 51 n. 13.

33. Peter Giles considers this also from the singer's point of view. He comes close to the notion of "vocal homosexuality" when he states that

> [t]he timbres of altos [male] and contraltos [female] do not mix well. Even on identical notes in the scale, the alto sounds higher and more piercing than the rather plummier contralto. Neither enjoys the sensation of singing next to the other (Giles, *The Counter Tenor,* 70).

34. Lang, *George Frideric Handel,* 169–170.

35. My references are to *Virgin Classics* VCT 7 90775–2 (1990), dir. Richard Hickox, with Arleen Auger (Poppea) and Della Jones (Nerone).

8

"WAS GEORGE FRIDERIC HANDEL GAY?"
On Closet Questions and Cultural Politics

Gary C. Thomas

*G*EORGE FRIDERIC HANDEL IS ONE of the towering figures of Western music. With the possible exception of Wagner, no other composer achieved the same level of fame and mythic stature in his own lifetime. By the time of his death an apotheosis was already well underway, which in turn facilitated a rich posthumous life as a British national institution, religious icon, hero revered by a musical cult (the Handelians), font of cultural nostalgia, and, finally, as Christopher Hogwood puts it, "a complete industry."[1] But if the romantic impulse to construct cultural heroes is human, the ironic counterimpulse to deconstruct them seems equally so: what is the reality behind the image, the truth behind the mask (inquiring minds want to know)? We thus get to enjoy our heroes twice, first in the putting on, then in the taking off, of their clothes; if anything, the latter is more pleasurable. Handel makes an especially interesting case study of our delight in dressing and undressing. For while as public figure he has been amply documented and examined, and his mythic image furbished and sufflated in the 230-odd years since his death, the man's private life has long been considered a mystery. One scholar's complaint in 1934 can stand for many:

> One would expect every detail of his life to be known and recorded, his every thought to be revealed with the pellucid clarity of his immortal strains. It is not so; to assemble the bare facts of Handel's life is a problem which has baffled the most laborious of his biographers, and his inward personality is more mysterious than that of any other great musician of the last two centuries.[2]

While Handel's silence about his private or "inner" being helped ensure an exalted afterlife as mythic icon and consumer commodity, it also worked to generate a lot of "mysteries" to be pondered, "puzzles" to be solved. Questions, trifling or serious, have flourished in the vast literature of Handel scholarship over the years: Did Handel meet Bononcini in Rome? (It's a good possibility;) Was Gustave Waltz Handel's cook? (Well, he might have been, for a while;) Why did Handel borrow? (For some very good reasons;) Was Handel insane? (Are you kidding?)[3] None has proved more insistent or troublesome, however, than the one euphemistically couched as his "relationship to women": did Handel sleep with them? or, in the form in which I am asking it, was Handel gay? The composer's interest, or noninterest, in the opposite ("apposite"?) sex has been a vexed question for biographers, music historians, and others from Handel's time to the present; it has constituted, in the words of Paul Henry Lang, a "problem [that has] puzzled his biographers for the last two hundred years."[4]

The first part of this essay examines the origin and history of the question itself—for I am far from the first to pose it—and will locate it in its proper discursive home, the closet. In the second section I pursue it in relation to "Handel's body" as a kind of countermythic strategy, that is, in terms of what we know of his material lived experience. In the last part, which is meant to mark the beginning of a conversation involving voices other than those of avowed (if postmodern) Handelians such as myself, I propose some points of departure for situating the "Handel question" on a larger ideological grid. My aim here is to map out some future directions for reading a denatured subject—a "homotextual Handel"—as a complex of dialectical relations involving his life, his work, and his audiences; in other words, to pose yet more questions. My project thus entails both a "deconstructive" moment (of a closed, romanticizing image) as well as a "constructive" one (of an open-endedly "multitextual" alternative), and these, like that texture of image and reality, life and work that is "Handel" himself, are inescapably political. What constitutes knowledge, who speaks for whom, and with what effects, are questions with political dimensions and consequences; language, as Foucault insisted, is linked not only to the knowing of things, but to human freedom.[5] Finally, although I believe my arguments will make a strong case that Handel was "gay,"[6] my main concern has not been to define, but to explore. I have tried to open a field of inquiry rather than close one off, to disrupt rather than suture. And realizing it is after all Handel we are talking about, I have endeavored to pursue these many and weighty questions in the ironic and gently subversive sense of the Emersonian motto: "I unsettle all things; nothing is to me sacred, nothing profane."

The Handel Question

To my knowledge, the first open mention in scholarly discourse of Handel in relation to homosexuality—where the two words "Handel" and "homosexual" stand side by side in print—is a brief reference in a 1981 article by the Enlightenment cultural historian George S. Rousseau. In a passage discussing the high number of bachelors among major and minor figures in the eighteenth century, Rousseau notes: "Of these several were apparently homosexual: Gray, Walpole, Beckford, Lord Hervey; others, like Newton, Handel, Gay, are questionable: and while one is constrained here to be speculative, one can at least say that the heterosexuality of these men has never been fully established."[7] Four years later, in a lengthy and ground-breaking essay on homosexuality in eighteenth-century England, Rousseau returned to the issue, this time rather more directly and polemically:

> When Handel replied to his sovereign's question about "the love of women" with a solecism about having no time for anything but music, George II apparently was satisfied; it is surprising that Handel's recent biographers should leave the matter there in this post-Freudian age. No one should suggest that Handel was homosexual without evidence, or even that his behavior was more homosocial than the norm for the age (difficult as this norm is to gauge): the point is rather that Handel's biographers have overlooked their subject's sexuality for reasons they never explicitly state. One can understand if a critical or thematic study of Handel's music should consider the composer's sexuality extraneous; yet biography, even when judged by the most puritanical criteria set out in the eighteenth century, has the duty to reveal the whole truth about the subject's life with at least a modicum of dispassionate objectivity.[8]

The issue was raised again the same year (the tricentennial of Handel's birth) in a new biography by Jonathan Keates, here not to pursue the question, but rather to foreclose it: "The assumption that as a lifelong bachelor [Handel] must perforce have been homosexual is untenable in an eighteenth-century context, when the vagabond life of so many musicians made marriage a distinct hindrance."[9] However, in the absence of any previous "assumptions" of Handel's homosexuality in the literature (and leaving aside for the moment Keates's peculiar rationale for its "untenability"), we are left to wonder on what his statement is based. Where did the question come from?

We begin with Handel himself. First, what about King George II's question to Handel about "his love of women," together with its reply "I have no time for anything but music"? While the exchange is interesting and clearly to the point—more for the blunt directness of the question ("you *are* attracted to women, *aren't* you?") than for Handel's evasive reply—no case will be made or broken on the basis of it. In any event, I have not been able to verify it.[10] I should note that Handel's reply, if he did say it, would only corroborate the view put forward by others that he simply was not interested in women (though with the obligatory subtext "of course I'd be *very* interested if only I didn't have all this damned music to write"). In its absence we are left with Handel's famous silence: far more than anything the composer said (or is reputed to have said), it was his silence that piqued the interest of the curious and contributed to the construction of the Secret. Handel's commentators, perhaps understandably frustrated, have only further contributed to its construction, through locutions such as: "Handel *firmly...barred the doors on the subject*" (Keates); "as an individual he remains *hidden*, his private life is rarely *exposed*, his letters are few and *unrevealing*"; he maintained an "*enigmatic* aloofness in matters of sex, politics, and religion" (Hogwood); "his amorous encounters were *as carefully screened from view* as were his political and religious inclinations" (Lang), and so forth (italics mine).

Apart from some anecdotal material, the sole references on this subject from reasonably reliable contemporaries of Handel are two statements found in the early biographies by John Mainwaring and Sir John Hawkins. Mainwaring, Handel's first biographer (he is usually credited with writing the very first biography of a famous composer) was a clergyman who may or may not have known Handel personally. Much of his information appears to have come secondhand, from conversations with John Christopher Smith, Jr., Handel's lifelong friend, protégé, and amanuensis, who of course did know him well. About Hawkins there is no doubt: he knew Handel personally, and probably quite well. Though he was thirty-four years Handel's junior, the myriad accounts contained in his mammoth *General History of the Science and Practice of Music* reveal Hawkins to have been a ubiquitous presence in the musical life of London who thus doubtless knew many who had been close to Handel during his lifetime.[11] The statements by both men are telling, and, since there is so little else to go on from Handel's contemporaries, I intend to examine them in some detail.

Thirty pages into his *Memoirs of the Life of the Late George Frederic Handel*, Mainwaring feels obliged to address the question head-on. In a passage accounting for the composer's "liberty and independency," Mainwaring tells us: "In the sequel of his life he refused the highest offers from persons of the greatest distinction; nay, the highest favours from the fairest of the sex, only because he would not be cramped or confined by particular attachments." [12]

We learn here two things: Because he cherished his liberty and independence so much Handel (1) refused to be bought off by even the wealthiest and most prestigious persons and, in like fashion, (2) refused sexual relations with even the most attractive of women. Given the eighteenth-century currency of the word "favours" as benign vocabulary for sexual seduction it is virtually impossible to read Mainwaring as referring to anything other than physical intimacy. (This is certainly how Mattheson read it, translating Mainwaring's phrase as "die schätzbaresten Winke des schönen Geschlechtes" [the most precious come-ons of the fair sex]).[13] Further implicit is the suggestion that although Handel refused such "come-ons" he nonetheless had his share of offers. Not surprisingly, Mainwaring also seems constrained to offer a reason, and while he may simply be invoking the long-standing misogynist theme that relationships with women are invariably traps for men (especially geniuses), it is also possible to read the statement the following way: "Handel, not wanting to be confined in a relationship with one woman (marriage or something other than marriage), therefore refused to sleep with any of the women who gave him the nod." And one might be furthermore inclined, at the risk of belaboring the phrase, to point out the defensive force of Mainwaring's "only," as in "Handel refused the sexual favors of women, but lest the reader jump to unseemly conclusions let me assure him that it was *only* because he didn't want to be cramped or confined." We end up with a fairly curious and, depending on how you read it, contradictory message since refusing sex with women while not wanting to be "cramped" and "confined" with any one in particular doesn't jibe. (Mainwaring certainly doesn't mean to suggest the opposite, that the man was so promiscuous he just couldn't settle down.) Why Mainwaring would even have bothered to slip in this inevitably question-begging and strangely (un)coordinate clause in the first place is not clear. (I mean, are getting support from the rich and famous and having sex with women all that parallel?) But on to Hawkins.

Hawkins's *A General History of the Science and Practice of Music* appeared in 1776, seventeen years after Handel's death. Though references to Handel are peppered liberally throughout the two large volumes, the main biographical material is contained in one of his usual "portraits," where we read the following:

> His social affectations were not very strong; and to this it may be imputed that he spent his whole life in a state of celibacy; that he had no female attachments of another kind may be ascribed to a better reason. His intimate friends were few; those that seemed to possess most of his confidence were Goupy, the painter, and one Hunter, a scarlet-dyer at Old Ford, near

> Bow, who pretended a taste for music, and at a great expense had copies made for him of all the music of Handel that he could procure. He had others in the city; but he seemed to think that the honour of his acquaintance was a reward sufficient for the kindness they expressed for him.[14]

A masterpiece of innuendo, and as disarming as it is suggestive, one wonders how long it took Hawkins to come up with it. But what is he trying to say? Even the most innocent attempt to read its surface brings us into difficulty: What exactly does Hawkins mean by "social affectations"? Simply that Handel didn't like socializing that much, i.e., he wasn't that drawn to people, or they to him? Or is it a reference to social propriety or formality of some sort (*Oxford English Dictionary:* "forced," "in fashion"), including, perhaps, concern for what other people were likely to think? Are we to read it then in this sense: Handel remained a bachelor his whole life because having little inclination for social ceremony he didn't feel the need to get himself a wife? Or perhaps this: being such a boor in public, he just couldn't manage to find someone who would marry him? Another problem lies in the meaning of the word "celibate." It usually denotes "single" or "unmarried"—its Latin root denotes this, as do all of the *Oxford English Dictionary* entries, for example—but is, of course, often used colloquially to mean "chaste." But "chaste" (he abstained from sex with anybody) can't be what Hawkins means, since in this context he seems to be offering an explanation or justification for why Handel never married (which everyone knows and knew). He is in any case rather speculative about it ("it may be imputed"). Of obviously much greater bearing on our problem are the phrases that follow: what does Hawkins want to signify by "female attachments of *another kind*"? What might this *better reason* be? Why all the ambiguity? It is hard not to read the passage in the following sense: Handel had no inclination, for whatever social reasons, to get married; now, as far as finding women to enjoy sex with (amours, paramours, visits to or by the ubiquitous London prostitutes, etc.) he didn't do that either, because of a better reason which I won't tell you because it's not fit to print. The language certainly indicates that Hawkins "knows something" and wants to communicate that he knows it, but the "something" is information he shrinks from naming openly because it cannot *be* named; or perhaps: "I know it and you know it, but it is something we just do not talk about." His next sentence ("His intimate friends were few…") is no help: rather than offering us a reason why, the "better reason" so tantalizingly invoked, it merely reiterates the sense of the preceding "His social affectations were not very strong," though the elision from "better reason" to "intimate [male] friends" who are then listed (some with names, others not) might have been Hawkins's way of hinting at the "reason." Of the scant testimony we have, this comes closest to suggesting that Handel was not interested in women sexually because he was gay, and this I offer as one possible (and I think compelling) reading, since it not only explains— rather than explains away—the posed but unanswered question (and the elision that follows it), but it is also utterly consistent with the prevalent construction of homosexuality (i.e., its eighteenth-century counterparts) as the "vice that cannot be named among Christians."

That Hawkins was himself inviting this interpretation of the "better reason" receives support from two subsequent references to the passage. The first appears as one of the vignettes in William Coxe's collection of Handel lore published twenty-three years later, where, in a passage that reads essentially as a gloss on Hawkins, we get the following:

> Handel contracted few intimacies, and when his early friends died, he was not solicitous of acquiring new ones. He was never married; but his celibacy must not be attributed to any deficiency of personal attractions, or to the source which Sir John Hawkins unjustly supposes, the want of social affection. On the contrary, it was owing to the independency of his disposition, which feared degradation, and dreaded confinement.[15]

Here, for whatever it may mean, "affectations" has become "affection." That aside, along with assuring us that Handel was an attractive, even convivial sort (he was not a boor), Coxe seems to be saying that when it came to "intimacies" Handel was basically a lone wolf, especially in his later years ("when his early friends died") and that such intimacies would have brought not only confinement but "degradation." But that this is further meant as a defense against the possible imputation of homosexuality is indicated in the continuation of the passage, where Coxe offers an anecdote (an antidote?) concerning two early marriage proposals (italic mine):

> *For* when he was young, two of his scholars, ladies of considerable fortune, were so much enamoured of him, that each was desirous of a matrimonial alliance. The first is said to have fallen a victim to her attachment. Handel would have married her; but his pride was stung by the coarse declaration of her mother, that she never would consent to the marriage of her daughter with a fiddler; and indignant at the expression, he declined all further intercourse. After the death of the mother, the father renewed the acquaintance, and informed him that all obstacles were removed; but he replied, that the time was now past; and the young lady fell into a decline, which soon terminated her existence. The second attachment, was a lady splendidly related, whose hand he might have obtained by renouncing his profession. That condition he resolutely refused, and laudably declined the

connection which was to prove a restriction on the great faculties of his mind.[16]

Here, as in Mainwaring, the idea resurfaces that women, marriage, or both, are millstones, confining to the spirit and degrading to the mind and that, thankfully, Handel was "resolute" in his praiseworthy refusal to be a party to it. One stumbles over the word "degradation," of course, a term that, according to the *Oxford English Dictionary*, had roughly the same (if not more severe) connotations in the eighteenth century as today. In what sense would marriage or other liaisons with women have constituted "degradation"? And attentive Freudians would certainly be loathe to let the conjunction of "degradation," "fear," and "dread" pass unremarked, and so let it be.

With the second of our two Hawkins commentators, Friedrich Chrysander, all this is preceded by a long and bizarre anecdote involving a mysterious lady admirer, a laurel wreath, and a poem, again by way of countering the imputation of "something being wrong."[17] When he finally gets around to Hawkins's statement—whether he included it purely out of German scholarly thoroughness, or for the primary purpose of containing the threat, is hard to tell—it is first qualified by a caution, then trumped by the "rewrite" of Coxe, or rather Coxe's assumed source, Smith:

> Of course he [Hawkins] is first of all giving only his own opinion, based among other things on hearsay and a certain personal acquaintance. But the young Smith, who must have known about it, and who willingly confirms the better part of Hawkins assumption, told his own [den Seinigen] a few things about the true circumstances and they have preserved the following account… [at which point we get a translation into German of the Coxe paragraph quoted above.][18]

It is well worth noting that when he comes to translate the phrase "better reason," Chrysander quite significantly (and deliberately, it would seem) alters its meaning: "daß er aber keinen weiblichen Umgang von anderer Sorte hatte, darf man besseren Grundsätzen zuschreiben." "Bessere Grundsätze" can only mean "better *principles*," not "better *reasons*." He, too, must have been troubled.

I have given so much attention to this passage in Hawkins largely because Handel scholars have given so little. In fact the most interesting thing about Hawkins's statement—more significant even than the messages it encodes— is the (chilling) fact that in all the many pages written about Handel subsequent to Coxe and Chrysander, in which, not surprisingly, references to Hawkins abound, *not one single biographical or musicological work even acknowledges the existence of this passage,* not even in those whose authors complain most loudly about the lack of "evidence."[19] Mainwaring's remark hasn't fared much better. For whatever else may be said about them, they do constitute evidence, and for the researcher pursuing the nettlesome question of Handel's "relationship to women" evidence that fairly leaps off the page.

Let us continue with, as it were, the question of the question, by surveying its configuration in the literature following Chrysander. For despite suppression of Hawkins on the subject (and Mainwaring too, for the most part), it lives on as a haunting presence, a "problem" in search of explanations. Fortunately for the gaiety of nations, such "explanations" are not lacking: even in the absence of what is inevitably demanded in the way of "hard" evidence (a notarized eyewitness account of Handel behind the scenes in flagrante delicto perhaps?), writers have labored to reach closure on the subject. What follows is a summary of four of the most common strategies for doing so.

First is what I shall call the Ladyfriend Trap, the discovery of female friends or secret affairs for men who did not otherwise seem to have or desire them. This is, of course, a strategy practiced not only by biographers, but often out of necessity and in the interests of passing (and thus surviving) by gay men themselves. But Handel's silence, the lack of documentable liaisons, and (should it have been considered) the testimony of Mainwaring and Hawkins have made this game infinitely harder to play. (And need it be said, even if heterosexual "affairs" could be documented, this might—and often does—mean nothing, especially with regard to the eighteenth century; human desire is rarely as tidy as our classifications.) Often the women remain nameless, and there is sometimes the suggestion that the interest is one-sided, as in Coxe's account of Handel's early women suitors; even when they are named the connections are tenuous. Thus Keates: "We can surmise that while in Italy he fell in love with the soprano Vittoria Tarquini, and it is not unreasonable to suppose that he may have felt attracted to certain of his leading singers such as Margherita Durastanti, Anna Strada and, in later years, Kitty Clive and Susannah Cibber."[20] (Of course it is only "not unreasonable" if viewed under the cosmic umbrella of enforced heterosexuality.) Paul Henry Lang tries to connect Handel erotically to at least four women, a Mme. Sbülens in Germany (one casual mention in a letter; Handel probably knew her father),[21] one Donna Laura, a "shadowy Iberian Princess" (they happened to be in the same place at the same time), in Florence the singer Vittoria Tarquini (along with Lucrezia d'André, another "Florentine belle in whom Handel became interested"), and other divas in London.[22] Of these, only the case of Vittoria Tarquini appears to have any substance, and it is questionable. Tarquini, known as "La Bombace" (the Bomb), was originally thought to have sung in Handel's first opera *Vincer se stesso è la maggior vittoria* (known usually by its shorter title *Rodrigo*), which was staged 1707 in Florence when Handel was twenty-two. Mainwaring, not long after the statement about Handel's refusal of female "favours," nonetheless records that Vittoria was quite interested in *him*, specifically that

> [s]he was a fine woman, and had for some time been much in the good graces of his Serene Highness [the Grand Duke Cosimo III of Tuscany; she was his mistress]. But, from the natural restlesness of certain hearts, so little sensible was she of her exalted situation, that she conceived a design of transferring her affections to another person. Handel's youth and come- liness, joined with his fame and abilities in Music, had made impressions on her heart. Tho' she had the art to conceal them for the present, she had not perhaps the power, certainly not the intention, to efface them.[23]

The passage says nothing about Handel's role here, unless the composer's was one of the "hearts" said to be "restless"; the notion that Handel was sleeping with her is based on a rumor that can be documented in a letter, recently discovered by Anthony Hicks, by the Electress Sophie of Hanover in 1710 in which is written "[Handel is] a good-looking man and the talk is that he is the lover of Victoria."[24] While it is possible that Handel was Vittoria's lover, most Handel scholars dismiss the idea as far-fetched. Hogwood says simply, "it is unlikely that Handel would have engaged with her on any other than professional terms," while Newman Flower, who admittedly wants to keep Handel innocent of any physicality whatsoever and who probably could not have known of Sophie's letter (though I suspect it would not have mattered to him anyway), notes dryly:

> She was a woman well advanced in middle age, with nothing more than an average voice, who would probably have been the last person to make any physical impression on Handel...At this period... Handel had no interest in women. Later, when he mellowed to that tenderness towards mankind which brought out some of the best of his melodies, he had a liking for feminine society. He became the genteel gallant—never quite the courtier. But whilst at Florence, at any rate, he can be quite safely exonerated from intrigue with an actress or any other woman.[25]

Handel still may have been sleeping with her, despite her age and voice, as Lang notes (by way of a gentle chide): "Our eminent and strait-laced histo- rian could not have been familiar with the traditional role middle-aged women have always played in the introduction of young men, especially artists, to the mysteries and delights of love." In any event, Lang is happy to conclude, "on this pleasant note the second Florentine visit ended..."[26]

Such difficulties with the Ladyfriend strategy have driven a number of writ-ers—faute de mieux—to what we may call the Mother Alibi. Psychologists predictably have diagnosed Handel's "problem" (and Brahms's too, by the way) rather coldly as an unnatural mother fixation (with "early rejection" by women an occasional cofactor, especially in German accounts), which made him incapable of passion for other women.[27] But many of the Handelians rather warmed to the idea of the composer's mother as his one and only. Waxing sentimental, if curiously incestuous, Flower for example writes:

> The affection of Handel for this simple German woman, who had borne him, increased with the years. She was the only woman who ever held any real place in his heart. His sisters were dead. He was mildly interested in his nieces, but the old lady of Halle had supreme command of that solitary affection he had for one of the opposite sex.[28]

Insofar as mother fixation has figured prominently in clinical etiologies of homosexuality, the Mother Alibi, like the bottomless Ladyfriend pit, far from removing the dreaded stigma, ends up again (however unintentionally) rein-forcing it.[29]

A third strategy, the Sexless and Celibate Syndrome, is another concept adduced, strangely enough, to establish Handel's normalcy. As Lang notes, it is much favored by the "pure" Handelians: "Flower called Handel 'sexless and safe' while others attributed his bachelorhood to a 'moral revulsion to carnal passion.'"[30] And R. A. Streatfeild wrote:

> [Handel was] a man of singular personal purity. In his time obscenity of language and unchastity of life were regarded as the most venial of sins, but from the typical faults of the age Handel was entirely free, and the disgust with which he regarded the sensuality that he saw rampant around him is, I think, to be read in *Samson* by those that have eyes to see.[31]

This line of thought may be traced back to Coxe, with its attendant confla-tion of bachelorhood with chastity, or perhaps to the now famous statement of Charles Burney—itself rife with suggestions of sexual sublimation—namely that

> Handel, with many virtues, was addicted to no vice that was injurious to society. Nature, indeed, required a great supply of sustenance to support so huge a mass, and he was rather epicurean in the choice of it; but this seems to have been the only appetite he allowed himself to gratify.[32]

Whatever the case, the "sexless" theory is not without its problems. Lang rejects the idea outright, as being disconcertingly abnormal in itself; with English Handelians such as Streatfeild and Flower clearly in mind, he bristles: "Many of the writers seem to regard celibacy as a higher and more spiritual state than marriage, which is a rather curious attitude coming from English Protestants."[33] The reference to English Protestants might well suggest that celibacy was connected in his mind—as well as in the minds of many stolid eighteenth-century Englishmen—with the Roman Catholic priesthood (i.e., not a good thing), and Handel had spent quite enough time in *their* company. In any event, it should be noted that the word "celibate," like "papist" and even "priest," had since the late sixteenth century functioned in the language as a pejorative synonym for sodomite. Whether this was in the minds of Flower or Streatfeild is unknown, but the attempt to preserve Handel in a state of safe (disembodied) sexlessness raises as many questions as it obviates. Handel was clearly unmarried, but was he (therefore) nonsexual?

The final strategy we can call the Aesthetic Fallacy, the idea that a composer, being in love with his Muse, has therefore no time for erotic relations with real human beings. This has been a favored explanation in Handel's case (especially, if the exchange with George II should be valid, because he said so). But it does little to clarify the problem of Handel's sexuality; if anything, it, too, further obscures it. That Handelians have embraced this notion of monkish aestheticism—the holy solitude of the artist—most vigorously should hardly surprise us. Flower wrote, for example, that "[h]is art was his life. No woman could have taken its place, or even shared that place. It drew from him everything he had to give."[34] But Percy M. Young is more skeptical, calling such a conclusion "curious," since bachelorhood "did not preclude the eighteenth-century gentleman from becoming acquainted with the delectable possibilities of female companionship. Pope, Gay, Congreve, Prior, Atterbury, and Savage were all bachelors: it was not unfashionable to avoid the *rigours* of matrimony."[35] Lang, who, as we have seen, found it necessary to posit actual sexual affairs with women in order to certify Handel as "normal," finally ends up blandly eliding the two. Not women, but "solitude" must have been his mistress after all: "One might say that he simply did not have time for serious engagement with women. Solitude for him was…his deepest inspiration…He saw no place for a woman in his scheme of things…" "How," asks Lang with disturbing misogynist overtones, "would any woman understand the single-minded pursuit of any idea that took possession of him?"[36] It might be noted parenthetically that Handel's inspired solitude did not preclude his spending an awful lot of time on banking and financial speculation, as well as eating and drinking—another of Burney's anecdotes tells of Handel leaving the table and the company of a friend to eat choice French dishes and swill fine wine in an adjoining room[37]—and fussing over his collection of exotic houseplants, a passion he shared with his friend Telemann. But Lang is not finished: apparently needing to reconcile this lofty notion with his insistence that Handel was a man of red-blooded passion he continues by arguing (with an admittedly oblique austerity, but at least veering toward the right track) that music is a form of sex: "There is a certain kinship," he declares, "between Eros and musical poetry. It is the *urge*, the *creative urge* that *drives* the composer to work, and the *pleasure he experiences while so engaged* is akin to erotic experience."[38] It hardly needs remarking that the notion of men taking erotic refuge in art has had in itself strongly homosexualizing connotations, particularly in the nineteenth century.[39] Because of such social codings—whether embedded in the discourse of Freudian psychopathology or Romantic aestheticism—Handel ends up here as well reimplicated in an association from which these authors presumably sought to extricate him.

At this point we have ample evidence if not to "answer" our question then at least to locate, on a discursive level, its origin: the closet. For despite the utter absence of the word "homosexual" (or any of its genealogical antecedents), it has been nonetheless everywhere actively present. As Eve Kosofsky Sedgwick has argued, the closet is an "epistemological" space where knowledge of a certain kind is generated—of a kind held by a given social body to be somehow marked as threatening.[40] Knowledge can be thought of as "closetworthy" in approximate proportion to its ability to threaten or contest manifest or dominant versions of the truth (some skeletons in the closet are more threatening than others). What is more, its production depends not on ordinary means but, as we have seen, on a series of specific discursive operations. On the most basic level closet knowledge depends on silence, an "absence" out of which is generated a discursively elaborated "presence," the secret. Then, as in Freud's "negation" or Foucault's "spiral"—mechanisms by which an object to be denied, repressed, or disciplined gains more, rather than less, presence and power—the secret is by the logic of "reverse discourse" further constituted and elaborated in a procession of alibis, justifications, or explanations: the "repressed," to put it in Freudian language, "returns." In other words, the question of Handel's homosexuality (Keates's "assumption") is constantly generated, not as a present surface of knowledge, but rather as an absent surfeit of it; a lack becomes an "excess"—knowledge is produced in "excess" of what is spoken, i.e., in its interstitial and subtextual spaces—everywhere, that is, except in the open. The closet is that space where silences speak, obfuscations reveal, absences signify, and negations posit.

Closet knowedge, existing in the nature of a threat, must therefore be held in check, and this is the function of the closet "door" ("held in check," rather than met with the force of annihilation, for the closet can be useful). What kind of a threat must homosexuality be in order to mobilize such elaborate means of containment; or in terms of our question: what is so threatening about a homosexual Handel? To grasp this we need to see that more is at stake than the reputation of a single man, however "great" he may be. Homosexuality keys into whole systems of representation and symbolic meaning; in Randolph Trumbach's words:

> [We] ought to study the historical forms of sexual behavior not simply because they are interesting in themselves, but rather because sexual behavior (perhaps more than religion) is the most highly symbolic activity of any society. To penetrate to the symbolic system implicit in any society's sexual behavior is therefore to come closest to the heart of its uniqueness.[41]

To get an idea of the magnitude of the role played by sexual deviance in Western symbolic systems, it will be useful to trace its genealogy back to the early modern period, i.e., to the generations directly preceding Handel. The first chapter of Alan Bray's *Homosexuality in Renaissance England* addresses this role in the abstract terms of "world view" or cosmology. Renaissance cosmology, he demonstrates, is a unified system with Heaven and Hell, with sin, corruption, the Devil, and all the rest, but with one exception: "homosexuality" (sexual deviance, "sodomy," the "sodomite") is not a part of it; rather, it represents the potential for its dissolution:[42]

> Homosexuality was not part of [the] law of nature. It was not part of the chain of being, or the harmony of the created world or its universal dance. It was not part of the Kingdom of Heaven or its counterpart in the Kingdom of Hell (although that could unwittingly release it). It was none of these things because it was not conceived of as part of the created order at all; it was part of its *dissolution.* And as such it was not a sexuality in its own right, but existed as *a potential for confusion and disorder* in one undivided sexuality. Hence the absence...of any satisfactory parallel for the contemporary use of "homosexuality" in the sense of an alternative sexuality.[43]

An important corollary to this scheme is that homosexuality nonetheless had a *use*: though contrary to the order of nature (*contra naturae ordinem*), it still served an important function as the "shadow" of order, as definition by the opposite, i.e., as a means of defining what "the good" was *not*. Bray is careful to distinguish between this elaborate cosmological system and the "ordinary" random behaviors that comprised the category of "sodomy." Nonetheless, the system and the moral imperatives based on it stood ever at hand, if in the background, to be deployed in the event of a major "outbreak" (since—significantly—this potential was thought to be contained in every man). A common trope is the comparison of such an "outbreak" to the Universal Deluge, the counterpart of "sodomy and buggery" in the world of Nature. And more:

> It was also the rationale of the claim that the celibacy of Roman priests was the cause of their alleged homosexual sins; the bulwark against sexual debauchery, in the minds of the Protestant reformers, was [therefore] marriage; that gone and all manner of sodomy and buggery would break forth.[44]

For those seeking to understand how homosexuality could have become as heavily (even cosmically) invested a sign in Western cultures, including for example the radical sociodiscursive dimensions of the AIDS "epi"-demic, such passages are rich in suggestion. What I want to stress is, first, the notion of a unified cosmos or *plenitude*; and, second, the "outsider" role played by sodomy not only as sexual deviance ("confusion"), but as an incommensurable threat to this plenitude.

While such notions may seem alien to most modern folk, they are still regularly invoked in crusades against homosexuality, whether by Roman Catholics, fundamentalist Christians, or (even) government institutions: the argument against lesbians and gay men in the U.S. military, for example, rests squarely on this footing (threat to "good order").[45] In Handel's time such a scheme rematerialized, alongside the orthodox version, in Leibniz's monadistic Great Chain of Being, a cosmology purged of its specifically Christian trappings in the interest of promoting Enlightenment deism and Philosophical Optimism ("the best of all possible worlds"), but which shared with its antecedent the central feature of a closed plenitude, an order liable to collapse should any aspect of it (Leibniz's "degrees" on the scale) be violated. Here is the idea in its famous versification by Alexander Pope, Handel's early colleague during his Burlington House years:

> Or in the full creation leave a void,
> Where, one step broken, the great scale's destroyed:
> From Nature's chain whatever link you strike,
> Tenth or ten thousandth, breaks the chain alike.
> ....
> And if each system in gradation roll,
> Alike essential to th'amazing Whole,
> The least confusion but in one, not all
> That system only, but the Whole must fall.[46]

Although this "enlightened" model assigns no specific role to sexual deviance as one of these potential disrupters of the Whole, the system recuperates the notion of the Order of Nature and emphasizes the necessity of controlling the passions, especially sexual ones, of subordinating them, that is, to the (complementary) Order of Reason. What Bray writes concerning the function of marriage as a bulwark against "confusion" in the Renaissance was no less potent an argument in the eighteenth century when the threat of libertine subcultures, including but not limited to homosexual ones, was perceived as becoming more virulent than ever.

Much about the "Handel question" can be explained if we see in it a microcosmic reflection of just such a tension between stability and rupture. Though different in degree, Handel's image is constituted as a plenitude, one that as time went on got constructed increasingly in terms not only of Romantic hero ("heaven-sent genius"), but also of British national identity and religious purity. The myth could hold together, indeed be fortified, by such accretions, even in the presence of minor flaws in an otherwise seamless fabric (Handel swore like a sailor? *Well, who didn't?*; Handel ate like a pig? *Hey, he was a big man!*; Handel was really a foreigner who talked with a thick German accent? *No matter; he was English at heart*, etc.). What it could not withstand was a force capable of undoing the whole thing, specifically the one flaw so destructive and incommensurate as to be unspeakable: that Handel was or even might have been—the question itself is sufficiently disruptive—queer. And it is precisely this threat that drove (and continues to drive) our love-sotted but "puzzled" Handel biographers to the various suppressive and repressive strategies of the closet: so much is at stake, for Handel's and (through any association with the question) their own public "respectability."

Few post-Enlightenment thinkers are likely to be moved specifically by the threat of gay men bringing about a Universal Deluge or undoing the "natural order of things";[47] still fewer, I imagine, subscribe to the doctrines of Philosophical Optimism. How then to account for the continuing persistence of homosexual panic? Put another way: Why in an enlightened age would not the possibility of a gay Handel be greeted if not with enthusiasm, then with "a modicum of dispassionate objectivity"? What is missing in our explanation?

The answer is that these systems and their latter-day counterparts, together with the strategies deployed in their support, are undergirded by an even more fundamental metasystem on which all patriarchies depend, and that is, of course, gender. To return to our Handel biographers: the issue is in reality not marriage, or chastity for that matter; when Keates baldly asserts that Handel was not homosexual because "in an eighteenth-century context the vagabond life of musicians made marriage a distinct hindrance" he falters, like Young and others before him, on two grounds: first, gay men from Handel's time through Stonewall (but *especially* in the eighteenth century) married more often than not, and for a variety of reasons (as a means of fulfilling social obligations, in order to pass, sometimes because they wanted a family, or because they genuinely enjoyed women); and second (and of much lesser significance) Handel's trips to Italy and Germany hardly qualify him as an itinerant. The real question is rather: Was George Frideric Handel a *man*? And this is where Lang correctly identifies the problem: *masculinity*. Writing in 1966 and reacting to almost two centuries worth of closet maneuvers intended to explain or deflect the question (but which, as we have seen, paradoxically succeeded only in more deeply reinforcing it), Lang clearly wants to clear up the "confusion" once and for all, to, as it were, tear this diseased plant out of Handel's garden, root and branch, and sow the field with salt. He thus bravely devotes three whole pages to "Handel and Women," and, although he casually admits to having no evidence for the many "peripheral love affairs" he attributes to the composer, and with Mainwaring and Hawkins safely out of sight, he does at least identify what the real issue is, which he calls a "comforting fact" (and which—significantly—explains his need for a "sexual" if "unsafe" hero): Handel, he assures us with enormous confidence, "was attracted to women in all stages of his life [because he was a] *man of normal masculine constitution*."[48] Let us turn now to the life of Handel the *man*.

Handel's Body

Before reaching the too easy conclusion that the Handel question is nothing more than the construction of biographers hopelessly afflicted with homosexual panic, that Handel is a "victim of discourse," let us remember that while he was "given" a life, a very richly embroidered one, he also "had" a life, that is, a body. So far our considerations have involved the erasure of that body beneath the heavy layers of eighteenth-century pomp and wiggery. Let us expunge the stuffy image conveyed by those late engravings and put in their place Philipp Mercier's portrait of a fortyish, still handsome composer in flaming cardinal-red robe and chapeau, quill in hand, leaning in relaxed pose on his harpsichord; here at least Handel, by all accounts a very attractive man (Mattheson glowingly describes him as "broad-shouldered, strapping, and muscular"), resembles a living creature with blood in his veins. Deconstruction can help us cut through the accretions of time in order to render our mythic text problematic; to reembody it we need the dialectical

172 ᵕᵛ GARY C. THOMAS

antidote to myth: material history. Like any human life, Handel's was lived out within a dense web of sociocultural relations and assumptions, including many that bear on the question before us. We must therefore remove our composer from the clutches of the panic-stricken and return him to the concrete social realities of eighteenth-century London and the Continent. Not only is Handel's public career here fairly well documented, but his private life turns out, upon examination, to be in many respects less "mysterious" than we have been led to believe.

Not insignificantly, the span of Handel's life coincides with an important development in the conception and practice of same-sex eroticism in the West: that is, the emergence alongside ordinary and more or less random sodomitical behaviors—which included many forms of unauthorized sex acts—of a distinct social role and identity for a certain kind of homo-erotic man, the so-called molly, and together with it, a corresponding social institution, the molly house. Facilitated, like the first gay bars in the U.S. after World War I, by social uprootedness attending industrialization and urbanization, the molly house provided an anonymous and convivial locus in which homoerotic men could congregate, drink, and dress up, and, in the back rooms, enjoy physical pleasure with each other, i.e., have sex. The existence of the houses helped solidify and shape a gay identity in the London scene, one that formed a part of a larger libertine subculture, and which roughly 150 years later would be taxonomized in clinical discourse as "the homosexual" or "the deviant." "Sodomy…that utterly confused category," wrote Michel Foucault, "was a category of forbidden acts [defined by the ancient civil or canonical codes]; their perpetrator was nothing more than the juridical subject of them. The nineteenth century homosexual became a personage, a past, a case history, and a childhood…The sodomite had been a temporary aberration; the homosexual was now a species."[49] But as Alan Bray has shown, the molly represents a significant intermediate stage in this historical trajectory. If the "sodomite" was a perpetrator of forbidden acts, the "molly" was one social identity for men who engaged in such acts, in other words, an eighteenth-century gay man.[50]

Together with the infamous London masquerades, the so-called "gentlemen's clubs," the assemblies of modish rakes, and the backstage theatrical milieu, the molly houses formed part of a rich and openly libertine subculture, a deliciously scandalous and much gossiped and written about feature of the London scene, Margaret Clap's house having been one of the more notorious.[51] In the aggregate they earned London the reputation in the minds of the prurient of being a vast machinery of sexual gratification, in the words of one writer, a sodomitical "Hell on Earth."[52] In the 1720s a set of ad hoc vice squads, known variously as the societies for the reformation of manners or for the prevention of vice, was formed to intimidate and terrorize the mollies, though—significantly—not to eliminate them. Intermittent pogroms were carried out, the more terroristic because random, and in the first half of the century numerous arrests and punishments took place.[53] These included imprisonment, the pillory, and execution. (Then, as now, being gay had dangerous consequences.) With the urban molly and the molly house two essential conditions of modern homophobia and homosexual panic had been supplied: a defined social identity and a visible and more or less coherent subculture, together with an obligatory stereotype: effeminacy.[54]

Molly houses were, however, but one manifestation of a larger social phenomenon, the coming to visibility of homosexual subcultures across a broad range of social classes. As Lawrence Stone notes:

> Homosexuality was apparently becoming more common, or at any rate more open, among the upper classes...By the early eighteenth century homosexual clubs existed for the upper classes in London...It also seems possible that the higher proportion of the social elite were indeed homosexuals. What is certain is that male homosexuality was practised and talked about more openly in the eighteenth century than at any previous time.[55]

Excluding boys' schools, churches, and monasteries, particularly Roman Catholic ones, which for centuries had been (and still are) associated with homoerotic activity, two other social institutions or milieux, in contrast to the molly house either removed from London and/or more private in character, attracted homoerotic men: the Grand Tour and the country retreat. Throughout the century the Grand Tour provided an opportunity for men of (mainly) the upper classes to escape the prying eyes and gossiping tongues of London polite society and indulge their passions, notably classical art and the "sodomitical vice," in the place that was thought of as synonymous with both: Italy. Though studies of travel literature including the Grand Tour abound, its erotic and especially homoerotic aspects have been overlooked or consciously suppressed, as Rousseau has shown in a recent article, "Love and Antiquities: Walpole and Gray on the Grand Tour." Here he describes one contemporary's account:

> As the anonymous author of *Reasons for the Growth of Sodomy in England* wrote in 1729, Italy was perceived to be the mother and nurse of sodomy: the place where men kissed each other, where Englishmen first learned the unnatural vices that permitted them to become catamites and pathics (i.e., objects of sport for older and usually richer men); the place where every man could easily procure a sex partner, where every churchman and politician...could find his Ganymede of any age; the place where anus and

castration were words not out of place in conversation (*casti* and *culo*). Throughout the century various English moralists warned that their country would soon rival Italy as the most sodomitical place on earth; to offer evidence the author of *Reasons for the Growth of Sodomy* pointed to the success in England of Italian opera and the theatre's decline into pantomime.[56]

Back at home, the aristocratic elites and other so-inclined men of means could steal off to their private hideaways—many of them designed after classical or Italian models, the Palladian being a much favored one—to enjoy the leisure and pleasure they claimed as their birthright. The pursuit of music, literature, polite conversation, gustatory indulgence, and physical intimacy appear to have been the regular fare.[57]

From the time of his early adolescence Handel's private as well as public life was carried out essentially within three of these milieux: the urban theater scene, the Italian sojourn, and the English country retreat. That is to say, Handel's social orbit coincided, and from an early age, with the most important private and public spaces occupied by homoerotic men of a certain social status and privilege, all of which were in one way or another associated with "Italianness." His first contacts with Italians came in the early 1700s in Germany (Hanover and Hamburg, possibly Berlin), though accounts of who, when, and where differ and cannot be established with precision.[58] Surely however his contacts with Agostino Steffani, a priest and then Capellmeister in Hanover, with Giovanni Battista Bononcini and Attilio Ariosti, both opera composers whom Handel probably met in Hamburg;[59] and especially with Prince Giovanni (Gian) Gastone de' Medici and his brother Ferdinand, were influential in Handel's decision to visit Italy, which he did (accompanied by an otherwise unknown man named von Binitz) in the autumn of 1706 at age twenty-one.[60] For a little over three years the budding composer spent time in Florence, Rome, and Venice, first as the guest of Gian Gastone and Ferdinand at the ducal court in Florence and then of various men and families of wealth and prestige, including in Rome the Marchese Francesco Ruspoli and the Cardinals Colonna, Pamphili, and Ottoboni, the latter of which maintained a lavish villa, Palazzo della Cancelleria, with a brisk musical culture. Ottoboni, one of a long list of cardinals from wealthy and influential Roman families, was particularly well known, some say "notorious," for attracting men like the famous young singer Paolucci and Arcangelo Corelli into his service (Corelli lived virtually his whole life with Ottoboni; Steffani, according to Hawkins, stayed there during his visits). Ottoboni's musical establishment was one of two institutions known as "Arcadian academies" flourishing in Rome at the time. The original academy, founded in 1690 for the purpose of cultivating the arts of music and poetry, comprised an international membership, including both men and women of prestige and influence, counts and countesses, cardinals, bishops, etc. Ottoboni's was a smaller and more private group under the musical direction of Corelli, and, although Handel was too young to become a member (he was not yet twenty-four, the minimum age), he was immediately introduced into this circle, which, according to C. F. Abdy Williams, "received him with open arms."[61] Apparently lacking women, this private Arcadia can be thought of as distinctly homosocial in nature. But what evidence is there to indicate that any or all of these men were homoerotic or homosexual? This is a thorny problem for the historian and before continuing I should like to address briefly some of its dimensions.

Until now we have been left rather hanging in the matter: between, on the one hand, gay popular history (in which we find lots of gay people, and virtually everyone is suspect) and, on the other, no history (total exscription, save for a few of the most "notorious"). Marion Ziegler's assertion, for example, that Gian Gastone, the last of the Medici line, was "one of the most open homosexuals in Europe in his day," like his speculation that Handel and Mattheson were probably lovers, is tendered without much in the way of supporting documentation.[62] But does this mean it is groundless? It is a difficult question because even when honestly sought, evidence is likely to be elusive and circumstantial; what there is of it has frequently been ignored, some of it (we are only now discovering) suppressed owing to unscholarly prejudice or cowardice. What is more, the burden of "proof" always rests with the "plaintiffs," whose claims are often dismissed under that catch-all rubric of "special pleading" (I daresay, "pleading" the heterosexuality of any of these men, especially the clergy, would be a much taller order). On the other side, the areas of supporting research that might help to sort out and contextualize questions such as mine by piecing together a history of homoeroticism and homosexual subcultures—Rousseau's work on sociosexual aspects of the Grand Tour, systematic studies of subcultural semiotics (code languages, systems of visual representation, etc.)—are now beginning to receive due attention.[63] The commonplace that scores of homoerotic or homosexual men have over the centuries sought and found refuge in the priesthood, for example, is not something one will read in an authorized church history (or in most scholarly books, for that matter); it is more likely to be a matter of insider knowledge, couched in the discourses of gossip and rumor. While such ways of speaking may be unreliable, at all events difficult to assess, they nonetheless must be taken into account when closet questions are at issue, for the simple reason that for gay people they have been among the few available avenues of communication and truth-telling.

As a means by which forms of subjugated knowledge—those disqualified as inferior or otherwise "unscientific"—function to challenge those judged to be authoritative, the "corrosive discourses" of gossip and rumor indicate at the very least the presence of alternative voices and versions of reality ("the church is full of homosexuals and everybody knows it"), which must then contend with existing and culturally sanctified claims to the truth ("there are no homosexuals in the church; there are no homosexuals in history").[64] In any case, gossip, whatever its claims to truth or reality, is a discourse available to be *used*, by someone for some purpose ("the talk is that he was the lover of Victoria"), and that purpose is in the end always political.

As it turns out, Ziegler's characterization of Gian Gastone appears to have been close to the truth: according to written accounts, the last of the Medici appears to have been a "rampant" sodomite and instigator of "bacchanalian orgies," at least later in his life.[65] And what of our cardinal(s)? To stay with Ottoboni: this central figure in Handel's Italian experience is described by the French diplomat de Brosses as a character "sans moeur, sans crédit, débauché, ruiné, amateur des arts, grand musicien" (without morals, without repute, debauched, decadent, lover of the arts, and a fine musician).[66] This is interesting as closet evidence, since every single one of the terms here could and in varying contexts did function as codewords for gay; taken together, the meaning seems incontrovertible. Put differently: it takes a willful *misreading* to understand the statement to mean anything other than "here's yet another queer cardinal." But when it comes to Rome, especially in the circles of courtesans, aristocrats, and clergy, we are not entirely at the mercy of conjecture or semiotic analysis: Rome was in point of fact the site of flourishing homosexual subcultures, many of which involved the clergy and music (an anonymous Dutch traveler wrote extensively of this in a work entitled *Intrigues Monastiques, ou l'Amour Encapuchonné* [1739], for example), and Handel would not be the first composer whose orbit coincided with them. Concerning Pietro Metastasio, for instance, Rousseau writes:

> Joseph Spence records that he came upon the "real history" of Metastasio, the greatest opera librettist of his time, while in Italy. According to Spence, Gravina, the unequivocally homoerotic Italian poet-critic, heard the eleven-year-old Metastasio playing music impromptu in the streets of Rome. On a whim he adopted the urchin as "son" and lover; nine years later he left the now twenty-year-old Metastasio a small fortune to set himself up as a librettist. Metastasio recognized his own sexuality; he gravitated to the court not only because of his vocation, but also because the court offered him economic security and sexual license.[67]

In general, travel literature is proving an important source for the uncovering of such "real histories." And such research may eventually enable us to answer another question that arises in the case of Ottoboni: to what extent exactly was his more "private" and homosocial Arcadia also a homoerotic venue?

The question is significant because strong connections between homosexual subcultures and the (loosely defined) "artistic Arcadia" already exist. Although obviously not the sole property of gay people, the idea of Arcadia, that mythic-pastoral *locus amoenus* (pleasant place) populated by shepherds and shepherdesses has a long and richly established history of homosexual appropriation. As Jacob Stockinger notes, gay people, like those of any subculture, have created minority codes out of majority symbols, minority "speech" within a majority "language"; and this is one such instance.[68] Rooted in classical antiquity and associated with pastoral genres (notably the eclogue) and poets (Anacreon, Theocritus, Virgil, e.g.), a cast of characters (Ganymede, Alexis, Corydon, etc.), and a whole system of poetic tropes (eating fruit, playing music, coquettry, love-making, and the like), "Arcadia" functioned as a literary displacement, through the playful and legitimizing disguise of the music-loving shepherd, of same-sex eroticism and desire (men *do* fall in love—with each other).[69] The Arcadia was also in many instances a real social space in which homosexual men or other "libertines," including participants in the Italian Grand Tour, could congregate and pursue their common interests, especially in Rome (the "City of Sodom"). In other words, as a symbolic sign system as well as a network of social spaces, the Arcadia articulated and filled the need of a small but cohesive international subculture.[70] Whatever else we are able to say about this institution and its semiotic code-world, none of it does anything but reinforce the network of material relations indicative of a homoerotic Handel, and this especially in light of the gaps in the historical record of these years.

When young George Frideric returned to England toward the end of 1710 he lived first with a Mr. Andrews of the London suburb of Barn-Elms (now Barnes). About this man we know very little, except that he also maintained a house in town and was possibly connected to a men's social group, the Kit-Kat Club.[71] Then, sometime in 1713 at age twenty-eight, Handel moved into what was certainly a homoerotic milieu, Burlington House in Piccadilly, the palatial residence of the young Richard Boyle, the Earl of Burlington, who also had a Palladian country retreat at Chiswick, and who became his patron. With Burlington he lived for three years, mingling with other residents and visitors, including Alexander Pope and John Gay, both "homosocial" if not homoerotic,[72] as well as the architect, landscape designer, and painter William Kent, about whom there can be no doubt. That men like Burlington, whom Lang aptly describes as an "English Arcadian," commissioned or designed these houses as in effect islands of Italian high culture, including many elements of the Italian Arcadia, is apparent not only in their architecture, but from the imagery that informs descriptions of it.[73] Gay's poem "Trivia," published January 1716, oft-quoted in Handel literature, indeed locates it as an island of beauty and respite near to but separate from the squalor of London:

> Yet *Burlington's* fair Palace still remains;
> Beauty within, without Proportion reigns.
> Beneath his Eye declining Art revives,
> The Wall with animated Picture lives;
> There *Hendel* strikes the Strings, the melting Strain
> Transports the Soul and thrills through ev'ry Vein;
> There oft' I enter (but with cleaner Shoes)
> For *Burlington's* belov'd by ev'ry Muse.[74]

What was Handel's life like in the Burlington household? Though Hogwood describes it as "regulated," the schedule hardly appears to have been crushing: plenty of time for composition, rest, walks in the country, gardening, music-making, and, of course, those long dinners and sparkling conversations about the arts. But this isn't entirely a matter of conjecture either. Consider the following description, contained in a letter by Pope to his confidante, a Mrs. Teresa Blount:

> I am to pass three or four days in high luxury, with some company, at my Lord Burlington's. We are to walk, ride, ramble, dine, drink, and lie together. His gardens are delightful, his music ravishing. [75]

The inventory of Arcadian pleasures in these sources is noteworthy, not least for their barely coded eroticism. Present in the space between "music" and "ravishing" lies the erotic body, and is there any reason to equivocate about the meaning of "lie together"? Do we imagine Pope really to have meant something on the order of: "we are to walk, ride, ramble, dine, drink, and lie together, all except for Handel, of course, who, being thoroughly shocked at such behavior, will doubtless repair to his room to sulk and play the harpsichord"? A distinctly Arcadian ambience is corroborated by the following couplets, again from a poem by Gay, describing Burlington's bucolic pastimes with his "friend" William ("Kentino") Kent, the artist he had met in Italy:

> While you, my Lord, bid stately Piles ascend,
> Or in your *Chiswick* Bow'rs enjoy your Friend;

Where *Pope* unloads the Bough within his reach,
Of purple Grape, blue Plumb, and blushing Peach.[76]

An innocent reading of these documents as "purely metaphoric" will be difficult to sustain in view of the larger homoerotic code system that informs it. Put differently: the metaphoric conventions, especially those having to do with "ravishing music," "enjoyment of the friend," "the eating of fruit," function in the sociodiscursive field of Arcadia precisely as mechanisms of homosexual concealment.[77] Still, Newman Flower (always wonderful) could insist that while Burlington

> was a rich idler, yet, unlike most rich idlers of his time he chose a branch of art and gave his riches to it, without expectation of reward. He had not been drawn into the throes of loose living. The ladies at the lesser theatres were common game, but not if he could help it in those productions with which he was associated. Drury Lane was a bawdy-house; the concert rooms were teeming with the mistresses of rich backers—ladies caught up for their pretty faces, and too often possessing voices which might have achieved something had they been capable of an honest pronunciation of the English tongue, or some semblance of melody. The clubs roared with merriment at the concert programmes which revealed the secret *amours* of those who should know better. But Burlington House was the home of the Arts, and it escaped the gibes.[78]

To this naive reading Lang gives his full assent when he writes in a passage as revealing as it is rife with Freudian negation: "Moreover, Burlington House and its master pass even Sir Newman Flower's closest scrutiny; he could not find any trace of 'loose living' that would have made the place and the company unfit for the future composer of *Messiah*." He continues, in what now must be read with at least a modicum of irony: "Handel lived there not unlike Corelli in the Ottoboni palace…"[79]

Biographers' interpretation of Handel's time in Burlington's household (and later at Cannons), where evidence of circumstantial homosexuality is difficult to suppress, has of course varied. Hogwood's description of their association is, for example, rather different from Flower's. Here, in the most recent scholarly biography of the composer,[80] the author remains either curiously neutral on the question of Handel's homosexuality, or, as in the following passage, subtly urges the reader to form such a conclusion on her own:

> As a noble amateur [the Earl of Burlington] preferred to initiate rather than execute. Amongst his circle of designers, the most favoured was

William Kent, whom he met in Rome during his first Italian visit in 1714. "Kentino" moved into Burlington House on his return to England and lived with the Earl for the remainder of his life; according to John Harris [author of *The Palladians*] "There is no reason not to presume a close homosexual relationship."

Hogwood immediately continues: "The atmosphere at Burlington House must have been familiar to Handel from his first Italian residence with Ferdinand de' Medici. His private life here, however, remains private even today; from his youth he retained an enigmatic aloofness in matters of sex, politics and religion."[81] Similarly, in his account of Handel's second patronage at yet another place of "retirement," this time Cannons, a Palladian palace owned by James Brydges, Earl of Carnarvon and later the Duke of Chandos, he coyly hints at the same thing: "Cannons...was [yet] another example of the 'regulated employment' that he had found with Ruspoli and Burlington, but [this one was] even further from the public eye."[82] Hogwood is correct in making the comparison, and the entire subject of the Grand Tour and the suburban or country retreat as sites involving homosexual subcultural activity, identity, and language is deserving of more detailed interdisciplinary study. With respect to the Handel question, the roles of plaintiff and defendant surely need to be reversed: In light of the composer's extensive and intimate association with demonstrably homosexual men and/or milieux, the question becomes this: on what basis can or ought one argue that Handel was everywhere he went an exception?

Conclusion: A Gay Handel

Whether at this point the question "Was Handel gay?" can be answered with iron-clad certainty remains, finally, a matter of interpretation. Though I have tried to represent the question as more interesting and important than whatever conclusions we might arrive at, and while I appreciate the perverse advantages of leaving it open-ended as opposed to comfortably "settled," I do believe Handel "by the preponderance of the evidence" to have been a gay man, though probably, like many others of his day, a conflicted one.[83] Not because he was single and silent; not because, in the absence of evidence of any erotic interest in women, those who knew him were silent or enigmatic about "it"; not because his commentators have filled those silences with alibi, fabrication, and prevarication, and ignored evidence; not because he chose to leave the provinces and live his life without complaint in the venues most closely associated with homoerotic men; not even because he loved opera and houseplants (history doesn't record whether he kept a cat)— not, that is, because of any one of these, each in itself perhaps subject to interpretation, but rather because of the overwhelming effect of their confluence, and because as an "explanation" it accounts without need of excuse for virtually every aspect of the composer's life (including, perhaps, that unseemly "eating problem"). Others may reach different conclusions, of course. More importantly, I hope to have removed at least the question from the closet—and perhaps all who love and want to "know" Handel, whatever their reasons, along with it—where it can be pursued openly and without dread; if not with dispassionate objectivity, then perhaps with a bit of humor. This itself would be a step in the direction of civilization.

That said, I must nonetheless confess to doubts about the question, at least about the terms in which it is framed. Like our hapless apologists who ended up reinforcing what they hoped to dismiss, by posing the question in these terms (and for whatever gains we may win by doing so—and they may be considerable), we too end up reinforcing rather than calling into question the binary logic on which it (and its closet home) depends. By attempting to decide ("yes" he was, "no" he wasn't; even "maybe" he was or wasn't) we give assent to the either/or–self/other frame that engenders ("engenders," indeed) homosexual panic and that in effect reinforces the enabling conditions of the closet itself. I realize that in arguing this way I am attempting to work both sides of the street at the same time—insisting on the one hand that a gay Handel gives us a better model, one capable of embracing rather than eras-ing contradiction, and of explaining, rather than explaining away, the Handel question, while now setting out to deconstruct that question. But I do in fact want it both ways: first, because a gay Handel functions at the political level to address and legitimate the urgent project of "gay history," by which I understand the history of same-sex eroticisms and behaviors, of sexual-cultural differences and resistances, the history, in a sense, of all men and women refracted through the dialectical lens of sexism, homophobia, and power—however continuous or discontinuous, however socially constructed, inflected, and materially contingent these polyvocal narratives, only now being written, in reality are.[84] And second, because an (admittedly and unapologetically essentialized) gay Handel responds to the terms in which the struggles for gay liberation are being waged at this (our) moment in his-tory, in the courts, in the voting booths, in the clinics, and in the streets. In these venues, "gay Handel" will be something of political use, a use inextri-cably bound up with the struggles, discursive and material, on two sides of the closet door.[85] Someday, perhaps, when the closet no longer exists, when the impoverishing binarisms that currently define and enforce it are gone, "gay Handel" might seem a quaint anachronism. But today is not that day.

On the other hand, and looking toward a postcloset future, the concept of a gay Handel may still help us call into question the single and culturally unproblematic plenitude the composer has been made to represent. Like "homosexuality" and "musicality," Handel too needs to be approached not as a fixed and posited "entity"—to be anatomized, taxonomized, policed, and "punished"—but rather as a site of dialectical tensions and relations in culture, with contradictions and connections, consonances and dissonances; in short, not as Handel, but as "Handel," a problem (and a very interesting one) of cultural studies, as in fact what "Handel" through the open pursuit of our question has already become: a *(homo)text*.[86] This homotextual Handel will take us beyond the closet questions with which so much of this essay has (necessarily) been preoccupied and into more engaging avenues of inquiry, notably involving what has thus far remained completely in the background: his music. Handel's silence ends where his music begins, and in the operas, oratorios, and other texts, the composer has left us a rich field of social discourse, the more powerful and effective because of its music, a complex "body" and site of cultural conflict and (one hopes) of renewed scholarly interest.

That a number of Handel's commentators have sought to deflect the issue of the composer's relationship to women onto his music is thus to their credit rather than otherwise. "Handel" *is* a relationship to women (and to many other things) in his music. Unfortunately, their purpose has been driven by the narrow—and futile—pursuit of a chimera, a "definitive answer" to the question. Lang, for example, after announcing that "the solution to this mystery must be sought…in the artist rather than the man,"[87] then proceeds to scour the operas and oratorios for "proof," in the form of "memorable" female characters, that Handel was attracted to women and was therefore normal, etc. "We may have no positive proof of Handel's love affairs," he writes, poised to clinch his argument, "but how could a man unacquainted with love compose the wondrous idyll known as the 'Nightingale Chorus' (*Solomon*), the lilting, seductive promise of an enchanting night?" (As though gay men are "unacquainted" with love, or "grief" for that matter; as though precisely the capacity to love one's own sex unconditionally isn't a large part of what being lesbian or gay means.) This same logic might have led Lang to wonder how a man unacquainted with the love of men could possibly have composed the moving lament of David over Jonathon ("For thee, my brother Jonathon" in *Saul*; a love described in the well-known biblical text as "surpassing the love of women"), or why Handel could designate as "far beyond" anything in *Messiah* the chorus "He saw the lovely youth" (*Theodora*), if he had never been in love with one.[88] But these escape his notice, and, anyway, what could not be proved on this basis? Such arguments, in both directions, come and go with the regularity of the tides. More recently, in February 1991, British music critic Nicholas Kenyon, now controller (i.e., head) of Radio Three, the British Broadcasting Company's classical music, drama, and cultural affairs station, tried to argue along similar lines, and with similar motivations:

> What "Susanna" argues for—and how piercingly apposite the subject turns out to be in the present age—is chastity. It is a portrait of virtue, of Susanna's unrelenting, passionately defended faithfulness in the face of ridicule from those who believe that she has abandoned it or cannot believe that she would wish to. (I wonder whether the scholars who debated, at the last American Musicological Society convention, the topic, "Was George Frideric Handel gay, and why the question matters" considered the evidence of this work that he might have been celibate).

To which music critic Joshua Kosman fired off the tart reply: "No such evidence was discussed, for one simple and obvious reason: it doesn't exist. 'Susanna' no more suggests that Handel was celibate than 'Messiah' suggests he was the Redeemer, or the Royal Fireworks Music that he was a Roman candle."[89] Kosman is clearly right in rejecting the simple equation text-equals-life (the old biographical fallacy; and thank goodness, considering all that goes on in Handel) as self-evidently contradictory, but especially when it is advanced as proof of something so specific, in this case that Handel himself lived like a monk (and, given the context, a heterosexual one at that—if there is such a thing—and does it need to be said yet again: being gay is not coterminous with "having sex"?). Such arguments lead only into that proverbial night where all cows are black. On the other hand, is it wrong to suggest that *Susanna* articulates *something* about celibacy (also *Theodora*: "The meanest of my guards with lustful joy shall triumph o'er her boasted chastity")? And what about those love triangles, all the erotic passion and its renunciation, the omnipresent conflicts between love and duty (in *Imeneo*, for example)? Handel's first Italian opera was titled *Vincer se stesso è la maggior vittoria* (to conquer oneself is the greatest victory). What is that all about? Why was this theme so prevalent then (and in some quarters, apparently, now)?

To answer this we need to broaden and complicate these questions, and pose new ones. As such disputes begin to demonstrate, Handel's texts are not, or should not be allowed to remain, a collection of dead "masterworks," preserved in some (an)aesthetic formaldehyde awaiting the cold metal of the formalist's knife; rather they are part of a whole field of social relations and discourses that participate in a complex and open-ended historical conversation. As such they do more than "reflect" the social formation of their time; in a tangible (sensually receivable) way, they actively *produce* it. We might therefore want to pose questions such as these: what and whose ideological interests were or are served—or subverted—by Handel's interventions in these larger historical conversations?; how did Handel manipulate the discursive codes available to him (and for what effects on which audiences?); how have these been used in history (by whom, and for what purposes?); finally, perhaps, who has permission to investigate them— only the guardians of the canon, or anyone intrepid, or foolhardy, enough to venture onto their turf? Happily, such questions are slowly moving toward the center of musicological research, thanks in no small measure to the work of feminist and cultural musicologists.[90] With respect to Handel scholarship, though his texts offer a veritable cornucopia of material waiting to be explored as cultural discourse, with the exception of studies such as Ruth Smith's on the the oratorio texts (and literally scores of suggestive points of departure in Winton Dean), Handel has remained essentially exempt.[91]

One problem calling for attention in a New Handel Studies will clearly be the conflicted status of "Italian" opera seria, especially in relation to the rise of "English" oratorio. Although a good deal of ink has already been spilled on this, much work remains before we understand it as a complex phenomenon, including musical considerations, in larger ideological terms. I have tried to show that virtually every aspect of the Handel question, including much of the evidence of his material life, intersects with a homosexual problematic, but nowhere is it more striking than in this specific sociocultural arena. In the following I would like to sketch briefly some of the questions a homotextual reading might engage.

A vast literature documents the fascination of the English public with things Italian, including both the promiscuously libertine carnival subculture as well as, in more refined circles, the decorous pursuit of Italianate high culture. Italian opera seria occupies, however, a curious and problematic position between these two poles. Though controversial from the beginning, it was nonetheless enthusiastically embraced, in some quarters even fetishized, for roughly a quarter of a century, after which it was essentially banished in favor of "English" music drama and oratorio. Representing more than a superficial debate over language, musical form, or the vagaries of "taste," the struggle surrounding this London entertainment must be understood as the site of a much broader ideological contest, around which competing sets of discourses, cultural values, and national politics coalesced.

(The opera was politicized from the outset, support for it tending to come from the Whigs, opposition for the most part from the Tories, who saw in it "evidence of a decline in national virtue and an excuse to proclaim a chauvinistic brand of patriotism."[92]) Embedded and conflated in these discourses—those "around" as well as "in" the musical texts themselves—and lying in many ways at their core, are issues of gender, sexuality, codes of morality and conduct, constructions of national identity, and the status of music itself (music and manhood). Handel, who in the summer of 1723 had moved into his own house in the heart of the city, and whose first artistic love for the next fifteen years was Italian opera (this even after he had been obliged—dragged kicking and screaming, as it were—to turn his creative energy to English oratorio) stood in many ways at the center of this conflict.[93] And the conflict, as I will try to show, stood at the center of him.

Let us consider first the nexus of music, gender/sexuality, and nation, that is, the construction of music, especially "Italian" music, variously as "extravagant," "decadent," "effeminate," and "un-English."[94] Suspicions inherited from the previous century (and earlier) concerning the art of music itself as time- and energy-wasting,[95] as an indulgent and effeminate pastime and trap—"alluring the auditorie to effeminancy," as Phillip Stubbes put it[96]—were revived and exploited in the debates. Commingled with these suspicions were the contradictory perception of opera as a foreign and exotically attractive (but "un-English") presence in the heart of the nation's capital coupled with the xenophobic conviction that Italians (or, rather, constructions of "Italianness") were somehow to blame for the rise of sexual libertinism, in particular for the establishment of a menacing homosexual subculture. The following remark by John Dennis, an early and persistent critic of Italian opera, is typical: Italian music, he declared in 1706, was "soft and effeminate, [an art which] emasculated and dissolved the Mind."[97] Twenty years later he was still insisting that this kind of music weakened men and damaged them as British subjects; he consequently urged British women to discourage their men from opera, or risk their husbands becoming homosexual. In the following passage, in which music and sodomy are virtually equated, Dennis rails against his music-sotted enemies of the state:

> If they are so fond of the *Italian* Musick, why do they not take it from the *Hay-Market* to their Houses, and hug it like their secret Sins there?...Is there not an implicit Contract between all the People of every Nation, to espouse one another's Interest against all Foreigners whatsoever? But would not any one swear, to observe the Conduct of these Persons, that they were protected by *Italians* in their Liberty, their Property, and their Religion against *Britons*? For why else should they prefer *Italian* Nonsense

to *British* Reason, the Blockheads of *Italy* to their own Countrymen, who have Wit; and the Luxury, and Effeminacy of the most profligate Portion of the Globe to the *British* Virtue?[98]

At the iconic center of this conflict, and functioning in a synecdochical relationship to it, that is, as an image in which all of these elements—xenophobia, gynophobia, and homophobia—coalesce, is the literal and metaphorical figure of the castrated male, the castrato. "In the opinion of some English," as Richard Leppert notes, "the castrati were the epitome of Italian-Continental degradation, or what Lord Chesterfield was later to refer to as 'that foul sink of illiberal vices and manners.'"[99] Like the carnival freak, the castrato was a heavily freighted signifier prompting highly ambivalent and conflictive reactions: as an exotic spectacle it seduced and entertained; as a gender-bending image of mutilated and sodomized Italian (non) masculinity it repulsed and threatened. One is put in mind of Aschenbach's phrase: "fascinated with loathing."[100]

When located on a larger cultural grid, the discursive nexus of Italian-homosexual-effeminate, with which constructions of opera are thoroughly saturated, can help us understand the necessity of an "English" oratorio as well as a mythical "English" Handel as antidotes. For the two are inextricable: Handel's image was nourished on the basis not of opera, but of oratorio, or, rather, specific oratorios like *Messiah* and *Israel in Egypt*. The former represented Handel as pure Christian, his music (dis)placed in the service of an anglicized Protestant God, and the latter, Handel as manly Briton (the English being of course the "chosen people"), his music now understood as defender of the British state, or as somehow embodying British*ness* per se.[101] What this amounts to, in other words, is the appropriation of both Handel and oratorio into vast second-order signifying systems working to suppress the Italian-homosexual-effeminate in favor of its ideological opposite (and "preferred reading"): the British–hetereosexual, if celibate–masculine.

That the oratorios refuse to be read this way will not be news to anyone who has studied their discourse, certainly not to Handel scholars who have rightly viewed with suspicion any attempts to make clear-cut distinctions between them and opera seria. While scholars may disagree on the reasons (or which reasons to emphasize) for the decline of opera in favor of oratorio, few dispute that Handel turned from opera seria only with great reluctance. Even Reinhard Strohm's suggestion that the composer was frustrated with its conventions to the point of working to alter them, strikes me as evidence of increasing rather than waning engagement with the form.[102] Some have even insisted that the oratorios are "operas in disguise." Though such arguments tend to rest more on musical rather than textual considerations, there is much in the texts themselves to support the notion. Even if the oratorios draw principally from religious (mainly Old Testament) sources, and make use of large choral ensembles appealing to subsequent aspects of British tradition (communal religious singing), they nonetheless constitute, no less than opera, a powerful theater of human conflict and desire. Take for example the following remarks by Winton Dean on *Semele*, in which both of these ideas surface:

> *Semele*, which Chrysander published as an oratorio though of course it is nothing of the sort, had been staged in Cambridge in 1925 but hastily returned to purdah, despite heavy bowdlerization of the words, because Handel showed uninhibited delight in the joys of sexual fulfillment. It escaped notice that the story with its punishment of hubris is unexceptionably moral.[103]

Streatfeild's reaction to the same "oratorio" demonstrates a similar contradiction. Streatfeild liked *Semele* (a lot), not, one is surprised to read, for its moralizing "punishment of hubris," but rather for "the same lightness of touch, the same ease and gaiety of inspiration, and the same sunny background of the fresh, laughing, pagan life of old Greece [as we find in *Acis and Galatea*]." Streatfeild was especially drawn to the choruses, which he admired for their dance measures, in particular "the *ravishing* love-chorus, 'Now Love, that everlasting boy.'"[104] We have already seen how he could, on the other hand, archly move apropos of *Samson* to purify his hero of "obscenity of language and unchastity of life," by claiming that "the disgust with which Handel regarded the sensuality that he saw rampant around him is…to be read in *Samson* by those that have eyes to see."[105] Well, what *was* Handel, Pagan or Puritan?[106] What do the conflicts in and about these operas and oratorios have to tell us? What do they tell us about "Handel"?

One of the things they remind us about Handel's music is that its (baroque) "affections" were polymorphously persuasive. Like rhetoric, the ancient doctrine "discovered" in the Renaissance and quickly appropriated by the composer's art ("what passions cannot music raise or quell"?), music has no inherently (essentially?) determinate subject matter and is available for use by anyone for any purpose. Handel's music could take pleasure in the world of pagan sensuality, "uninhibited delight" in the joys of sex, only to turn to the "punishment of hubris." It could bewail the loss of a beloved friend through the injustices of political struggle, while elsewhere (in the Coronation anthems, say) working to make "inequality seem noble and hierarchies seem thrilling."[107] In the same way that it is often difficult to "see" the difference between a baroque church and a baroque theater, it is difficult to "hear" the difference between opera and oratorio. That Handel's "Italian" music could be turned into an ideologically acceptable, indeed politically useful, vessel, is not therefore to be wondered at.[108] What remains problematic are the antagonistic cultural meanings encoded there ("puritanical" aims, "pagan" means, e.g.), the socially overdetermined forces that controlled (or attempted to control) their production and later interpretation, and the political ends these processes served and continue to serve.

When viewed from a point of sufficient abstraction, affinities among the contested and culturally suspect quantities of musicality, Italianicity, and homosexuality emerge with rather striking clarity. Operating as loose correspondences in a relation of opposition (manifest image versus latent reality; control versus indeterminacy; order versus dissolution, and so forth), they stand ready for their social and ideological appropriation: musicality as an "effeminizing" and "indeterminate" property to be controlled and channeled; Italianicity , constructed from the I/eye of the English as a "confusion" of attraction and loathing, in need of a firm, anglicizing hand from above (Grand Tour as "educational experience," but also "forbidden pleasure"; country retreat as "gentlemanly retirement," but also secret Italian Arcadia, island of "loose living"; castrato as spectacle, but also threat; etc.); homosexuality, which emerges here as perhaps the central term, linking the musical, the effeminate, and the Italian/pagan, stands in need of disciplined suppression, if not total erasure.

The ideological work performed through these discursive operations serves a single, overarching aim: the support and maintenance of (in this case) Anglopatriarchal authority and control. The mechanism involved is, in Sedgwick's formulation, a "coercive double-bind" affecting not just gay men, but all men across the homosocial-homosexual spectrum. The double-bind is paradoxical in the sense that in order to maintain patriarchal control men must of necessity bond with each other in various competitive modalities and configurations of power ("over" women, "against" the effeminate), while not crossing the fine and often invisible line into the "dangerous," noncompetitive, and sensual ("feminizing") modalities of physical and emotional love. In order to accomplish this, the concept of "man"—including constructions of the manly and the masculine—must be clearly and unambiguously definable and recognizable, hence the need for a social and cultural Other (women, queers, cultural "decadents") through and from which "real" men can identify and know themselves as different. Such feminized Others, coded variously as weak rather than strong, diseased rather than healthy, as the soft, the fluid, and the indeterminate ("hermaphroditic," e.g.), as opposed to the hard, the solid, and the cleanly defined, etc., are at all costs to be resisted, repressed, and controlled, but also made use of (since they are needed). The confusing paradox of men who bond emotionally, lovingly, and pleasurably with other men, who are desirous of being penetrated ("ravished") as well as penetrating, that is, who disrupt received and totalizing somatic and gender boundaries, and in whom therefore the inherited scripts of the Fathers are subverted, is anathema to patriarchy; it is its shadow, the *unheimlich* itself. Is this the ultimate "threat" of homosexuality (and music)—the dissolution of sacred borders and boundaries—a Universal Deluge after all?[109]

It is significant that modern homosexual panic, that disease of the closet, arose in conjunction with revolutionary Enlightenment challenges to the old religious and political orders. The "vacuum" created by the "death of," or at the very least threat to, the old gods and (in most cases) monarchies would henceforth be filled by mere "men." If the power and authority wielded by those now defunct or moribund hierarchies had been formerly "received" as a function of a divinely ordained and fixed *natural order*, the successive incarnations of patriarchy could no longer depend on that (now deconstructed) category of the natural (the deconstruction or demystification of which had in effect created the dearth). Rather, it would depend, and ever more urgently, on the *discursively naturalized image* of gendered power, the *image* of the manly, the masculine, the heroic, etc. The modern homosexual closet, a space in which the exotic fluidity of "deviance" and "deviants" can be located and panoptically controlled, is an effect of this on-going crisis of masculinity, of the need for continual discursive reinforcement of the *categorical image*. From here the amorphous threat of the "homosexual" can be displaced at will, i.e., wherever useful. As Sedgwick notes:

> European society may or may not have actually "needed" for there to be homosexual men. What it did need—or, to put it less functionalistically, what its constituent interests found many ways to use—was a disproportionate leverage over the channels of bonding between all pairs of men.[110]

Ways, that is, of keeping them in line, creating taxonomic and social borders between "the manly" and "the unmanly" (indeed, the "masculine" in sharp contradistinction to the "feminine"), and so maintaining the necessity of the closet. That is why the closet is so useful and its destruction more anxiety-provoking even than its continued maintenance. For in its deepest recesses the closet harbors its final secret and ultimate threat: that "manliness," that always vulnerable plenitude in constant need of discursive renaturalization and reinforcement, that illusion on which modern patriarchal control is so utterly dependent, will finally be unmasked as the truly "unnatural" and "perverse" image that it is.

Handel, whose life coincided with these revolutionary paradigm shifts, whose texts are in many ways complex and eloquent negotiations of them, and who is therefore the first modern composer whose sexuality could pose a "problem" in the terms that it did, strikes me as a living simulacrum of this coercive double-bind. Like the oratorio whose musical "body" betrays the masks of its ideological appropriation, and the masculine persona whose mythic solidity belies its neurasthenic vulnerability, Handel's physical and musical bodies impede the suture required to maintain the safe and comforting, disciplined object we've come to know as his image. Our own Handel cannot be Mainwaring's, Flower's, Lang's, or even Hogwood's; the past, however comfortable, is not for living in. Out of the widening spaces of a fissured closet there may, however, emerge in their stead a new polyvocal subject, a "Handel" finally more intelligible, more human, more interesting, and maybe even more amusing, than we ever imagined.

Notes

I wish to thank Susan McClary, my friend and erstwhile colleague at the University of Minnesota, for inciting me to this. Thanks also to Philip Brett, Elizabeth Wood, and Richard Leppert for valuable criticisms and suggestions, some of which have been incorporated, others perversely ignored. I hereby absolve each of them of any responsibility for the essay published here.

1. "Even in his own lifetime Handel passed from being an individual to an institution, and eventually a complete industry." Christopher Hogwood, *Handel* (London: Thames and Hudson, 1984), 7.

2. Edward J. Dent, *Handel* (London, 1934; reprint Port Washington, N.Y./London: Kennikat Press, 1972), 9.

3. On Bononcini: Rita Steblin, "Did Handel Meet Bononcini in Rome?," *Music Review* 45 (1984): 179–93; on Waltz: William C. Smith, "Gustavus Waltz: Was He Handel's Cook?" in *Concerning Handel, His Life and Works* (London: Cassell, 1948): 165–94; on musical borrowings: John H. Roberts, "Why Did Handel Borrow?" in: *Handel, Tercentenary Collection* (Ann Arbor, London: UMI Research Press, 1987): 83–92; on insanity: William A. Frosch, "Moods, Madness, and Music. II. Was Handel Insane?," *Musical Quarterly* 74 (1990): 31–56.

4. Paul Henry Lang, *George Frideric Handel* (New York: W. W. Norton, 1966), 543.

5. This is a central theme in, e.g., Foucault's *The Order of Things: An Archeology of the Human Sciences* (New York: Vintage, 1973).

6. Footnotes explaining one's terms are by now a virtual commonplace in essays such as this, and here is mine. I realize the word "gay" in this (eighteenth-century) context is a matter of dispute, but so is the entire semantic field of same-sex desire, as well as being confused and mobile. To me, this is a happy sort of fluidity, one that may eventually lead out of the prison house of binary taxonomy altogether. In the meantime we need language in order to speak about a subject. I use a lot of the available language, impoverished

though it might be, to signify various aspects of same-sex eroticism and culture, includ-ing "homosexual(ity)" (a nineteenth century invention), "sodomite" (a biblical term), "homosocial" (twentieth-century cultural theory), etc; (a helpful guide for eighteenth-century studies is to be found in footnote 1 of George S. Rousseau's "The Pursuit of Homosexuality," discussed further on). The word "gay" is used to signify homoerotic desire, that is (in this case), men desiring to bond in emotional and physical intimacy with other men, whether sexually "consummated" or not, subject to and shaped by the social conditions and discursive codes and constructions prevalent in the specific time and place of history in which they lived. Thus, just as one can speak of eighteenth century black slaves without changing the word "blacks" or "Afro-Americans" to Negroes or niggers—both words current at that and later times—so, I believe, one can speak of gay people in eighteenth-century London, when a more or less modern conception of homo-sexual identity was in formation ("gay" being an acceptable and preferable alternative to the contemporary, but roundly denigrating terms "sodomite," "catamite," "pathic," "molly," etc.). The term "gay" also has a comfortable historical bagginess about it, having probably originated in marginal bohemian subcultures ("theater people"), and, like "bohemian," it is infused with positive connotations ("unencumbered," "libertine," "creative," "outsider," etc.). I use "gay," and "queer," as words chosen from history by gay people themselves at different stages of their self-realization, and appropriated and rehabilitated for their own uses. While this usage is grounded in a post-Stonewall gay-liberation consciousness, I see no reason to limit its reference only to certain men and women (the uncloseted, for example) or to a specific period of time (1969 on). In view of the rich amorphousness of sexual desire, it is hardly surprising that rational discourse has had such a tough time of it (as opposed to music, say, which has found eloquent and differentiated means for its expression), and had I begun thinking about this topic in 1992 rather than 1990, when it was presented as a paper before the American Musicological Association, I might have chosen the word "queer" for the title. At the time "gay," at least in relation to Handel, seemed impertinent enough.

7.   Quoted from G. S. Rousseau, "Threshold and Explanation: Social Anthropology and the Critic of Literature in the Age of Post-Disciplines," in *Enlightenment Crossings: Pre- and Post-Modern Discourses, Anthropological* (Manchester: Manchester University Press, 1991), 159. The essay originally appeared as "Threshold and Explanation: The Social Anthropologist and the Critic of Eighteenth-Century Literature," in *The Eighteenth Century: Theory and Interpretation* 22 (Spring 1981): 127–52.

8.   "The Pursuit of Homosexuality: 'Utterly Confused Category' and/or Rich Repository?" in Robert Purks Maccubbin, ed., *'Tis Nature's Fault: Unauthorized Sexuality during the Enlightenment* (Cambridge: Cambridge University Press, 1985): 135.

9.   Jonathan Keates, *Handel: The Man and His Music* (New York: St. Martin's, 1985), 22. Though not named, homosexuality is strongly hinted at in a short but engaging sketch of Handel's life by Klaus Häfner ("eine schicksalhaft angeborene Veranlagung" [a fateful, inborn predisposition]) as a parallel case to Johannes Brahms. "Georg Friedrich Händel," in *Georg Friedrich Händel. Ausstellung aus Anlaß der Händel-Festspiele des Badischen Staatstheaters, Karlsruhe 1985* (Karlsruhe: Bad. Landesbibliothek, 1985): 8–10.

10.   As his reference for the supposed exchange between Handel and King George II Rousseau cites German musicologist Walter Serauky's *Georg Friedrich Händel, Sein Leben—Sein Werk* (Kassel/Basel: Bärenreiter, 1956), vol. 3, 612. Although a likely vicinity in which to find such matter—the section deals with Handel's relations with both men and women—this specific reference is not there, or to my knowledge anywhere else in Serauky's three-volume work. I consulted Rousseau, who suggested that his notes, taken in Europe,

may have been in some disarray with regard to Handel. However, he continues in the belief that Handel's homosociality is virtually guaranteed when the entire life is viewed on balance. Rousseau's article is reprinted as "The Pursuit of Homosexuality" in *Perilous Enlightenment: Pre- and Post-Modern Discourses, Sexual, Historical* (Manchester: Manchester University Press, 1991), 2–43, a companion volume to *Enlightenment Crossings* (noted above) and *Enlightenment Borders: Pre- and Post-Modern Discourses, Medical, Scientific* (Manchester: Manchester University Press, 1991).

11. Sir John Hawkins, *A General History of the Science and Practice of Music* (London, T. Payne, 1776; new edition with the author's posthumous notes, London, 1875; reprint Graz, Austria: Akademische Druck- u. Verlagsanstalt, 1969), 2 vols. On Hawkins's relationship to Handel, see J. Merrill Knapp's foreword, v–xii.

12. John Mainwaring, *Memoirs of the Life of the Late George Frederic Handel* (London: R. and J. Dodsley, 1760); reprint with foreword by J. Merrill Knapp (New York: Da Capo Press, 1980), 28–29.

13. In his translation of Mainwaring's biography published one year later Johann Mattheson, who knew Handel from the age of eighteen and was at pains to correct the author wherever possible (in 1761 Mainwaring's work was still anonymous), obviously says nothing to contradict him on this issue. *Georg Friderich Händels Lebensbeschreibung* (Hamburg, 1761); reprinted in Bernhard Paumgartner, *John Mainwaring, Johann Mattheson, Georg Friedrich Händel* (Zürich: Atlantis Verlag, 1947), 39.

14. Sir John Hawkins, *A General History of the Science and Practice of Music*, vol. 2 911–12.

15. William Coxe, *Anecdotes of George Frederick Handel and John Christopher Smith* (London, 1799; reprint with new introduction by Percy M. Young, New York: Da Capo Press, 1979), 28.

16. Coxe, *Anecdotes*, 28–29.

17. Friedrich Chrysander, *G.F. Händel* (Leipzig: Breitkopf & Härtel, 1858–67; 2nd ed., 1919; reprint Hildesheim: Olms, 1966). The passage in question is in Chrysander's second volume, which appeared in 1860 and was immediately reprinted, under the heading "Händels Verhältniss zu den Damen," in the *Niederrheinische Musik-Zeitung für Kunstfreunde und Künstler*, no. 25 (Cologne, 22 June 1861): 197–99.

18. Chrysander, *G.F. Händel*, 118. "Zwar wenn Hawkins sagt: 'Seine geselligen Gefühle waren nicht sehr stark, und daher mag es kommen, daß er sein ganzes Leben im Cölibat zubrachte; daß er aber keinen weiblichen Umgang von anderer Sorte hatte, darf man besseren Grundsätzen zuschreiben"—: so ist dies zunächst nur seine eigne Ansicht, indeß auf Hörensagen und eine gewisse persönliche Bekanntschaft gegründet. Aber der jüngere Schmidt, der es wissen mußte, und der den besseren Theil von Hawkins' Vermuthung willig bestätigte, erzählte den Seinen mancherlei über das wahre Verhältniß, und diese haben uns folgendes davon aufbewahrt."

19. One is reminded of Galileo's colleague at the University of Padua, who refused to look into the scientist's telescope: either what Galileo claimed to see wasn't there, or if it was, it would be very dangerous to look at it. My research includes the following: V. Schoelcher (1857); W. S. Rockstro (1883); C. F. Abdy Williams (1901); P. Robinson (1908); R. A. Streatfeild (1910); R. Rolland (1920); H. Leichtentritt (1924); J. Müller-Blattau (1933); E. J. Dent (1934); P. M. Young (1947); W. C. Williams (1948); W. Serauky (1956–8); N. Flower (1959); O. E. Deutsch (1959); S. Sadie (1962); P. H. Lang (1966); W. Dean (1980); W. Siegmund-Schulze (1984); C. Hogwood (1984). Keates's biography forms an exception, in that here the Hawkins statement is deliberately misconstrued. Early in the book Keates notes the following: "Handel's rejection of marriage to Margreta Buxtehude raises the general and hitherto unresolved issues of his relations with women. There is, alas,

practically no documentary evidence regarding this aspect of his private life, and he is the only major composer of the last three centuries firmly to have barred the doors on the subject" (22). That he is clearly familiar with Hawkins is indicated when he later makes the phrase "social affections" ("affections" rather than "affectations" comes from Coxe, but "were not very strong" is Hawkins) refer to food rather than sex: "[All these instances of Handel's love of food] rule out any idea of a recluse whose 'social affections were not very strong.'" [265] A second allusion is found one page later, here elided with a phrase taken from some annotations scribbled in the margins of a copy of Mainwaring, in which their author—some think King George III—wrote: "G. F. Handel was ever honest, nay excessively polite, but like all men of sense would talk all, and hear none and scorned the advice of any but the Woman He loved, but his Amours were rather of short duration, always within the pale of his own profession, but He knew that without Harmony of souls neither love nor the creation would have been created and Discord ends here as certainly as the last Trumpet will call us from our various Pleasures..." Keates writes: " 'Social affections' had brought him friends among the nobility as well as 'within the pale of his own profession,' and his summers seem by now to have established a fairly regular pattern... [266]," where, in other words, it might vaguely support the idea (suggested in the annotations) that Handel did have affairs with women. Keates, *Handel*, pages as noted. The assertions in the annotations themselves cannot be taken as "documentary evidence," especially the notion that Handel "scorned the advice of any but the Woman he loved"—which, by the way, Newman Flower read as "his Muse"—since this is so out of sync with the many references to Handel's independence, especially in matters professional. Though of course anything is possible, that Handel was frequently or even occasionally involved with women ("within the pale of his own profession" being a reference to singers?) seems unlikely in light of Mainwaring and Hawkins; that he was enamored to the point of taking their "advice" seems utterly bizarre given what we are told of his relationship with his singers (cf. Coxe's anecdotal remark: "If Handel was little disposed to submit to the caprice of the male performers, he was not of a temper patiently to endure the disturbance arising from female squabbles for precedence; and still less, to have his views thwarted by their peevishness, or non-compliance with rules which he had thought necessary to prescribe." Coxe, *Anecdotes*, 18). More important is the question of authorship: if it was the king, a case made essentially on the basis of "a remarkable similarity to [the handwriting] of a contemporary concert bill written by George III" (but undermined by other circumstances), one wonders how the king might have gained such information about the composer, who was fifty-three years his senior and who had died one year before George's ascension to the throne. What is more, the king as an ardent member of the first wave of "Handelians" was not above intervening when the composer's public image was at stake. See for example K. S. Grant's account of George's "help" in the writing of Charles Burney's pamphlet on the 1784 celebration of Handel (*An Account of the Musical Performances...in Commemoration of Handel* (London, 1785) in *Dr. Burney as Critic and Historian of Music* (Ann Arbor: UMI Research Press, 1983), 154ff. On the annotations see William C. Smith, "George III, Handel and Mainwaring," *Musical Times* 65 (1924): 789–95.

20. Keates, *Handel*, 22.

21. See Otto Erich Deutsch, *Handel, a Documentary Biography* (London: Adam and Charles Black, 1955), 12, 275–76, 415. Mme. Sbülens was in all likelihood the daughter of Johann Wilhelm Sbüelen, who Deutsch surmises to have been Handel's friend and agent in Hamburg.

22. Lang, *Handel*, 84ff., 543–46. On Lucrezia: "Among the cantatas of this period [first Italian journey], *La Lucretia* is by far the most accomplished—and ardent—which lends some credence to the rumoured love affair with Lucrezia d'André, a diva at the court, for whom

it was composed." Lang, *Handel*, 63 and 85. Documentation for this rumor has thus far eluded me. Strangely enough, Lang fails to seize on an obscure reference in a letter of 13 July 1719 from Paolo Antonio Rolli to the Abbate Giuseppe Riva: "The Denys woman, alias Sciarpina, has already sung twice at the Princess's [of Wales]. She is certainly helping herself along! The Man loves and hides his feelings: but *quousque tandem?*" Quoted from Deutsch, *Handel, a Documentary Biography*, 92–93. There are two problems here: the woman is unidentified, neither the name Denys nor the alias appearing to my knowledge anywhere else in the literature; and, too, the identity of "[t]he Man" as Handel is not absolutely certain (Deutsch notes simply that " 'L'Uomo,' the man, or rather the monster, usually means Handel in Rolli's letters"). Handel commentators are in general troubled by the lack of gossip indicative of affairs with women. See Smith, "George III, Handel, and Mainwaring," 793–94, and Dent, *Handel*, 128: "In an age when all opera-houses were, with some truth, regarded as centres of sexual promiscuity, it is indeed remarkable that not the least evidence exists, with one solitary exception [the marginal notes in the Mainwaring copy], that Handel was ever even alleged to have had an illicit love-affair."

23.   Mainwaring, *Memoirs*, 50–51.

24.   Hogwood: "Further doubt is cast on Mainwaring's story by the fact that [Vittoria's] name does not appear on the cast list printed in the libretto [of *Rodrigo*]. But the rumour revives with the recent discovery by Anthony Hicks of a letter written in 1710 by the Electress Sophie of Hanover, referring to Handel as 'a good-looking man and the talk is that he is the lover of Victoria…'" *Handel*, 39.

25.   Newman Flower, *George Frideric Handel, His Personality and His Times* (London: Cassel and Co., 1959), 84–85.

26.   Lang, *Handel*, 86.

27.   The early rejection idea is most thoroughly (if skeptically) aired in Serauky, *Georg Friedrich Händel*, vol. 3, 611–12.

28.   Flower, *Handel*, 177.

29.   Percy M. Young seems to have sensed this when he moved to disparage the idea: "A not unnatural affection for an estimable mother and a later aversion to the bonds of holy matrimony have been construed into psychological jargon as 'mother fixation.'" Percy M. Young, *Handel* (London: J. M. Dent, 1947), 5.

30.   Lang, *Handel*, 543.

31.   R.A. Streatfeild, *Handel* (London: Methuen, 1910), 305.

32.   Charles Burney, 1785; quoted in Hogwood, *Handel*, 41 (note caution on Burney's representation of Handel in the 1785 *Account of the Musical Performances…*, note 19 above).

33.   Lang, *Handel*, 543. My guess is Lang never heard the chant "Two, four, six, eight, not all…"

34.   Flower, *Handel*, 85.

35.   Young, *Handel*, 50 (italics mine). Curiously, Young attacks as "rude insinuation" one of the very few specific references linking Handel to a named woman; it is a fairly casual remark contained in the famous attack on Handel and Robert Walpole published under the name of Paolo Rolli in the *Craftsman*, 7 April 1733, in which the singer Strada del Po is named as being "much in [Handel's] favour." Deutsch, *Handel, a Documentary Biography*, 311.

36.   Lang, *Handel*, 544.

37. Charles Burney, quoted from Hogwood, *Handel*, 130.

38. Lang, *Handel*, 544. Italics mine.

39. See for example Richard Dellamora, *Masculine Desire: The Sexual Politics of Victorian Aestheticism* (Chapel Hill: University of North Carolina Press, 1990) and Richard Jenkyns, *The Victorians and Ancient Greece* (Cambridge, Mass.: Harvard University Press, 1980).

40. See Eve Kosofsky Sedgwick, *Epistemology of the Closet* (Berkeley: University of California Press, 1990), especially "Introduction: Axiomatic" and chapter 1, "Epistemology of the Closet."

41. Randolph Trumbach, "London's Sodomites: Homosexual Behavior and Western Culture in the 18th Century," *Journal of Social History* 11, no. 1: 24.

42. Here we see also the conceptual root of the code word "dissolute."

43. Alan Bray, *Homosexuality in Renaissance England* (London: Gay Men's Press, 1982), 25. Italics mine.

44. Bray, *Homosexuality in Renaissance England*, 26.

45. Philosopher Richard D. Mohr has shown that the antigay stance of the Roman Catholic Church is based wholly on the argument of natural order: "Since the thirteenth century, naturalness had been the ethical engine of Catholic doctrine. If strong popular objections to homosexuality were allowed to fade, Catholic doctrine would lose any link with ordinary morality and so would, as a mode of thought, become no more than an intellectual oddity of, at most, historical interest." Quoted from Richard Mohr, *Gays/Justice. A Study of Ethics, Society, and Law* (New York: Columbia University Press, 1988), 35. See the same author's "Why the Catholic Church Can't Give up Its Antigay Position," *The Advocate* 20 January, 1987, no. 464: 9.

46. Alexander Pope, *An Essay on Man*, Epistle I, lines 243–50.

47. Though not as few as one might hope. As of this writing a powerful backlash is underway in the U.S., including a dramatic increase in hate crimes (gay bashing) and the introduction of bills and ballot referenda that aim to reverse the hard-won legal protections of the last decade. In November 1992, for example, citizens of the State of Colorado passed a referendum prohibiting laws that protect gay people from discrimination; similar measures are being advanced in other states across the country.

48. Lang, *Handel*, 543–44. "Considering the extremely wide range of the characters of Handel's heroines, and the infinite nuances in their femininity, it seems incontrovertible that he must have been a man not only of normal masculine constitution but one attracted by and sensitive to feminine charms, as is borne out by his marked predilection for the women among his friends." See also an earlier passage (63): "While some of his biographers are very much pleased that no love affair can be ascribed to Handel with absolute certainty—a pious man does not trifle with women—one notices that from Hamburg to London there are entr'actes in Handel's busy and studious life where many signs point to the comforting fact that he was an ordinary healthy mortal." And also Hugo Leichtentritt: "Die ganze Erscheinung Händels atmete Männlichkeit im höchsten Maße. Imponierende Würde, Macht gingen von ihm aus. Die künstlerische Arbeit war als der eigentiche Zweck seines Daseins ohne jede Möglichkeit der Mißdeutung für jedermann offensichtlich..." (Handel's whole appearance exuded manliness in the highest degree. Impressive dignity, power emanated from him. Artistic production was the true purpose of his life, obvious to everyone and without *any possibility of misinterpretation*) *Händel* (Stuttgart/Berlin: Deutsche Verlags-Anstalt, 1924), 227 (italics mine). See also (anonymous) "Manliness in Music," *The Musical Times*, 1 August 1889: 461, "No musician need

be unmanly; and the best have almost invariably been remarkable for a robustness of mind and character, if not of physique. Travel and adventure and a love of Nature have, in a great many cases, proved powerful incentives to the genius of composers. They have often been combative, contentious, even pugnacious. There was no lack of virility in the character of Beethoven. Handel was made of sturdy stuff, capable of volcanic explosions of fury. His extraordinary recuperative energy may best be gauged by the fact that he wrote his finest work after a paralytic seizure. Here, surely, was no lack of physical energy." My thanks to Malcolm Brown for calling this obscure article to my attention.

49. Foucault continues in this oft-cited passage: "Nothing that went into his total composition was unaffected by his sexuality. It was everywhere present in him: at the root of all his actions...written immodestly on his face and body because it was a secret that always gave itself away. It was consubstantial with him, less as a habitual sin than as a singular nature..." Michel Foucault, *History of Sexuality. Volume I: An Introduction*, trans. R. Hurley (New York: Vintage, 1980), 43 and 101.

50. Randolph Trumbach has called attention to the similarities between eighteenth- and twentieth-century gay subcultures: "That subculture bears an extraordinary resemblance to those described in the 20th century sociological literature. There are the same meetings in parks, latrines and bars. There is a similar specialized argot. There are similar forms of effeminacy. There is the same range of age and occupations. There is the same presence of both married and single men [etc.]," "London's Sodomites: Homosexual Behavior and Western Culture in the 18th Century," *Journal of Social History* 11, no. 1: 23. Evidence suggests that molly houses were frequented by men of the middle and lower classes, mainly merchants, urban bureaucrats and functionaries, and also laborers. That sailors and seamen on leave would also have been welcome patrons is possible in light of recent research (some of it contested) showing that certain groups of sailors and buccaneers had formed homoerotic communities at sea, not, as has been uncritically assumed (on the model of the incarcerated criminal) out of necessity, but rather out of choice. See B. R. Burg, *Sodomy and the Pirate Tradition. English Sea Rovers in the Seventeenth-Century Caribbean* (New York: New York University Press, 1984).

51. On the molly house see Rictor Norton, *Mother Clap's Molly House: The Gay Subculture in England 1700–1830* (London: Gay Men's Press, 1992). In terms of a broader cultural problematic, perhaps the most interesting of all these venues however is the masquerade, a social institution closely associated with its Italian relatives, carnival and opera. The masquerade was a site of all sorts of "unauthorized" sexual activity, "brought on" (so the antimasquerade writers of the period alleged) by the practice of transvestism, which of course also served to conceal the identities of the merry and liberated revelers. Whether Handel joined in the London masquerades, a lucrative business venture of his sometime associate John Jacob Heidegger, is not known, though Mainwaring tells us that Handel was first "discovered [by Domenico Scarlatti] in Venice at a Masquerade, while he was playing the harpsichord in his visor." Mainwaring, *Memoirs*, 51. On the London masquerades see Terry Castle's excellent *Masquerade and Civilization* (Stanford, Calif.: Stanford University Press, 1986).

52. Anonymous, *A Hell upon Earth, or, The Town in an Uproar...Occasion'd by the Late Horrible Scenes...of Sodomy, and Other Shocking Improprieties* (1729). Such tracts flourished; see G. S. Rousseau, "The Pursuit of Homosexuality," especially 141–56.

53. "For the elaboration of secular power over male bonds, then, it made sense that the molly-house persecutions be pogromlike in nature, that the distinctly homosexual man not know whether or not to expect to be an object of legalized violence." Eve Kosofsky Sedgwick, *Between Men: English Literature and Male Homosocial Desire* (New York: Columbia University Press), 88.

54. The literature on the "revolution" of gender, sexual identity, and behavior in eighteenth-century England is impressive, and growing. Of central importance are the various studies by historian Randolph Trumbach, too numerous to list here. The most relevant to this present topic: "The Birth of the Queen: Sodomy and the Emergence of Gender Equality in Modern Culture, 1660–1750," in Martin Duberman, Martha Vicinus, George Chauncey, Jr., eds., *Hidden from History: Reclaiming the Gay and Lesbian Past* (New York: New American Library, 1989): 129–40; "Sodomitical Assaults, Gender Role, and Sexual Development in Eighteenth-Century London," in Kent Gerard and Gert Hekma, eds., *The Pursuit of Sodomy: Male Homosexuality in Renaissance and Enlightenment Europe*, (New York: Haworth, 1989): 407–32; "Gender and the Homosexual Role: the 18th and 19th Centuries Compared," in Dennis Altman, et al., eds., *Homosexuality, Which Homosexuality* (London: Gay Men's Press, 1989): 149–70; "Sodomy Transformed: Aristocratic Libertinage, Public Reputation and the Gender Revolution of the 18th Century," *Journal of Homosexuality* 19 [1990], no. 2: 105–24.

55. Lawrence Stone, *The Family, Sex and Marriage in England, 1500–1800* (London: Weidenfeld and Nicholson, 1977), 541–2. It must be noted that "openly talked about" means "in decidedly negative terms" (such as in the antisodomy tracts). Sexual deviance was not a topic of polite conversation; in most forms of social discourse it remained, well into the nineteenth century and beyond, the "unmentionable vice."

56. George S. Rousseau, "Love and Antiquities: Walpole and Gray on the Grand Tour," in *Perilous Enlightenment*, 176–77. This article begins to answer to Rousseau's own challenge posed a few years earlier: "So much has been written about the grand tour that a false impression arises that all has been said. Nothing could be further from the truth; in the homosexual domain the search has not even begun. Prudery, cowardice, and reticence have combined to deter scholars. Yet this is one field of investigation where extant annals await to be tapped if only the scholars will dig in." Rousseau, "Pursuit of Homosexuality," 157.

57. Like the Grand Tour, the country house or villa appears to have constituted a kind of micro-culture in itself, a place of "retirement," a means by which "the proprietor could physically develop the necessary dimensions of his subjectivity—the study, the music room, the art collection, the emblematic landscape. The villa as a type also provided the means by which an emerging professional and mercantile elite could spatially define their social identity as distinct from both the entrenched country establishment and urban corruption." (John Archer, University of Minnesota, from his forthcoming study *"Retirement" and the Constitution of the Self: The Eighteenth-Century English Compact Villa*; cited with author's permission.) The socio-sexual aspects of this emerging identity and subjectivity are worthy of further study. One wonders for example about the relationship of design and execution of the Palladian house to the kind of heterodox social activities it seems to have supported.

58. See accounts in Hogwood, *Handel*, and Young, *Handel*.

59. Hamburg was known as the "Venice on the Elbe" presumably because of the water and the opera, at the head of which was the "dissolute" Reinhard Keiser. Hogwood, *Handel*, 22.

60. C. F. Abdy Williams, roughly following Mainwaring, claims Handel went to Italy at the direct invitation of Gian Gastone in 1705, in *Handel* (London: J. M. Dent, 1901), 30 (though this claim is disputed: see. R. Strohm, "Händel in Italia: Nuovi Contributi," *Revista italiana di musicologia* 9 [1974]: 154–55). Incidentally, the reference to "von Binitz" (not Binitz) comes from Mattheson's account (and was not, as Hogwood claims, "ennobled by later biographers to 'von Binitz'" [*Handel*, 31]).

61. Williams, *Handel*, 38.

62. Marion Ziegler, "The Great Gay Composers," in Dennis Sanders, ed., *Gay Source. A Catalogue for Men* (New York: Coward, McCann & Geoghegan, Inc., 1977), 84. Handel, who usually does not make it onto such lists (*The Gay Book of Days* by Martin Greif [Secaucus, N. J.: Lyle Stuart, 1982] being an exception) is surprisingly the featured composer in this article. Ziegler believes Handel to have been the first major composer in the West whose homosexuality is not in doubt. Also "identified" or "suspected" in the article are the following: Mattheson, Steffani, one or both of the Smiths, Thomas Arne, Telemann, Jennens, and others. I wish to thank J. Peter Burkholder for acquainting me with Ziegler's essay.

63. On semiotics, see, for example, Raymond Bentman, "Thomas Gray and the Poetry of 'Hopeless Love,'" *Journal of the History of Sexuality* 3/2 (October 1992): 203–22; also Harold Beaver, "Homosexual Signs," *Critical Inquiry* 8, no. 1 (Autumn 1981): 99–119.

64. This area of discourse analysis is currently among the projects of my colleague, Bruce Lincoln, whom I would like to thank here for his helpful thoughts as well as for the felicitous locution "corrosive discourses."

65. See Rousseau, "Pursuit of Homosexuality," 159.

66. Quoted in Hogwood, *Handel*, 32.

67. Rousseau, "The Pursuit of Homosexuality," 152–53.

68. Paraphrased from Jacob Stockinger, "Homotextuality: A Proposal," in Louie Crew, ed., *The Gay Academic* (Palm Springs, Calif.: ETC Publications, 1978), 145.

69. See Byrne R. S. Fone, "This Other Eden: Arcadia and the Homosexual Imagination," in Stuart Kellogg, ed., *Essays on Gay Literature* (New York: Harrington Park Press, 1985), 13–34. Fone's article briefly surveys the literary tropes of Arcadia in a selection of literature from Richard Barnfield through E. M. Forster. He sees them as serving three main functions:

> 1) to suggest a place where it is safe to be gay: where gay men can be free from the outlaw status society confers upon us, where homosexuality can be revealed and spoken of without reprisal, where homosexual love can be consummated without concern for the punishment or scorn of the world; 2) to imply the presence of gay love and sensibility in a text that otherwise makes no explicit statement about homosexuality; and 3) to establish a metaphor for certain spiritual values and myths prevalent in homosexual literature and life, namely, that homosexuality is superior to heterosexuality and is a divinely sanctioned means to an understanding of the good and the beautiful, and that the search for the Ideal Friend is one of the major undertakings of the homosexual life. Only in this metaphoric land can certain rituals take place, rituals that celebrate this mythology. (13)

While Fone's approach is thus problematically essentialist, his work (begun earlier in the anthology *Hidden Heritage: History and the Gay Imagination* [New York: Irvington Publishers, 1981]) identifies an area important to the understanding of gay subcultural sign systems. For a more detailed examination of Arcadian elements in Renaissance discourse, see Bruce R. Smith's excellent and readable *Homosexual Desire in Shakespeare's England. A Cultural Poetics* (Chicago: University of Chicago Press, 1991), especially chapter 3, "The Passionate Shepherd."

70. As Harold Beaver notes in his article, "Homosexual Signs": "Alice is unwilling to admit that a corporate fiction can validate her private fiction; and that private fiction confronts the pervasive public fictions of social life. But all signs imply a system. It is the system

alone that makes them significant. It is the system alone that sustains all subversive, or liberating, forces. So homosexual signs, too, must imply some sort of system. Plato, in the *Phaedrus* and the *Symposium,* elaborated one such system. Possibly Lacan today supplies another. Nothing else quite answers the need." In *Critical Inquiry* 8, no. 1 (Autumn 1981): 114. On sociocultural aspects of Italy and the Grand Tour, see in addition G.S. Rousseau's "Love and Antiquities," and sections 6 and 7 of the same author's "Pursuit of Homosexuality," 151–61.

71. Hogwood, *Handel,* 66. Information about Mr. Andrews is scarce; he doesn't even seem to have a first name, though Hogwood connects him with the Kit-Kat Club, a Whig social group that combined politics and the arts. Further clues to the identity of Andrews might eventually be found through this channel.

72. On the question of Alexander Pope and others, see George S. Rousseau's perceptive article "Threshold and Explanation: Social Anthropology and the Critic of Literature in the Age of Post-Disciplines," in *Enlightenment Crossings,* 142–68.

73. The literature on the importation of Italian culture to England is growing. See, for example, John Dixon Hunt, *Garden and Grove: The Italian Renaissance Garden in the English Imagination 1600–1750* (Princeton, N. J: Princeton University Press, 1986).

74. John Gay, *Trivia, Or, The Art of Walking the Streets of London,* quoted from Vinton A. Dearing, ed., *John Gay, Poetry and Prose* (Oxford: Clarendon Press, 1974), vol. 1, 157.

75. "Pope to Mrs. Martha Blount" (dated 1716), in Whitwell Elwin and William J. Courthope, eds., *The Works of Alexander Pope* (London: John Murry, 1886), vol. 9, 264. Also Streatfeild, *Handel,* 68–69.

76. Gay, *An Epistle to the Right Honorable the Earl of Burlington* ("A Journey to Exeter," 1716), quoted from Dearing, ed., *John Gay, Poetry and Prose,* vol. 1, 203.

77. Cf. Fone's description of Daphnis and Corydon in Richard Barnfield's "The Affectionate Shepherd" (published anonymously in 1594): "Daphnis is far richer than Corydon, for not only does he have sheep, he has a garden plot full of herbs and 'Sweet smelling beds of lilies, and of roses, / Which rosemary banks of lavender encloses.' Multitudes of flowers will be Ganimede's, as well as gifts: 'sweet smelling arbours made of eglantine / Should be thy shrine, and I would be thy dove. / Cool cabinets of fresh greene laurell boughs,' and 'apples, cherries, peares, plumbs, / Nuts, walnuts, fil-reads, chestnuts.' Indeed, Daphnis will do anything for Ganimede if he will ' pittie my complaint...All these and more Ile give thee for thy love...'" "This Other Eden," 14–15.

78. Flower, *Handel,* 117.

79. Lang, *Handel,* 127.

80. I exclude Keates. His account contains neither bibliography nor citation apparatus. By contrast, Hogwood (with the assistance of Handel scholar Anthony Hicks) endeavored to produce a new account of Handel's life based as closely as possible on primary sources, including materials recently become available to scholars, such as documents from the Ruspoli archives.

81. Hogwood, *Handel,* 68.

82. Hogwood, *Handel,* 73.

83. Cf. Bentman's description of the poet Thomas Gray: "Gray did not have the resources of the aristocrats who fled from England; or the power of Hervey, who could live in defiance of public opinion; or the wealth of Beckford, who could live in luxurious isolation. He had little choice but extreme discretion or silence to deal with his desires." "Thomas Gray and the Poetry of 'Hopeless Love,'" 213.

84. Cf. Randolph Trumbach: "The history of sodomy in the eighteenth century is not simply the history of repression. It encapsulates the history of all society. It can provide a key to unlock the mysteries of the history of gender, sexuality, individual identity, human society's relationship to the physical world, and even (it has been claimed) the mysteries of the rise of modern capitalism." "Sodomitical Subcultures, Sodomitical Roles, and the Gender Revolution of the Eighteenth Century: The Recent Historiography," in Maccubbin, 'Tis Nature's Fault, 109.

85. I hope it is clear that the burden of this essay is not, as some have alleged, to secure historical "role models" for lesbians and gay men; the issues involved in the pursuit of a gay Handel are more interesting and profound than that. At the same time we ought to be slow to dismiss the idea of "famous men and women who were gay" out of hand. For each of these is part of the complex narrative I'm calling "gay history." This is a proud and tragic history, one that has been erased, covered up, or prevaricated about for long enough. If Handel belongs on the long and impressive list of queer men and women (in vast disproportion to their numbers), who have created, performed, cultivated, and adored music I want to know about it and talk about the ways in which that might be meaningful. And if this knowledge gives one hate-mongering bigot pause, or makes one young lesbian or gay man proud, then so be it; for that alone the effort will have been worth it.

86. To my knowledge, the term "homotextuality" was first used by Stockinger in the article cited above, "Homotextuality: A Proposal."

87. Lang, Handel, 543.

88. Recounted by Thomas Morell, librettist of Theodora; quoted from Streatfeild, Handel, 205.

89. Nicholas Kenyon, "Virtue All Around in Handel's 'Susanna,'" New York Times, 10 February, 1991; Joshua Kosman, letter to the editor, New York Times, 24 March, 1991. There was in fact no "debate," only the usual questions following the paper; Kenyon seems not to have wanted to dignify the exercise in any way, least of all by naming the author.

90. In, for example, the following: Susan McClary's Feminine Endings: Music, Gender, and Sexuality (Minneapolis: University of Minnesota Press, 1991); Lawrence Kramer's Music as Cultural Practice, 1800–1900 (Berkeley: University of California Press, 1990); Richard Leppert and Susan McClary, eds., Music and Society: The Politics of Composition, Performance and Reception (Cambridge: Cambridge University Press, 1987); John Shepherd, Music as Social Text (Cambridge: Polity Press, 1991); and others.

91. Ruth Smith, "Intellectual Contexts of Handel's English Oratorios," in Christopher Hogwood and Richard Luckett, eds., Music in Eighteenth Century England. Essays in Memory of Charles Cudworth (Cambridge: Cambridge University Press, 1983), 115–34. See also the engaging line of inquiry pursued in Philip Brett and George Haggerty, "Handel and the Sentimental: The Case of 'Athalia,'" Music and Letters 68 (1987): 112–27. By Winton Dean see: Handel's Dramatic Oratorios and Masques (London: Oxford University Press, 1959; reprint 1966, 1972). On Theodora for example: "Where Morell's Romans, except in their last chorus, are brutal and licentious, Handel's are care-free children of nature. His absolute refusal to find anything repulsive in their sexual appetites is one of the most striking features of the oratorio… The fact that his vision could comprehend the Christian and the pagan view of life…is a tribute to his stature as an artist. It is also a pretty sure indication that elements of both were at large in his character" (560).

92. Richard Leppert, "Imagery, Musical Confrontation and Cultural Difference in Early 18th-Century London," Early Music 14 (1986): 330.

93. Winton Dean represents this view most vigorously, but the issue is far from settled. See for example Carole Taylor, "Handel's Disengagement from the Italian Opera," in *Handel Tercentenary Collection* (Ann Arbor: UMI Research Press, 1987), 165–81.

94. For a taste of the same wine in a different bottle see: David Hilliard, "Unenglish and Unmanly: Anglo-Catholicism and Homosexuality," in *Victorian Studies* 25 (1982): 181–210.

95. And sapping (as in *Dr. Strangelove*) of "precious bodily fluids"? Cf. Flower, "[Music] drew from [Handel] everything he had to give," *Handel*, 85.

96. Phillip Stubbes, the English pamphleteer, in *The Anatomie of Abuses* of 1583. The entire passage, leaning on ancient authorities, reads in full:

> I Say of Musicke as Plato, Aristotle, Galen, and many others have said of it; that it is very il for yung heds, for a certeine kind of nice, smoothe sweetnes in alluring the auditorie to niceness, effeminancie, pusillanimitie, & lothsomnes of life, so as it may not improperly be compared to a sweet electuarie of honie, or rather to honie it-self; for as honie and such like sweet things, received into the stomack, dooth delight at the first, but afterward they make the stomack so quasie, nice and weake, that it is not able to admit meat of hard digesture: So sweet Musick at the first delighteth the eares, but afterward corrupteth and depraveth the minde.... . But being used in publique assemblies and private conventicles, as directories to filthie dauncing, thorow the sweet harmonie and smoothe melodie therof, it estraungeth the mind, stireth up filthie lust, womanisheth the minde, ravisheth the hart, enflameth concupiscence, and bringeth in uncleannes.

Phillip Stubbes, *Phillip Stubbes's Anatomy of Abuses in England in Shakespeare's Youth, A.D. 1583*, ed. F. J. Furnivall, 2 vols. (London: N. Trubner & Co., 1877–82), vol. 1: 169–70. One wonders what the good Stubbes would have thought of almost anything in Handel.

97. Quoted from Leppert, "Imagery, Musical Confrontation and Cultural Difference," 337. Cf. poem, published in Steele's *Miscellany* and which, according to Hawkins, "bespeaks the general sentiments of the English with regard to the Italian opera and singers":

> Begone, our nation's pleasure and reproach!
> Britain no more with idle trills debauch,
> Back to thy own unmanly Venice sail,
> Where luxury and loose desires prevail;
> There thy emasculating voice employ,
> And raise the triumphs of the wanton boy.
> Long, ah! too long the soft enchantment reign'd,
> Seduc'd the wise, and ev'n the brave enchain'd;
> Hence with they curst deluding song! away!
> Shall British freedom thus become they prey;
> Freedom which we so dearly used to prize,
> We scorn'd to yield it—but to British eyes.
> Assist ye gales, with expeditious care,
> Waft this prepost'rous idol of the fair;
> Consent ye fair, and let the trifler go,
> Nor bribe with wishes adverse winds to blow:
> Nonsense grew pleasing by his syren arts,
> And stole from Shakespeare's self our easy hearts.

Quoted from Hawkins, *A General History,* vol. 2, 809.

98. Quoted in Leppert, "Imagery, Musical Confrontation and Cultural Difference," 337.

99. Leppert, "Imagery, Musical Confrontation and Cultural Difference," 331.

100. On the castrati see Marjorie Garber, *Vested Interests: Cross-Dressing and Cultural Anxiety* (New York: Routledge, 1992).

101. Cf. Donald Burrows's review of H. C. Robbins Landon's *Handel and His World:* "The tone of the chapters dealing with the 1730s suggests an old-fashioned approach: the underlying message seems to be 'why doesn't Handel stop writing these silly operas and get on with the oratorios as nature intended,?'" *Musical Times* 126 (1985): 91.

102. Reinhard Strohm, "Handel and His Italian Opera Texts," in *Essays on Handel and Opera* (Cambridge: Cambridge University Press, 1985), 78 ("In fact Handel was searching in different directions for ways of escaping from the conventions of the traditional *dramma per musica*").

103. Winton Dean, "Scholarship and the Handel Revival, 1935–85," in Stanley Sadie and Anthony Hicks, eds., *Handel. Tercentenary Collection* (Ann Arbor: UMI Research Press, 1987), 7.

104. Streatfeild, *Handel,* 307. Italics mine.

105. Streatfield, *Handel,* 305.

106. Handelians know what is coming: "[Handel] was a good old Pagan at heart, and (till he had to yield to the fashionable Piety of England) stuck to Opera, and Cantatas, such as Acis and Galatea, Milton's Penseroso, Alexander's Feast, etc., where he could revel and plunge without being tied down to Orthodoxy. And these are (to my mind) his really great works: these, and his Coronation anthems, where Human Pomp is to be accompanied and illustrated." Edward Fitzgerald, *Letters and Literary Remains,* ed. William Aldis Wright (London: Macmillan, 1902); quoted in Hogwood, *Handel,* 256.

107. The phrase is taken from John Berger, *Ways of Seeing* (London: Penguin, 1972), 29.

108. Cf. José Maravall, *Culture of the Baroque: Analysis of a Historical Structure,* trans. Terry Cochran (Minneapolis: University of Minnesota Press, 1986), 58:

> The culture of the baroque is an instrument to achieve effects whose object is to act on human beings and which is designed to ensure that they behave, among themselves and with respect to the society of which they are a part and the power that controls it, in such a manner that the society's capacity for self-preservation is maintained and enhanced... In sum, the baroque is nothing but a complex of cultural media of a very diverse sort that are assembled and articulated...so as to succeed practically in directing them and keeping them integrated in the social system.

109. Cf. Naomi Scheman's perceptive analysis:

> [Male] homophobia attaches with greatest force not to the general idea of sexual desire for another man but to the specific idea of being in the receptive position sexually. Given a culturally normative definition of sexuality in terms of male domination and female subordination, there is an understandable anxiety attached to a man's imagining another man's doing to him what men are expected to do to women: Real men...are not supposed to allow themselves to be fucked. (Thus in men's prisons, the stigma attaches not to rapists but to their victims.)

Male homophobia combines this anxiety with its corresponding desire, that of being, as we might say, ravished, or swept away. It's notoriously difficult to speak—or think—clearly about such desires or pleasures, a difficulty made apparent by the intertwinings of rape and rapture (which themselves share a common Latin root) in the Oxford English Dictionary's definition of ravish."

Naomi Scheman, "Though This Be Method, Yet There Is Madness in It: Paranoia and Liberal Epistemology," in Louise M. Antony and Charlotte Witt, eds., *A Mind of One's Own: Feminist Essays on Reason and Objectivity* (Boulder, Colo.: Westview Press, 1993): 150–51. For a different reading of the same anxiety, see Michel Foucault:

[A neat image of homosexuality] annuls everything that can be uncomfortable in affection, tenderness, friendship, fidelity, camaraderie and companionship, things which our rather sanitized society can't allow a place for without *fearing the formation of new alliances and the tying together of unforeseen lines of force.* I think that's what makes homosexuality 'disturbing': the homosexual mode of life much more than the sexual act itself. To imagine a sexual act that doesn't conform to law or nature is not what disturbs people. But that individuals are beginning to love one another— there's the problem.

Conversation, "Friendship as a Way of Life," published in *Foucault Live* (New York: Semiotext(e), 1990), 205. Italics mine.

110. Eve Kosofsky Sedgwick, *Between Men: English Literature and Male Homosocial Desire* (New York: Columbia University Press), 88.

9

CONSTRUCTIONS OF SUBJECTIVITY IN SCHUBERT'S MUSIC

Susan McClary

Prelude 1: I Lost It at the Y

*A*LTHOUGH THIS ARTICLE APPEARS here for the first time in printed form, it already has a substantial public history—one that needs, I think, to be addressed. I wrote it initially for a panel on gay issues held at the 1990 meeting of the American Musicological Society: the first such session ever authorized by the AMS. Because I had begun developing methods for analyzing music with matters such as gender in mind, I was invited to discuss how a composer's sexuality might be relevant to the music itself.

I chose Schubert, for two reasons. First, Maynard Solomon's "Franz Schubert and the Peacocks of Benvenuto Cellini" had recently appeared in a prestigious journal.[1] Like many musicologists at the time, I found his arguments persuasive, and I took as more or less established that Schubert had engaged in same-sex erotic activities.[2] The task I set myself for this panel, then, was to explore the question of whether or not his music responded in any way to his sexual orientation.

My second reason was independent of Solomon's work. For some time before his articles concerning Schubert appeared, I had encountered several musicians and listeners (many, but not all of them, gay) who asked *on the basis of the music itself* whether Schubert was gay: there was something about the sensibility projected in his music that led them to intuit some connection. Since I am interested in the ways music engages in constructions of gendered subjectivity—and since I too had long perceived a remarkable difference in

Schubert's musical procedures—I saw this paper as an occasion for examining this issue in a public forum. I must emphasize, however, that without Solomon's publications I would not have framed this project in terms of sexuality per se, for I do not believe that one can discern a composer's sexual orientation (or gender or ethnicity) merely by listening to the music.

While the panelists all felt a bit apprehensive about adverse reactions from those who had already branded our session sensationalistic, we also knew that a considerable number of gay and lesbian scholars would attend and lend support. Accordingly, we prepared our presentations with this latter part of the audience in mind. In retrospect, I must say that I have never participated in a more exciting event. Positive reactions overwhelmed any opposition that surely was lurking in the hall, and it seemed that queer musicology had finally arrived.

About a month later, I received an invitation from Joe Horowitz to present my talk at the annual Schubertiade at the 92nd Street Y in February 1991. I agreed—in part because I had no idea what the 92nd Street Y is. In the Midwest whence I hail, the "Y" in any given town is simply a community center—indeed (as the Village People's anthem "YMCA" proclaims), a place to which men often go for anonymous sex.

Too late I discovered that the Y on 92nd Street is a YMHA (Hebrew) and, moreover, that it is a venerated venue for High Culture events, with the Schubertiade as a yearly event of particular gravity. Who knew? What's more, the 1991 Schubertiade had to be postponed until 1992, by which time the general climate in the country had shifted: backlash—in a word—was in full swing. The AMS meetings in fall of 1991 had witnessed a Schubert session at which audience members seized the mike and made pronouncements in "defense" of Schubert's reputation. Ominous clouds had begun to gather.

In the month before I was scheduled to deliver the talk in New York, I scrambled to devise some version of this project that would not instantly alienate the Schubertiade clientele. The paper adopted a tone of calm reassurance. I pulled my punches; I was practicing Safe Text, and it was boring. Yet I wanted to make the best possible case to an audience predisposed to hostility.

How hostile I had no idea until I arrived at the fateful site and discovered just how hostile hostile can be. Since the Schubertiade lasted an entire day, I had several occasions to stand in a long line in the women's room, where I was privy to unrelieved carping about this woman who was "determined to drag our Schubert through the mud." Solomon's article had been circulated in advance, and some of those who spoke during the course of the day deemed it appropriate to take gratuitous swipes at him ("a pornographer"), with the obvious approval of the crowd.

By the time my slot rolled around after dinner (dessert, anyone?), the cause was clearly hopeless. But I gave the paper anyway. Nothing much happened, except for some audible squirming during the musical examples (I played excerpts from the "Unfinished" Symphony and presented a voice-over in which I invited them to hear their beloved passages in a somewhat different way). The questions afterward were polite, although one person stood up and announced that *Schubert could not have been homosexual* (applause), while another proposed that Schubert's alleged alienation might have been merely the product of his being a "short, fat man." Many audience members latched onto this latter explanation as though it were a life raft in the middle of the ocean. Although I spotted a few gay people in the crowd, they remained silent—quite understandably—during the hailstorm. I went home, relieved it had not been worse.

In fact, it was only beginning. Two days later the *New York Times* published the first of three reactions to the paper. Working from an early draft the staff at the Y happened to have had on hand, Edward Rothstein reported on the event as a whole, with a somewhat skeptical account of my contribution. He too preferred the "short, fat" explanation. Two weeks later, Rothstein's column in the Sunday edition of the *Times* presented a more antagonistic treatment of my arguments, followed the next day with a smug parody by his colleague Bernard Holland.[3]

Still operating under the illusion that the New York establishment was basically liberal, I wrote a reply, as did Philip Brett and Elizabeth Wood. We waited. Every Sunday I dutifully bought the *Times* to see our letters. Nothing. Finally some phone calls confirmed that the *New York* ("All the News That's Fit to Print") *Times* had not seen fit to print our answers. Nor were they willing simply to admit it: the editor first claimed to have received no letters; next that they had been lost; then that they had been personal letters to Rothstein, who was answering them personally; finally that because they addressed columns in both Sunday and weekday editions they could not be run in either.

By now, this talk was the most notorious queer text in musicology, even though it was not available for anyone to see. The ensuing controversy took place with no trace of my arguments except as the *Times* had reported them. At this point, Paul Attinello suggested that the *Gay/Lesbian Study Group Newsletter* (of which he is an editor) print my speech, so that at least other musicologists concerned with such issues could read my words as I had delivered them. Consequently, that talk—which was tailored specifically for a resistant audience—now exists in the public domain and may be consulted.[4]

Prelude 2: So—Was He or Wasn't He?

Just as *Queering the Pitch* was going to press, Solomon's findings came under severe attack—most pointedly by Andreas Mayer and Rita Steblin, both of whom question matters of translation and issues of historical accuracy in Solomon's article.[5] Whatever the scholarly merit of their research, both are expressly motivated by the need to rescue Schubert from any affiliation with homosexuality.[6] And while their aversion to gay issues does not in itself invalidate the evidence they bring forward, I am saddened to see the debate carried out in terms of such animosity, for it indicates that many scholars still regard same-sex erotic activities as pathological.

I will respond directly to this debate elsewhere,[7] but I want to go on record here as admiring the seriousness, grace, and courage with which Solomon has introduced questions concerning misogyny in Beethoven, homophobia in Ives, or homoeroticism in Schubert into a discipline that has steadfastly refused to address such issues.[8] *Even if* the cases he has presented turn out not to be as airtight as they initially seemed—or, conversely, if they stand up perfectly well under scrutiny—it seems clear to me that Solomon's work has proceeded from the concerns about gender and sexuality that are now studied as a matter of course in the other humanities. His is not some nefarious plot to besmirch the images of our dearest icons, but rather an attempt at factoring in certain crucial dimensions of human life as they intersect with cultural expression.

Until the smoke clears from this controversy, however, we cannot simply assume that we know Schubert was inclined to sexual relations with other males. And—as I mentioned above—my original argument linking Schubert's music and sexuality relied upon what I took to be corroboration from external sources. So why proceed with the publication of this article?

First, my initial positions concerning Schubert's music and sexuality are already a matter of public record, and I cannot retreat from this topic without some kind of public statement. Second, my actual arguments about Schubert's music—for all the sensationalism whipped up in the press in response to them—never have had anything to do with actual sexual behavior; in some sense, I don't really care whom Schubert slept with. My project addresses, rather, his particular constructions of subjectivity, and I still stand by these arguments (thus the change in title), whatever Schubert's preference in bed partners may have been. Finally, some of the idiosyncrasies in Schubert's music—whether criticized or embraced—have long been perceived as having something to do with masculinity. Thus even if we were to declare a moratorium on the subject of Schubert and sexuality, these questions would not go away. The theoretical issues raised by this case are central to research concerning gender, sexuality, and subjectivity in music, and they deserve serious treatment—even in the unlikely event that hard evidence emerges proving that Schubert was involved exclusively with women.

The following article pursues most of the same arguments as its predecessors—indeed, the framing of the article, the readings of the compositions, and the discussions concerning subjectivity have been left virtually unchanged. The alterations principally involve the issue of sexuality itself, which now is articulated more provisionally than in earlier versions.

In 1987 I asked my undergraduates at the University of Minnesota to write short critical analyses of the second movement of Schubert's "Unfinished" Symphony. While I requested that they make a point of some sort in their essays, I was primarily concerned that they demonstrate their ability to deal with keys, themes, and formal structure. A couple of days before the papers were due, a small group of students arrived at my office looking perplexed. They asked shyly if I had been holding back any pertinent information concerning Schubert. When I asked them to elaborate, I was greeted by an embarrassed silence; but finally a young man (whom I knew to be a gay activist) blurted out: "Was Schubert gay?" Since I was not yet familiar with Maynard Solomon's work on Schubert,[9] I had no information to offer them. But I did ask why they had reached such a conclusion. Their answer: Schubert's procedures in this movement diverged so willfully from what they took to be standard practices and in such particular ways that they could find no other explanation.

My students were by no means the first to suggest a link between Schubert's stylistic idiosyncrasies and his sexuality—or at least his masculinity. As David Gramit has shown, critics since Robert Schumann have often characterized Schubert and his music as "feminine," as somehow lacking in the manliness associated with Beethoven.[10] By contrast, my students—some of whom are themselves gay—did not regard the unusual features of Schubert's music as evidence of insufficient manliness. Nor were they trying to sniff out a scandal about Schubert's private life; there was nothing prurient in their question. Rather they perceived in his music a different sensibility, and they wanted to include Schubert as one of a number of homosexual artists who have sought to counter a long history of pernicious cultural stereotypes by producing images of, by, and for themselves.

Their question belonged, in other words, to a branch of research just starting to emerge, as scholars such as Michel Foucault have begun to reveal the
staggering range of explanations for and responses to same-sex erotic practices in many parts of the world and at various times in history.[11] Because
the Christian West has usually branded these activities as illicit, persons
attracted to others of their own sex tend not to appear in historical documents except in trial records or in descriptions that paint them as sordid and
deviant. We are only now investigating the ways in which such people have
understood themselves as individuals and as members of communities or
subcultures—and now only because the relative tolerance of the last two
decades has permitted scholars to venture into this previously unspeakable
terrain, to pursue lines of inquiry earlier generations would have regarded as
professional suicide.

Maynard Solomon's essays argue that Schubert circulated within such a
subculture in early nineteenth-century Vienna. Basing his arguments on
Schubert's journal entries, on accounts of Schubert by his acquaintances,
and on letters among Schubert and his friends, he claims that Schubert probably engaged in sexual activities with other males. More important for my
purposes, he suggests that this aspect of Schubert's life was central to his
understanding both of himself and of his principal affectional and social
relationships.[12]

But although he deems it appropriate to explore these aspects of
Schubert's personal life, Solomon warns readers not to try to relate his findings to Schubert's music itself, and with good reason: many people still
simply assume that gay men—along with whatever they produce—will be
unmanly and, therefore, flawed. Malcolm Brown has demonstrated that
when Tchaikovsky's homosexuality came to light, labels such as "hysterical,"
"effeminate," and "structurally weak" began to proliferate in descriptions of
his music.[13] So long as homosexuality itself is understood as a defect, we
seem to have only two choices: either this inclination is irrelevant to the
music or—to the extent that it exerts any influence—it makes the music
defective as well.

But what of artists who refuse to find their sexualities shameful? An assort-
ment of positions exists, even among gay people today. Many (especially those
of the pre-Stonewall generation) insist that one cannot discern sexual orientation by listening to the music that person produces; they strive to keep that
aspect of their lives separate from their work, in part to resist essentialist pro-
jections. And they are right to insist that a gay man may compose however he
pleases—just as a black musician may work within serialism without a hint
of African-based rhythms, a woman may write in an aggressive manner, or a

white male may attempt to invoke the tone of a lesbian blues singer in his own compositions. Music *need not* reveal anything personal about the composer (although the discursive decisions a composer makes—such as avoiding certain available options, affiliating with others—always signify).

Yet some artists *choose* to make a difference based on sexuality, gender, or ethnicity in what they produce. This has been especially true during the last twenty years, when the consolidation of African-American, Latino, feminist, lesbian, and gay networks has made such self-affirmation both viable and (for some, at least) politically desirable.[14]

When we turn to earlier periods in history, however, we are much less likely to discover evidence of such practices, for the necessary social conditions usually did not obtain. Moreover, the publicly oriented priorities of the arts before 1800 or so tended to preclude personal expression as an artistic goal. Consequently, it would be pointless to seek traces of gay self-identification in the motets of sixteenth-century composer Nicholas Gombert.

But it was around Schubert's time that representations of "the self" began to become prominent in the arts. By the 1830s a few writers who engaged in same-sex eroticism—most notably Théophile Gautier—had started presenting alternative constructions of gender, desire, and pleasure, making their sexual orientations a deliberate (i.e., not inadvertent) dimension of their work.[15] Thus the historical conditions by themselves do not preclude the possibility that Schubert too was such an artist, albeit one of the earliest. And whatever his sexual preferences, Schubert's music challenged standard narrative schemata in ways that invite us to reflect on his particular articulations of subjectivity.

Of course, in order to consider Schubert's music as participating in any kind of representation, we have to be able to perceive the genres within which he worked as having something to do with the social world. Unfortunately, instrumental music has been defined for nearly two hundred years as self-contained, available only to the concerns of formal analysis. By maintaining this stance (which may seem quite neutral at first glance), the discipline has prohibited not only questions about sexuality, but *all* studies that would treat music as an active component of culture.

This is not the place to present a full theory of music and social meaning, though I have explained elsewhere my reasons for trying to pry open this music that has been sealed off from criticism.[16] My methods involve paying attention to semiotics, narrativity, genre, reception history, and cultural theory. Rather than protecting music as a sublimely meaningless activity that has managed to escape social signification, I insist on treating it as a medium that participates in social formation by influencing the ways we perceive our feelings, our bodies, our desires, our very subjectivities—even if it does so surreptitiously, without most of us knowing how. It is too important a cultural force to be shrouded by mystified notions of Romantic transcendence. As I proceed through the following discussion, I will sketch my rationales and point to other places where the reader might look for further evidence. But I want to make it clear from the outset that my approach—far from being standard musicological fare—is being developed here partly in tandem with the topic at hand.

Schubert lived at a critical moment in European history, when the ideals of the emerging middle class were replacing the rigid structures of the ancien régime. During this period of radical social transition, many of the concepts we now take for granted as fundamental—such as identity and masculinity—were still very much in flux. The versions of these concepts we now tend to accept as universal were constructed at this time, in part within the context of the arts: as Terry Eagleton has demonstrated, the aesthetic realm served as one of the principal sites where competing models of the individual and subjectivity could be explored.[17]

In literature the privileged genre was the bildungsroman (roughly translated, the novel of character development) in which a protagonist such as Wilhelm Meister or David Copperfield struggles to learn the ways of the world, to nurture inner resources, to reach maturity. Some of these novels involve female subjects (as in Jane Austen), but the genre more typically concerns the shaping of the new masculine subject. Through such novels, we learn how the proper bourgeois male was to acquire the strength of purpose to forge an autonomous identity, but also to cultivate the sensitivity that made middle-class men worthier than the aristocrats they were displacing.[18]

The musical equivalent of the bildungsroman was not opera, which always remains grounded in social interaction, but rather the seemingly abstract sonata procedure that organizes most classic and romantic instrumental music.[19] Sonata movements, which started to appear in the mid-eighteenth century, typically trace the trajectory of an opening thematic complex that passes through episodes of destabilized identity but arrives finally at the reconsolidation of the original key and theme. In its earlier manifestations, sonata was a relatively "objective" process: the dynamic qualities of the tonal schema that fueled it made each movement seem daring in its departures from certainty, yet ultimately reassuring as it displayed its ability to attain—as though by its own efforts—security and closure.

As this standard process became familiar, composers started modifying it in a variety of directions. Mozart, for instance, began to inflect his movements in such a way as to introduce subjective expression into the more objective formal plan of sonata. That is, he worked at striking a balance between the goal-oriented narratives that propel his pieces and the lyrical passages that suggest depth, sensitivity, interiority. In doing so, Mozart not only reflected, but actively participated in, the cultural shaping of the masculine self at this moment in history.[20]

Beethoven and Schubert belonged to successive generations, and while they continued to mine the potentials of sonata procedure, their approaches differed considerably both from Mozart and from each other. Beethoven's solutions were widely accepted as virtual paradigms, especially the one presented in the Third Symphony (the *Eroica*). In the opening movement of this celebrated symphony, the subjective force of the principal theme hammers away, apparently making its own formal pathway as it goes. Any distraction from its agenda—especially the tender motives that keep cropping up during the exposition—must be resisted or annexed for the sake of satisfactory self-development. When the subject finally appears in its definitive form in the coda, the listener can scarcely help cheering the strength and self-denial that made this hard-won, heroic identity feasible. When critics refer to the virility of Beethoven's music, they have in mind this kind of narrative and those types of gestures.

To be sure, Beethoven himself offered many other versions of subjectivity: one thinks immediately of the slow movement of the Ninth Symphony or the cavatina from op. 130 as instances of extraordinary openness, tenderness, and vulnerability. In fact, compositions such as op. 127 seem to try quite deliberately to critique the heroic model later so firmly associated with Beethoven's name.[21] But it is the phantom of the *Eroica* that haunts music criticism throughout the rest of the century and up until the present.[22] This is the standard against which everyone else is measured and—more often than not—found wanting.

Schubert's strategies are quite different from those of the *Eroica*. But they differ not because he was incapable of producing heroic narratives along the lines Beethoven had charted (nothing would have been easier than following that model, which was already available), but rather because he evidently wanted to explore other possibilities.[23] Unfortunately, Schubert's music was little known during his own day, and by the time it came to the attention of the greater public, compositions such as the *Eroica* had already been embraced not merely as *the* standard in music, but also as *the* model of German manhood. Thus began the tradition of casting Schubert as "feminine," in direct comparison with the hypermasculine figure Beethoven had become in the popular imagination. As Sir George Grove wrote:

> Another equally true saying of Schumann is that, compared with Beethoven, Schubert is as a woman to a man. For it must be confessed that one's attitude towards him is almost always that of sympathy, attraction, and love, rarely that of embarrassment or fear. Here and there only, as in the Rosamund B minor Entr'acte, or the Finale of the 10th symphony, does he compel his listeners with an irresistible power; and yet how different is this compulsion from the strong, fierce, merciless coercion, with which Beethoven forces you along, and bows and bends you to his will.[24]

Yet Schubert—no less than Mozart or Beethoven—was constructing models of male subjectivity. His have been read as "feminine," largely because subsequent generations have learned to reserve the term "masculine" for only the most aggressive formulations. And this speaks volumes for our limited notions of gender.

Before we leave the comparison, it is important to emphasize that Beethoven was scarcely a champion of heterosexuality, even if he did succeed in constructing what has been accepted as an ideal of masculinity in music. As Solomon's biography makes clear, this man was highly conflicted with respect to his sexuality: he never managed to sustain an intimate relationship, and his inclinations were decidedly homosocial—often expressly homoerotic.[25] Consequently, we have to be careful not to position him as "straight" in opposition to Schubert, but rather to bear in mind that both men may have been drawn to same-sex activities. The differences between them could be the result of Schubert's acceptance and Beethoven's horror of sexuality. We might hear Beethoven's greater tendency to violence not as strength or confidence, but as overcompensation for fears of inadequacy—fears that not only influenced Beethoven's self-image, but that plague bourgeois masculinity in general.[26] In any case, what is at issue is not Schubert's deviance from a "straight" norm, but rather his particular constructions of subjectivity, especially as they contrast with many of those posed by his peers.

It might be argued that the project of interrogating these aspects of Schubert's music ought to be delayed until the rest of the paradigm is complete. But while we need to know a great deal more about images of gender and narratives of desire within the whole repertory, it makes sense to start with Schubert, whose music has been heard by so many as making some important difference with respect to sensibility. Because we have a history of critics fretting about Schubert's masculinity and his music, his example offers us rare access into what nineteenth-century culture thought was at stake in "absolute music." As Eve Kosofsky Sedgwick has taught us, issues of sexuality are not at the margins of culture during this period, but are centrally what is being contested. Accordingly, studying Schubert can help us unlock the entire repertory.[27]

Let us turn to the second movement of the "Unfinished" Symphony. What is remarkable about this movement is that Schubert conceives of and executes a musical narrative that does not enact the more standard model in which a self strives to define identity through the consolidation of ego boundaries. Instead, each of several moments within the opening theme becomes a pretext for deflection and exploration: the passage drifts through time by means of casual, always pleasurable pivots that entice the E-major theme variously to C# minor, G major, E minor, and then—without warning or fanfare—back to E major (example 1).

This is *not* how one ordinarily establishes one's first key area. In a Beethovenian world, such a passage would sound vulnerable, its tonal identity not safely anchored; and its ambiguity would probably precipitate a crisis, thereby justifying the violence needed to put things right again.[28] Yet Schubert's opening section provokes no anxiety (at least not within the music itself—critics are another matter): it invites us to forgo the security of a centered, stable tonality and, instead, to experience—and even *enjoy*—a flexible sense of self. To be sure, a "proper" subject soon enters, stomping between tonic and dominant to solidify identity as it is more typically construed (example 2). It also soon turns grim, as it stakes out C# minor with the same cadential decisiveness. But the heroic posturing of this passage—clearly not to be heard as protagonist—suddenly yields to the opening materials, quietly proceeding as before. This abrupt intrusion of authority throws the principal theme and its porous ego into even greater relief.

The second key area is perhaps even more remarkable. Its single motive passes through a succession of transformations, from timid quaking (example 3a), to greater confidence (example 3b), to violent Sturm und Drang (example 3c). Yet despite the radical changes in the affective clothing of the theme and its twisting harmonies that appear to seek relief, its tonal position remains stuck on C#/D♭. Stable identity and the security of tonal center are here presented as a kind of prison from which subjectivity cannot escape, regardless of how much it strains. But with the final transformation, the motive splits into two personae that interact and together reach ravishing cadential unions (example 3d). It abandons its rigid key identity and floats easily from D major, to G and C, and back—through a sleight-of-hand modulation—to E for the recapitulation.

This second theme resembles in certain respects the first section of Schubert's Impromptu in C Minor, op. 90, no. 1, in which the theme becomes increasingly violent and yet can find no escape.[29] In the impromptu, a pivot leads to a flexible second subject that—while beautiful—cannot survive within the bleak world already defined by the opening. By contrast, in the second movement of the "Unfinished" it is the flexible opening theme that sets the terms, and the rigid second theme reaches its release by emulating the liberatory ideals of the first.

Significantly, while the recapitulation presents the first three transformations of the second theme more or less as before (albeit transposed), the final version is no longer necessary: it has merged with the opening materials, which reappear to close off the movement. The fusion of the two is most evident near the end, when the riff that previously led into the second theme is met instead by the opening (example 4). As they pass through a mysterious enharmonic pivot between E and A^b major, the two themes become interchangeable.[30]

It is finally the mediant of E major (g#/a^b), rather than its tonic or dominant, that provides the key to transcendence in this movement. This pitch was generated almost as though in a dream at the beginning of the movement: while the previous movement had ended by repeating over and over the futile cycling from b through c# to d, never managing any progress, the second opens with what can be heard as a continuation of that scalar trajectory, e-f#-g#, with this final pitch marking both the escape from the brooding key of B minor and the vulnerable status of the new key. So long as the g# remains, the utopia can continue to prevail; but with the erasure of that g# would come the return (conventionally speaking, the *inevitable* return) of B minor and the loss of the fragile world that has been constituted here. At the close, the melody holds onto the g#; it descends briefly to f# as though toward cadence on e, but then deflects back up to g#. An arpeggiated tonic triad arises from this pitch—harmonic certainty is assured—but the melody itself refuses to be grounded.[31]

Theodor Adorno compared Schubert's musical procedures with the facets of a crystal, noting that Schubert often shuns dynamic narrative and instead assembles compositions from clusters of similar motives.[32] Predictably, Adorno was unnerved by this "deviance" and saw it as evidence that Beethoven's celebrated synthesis between dynamic process and subjective identity was unraveling. Carl Dahlhaus has described Schubert's strategies in

Example 1

Example 1, continued

Example 2

Example 3a

Example 3b

Example 3c

Example 3d

Example 4

similar terms:

> The teleological energy characteristic of Beethoven's contrasting derivation
> is surely not absent in Schubert, but it is perceptibly weaker. Conversely,
> Schubert's procedure gains an element of the involuntary: the link between
> the themes is not deliberately brought about; it simply happens.[33]

Dahlhaus goes on to defend Schubert's artistry by arguing that his personae are *purposely* weak and involuntary. Yet despite this qualification, he still uses negative adjectives—"involuntary" and "weaker"—to describe Schubert's difference from Beethoven, his invariable yardstick.

It is important to remember, however, that Schubert's solutions required him to rework virtually every parameter of his musical language: he did not, in other words, slide passively or unwittingly into his imagery. Lawrence Kramer has written in detail about the ingenuity with which Schubert crafted his new harmonic language. Although we often speak of Schubert as if he managed to transmit his own subjective feelings directly into his music, these "feelings" had to be constructed painstakingly from the stuff of standard tonality.[34]

The second movement of the "Unfinished" appears to drift freely through enharmonic and oblique modulations, rather than establishing a clear tonic and pursuing a dynamic sequence of modulations; identities are easily shed, exchanged, fused, and reestablished, as in the magical pivot between E and A^b major near the end. But this illusion of drifting was not easy to accomplish, either conceptually or technically. In this movement, Schubert pushes the formal conventions of tonality to the limits of comprehensibility. Instead of choosing secondary keys that reinforce the boundaries of his tonic triad, Schubert utilizes every pitch of the chromatic scale as the pivot for at least one common-tone deflection. The tonic always rematerializes, but never as the result of a crisis. On some level, centered key identity almost ceases to matter, as Schubert frames chromatic mutation and wandering as sensually gratifying.[35]

To be sure, the exploration of chromaticism is one of the principal projects of nineteenth-century music. But not all chromaticism works the same way.[36] We usually credit the *Tristan* prelude with initiating the dissolution of tonality, but at least Wagner relies on a conventional association between desire and cadence: he imbues his chromaticism with a mixture of pleasure and pain as it continually defers the longed-for and dreaded telos. By contrast, Schubert tends to disdain goal-oriented desire per se for the sake of a sustained image of pleasure and an open, flexible sense of self—both of which are quite alien to the constructions of masculinity then being adopted as natural, and also to the premises of musical form as they were commonly construed at the time.

In this, Schubert's movement resembles uncannily some of the narrative structures that gay writers and critics are exploring today. Literary theorist Earl Jackson has recently identified several traits of what are usually taken as standard modes of narrative organization—traits that (not coincidentally) correspond to commonly held ideals concerning masculinity. These include clear dichotomies between active and passive roles, constant reinforcement of ego boundaries, and avoidance of experiences such as ecstasy or pleasure that threaten to destabilize the autonomous self. By contrast, Jackson describes gay male sexuality in terms of "a dialectic based on an intersubjective narcissism...in which self and other intermesh":

> Subjectivity within male coupling is episodic, cognized and recognized as stroboscopic fluctuations of intense (yet dislocated, asymmetrical, decentered) awareness of self-as-other and self-for-other...[Gay] male sexuality...is a circulatory system of expenditure and absorption, of taking/giving and giving/taking...The gay male body is polycentric and ludic, sexually actualized as a playground.[37]

Of course, even if Schubert's music strongly resembles some contemporary structures by gay artists, we must be wary of assuming that he must therefore have been gay. Gay men are quite capable of producing narratives of a more rigid sort, while heterosexuals might write in ways that resemble Schubert. Yet the association of the standard model with "proper" masculinity has a very long cultural history: Schubert has been labeled "feminine" precisely because he does not conform with the traits Jackson lists as premises of the assumed norm. But the characteristics Jackson admires as typical of narratives by gay men—excess, pleasure, play, porous identities, free exchange between self and other—have little to do with "femininity," nor are they accidental; they actively construct an alternative version of the masculine self. If an earlier period had no way of comprehending Schubert's music other than labeling it "feminine," Jackson presents a model for understanding Schubert's strategies as participating in the cultural construction of masculinity.

Interestingly, while Jackson's work was not yet available at the time, the characteristics he lists are also the elements my students pointed to when I asked why they thought Schubert might have been gay: they understood Schubert to be *refusing* the heroic narrative along with the rigidly defined identity it demands.[38] And I suspect that these associations account for why so many musicologists—myself included—were so willing to accept Solomon's results: Solomon's revelation that Schubert was drawn to same-sex eroticism was but the missing piece of a puzzle that now made all the sense in the world.[39]

We also have to be wary of trusting correspondences between cultures as distant from ours as early nineteenth-century Vienna, about which we know very little concerning sexual practices. Literary historians have traced attempts at depicting a homosexual sense of self only as far back as Gautier's *Mademoiselle de Maupin* (1835), and his solutions differ considerably from

Schubert's. Even Oscar Wilde was circumspect about what would count as homosexual subjectivity: his characters who exhibit signs of perversity tend to be masked and displaced, as in the case of *Salome*.[40]

Only very occasionally (most notably since the emergence of a visible gay movement in 1969) has this community been free to produce alternative constructions of desire and masculinity openly. Jackson developed his theories in conjunction with the fictional works of Robert Glück, who is regarded as a pioneer in what is called the "new narrative"; but Glück does not even pretend to represent all the varieties of gay subjectivities available today, much less some kind of transhistorical "gay sensibility." If Jackson's discussion of Glück has proved useful for this project, it is because Glück's strategies resemble so strongly what I had already perceived in and written about concerning Schubert's music. And it does seem clear that Schubert— for whatever reason—was producing constructions of male subjectivity that differed markedly from most of those that surrounded him.

Movements such as the second movement of the "Unfinished"—as well as sections of many other compositions—celebrate such differences as utopian: in these, the field is established by pleasurable free play, and the forces that threaten to disrupt are successfully defused. But there was another side to Schubert: a side that produced victim narratives, in which a sinister affective realm sets the stage for the vulnerable lyrical subject, which is doomed to be quashed. This is true, for example, of the first movement of the "Unfinished" Symphony.

What distinguishes these from standard movements is that they invite the listener to identify with a subject that stands in the subordinate position, rather than with the opening complex. Critics and listeners have long associated such themes with Schubert himself. Thus in his review of the first performance of the "Unfinished" Symphony (1865), Eduard Hanslick describes the exposition of the opening movement as follows:

> After that yearning song in minor, there now sounds in the cellos a con-
> trasting theme in G major, an enchanting passage of song of almost
> *Ländler*-like ease. Then every heart rejoices, as if Schubert were standing
> alive in our midst after a long separation.[41]

When these subordinate themes—the beautiful tunes—are destroyed, there is no triumph of the self, but rather its victimization at the hands of a merciless fate.

I have written elsewhere about how such movements can be heard as symptomatic of the pessimism that prevailed in European culture in the 1820s: it is possible to back up such an explanation by comparing Schubert's tragic narratives with those that began to appear in literature at the same time.[42] Likewise, Kramer ties Schubert's idiosyncrasies to certain notions of subjectivity that circulated widely in early Romanticism.[43] In other words, we could regard these aspects of Schubert's music as culturally motivated rather than personal.

But at a time when art was concerned with self-expression, personal explanations also might well be considered. Solomon has pointed to the possibility of childhood trauma in explaining Schubert's dark side. Others, such as theorist Edward T. Cone, have linked such narratives to Schubert's reactions to his syphilitic condition, which brought him years of physical anguish and finally death.[44] As Schubert wrote in March 1824:

> Imagine a man whose health will never be right again, and who in sheer despair over this ever makes things worse and worse, instead of better; imagine a man, I say, whose most brilliant hopes have perished, to whom the felicity of love and friendship have nothing to offer but pain at best, whom enthusiasm…for all things beautiful threatens to forsake.[45]

Later the same year he wrote this slightly more accepting account of his situation:

> True, it is no longer that happy time during which each object seems to us to be surrounded by a youthful radiance, but a period of fateful recognition of a miserable reality, which I endeavor to beautify as far as possible by my imagination (thank God). We fancy that happiness lies in places where once we were happier, whereas actually it is only in ourselves.[46]

Both of these testify to Schubert's sense of estrangement from former good times and his immersion in "miserable reality." He still tries to envision beauty; at times he succeeds. But "miserable reality" often gets the upper hand in his musical narratives.

But Schubert might also have been predisposed to producing such narratives because he experienced alienation as a man whose pleasures were deemed illicit by his social context. As I mentioned above, it was suggested at the 92nd Street Y Schubertiade that Schubert's victim narratives might have been inspired by the fact that he was "short and fat," an explanation quickly seized as a preferable explanation to one grounded in sexuality. Yet it is important to notice that what gets punished in these narratives is an extraordinarily open form of pleasure (I must confess to being unsure what would count as the musical representation of "short and fat," but I think I can recognize pleasure when I hear it). Although we may never be able to ascertain why, some of Schubert's constructions—like narratives produced by many homosexual writers, including Marcel Proust, André Gide, Radclyffe Hall, Tennessee Williams, or James Baldwin—often present a tragic vision of the world in which the self and its pleasures are mutilated by an uncomprehending and hostile society.[47]

The hopelessness of the first movement of the "Unfinished," however one reads it, makes the vision of human interaction in the second all the more extraordinary. Because a conventional return to the overarching tonic B minor for subsequent movements would have returned us necessarily to "miserable reality," would have canceled out the g#/a^b so tentatively established at the end of the movement, Schubert may well have been reluctant to complete this symphony.

Hanslick described the end of the movement as follows:

> As if he could not separate himself from his own sweet song, the composer postpones the conclusion of the [andante], yes, postpones it all too long. One knows this characteristic of Schubert: a trait that weakens the total effect of many of his compositions. At the close of the Andante his flight seems to lose itself beyond the reach of the eye, nevertheless one may still hear the rustling of his wings.[48]

Here once again we find the most loving of insights ruptured by a disclaimer that attempts to distance the anxious critic from the object of desire. I would prefer to say that Schubert concludes with a gentle yet firm refusal to submit to narrative conventions that would have achieved closure only at the expense of his integrity.

Standard accounts from Schumann to Dahlhaus warily label Schubert's music as sentimental, feminine, or weak, even as they mean to praise him. In other words, Solomon and I did not introduce the issue of sexuality into Schubert interpretation: Schubert has long been coded covertly as "effeminate" and downgraded accordingly. But Solomon's research invites us to read this dimension of Schubert's life and music in the affirmative terms made available by gay and feminist theory. For with recent scholarship, we can begin to see how culture has privileged certain models of masculinity and narrative structure, and it becomes easier to recognize and value alternatives. What has been perceived in Schubert's music as defective may at last be heard as purposeful, ingenious, and liberatory—and this is so whether or not he was actually involved in same-sex erotic activities.

Needless to say, Schubert's music need not be heard as having anything to do with sexuality; as we have seen, his idiosyncratic procedures can be interpreted along many other lines as well. I am not interested in dismissing other ways of appreciating this repertory, nor would I want to see his or anyone else's music reduced to nothing but evidence of sexual orientation. Moreover, it is possible to imagine women or heterosexual men devising similar strategies: male or female homosexuality is neither a necessary nor sufficient condition for the production of such narratives.

What does seem clear, however, is that Schubert was constructing images that later were marginalized, but that many of us today prefer to the more aggressive, heroic models that have prevailed. And while his music does not reduce to a simple allegory of sexuality, at the same time, his particular experiences of self, intimacies, and (perhaps) social disapproval might well be understood as factors in the formal procedures he designed. If we hear Schubert's music as offering deliberate counternarratives, we can learn much about how music participated in shaping notions of gender, desire, pleasure, and power in nineteenth-century culture. And we can stop the shameful practice of apologizing for his magnificent vision.[49]

Notes

1. Maynard Solomon, "Franz Schubert and the Peacocks of Benvenuto Cellini," *19th-Century Music* 12, no. 3 (Spring 1989): 193–206.

2. A word on terminology. There are no suitable words for an early nineteenth-century male who had sexual relations with other males. "Homosexual" is anachronistic because it comes from a later historical moment; it also implies an essential and clinically pathological condition. "Gay" comes from an even later time and represents a radically different political environment. Terms from earlier times tend to indicate only that a given individual commits particular kinds of acts (a "sodomite" is merely someone who commits sodomy). Thus while "same-sex erotic activities" is cumbersome, I use it rather than the easier (though misleading) alternatives. The term "queer" has been appropriated recently by many scholars working in this field, both despite and because of its usually pejorative connotations. In addition to its political implications, "queer" also has the advantage of side-stepping the quagmire of clinical terminology to designate identities, activities, or areas of research that resist hegemonic models of sexuality.

3. Edward Rothstein, "Was Schubert Gay? If He Was, So What?" *New York Times* (4 February 1992); "'And If You Play "Boléro" Backward...'" (16 February, 1992); and Bernard Holland, "Dr. Freud, Is It True That Sometimes, Tea Is Only Tea?" (17 February, 1992).

    Holland has continued his crusade of trying to render irrelevant such trivialities as gender, race, and sexuality. In a column "Social Cause As Weapon and Shield" (New York Times, Arts and Entertainment, 9 August, 1992), he advocates critical approaches that deliberately avoid taking such issues into account: "I would also hope that the shape and tone of Robert Mapplethorpe's photography might transcend worry about his sex life." As if part of the point of Mapplethorpe's work were not to insist on his sexuality, as if anyone besides Holland and Jessie Helms were "worrying" about that.

4. *Gay/Lesbian Study Group Newsletter* 2, no. 1 (April 1991): 8–14. This issue also contains the unprinted responses to the *Times* from Philip Brett, Elizabeth Wood, and myself.

5. Andreas Mayer, "Der Psychoanalytische Schubert: Eine kleine Geschichte der Deutungskonkurrenzen in der Schubert-Biographik, dargestellt am Beispiel des Textes 'Mein Traum,' " in *Schubert durch die Brille* 9 (1992): 7–31; Rita Steblin, "Franz Schubert und das Ehe-Consens Gesetz von 1815," *Schubert durch die Brille* 9 (1992): 32–42; and "Schubert's Sexuality: The Question Re-Opened," forthcoming in *19th-Century Music*, with a response by Solomon.

6. For instance, Mayer accuses Solomon of conforming to a "p.c." agenda in his scholarship (20–21) and links him (30, n. 45) with Leonard Jeffries—the professor of African-American Studies at City University of New York who was removed as chair as the result of anti-Semitic statements made in conjunction with his Afrocentric theories.

7. The editors of *19th-Century Music* have solicited reactions from Edward T. Cone, Robert Winter, and myself, and these will appear in the same issue with Steblin's article and Solomon's rebuttal. To put the matter briefly, some of Steblin's arguments—especially her detection of a couple of questionable translations in Solomon and her discussion of Viennese marriage-consent laws—are well taken. But others reveal a lack of sensitivity to the range of behaviors that might well occur within a subculture organized around shared homoerotic interests—especially at a time when the public affirmation of such interests was not yet possible. For instance, the fact that Schubert and others of his circle had women friends and considered or even entered into marriages does not necessarily mean they were not also involved in male-male sexual activities. While her article raises enough questions to warrant a reexamination of the situation, I do not believe it succeeds in discrediting Solomon's position. Moreover, the overkill quality of her attack makes it clear that she finds utterly intolerable the possibility that Schubert might have been attracted to other men.

8. See his *Beethoven* (New York: Schirmer Books, 1977) and "Charles Ives: Some Questions of Veracity," *Journal of the American Musicological Society* 40 (1987), especially 466–69.

9. Solomon first wrote about Schubert's sexuality in "Franz Schubert's 'My Dream,'" *American Imago* 38 (1981): 137–54, and this article received considerable attention from the gay community. Thus it is quite possible that my students had already heard reports of Schubert's homosexuality.

10. David Gramit, "Constructing a Victorian Schubert: Music Biography and Cultural Values," paper presented for the 1991 meeting of the American Musicological Society, forthcoming in *19th-Century Music*. My thanks to Gramit for providing me with a copy of this paper. This tradition began with Robert Schumann's essay on Schubert's C major Symphony, throughout which Beethoven and Schubert are paired in terms of virility versus "womanliness." And the tradition lives on: Joseph Horowitz's preview article in the *New York Times* for the Schubertiade (19 January, 1992) had "Schubert and the Eternal, Inescapable Feminine" emblazoned across the page as a headline. See below for more on Schubert's image as "feminine." Note that neither Solomon nor I suggest that Schubert was feminine.

See also Eve Kosofsky Sedgwick, *The Epistemology of the Closet* (Berkeley/Los Angeles: University of California Press, 1991). Sedgwick argues that we cannot properly study twentieth-century culture without taking sexual orientation into account, for many of the debates that spawned modernism were reactions to what was perceived as the increasing homosexual presence in the arts. Gramit's article suggests that such tensions—or at least anxieties concerning virility—pervaded much of the nineteenth century as well.

11.   Michel Foucault's *History of Sexuality* is the pioneering work in this area. He died, unfortunately, after completing only the first three volumes of this vast project. See also Martin Bauml Duberman, Martha Vicinus, and George Chauncey, Jr., eds., *Hidden from History: Reclaiming the Gay and Lesbian Past* (New York: New American Library, 1989); and David Greenberg, *The Construction of Homosexuality* (Chicago: University of Chicago Press, 1988).

12.   For a neutral account of Schubert's companions and their ideals, see David Gramit, "The Intellectual and Aesthetic Tenets of Franz Schubert's Circle," Ph.D. dissertation, Duke University, 1987. Gramit presents the following summary of the foreword to one of their yearbooks (1817–1918): "through diligent study of the good, the true, and the beautiful, youths would mature to men who were manly, noble, and beneficial to society as a whole" (38).

While Steblin offers this quotation as evidence of the circle's nonsexual interests, this description fits perfectly within Dorianism: a widespread trend in nineteenth-century Germany and England in which platonic (i.e., homoerotic—as in Plato—rather than strictly nonsexual) relationships between older mentors and younger males were encouraged. The most famous manifestation of such practices is Wilde's Dorian Gray. For a historical and theoretical examination of Dorianism, see Richard Dellamora, *Fin de Siècle/Fin de Siècle: Sexual Politics and the Sense of an Ending in Late 19th- and 20th-Century Writing* (New Brunswick: Rutgers University Press, forthcoming).

13.   Malcolm Brown, paper presented at the 1990 meeting of the American Musicological Society.

14.   This is not to suggest that identity politics are entirely risk-free. A huge bibliography now exists in which theorists affiliated with marginalized groups weigh the benefits and dangers of what has been called "strategic essentialism." See, for instance, Gayatri Chakravorty Spivak, *In Other Worlds: Essays in Cultural Politics* (New York: Routledge, 1988); Judith Butler, *Gender Trouble: Feminism and the Subversion of Identity* (New York: Routledge, 1990); Drucilla Cornell, *Beyond Accommodation: Ethical Feminism, Deconstruction, and the Law* (New York: Routledge, 1991); Jonathan Dollimore, *Sexual Dissidence: Augustine to Wilde, Freud to Foucault* (Oxford: Oxford University Press, 1991); and Kwame Anthony Appiah, *In My Father's House: Africa in the Philosophy of Culture* (Oxford: Oxford University Press, 1992).

15.   I have learned a great deal from discussions with Richard Dellamora on the history of such constructions in literature. See his *Masculine Desire: The Sexual Politics of Victorian Aestheticism* (Chapel Hill: University of North Carolina Press, 1990) and *Fin de Siècle*. For other recent theoretical work on gay and lesbian self-representation in culture, see Dollimore, *Sexual Dissidence*; Diana Fuss, ed., *Inside/Out: Lesbian Theories, Gay Theories* (New York: Routledge, 1991); and the special issue, "Queer Theory: Lesbian and Gay Sexualities," in *differences* 3 (Summer 1991), Teresa de Lauretis, guest editor.

16.   See particularly the first chapter of my *Feminine Endings: Music, Gender, and Sexuality* (Minneapolis: University of Minnesota Press, 1991). For sample case studies, see also "The Blasphemy of Talking Politics during Bach Year," in Richard Leppert and Susan McClary,

eds., *Music and Society: The Politics of Composition, Performance and Reception* (Cambridge: Cambridge University Press, 1987); McClary, "A Musical Dialectic from the Enlightenment: Mozart's Piano Concerto in G major, K. 453, Movement 2," *Cultural Critique* 4 (1986): 129–69; and McClary, "Narrative Agendas in 'Absolute' Music: Identity and Difference in Brahms' Third Symphony," in Ruth Solie, ed., *Music and Difference,* (Berkeley and Los Angeles: University of California Press, 1993).

17.   See Terry Eagleton, *The Ideology of the Aesthetic* (Oxford: Basil Blackwell, 1990).

18.   For a superb study of the bildungsroman as a terrain where these issues are worked through, see Franco Moretti, *The Way of the World: The Bildungsroman in European Culture* (London: Verso, 1987). For an insightful discussion of how German-speaking intellectuals and artists of this time developed notions such as *Kultur* and *Bildung* in direct counterdistinction to French *civilisation,* see Norbert Elias, *The History of Manners,* trans. Edmund Jephcott (New York: Pantheon, 1978), 1–50.

19.   For a similar position, see Leonard B. Meyer, *Style and Music: Theory, History, and Ideology* (Philadelphia: University of Pennsylvania Press, 1989): "In 'pure' instrumental music, the strategies chosen by composers to create unity were responsive to the tenets of Romanticism...Even in the absence of an explicit program, motivic continuity created a kind of narrative coherence. Like the chief character in a novel, the 'fortunes' of the main motive—its development, variation, and encounters with other 'protagonists'—served as a source of constancy throughout the unfolding of the musical process" (201).

20   This conception of sonata and Mozart's specific contributions are developed at length in my "Narratives of Bourgeois Subjectivity in Mozart's 'Prague' Symphony," in Peter Rabinowitz and James Phelan, eds., *Understanding Narrative* (Ohio State University Press, forthcoming).

21.   I am now writing an article on Beethoven's implicit critiques of the heroic model.

22.   See Sanna Pederson, "The Task of the Music Historian: or, The Myth of the Symphony after Beethoven," unpublished paper. I wish to thank Ms. Pederson for permitting me to see a copy of this paper.

23.   For a similar argument concerning the songs, see Lawrence Kramer, "The Schubert Lied: Romantic Form and Romantic Consciousness," in Walter Frisch, ed., *Schubert: Critical and Analytical Studies* (Lincoln: University of Nebraska Press, 1986), 200–36.

24.   Sir George Grove, *Beethoven, Schubert, Mendelssohn* (London: Macmillan, 1951), 238. The essays are reprinted from the first edition of the *Grove Dictionary of Music and Musicians* (1882). I doubt that his description of Beethoven is meant to sound negative.

25.   Solomon, *Beethoven.* The extraordinary history of scholars fetishizing the letter to the "immortal beloved" dramatizes how desperately we have wanted to prove Beethoven's "normality." That all we have is a single letter to an unidentified person that perhaps was never sent shows the poverty of Beethoven's personal life. Schubert's was incomparably richer.

26.   See again Eagleton, *The Ideology of the Aesthetic,* and Moretti, *The Way of the World,* for the contradictions faced by males during this period. For theoretical accounts of masculinity and its discontents, see Victor J. Seidler, *Rediscovering Masculinity: Reason, Language and Sexuality* (London and New York: Routledge, 1989); Jessica Benjamin, *The Bonds of Love: Psychoanalysis, Feminism, and the Problem of Domination* (New York: Pantheon, 1988); and Kaja Silverman, *Male Subjectivity at the Margins* (New York: Routledge, 1992).

27.   Given the sexual ambiguity of so many of its foremost practitioners, we might even

consider the nineteenth-century German symphony—the music that dare not speak its meanings—as a genre of the closet.

28. In a sense, of course, Beethoven resists conventional procedures far more explicitly than Schubert. He marks his departures from usual practices as dramatic events, virtually declaring war on the norms that would constrain him. Yet his transgressions rarely pass without reaction: his narratives both celebrate and punish deviation, in accordance with the contradictory pressures informing masculinity since the early nineteenth century. Even the cavatina in op. 130 and the third movement of the Ninth Symphony (mentioned earlier as open, vulnerable constructions) are met with responses of unparalleled violence: respectively, the Great Fugue and the ripping dissonances that open the finale of the Ninth. Beethoven upholds the Law even as he violates it; by contrast, Schubert simply "changes the subject" (pun intended).

29. See my discussion of this piece in "Pitches, Expression, Ideology: An Exercise in Mediation," *Enclitic* 7 (Spring 1983): 76–86.

30. It is interesting to note that Schubert liked to intertwine his name with that of his intimate friend Franz von Schober, creating the fusion "Schobert" (Solomon, "Franz Schubert and the Peacocks," 198). Beethoven occasionally works through similar pivots: see, for instance, the end of the variation movement in op. 127. Here too some kind of union is at issue, but it appears to be linked to the quasi-religious experience in the middle of the movement. By contrast, Schubert's movement bears no semiotic references to anything sacral—except, perhaps, this moment.

31. See the quotation by Eduard Hanslick below.

32. Theodor Adorno, "Schubert," *Moments Musicaux* (Frankfurt: Suhrkamp, 1964).

33. Carl Dahlhaus, "Sonata Form in Schubert: The First Movement of the G-major String Quartet, op. 161 (D. 887)," trans. Thilo Reinhard, in Frisch, *Schubert*, 8–9.

34. Kramer, "The Schubert Lied."

35. Literary theorist Ross Chambers has recently been theorizing narrative digressions of this sort as formal expressions of subversive, antipatriarchal desire. I wish to thank Chambers for sharing his insights with me in conversation.

36. For yet other alternatives, see the discussions of chromaticism in chapters 3 and 4 in my *Feminine Endings*, and in my *Georges Bizet*, Carmen (Cambridge: Cambridge University Press, 1992).

37. Earl Jackson, Jr., "Scandalous Subjects: Robert Glück's Embodied Narratives," "Queer Theory" issue of *differences*, xv and 118–19. Jackson continues: "Understanding the extensions of these subjects into narratives which at once reflect and constitute them requires a narratology that takes into account the politics of sexual difference and the roles sexualities play in the generation of narrative form" (119).

38. I have been gratified to hear from a number of gay men who testify to their having long heard Schubert along these lines. My thanks especially to composer Byron Adams and literary theorist/historian Wayne Koestenbaum.

39. See, for instance, Richard Kramer, review of *Drei grosse Sonaten für das Pianoforte* and *Der Graf von Gleichen*, in *19th-Century Music* 14 (1990): 215.

40. On Wilde, see Dollimore, *Sexual Dissidence*, and Neil Bartlett, *Who Was That Man? A Present for Mr Oscar Wilde* (London: Serpent's Tail, 1988). I wish to thank Mike Steele for introducing me to Bartlett's book.

41. Hanslick, quoted in Martin Chusid, ed., Norton Critical Score of the "Unfinished"

Symphony (New York: W. W. Norton, 1971), 114.

42. See the account in my "Pitches, Expression, Ideology."

43. Kramer, "The Schubert Lied."

44. Edward T. Cone, "Schubert's Promissory Note," *19th-Century Music* 5 (1982): 233–41. Cone discusses a *moment musical* in which a gentle, happy-go-lucky theme makes contact with another key, only to have the contamination of that key destroy the initial theme. He argues that such a formal plan cannot be explained without recourse to something beyond structural analysis, and he posits Schubert's syphilis as the key to this chilling composition. See also William Kinderman, "Schubert's Tragic Perspective," Frisch, *Schubert*, 65–83.

45. Otto Erich Deutsch, *Schubert: A Documentary Biography*, trans. Eric Blom (London: Dent, 1946), 339.

46. Deutsch, *Schubert*, 484.

47. Note that I am not reading this movement (as Rothstein suggested in his review) as the story of *A Streetcar Named Desire*, with Schubert playing the Blanche Dubois role. I am merely pointing out that something of the abjectness in this narrative runs through a number of prominent literary works as well. Nor is this a Freudian reading: I am claiming that Schubert is quite deliberately channeling his materials to produce such a narrative through a public discourse.

48. Hanslick, as quoted in Chusid, Norton Critical Score, 115.

49. I wish to thank Byron Adams, Paul Attinello, Philip Brett, Peter Burkholder, Ross Chambers, Richard Dellamora, David Gramit, George Haggerty, Joseph Horowitz, Owen Jander, Wayne Koestenbaum, Lawrence Kramer, Richard Kramer, Fred Maus, Tom Plaunt, Eve Sedgwick, Gary Thomas, Robert Walser, and James Westby for reading various versions of this paper and making invaluable suggestions.

10

EROS AND ORIENTALISM IN
BRITTEN'S OPERAS

Philip Brett

I N WHAT SEEMED A RATHER BOLD GESTURE during my student days at
King's College, Cambridge, I persuaded a friend of mine with one of
those classic Cambridge baritone voices to perform with me in a College
Music Society concert the *Four Indian Love Lyrics* of Amy Woodforde-
Finden. This was the closest I could have been said ever to have come, as a
highly repressed and not-at-all gay boy, to camp. Any success it might have
had as camp, however, was entirely owing to my straight baritone friend,
who did incredibly unsuspected and virtually obscene things to the articulation of such phrases as "Pale hands, pink-tipped" in the song "Pale Hands I
Loved beside the Shalimar."

Those who know the songs presumably know them for what they are
usually taken, a brand of popular turn-of-the-century kitsch. In the erotic
lyrics, written by a woman with the male nom de plume of Laurence Hope,
the gendered female figure exists in a lightly masochistic relation to the dominant male ("Less than the dust beneath thy chariot wheel, / Less than the
rust that never stained thy sword, / Less than the trust thou hast in me, my
Lord: / Even less than these, even less than these!"). Woodforde-Finden com-
plements their brand of sexual fantasy with a musical style that embodies
the exotic in the simplest of ways—a modal inflection here and there, a
vaguely "Eastern" ornament in the melodic line—but otherwise wavering
somewhere between late nineteenth-century Italian operatic rhetoric and
the Sullivan of Gilbert and Sullivan. Their undying appeal has led Boosey &
Hawkes to reissue them quite recently.[1]

After the performance, a don whom I liked and who I knew had been in
the Indian civil service came up to us with port on his breath and tears in his

eyes. "I haven't heard those songs since India, where they were often sung at the club," he explained. It has dawned on me since that in that setting, men and women, servants of the British raj, would have been applauding and thereby sharing in the performance by one of their own kind of songs hinting at species of erotic acts that though they might have performed they could never admit to. These erotic fantasies, however, could be displaced onto an Indian persona. Of course, this persona bore no relation to any real Indian, either those standing silently as servants ready to do the sahib's bidding at the club, or those who, far vaster in number than the British masters, would in ordinary circumstances hardly be noticed by them: one thinks of the terrifying anonymity to which Harry Coomer finds himself consigned when he becomes Hari Kumar in his native country in Paul Scott's *Raj Quartet*. Nor had the songs necessarily to be linked to India itself, for anywhere south of the Pyrenees and east of East Grinstead would do: among Woodforde-Finden's other works are a cantata, *The Pagoda of Flowers* (1907), located in Burma, and a song cycle entitled *A Lover in Damascus* (1904). She and her reception belong to a phenomenon in which Far, Middle, and Near East coalesce into what Edward Said calls "one of [Europe's] deepest and most recurring images of the Other."[2] It is the phenomenon that he calls orientalism.

Orientalism, in Said's usage, is the negative term of one of those many "binarisms" whose deconstruction in recent years has helped us to understand more about the culture of Europe and Northern America. In the context in which I have raised the topic, that of the erotic, musical, and colonial, we can see all at once the projection of a male fantasy of the feminine, and the identification of a subject race that, according to the imperialist fantasy, is begging to be subjected. Said sees orientalism as bound up with questions of power, that of rulers over subject races (207); of gender, because orientalism as an academic discipline "was an exclusively male province" (207); and of sexuality. In a sentence that indicates one of Said's few failures of nerve, he writes: "Why the Orient seems still to suggest not only fecundity but sexual promise (and threat), untiring sensuality, unlimited desire, deep generation energies, is something on which one could speculate" (188).

Nineteenth- and early twentieth-century music is, of course, deeply implicated in the general Eurocentric perception of the Orient, particularly in France and Britain, the countries Said points to as having the longest tradition of orientalism. A recent study by Ralph P. Locke of Saint-Saëns's *Samson et Dalila* indicates in extensive detail its musical consequences in French nineteenth-century opera, from Félicien David onward, and its reverberations in modern American culture up to and including Bernstein's *West Side Story* (1957).[3] Susan McClary's work on *Carmen* raises the issue in a feminist context, prompted by the portrayal of the title figure in the typical alluring-but-forbidden model of the exotic female Other.[4] British music remains to be studied in this respect: among composers there are obvious candidates like Delius and Granville Bantock, but the repertory will undoubtedly reveal a great deal more with careful combing—even the severe Holst wrote an "oriental suite" entitled *Beni Mora*.[5] In this essay I want to focus on rather specific examples of what I see as orientalism in the music of Benjamin Britten.

In the last decade, Donald Mitchell has revealed the extent of Britten's involvement in the musics of Asia, and Mervyn Cooke has charted the provenance of Britten's musical derivations quite precisely in even more recent work.[6] Britten's first exposure to this music, according to their accounts, was through the Canadian composer Colin McPhee, who had spent a good deal of the 1930s in Bali, and had become an authority on its music.[7] The two met early in Britten's American sojourn at the Long Island home of the Mayer family, where they were both welcomed like many other gay men in music and literature whom Elizabeth Mayer entertained and befriended.[8] The same age as Aaron Copland, another member of the Mayer's circle, and a generation older than Britten, McPhee was a prickly customer with a history of depression, drinking, and sponging off his friends. Yet the two hit it off well enough for Britten to make a special farewell visit to McPhee in October 1941 when the latter had a residency at Yaddo, an artists' retreat at Saratoga in upstate New York,[9] and it transpires that the Canadian composer tried, along with Copland, to influence the younger Englishman to a greater degree than has previously been recognized. In a letter to Elizabeth Mayer, McPhee refers to an article he has been writing—and the reactions of its subject:

> Ben seems to have winced at quite a few passages; I am glad of it. We've talked this all out before, but if (even if it doesn't get published) my negative phrases can help him, it will have been worth while. No one but Aaron has ever picked certain things in Ben to pieces—that is *not* what I mean—we don't want to do that, but try to make him see the futility of certain things. I understand Ben so well, and his fear that he can't. If he is only wanting a career (and I know that is not it), and a career that I know would be very short, then he need not change. But if he wants to survive, to be played with love later on, even during the later years of his life, he must search deeper for a more personal, more <u>interesting</u> idiom. Alas, this is so; in the order of today good craftmanship is *not* enough—that is why I can't, won't write.[10]

One aspect of the "more personal, more interesing idiom" that causes Britten's music "to be played with love" even to this day derives from the very music of Indonesia that McPhee championed so fiercely, and it is worth asking how the far less successful Canadian composer made such an impression, with immediate as well as long-range consequences, on the younger Englishman.

One area of mutual respect must have been established through piano playing, for McPhee had been a concert pianist and was probably a closer match for Britten in this respect than others of the circle. At any rate, Britten played with McPhee the latter's *Balinese Ceremonial Music*, a set of four pieces transcribed for two pianos, four hands; in 1941 they recorded them for the publisher, Schirmer. McPhee inscribed a copy "To Ben—in the hope that he'll find something in the music, after all." Ben indeed already found something in their heterophonic technique and exotic sound with which to characterize the "blue moon" episode of *Paul Bunyan* in the same year. And whatever ambivalence McPhee sensed must be weighed against Britten's playing the pieces again in a Wigmore Hall concert with Clifford Curzon in 1944 after his return to England; they had undoubtedly left their mark. Furthermore, as Bayan Northcott first discovered, sonorities from one of them turn up in the *Sunday Morning* interlude of *Peter Grimes*, which otherwise looks toward another exotic model, the coronation scene of Mussorgsky's *Boris Godunov*, to produce its sonorous picture of an English Sabbath.[11] Similar traces of "Asian" sonorities can be found or sensed in subsequent pieces, but it is not until *The Turn of the Screw* (1954) that, as we shall see, they become attached to a dramatic trope.

As Britten became more involved with these sonorities, the passages containing them became less recognizably related to the "pure gamelan" of McPhee's transcriptions and more generally "exotic." On hearing the examples for this paper, some listeners have resisted the suggestion that they owe anything to gamelan music at all, possibly because of the nature of my interpretation. Yet I am not proposing any new musical identification at all. Every passage mentioned in this essay has been heard and marked as exotic, oriental, or quasi-oriental by other Britten critics, principally Cooke, Mitchell, and Palmer. And it is Mitchell and Cooke who have invested the Britten-McPhee relationship with primary importance in the matter. Britten seems not to have been involved with other American composers of gamelan-inspired music, such as Cage, Cowell and Harrison, though gamelan is a gay marker in American music, as Stevan Key has pointed out to me.[12]

As it turns out, there is a European counterpart who may have helped significantly to reinforce the initial impact of gamelan on Britten—a homosexual composer much closer to camp in his aesthetic than the severe Englishman would ever have allowed himself to be, but one whom Britten nevertheless befriended, supported, and admired. Francis Poulenc's

Concerto for two pianos in D minor, written the year after the 1931 Exposition Coloniale de Paris at which he heard a Balinese gamelan, contains a passage at the end of the first movement that is closer than McPhee's transciptions to the sound of Britten's post-1956 gamelan music. The passage is heralded by the only eerie moment in this ebullient score, and subtle allusions to it occur at the end of each of the other two movements; the two composers were the soloists in a performance at the Albert Hall on 6 January 1945. The previous summer, Poulenc had finished his first opera, *Les Mamelles de Tirésias,* in which, just after the Theatre Director urges the audience to "make children—like you never have before" at the very end of the prologue, there occurs another "Balinese" moment that, like the two fleeting allusions at the close of the second and third movements of the Concerto, is much closer to the kind of pseudogamelan effect I am principally concerned with here. I do not know whether Britten saw the score then, but he thought highly enough of the work to present its first English performance at the Aldeburgh Festival in 1958 and to play the piano part himself.[13]

In 1955–1956, Britten, Pears, and their friends the Hesses went on a world tour during which the composer heard not only Balinese gamelan music, whose technique—which he found "about as complicated as Schönberg"— he now became involved with, but also Japanese music drama.[14] The first of these exposures bore immediate fruit in the 1956 ballet, *The Prince of the Pagodas,* in which the Pagodas themselves are depicted in gamelan music. Much later, in 1964, came *Curlew River,* the opera (comparatively long in gestation) that demonstrated the full extent of Britten's engagement with the Japanese Noh drama. After this point, Asian music, particularly Balinese gamelan music, turned up with great frequency in Britten's works, making its most extensive appearance, possibly, in *Death in Venice.*

The revelation of the extent of Britten's engagement with Asian musics was important if only because it revealed the parochialism of those critics who, in a curious evocation of the imperialist vision of London as the center of a Eurocentric world, saw (and still see) Britten as having cut himself off in his later years, to the detriment of his musical development. This anxiety, revealed in a particularly virulent attack by Tom Sutcliffe, music critic of the *The Guardian,* in the television documentary series *J'accuse* on Channel 4 during the spring of 1991, has strong links to concerns over his "going native"—for every British critic who accepts gamelan and heterophony as part of Britten's language there is another who loathes what they represent.[15] But the revelation of Asian influences also opened up new ways to explore the dramaturgy of the operas. In an essay of 1985 in the *Cambridge Opera Handbook* on *The Turn of the Screw,* Christopher Palmer made the association, crucial for my purposes here, between the gamelan-like sonorities and pentatonic melodic shapes on the one hand, and the opera's treatment of erotic desire and sexuality on the other.[16]

The musical organization of *The Turn of the Screw* is closely, even obsessively, worked out. No other Britten score is so tightly ordered, no scheme of his more imaginatively devised to produce a musically claustrophobic quality. The composer may well have realized that the "technical skill [that] always comes from the bourgeois side of one's nature" could—and must for him—be made to produce something more powerful and dramatically compelling than the "large unfeeling corpses" Auden had warned Britten about in a famous letter.[17] The fifteen interludes that punctuate the scenes consist of a set of variations on a theme that is announced at the beginning, immediately after the expressive Prologue. Consisting of three phrases of four notes each, this theme can be reduced to a set of rising fourths (or falling fifths) followed by falling thirds (or rising sixths), which cover all twelve notes of the chromatic scale. The first six notes, if laid out stepwise in the order 0-2-4-1-3-5, make the first six notes of the A major scale; the last six, if similarly arranged (6-8-10-7-9-11), cover the hexachord E-flat–C, suggesting E-flat or A-flat. As it turns out, A major and A-flat major are the two polar keys of the opera, the first signifying, in the broadest terms, the Governess's world, the latter the influence of the ghosts. The tonality of the interlude/variations and of their subsequent scenes in act 1 ascend from the one to the other; those of act 2 descend by an exactly inverted path. Almost every other thematic aspect of the work is somehow derived from this main theme, often in a way that is deliberately ambiguous. (See example 1.)

Example 1

Perhaps because of the organicist ideology underlying most music analysis, or because of a fairly simple-minded wonder that comes over most commentators on encountering a theme in Britten's music incorporating all twelve notes of the chromatic scale, no one pays attention to the actual musical effect generated by this passage—and again when the theme is heard in a similar juxtaposition at the beginning of act 2. The dynamics, the phrasing, the prolongation of each pitch, and the steady rise in pitch level associated with an

Example 2

exactly reiterated rhythm, all culminating in a 3/2 measure prolonging the twelve-note dissonance almost unbearably, lead the ear to hear the passage as an introduction, a giant upbeat if you will, to what happens next, at figure 1 (see example 2). The portentous quality of the gesture is scarcely matched, of course, by what follows—a theme played by flute, clarinet, and the two violins over an internal pedal on A, and therefore not fully foregrounded.[18] Most notable perhaps is its disturbingly asymmetrical rhythm, which is taken over completely by the timpani and tenor drum as the main element of the first scene, "The Journey," suggesting all at once the uneven roll of the carriage wheels, the palpitations of the Governess's frightened heart, and intimations of sensuality, the first delicate hint of exoticism in the score. *This* journey, evidently, is going to take us somewhere further than an English house in the country. The second theme, which Peter Evans ingeniously derives from the twelve-note series by filling in the inverted version of its first five notes, is equally important in the construction of the work and even more important dramatically than the twelve-note theme that precedes it. It migrates from character to character, subtly changing under the pressure of the dramatic situation.

It first attaches itself to the Governess, charting the significant moments that reveal her state of mind, from her fear of the task at hand in scene 1 and her arrival in scene 2 (where it hangs in the air on the high violins like a nervous thread), through her increasing "knowledge" of the situation and the awareness of her need to shelter the children as act 1 proceeds, to her ultimate realization, in scene 7 of act 1, that she "neither shields nor saves them." In act 2, it accompanies her growing recognition of failure, and of her sense of becoming tarnished in her efforts: "I have failed, most miserably failed, and there is no more innocence in me." Finally it occurs, plainer and perhaps coarser without its ironic final twist, as the Governess declares possessively at the opening of the passacaglia in the final scene, "O Miles, I cannot bear to lose you. You shall be mine and I shall save you."

The theme also attaches itself to the not so ghostly ghosts. Their most important enunciation of it occurs in the first scene of act 2, where its original association with the twelve-note theme is reproduced. Here, the introductory feeling of the twelve-note theme is intensified by a gradually increasing harmonic rhythm as well as by growing rhythmic activity in the bass toward its climax-provoking end. When the second theme arrives, it is in the ghosts' key of A-flat, and it is sung to the words that Myfanwy Piper, the librettist, imported from Yeats's "Second Coming": "The ceremony of innocence is drowned." It is precisely at the arrival of the second theme and Yeats's memorable phrase that the pseudogamelan effect that Palmer identified occurs, provided here by flute, harp, and celesta over gurgling woodwind trills, with gong and cymbal strikes reinforced by string pizzicati on the downbeat of each 3/2 bar (see example 3).

Example 3

The water imagery that Christopher Palmer writes about is likely to have arisen because Britten, who liked concrete images, responded to the word "drowned"; yet, as Palmer notes with respect to the last scene of act 1, in which a similar sound is projected, this imagery is directed, surely, toward the particular meaning of loss of innocence associated with erotic, or even purely sexual, practices.[19]

Since sex, once discerned, is so willful in its signification, and so easily gets out of hand (as it does, rather, in Palmer's account), it is wise to look first toward the historical context for a specific practice that might in particular apply to a tale such as this by Henry James and its transformation into an opera by Britten. In view of the "sexual awakening" theme here, and the involvement of children with supervisory adults in a nineteenth-century setting, masturbation is an inescapable choice. As Michael Moon has pointed out in his work on what he calls "the anti-onanist terrorist writing" of America in the nineteenth century, its target became increasingly "the *social* pursuit of this nominally solitary activity" (my italics). Its discourse, he continues, "crystallizes around the figure of the depraved individual—servant, older relative, or older child—who, by teaching the young to masturbate, introduces sexual difference and sexual desire into what American moral-purity writers represent as the previously innocent—which is to say asexual—homosocial environments to which the young are committed."[20]

The Turn of the Screw, written half a century after the inception of the antimasturbation campaign, which came to be an antihomosexual campaign through the mechanism noted above, is for Moon a prime example of that mechanism:

> One has only to recall how much in the tale turns on the mystery (or non-mystery) of little Miles's having been sent down from school for shocking misconduct toward some of his schoolmates—conduct into which he may have earlier been initiated by the literally haunting figure of Peter Quint—to perceive how resonant the figures of the boy and his corrupter, figures first disseminated on a mass scale in male-purity discourse, remained in the imaginations of James and many of his readers.[21]

It is surely not stretching the point to add the composer to those "readers," for if antimasturbatory literature and the homophobic myths associated with it were still widely circulated during my own childhood in Britain, how much more present would they have been in the 1920s when Britten was reaching puberty? Indeed it appears that he told two of his librettists separate horror stories of childish corruption close to home, one about his being raped by a master at school, the other about his being implicated in some obscure way in the mechanics of his father's homosexual desire.[22]

Whatever we make of these stories, whether true or strongly present in the composer's imagination as figured forth to his librettists, the music itself lends substance to the notion of Quint as corrupter, and we may remember that it was Britten himself who insisted to Piper that he "should sing—and sing words (no nice anonymous, supernatural humming or groaning)."[23] What we hear Quint sing in his first vocal entry, however, is a perverse transformation of what we have been calling the second theme (largely by an elaboration around the flattened seventh, the "blue note" of the original) into something preliterate. If we listened for a word, which I doubt anyone does on encountering this passage in the theater, we would hear the possessive, self-involved, long-enunciated "my," closing only at its moment of dying pleasure into the name of the Other whom it calls "Miles." This is a voice from Lacan's imaginary, rather than symbolic, order, conjuring up an echo of the original cry that objectifies the voice into an instrument of pleasure, or the mother's voice, from which the child first feels the pangs of separation.[24]

According to the Earl of Harewood, the extraordinary cantilena in scene 8 (example 4) was suggested to Britten by the sound of Pears singing a Perotin monody, but most auditors apprehend the exotic, something—in Wilfred Mellers's account—"recalling flamenco music and Moorish cantillation."[25] We have only to remember the tendency to conflate various parts of the East to appreciate the orientalism of the gesture. Mellers and Palmer hear Quint's cantilena as "open[ing] magic casements" for Miles: in his ultra–gay-male–affirmative account Clifford Hindley hears it as, simply, "love."[26] But, given the orientalist context, the landscape onto which those magic casements open must be one of dread as well as allure; for orientalism is one of the means by which desire unacceptable to or feared by the (Western) Subject can be projected on to the Other. As if to confirm this diagnosis, this vocal entry of Quint's, placed very carefully near the end of the first act, is heralded by and intertwined with echoes of variation 7, the first place in the score in which the pseudogamelan sounds fully assert their presence—sonorities derived from an encounter fifteen years earlier that Britten was now using to conjure up the distant world that the problematic McPhee had extolled and to delineate a character he himself had perhaps adumbrated.[27] In short, given the difference of the homoeroticism portrayed here, Britten's strategy belongs to the same cultural context as the lyrical effusions of Amy Woodforde-Finden, however distinct the musical effect.

Five years after *The Turn of the Screw*, in composing *A Midsummer Night's Dream*, Britten had recourse to a similar strategy in portraying Oberon. "If it is an accident that E flat is the key both of the immortals in *A Midsummer*

Night's Dream and of Quint's evil in *The Turn of the Screw*, it is the kind of accident that happens only to genius," writes Wilfred Mellers in rhetoric characteristic of Britten criticism.[28] If Quint is marked as homosexual and

Example 4

threateningly so by his "oriental" music, then Oberon is similarly designated by his countertenor voice; as Wayne Koestenbaum points out in a recent essay, the association of *falsetto* with unnaturalness and perversity in the singing manuals of the nineteenth century prefigures the discourse of homosexuality.[29] Furthermore, Oberon at his most threatening and evil, as he evades the fairy sentinel to dispense the erotic binding power embodied in the juice of the flower, sets off another stylized pseudogamelan, with the ever-prominent celesta aided by harp and glockenspiel and with pianissimo tremolo strings set off by the pizzicato double basses playing a derivative of the melody in canon (example 5).

The device of the exotic attached to Oberon and Quint may have been simply aimed at capturing aspects of Shakespeare and James. The transgressive, carnivalesque atmosphere of the wood outside Athens could be apprehended by a post-Freudian composer in such a way as to suggest a positively Bahktinian reading. Similarly, Britten would have pondered long and hard over how to recreate James's effect—Piper's view, after all, stated unequivocally, is that "neither Britten nor I ever intended to interpret the work, only to re-create it for a different medium."[30] What James set out to do, of course, was to liberate the old Gothic horror story from its reliance on apparitions by forcing the reader into the hot spot: "make him think the evil, make him think of it for himself, and you are released from weak specifications," James wrote in a preface to the New York edition of the tale.[31] In pushing for resolution in interpretation, then, we are lost, whether we subscribe to a "first story" in which the children are corrupted by the ghosts, or a "second story" in which the Governess in her hysterical condition conducts a battle for the children against an imagined foe. The reader who accepts the "first story" creates the subjective horror of deceitful evil in innocent-seeming children; the one who accepts the "second story" creates a monstrous predator in the guise of womanly protector. The one springs from and endorses homophobia, the other misogyny. Between these two positions, moreover, there is little room to move.[32]

The opera offers a focal character in the Governess. But she is distanced through James's framing device, which Britten, despite his liking for such frames, adopted at a comparatively late stage. Moreover, she is implicated in Quint's identity (in whatever way the listener likes to imagine) through the common basis of the theme they share, projected though it is in musically different ways. Britten himself could readily have found points of identification with both of them. But I should like to imagine him for a moment cast as Miles. The perceptively offensive Wystan Auden once wrote to the composer to say "You see, Bengy dear, you are always tempted...to build yourself a warm nest of love (of course when you get it, you find it a little stifling) by playing the lovable talented little boy."[33] Miles playing mock Mozart/Czerny to win the attention of his indulgent female wardens (in act 2, scene 6)

Example 5

conjures up Auden's image rather evocatively. Seen from Miles's vantage point of abjection ("I am bad, aren't I?"), moreover, the ambiguities of the tale recede a little as we see the lovable boy caught between a dominating lover and a possessive mother in a struggle that no side wins and that ends inevitably in death—a catharsis even more intense than the capitulation of Peter Grimes to society's persecution and his own internalized oppression.

But there is also a good deal that Britten may have perceived of himself in Quint. The composer's own attraction for boys between the ages of about twelve and sixteen was strong: David Hemmings, the Miles in the original production of the opera (and on the recording conducted by Britten), apparently became the focus of one of the most powerful of his attachments, which, like many of their kind, were reportedly tender and fatherly, occasionally passionate, but involving no sexual exploitation.[34] With his own childhood experiences in mind, Britten must have felt keenly the knife-edge balance on which such behavior rested. In *Peter Grimes* he had originally set out to portray a child abuser, a figure slowly but surely eradicated as work on the opera proceeded and supplanted by a worst-case scenario of another and more general kind—the outsider whom society hounds to death on no legal or moral grounds, an outsider represented most viably in that case by "the homosexual."[35] By means of James's tale he was able a decade later to return to the original theme, and also at the same time to exorcise—as he had in *Grimes*—a darker side of his own reality.

How then do we conceptualize an attitude toward the orientalism by means of which Britten casts such a web of ambiguity around Quint and Oberon, the powerful and predatory, but also alluring, figures who haunt the two last operas before an Eastern mode was adopted by Britten in earnest? Let me begin by making a distinction. Britten's is not comparable to the authorial anxiety exhibited in the *Alexandria Quartet*, in which, according to Joseph Boone's deconstructive reading, "the imaginary geography of Durrell's eroticized Egyptian landscape helps to throw the modernist and masculinist tenets of his text into disarray" and to "overwhelm the coherence of its representations of masculine heterosexual competence." In Durrell, as in the case of Flaubert, which Said discusses without revealing the threat of pederasty, "the exotic otherness of sexual 'perversion' [i.e., homoeroticism], is figured as the threat of erasure, the negation of artistic vitality or 'sap.'"[36] This is not true of Britten, who rather indicates a rich if dangerous enchancement of life and art beyond the world that imprisons him (and Miles). Nor is his strategy that of feminizing the Other, so typical of orientalist responses. After his cantilena, Quint emerges in a series of quite specifically phallic, if veiled, personae—"the riderless horse, snorting, stamping"; the hero highwayman; King Midas—before relapsing back into less personified images—the hidden life; the unknown gesture; the soft persistent word.

One way of looking at Britten in this regard is to put him a little farther down the line from Durrell on a continuum of sexuality. What if the coherence here is represented by consenting homosexual love between two adults, as represented by his life with Peter Pears; the exotic otherness and threat of erasure by pedophilia, the love of "thin-as-a-board juveniles" with which Auden taunted Britten.[37] Orientalism in its sexual mode in these two operas is, after all, attached exclusively to boy lovers, boy dominators, or boy seekers, that is to Quint and Oberon. This connects in turn to the pederasty that (as Boone notes) Said evades discussing in his account of Flaubert. The very dust-jacket picture of Said's book is Gérôme's "The Snake Charmer," depicting a naked boy entwined with a snake facing a crowd of men, who (it is suggested to the implicated Western male gaze) are enjoying the spectacle of a titillation offered to the spectator only in the form of graceful buttocks.

On the other hand, Britten was himself identified, through a process that links the oriental to elements in Western society—such as delinquents, the insane, women, the poor, and, of course, homosexuals—as "lamentably alien," to use Said's phrase. He was not the representative of a male hetero-sexist order, like Durrell, but of a group that, in the period of the operas under discussion, was particularly at risk of persecution as a result of the defection of Burgess and Maclean to the USSR and the subsequent intervention of the CIA into British domestic policing. Britten began composing *The Turn of the Screw* on March 30, 1954, less than a week after the conclusion of the notorious trial that resulted in the imprisonment of Lord Montagu, Michael Pitt-Rivers, and Peter Wildeblood; Humphrey Carpenter has turned up evidence that some time in January of the same year (or slightly earlier), Britten was interviewed by Scotland Yard, whose gentleman's agreement with the leisured classes was terrifyingly abrogated during this period, as part of their "definitely stepping up their activities against the homosexuals."[38] Do we understand, then, the demonizing of the homosexual through the orien-talism of these works as a means of expressing fear, shame, and defiance all at once? Are we to invoke a particularly complicated configuration of the dynamics of oppression to explain away the case?

However one theorizes the Britten syndrome outlined here—or that of Amy Woodforde-Finden and Laurence Hope, which is promisingly compli-cated owing to their gender—a fresh view should probably be taken of Britten's subsequent operatic musical relations with the East. An important note by the librettist of *Curlew River*, William Plomer, shows how uncom-fortable he was with the original idea for that opera of making it simply a translation of *Sumidagawa*, preserving the Japanese locale and character names. Britten also shows, in a letter of April 1958, how increasingly worried he became about the idea of creating a pastiche of a Noh play.[39] In insisting on the move into a comparable Western tradition, that of the mystery play, Britten opened up conditions in which he was able to pay homage to an Eastern tradition by adapting and imitating some of its musical and dramatic procedures without patronizing it, and without using it as a vehicle for the projection of Western fantasies. It is a project that tries hard to avoid the colonizing impulse, though of course it reflects the romantic utopianism also associated with the phenomenon of orientalism in the West.

When Britten returned to mainstream opera, he reverted to the deployment of gamelan music—this time notably closer to the original model—to denote moments of significance. In *Owen Wingrave* the gamelan makes a special appearance for Owen's biggest aria, his lyrical statement of belief about peace. In view of the earlier works the use is suggestive, so that when we hear the character exclaim, at the climax of the aria, before the emergence of the ghosts who are to seal his doom, that "peace is love," we may be pardoned for wondering what kind of love is involved. The use suggests the nonspecific erotic sensualism of the pagodas, those warm, slightly phallic but nonthreatening presences in the earlier ballet, *The Prince of the Pagodas* (1956). The suggestion of polymorphous perversity they entail points us in the direction of a world of prepubescent sensuousness, again preverbal, at a stage before entry into the symbolic order symbolized in the ballet by the phallic trumpet motif with which the prince emerges from the salamander. Owen is regressing into Britten's world of what has been called by the commentators "innocence," but which is beyond innocence and guilt, and is rather "nescience," the presymbolic state hymned in "A Time There Was" of *Winter Words*, and indicated in Britten's music either by aggressively triadic tonality or by these echoes of the East.

The difference from the pseudogamelan of *The Turn of the Screw* and *A Midsummer Night's Dream* is striking, and it is further emphasized by a reversal in the assignment of the gamelan in Britten's last opera, *Death in Venice*. Here the orientalism is mapped not onto the adult male lover, but onto the distant, inarticulate figure of the boy who is beloved. Not only is this dramatically apt, since Aschenbach, through whom we as audience perceive Venice and Tadzio, would naturally project them in the image of orientalism, but it allows for a wider critique of the European dialogue of Self and Other. Like *A Passage to India* in Sara Suleri's brilliant reading, it could be said to be "both an engagement with and a denial of a colonial homoerotic imperative."[40] As the slowly circling figure of Tadzio leaves Aschenbach crumpled onstage at the end of the opera, we are reminded of the forces tearing Fielding and Aziz apart during their near engagement at the end of E.M. Forester's novel. For two generations of upper-middle-class Englishmen, trained in the humanist liberal tradition that promised so much and performed so little, the climax of their creativity coincided with a scene of denial and pessimism.

Notes

This paper was first delivered at the Royal Music Association's twenty-seventh annual conference (entitled "Music and Eroticism") at Oxford in March 1992. I am grateful to John Milsom for urging it into existence and to Katherine Bergeron and Sue-Ellen Case for ideas on which it could grow.

1. With an informative introduction by Andrew Lamb, dated 1990; the firm first published the songs in 1903.

2. Edward Said, *Orientalism* (New York: Random House, 1978), 1.

3. "Constructing the Oriental 'Other': Saint-Saëns's *Samson et Dalila*," *Cambridge Opera Journal* 3, no. 3 (1991): 261–302. The author's strongly interdisciplinary approach, fixing the context especially well with reference to painting (Delacroix, Vernet, Gérôme, Regnault, and others, whose orientalism has been explored in specifically feminist terms by the art historian Linda Nochlin) includes the specific challenge: "a truly critical feminism may need to *face the fact* that an opera from 1877…cannot be fully recuperated into a modern conception of *how a self-respecting woman should conduct herself*" (my italics, 290–91). Her music and words written for her by men in the nineteenth century, Delilah is not likely to be subversive of the patriarchal order—though the composer's attachment to the "inversion" model of homosexuality, not explored by Locke, may have contributed to the ambiguity he senses in the portrayal of that most famous Philistine, whom Saint-Saëns himself may well have identified with in certain moods and certain costumes. For an account of the amazing closet performance on the stage of the Moscow conservatorium in 1875 in which Saint-Saëns, "with his long experience of impersonating Gounod's heroines," mimed Galatea to the Pygmalion of Tchaikovsky (with whom he had struck up an "amusing friendship"), see James Harding, *Saint-Saëns and His Circle* (London: Chapman & Hall, 1965), 141–42; I am indebted to Byron Adams for this reference.

4. *Georges Bizet: Carmen*, Cambridge Opera Handbooks (Cambridge: Cambridge University Press, 1992), especially 29–43, 51–61; 33–34 are especially important for my argument here because they make the point that "not all 'Orientals' were located in imaginary lands." To McClary's two marked categories, gypsies and Jews, I would, of course, add homosexuals (the third category victimized by the Nazis).

5. (1909–1910, first performed, 1912). I am indebted to my colleague Byron Adams for drawing my attention to this work, which has drawn a mixed reception from Holst critics.

6. Donald Mitchell, "What Do We Know about Britten Now?" and "Catching on to the Technique in Pagoda-Land," in Christopher Palmer, ed., *The Britten Companion* (London: Faber & Faber, 1984), 39–45 and 192–210. Mervyn Cooke, "Britten and the

Gamelan: Balinese Influences in *Death in Venice*," in Donald Mitchell, ed., *Benjamin Britten: Death in Venice* (Cambridge: Cambridge University Press, 1987), 115–28; and "Britten and Bali," *Journal of Musicological Research* 7, no. 4 (1988): 307–39. See also Cooke's Ph.D. thesis, *Oriental Influences in the Music of Benjamin Britten* (Cambridge, 1988), which includes a discussion of Japanese as well as Balinese influences.

7.   McPhee recounted his experiences in *A House in Bali* (New York: John Day, 1946; reprinted New York: Oxford University Press, 1987); his treatise *Music in Bali* (New Haven: Yale University Press, 1966; reprinted New York: Da Capo Press, 1976) is still consulted.

8.   A page from the Mayers' visitor's book shows Britten and Pears's names appearing for the first time on 21 August 1939, followed shortly by that of McPhee on 7 September; see plate 115, Donald Mitchell and John Evans, *Pictures from a Life: Benjamin Britten 1913–1976* (London: Faber & Faber, 1978); the book also contains photographs of McPhee and Britten together in the garden at Amityville and of the score of *Balinese Ceremonial Music*, mentioned below, that McPhee gave to Britten. For two different accounts of life at the Mayers, see Donald Mitchell and Philip Reed, eds., *Letters from a Life: Selected Letters and Diaries of Benjamin Britten* (London: Faber & Faber, 1991), vol. 2, 679–83 (also 724 for Britten's own account), and Humphrey Carpenter, *Benjamin Britten: A Biography* (London: Faber & Faber, 1992), 133–36. McPhee was treated for depression by Dr. Mayer, a psychiatrist; he also taught Elizabeth Mayer the piano; see Carol J. Oja, *Colin McPhee: Composer in Two Worlds* (Washington, D.C: Smithsonian Institute Press, 1990), 154–57, 179–80.

9.   The visit is referred to in a letter to Britten of 1 Oct(ober) (1942) from McPhee (in the Britten-Pears Library at Aldeburgh). After opening with "just a brief note to say I love you and think of you often" McPhee writes that "by the time you get (if you do) this letter, it will be just a year since you so very sweetly came to Saratoga." Written from Woodstock, where Copland lived and where Britten and Pears rented accommodation when they first arrived in the States, the letter goes on to give news of Marc Blitzstein, Victor (Kraft, Copland's lover), Oliver (Daniel who worked at CBS), David Diamond, and M(argaret) M(ead). These were McPhee's friends, of course—Copland and Daniel lent him money endlessly as well as promoting his work—but it is interesting to speculate that Britten may have met Margaret Mead through McPhee. McPhee gave his own birth date as 1901, but Carol J. Oja has verified the date 1900 from his birth certificate; see Oja, *Colin McPhee*, 1.

10.   Postmarked 10 July 1941 and written from Yaddo (italic letters printed with the red ribbon of the typewriter). Britten had put McPhee in touch with the editor, David Ewen (see letter 309, Mitchell and Reed, *Letters from a Life*, vol. 2, 907–8). According to a further letter of McPhee's to Elizabeth Mayer, on 30 October: "Ewen's book has been given up, and I am glad, for though I hope to publish something about Ben, in the same tone, I would like to develope [sic] it more. The other thing was too hasty."

11.   As indicated in David Matthews, "Act II Scene 1: An Examination of the Music," in Philip Brett, ed., *Benjamin Britten: Peter Grimes* (Cambridge: Cambridge University Press, 1983), 122–24. Further on the pre-1954 music see Cooke, "Britten and Bali" and *Oriental Influences*.

12.   Private communication.

13.   For an account of Britten's relations with Poulenc, see Mitchell and Reed, *Letters from a Life*, 1249–50. The two composers gave a further performance of Poulenc's two-piano Concerto on 16 January 1955 at the Royal Festival Hall in London; see Sidney Buckland,

trans. and ed., *Francis Poulenc: "Echo and Source," Selected Correspondence 1915–1963* (London: Victor Gollancz, 1991), 228 and 393. Peter Pears sang the part of the Husband in the Aldeburgh production of *Les Mamelles.*

14. Cooke, "Britten and Bali," 320.

15. Sutcliffe describes Aldeburgh, Britten's home and the place where he held his music festival, as "a haven isolated from the radical intellectual milieu Britten enjoyed in the thirties in London." Like many other observations in the program this has the ring of truth—Britten certainly became increasingly conservative as he aged; what is extraordinary is the anger expressed against the composer for not measuring up to the examples of Elgar and Vaughan Williams, for not being the national composer he was expected to be, and, ultimately, for exploiting an "emperor's clothes" situation. Thus the church parables, described as "a new brain-wave recipe mixing plainchant and monks and Japanese Noh theatre and percussive Balinese timbres" are "proof enough that Britten was producing exactly the emotional corpses that Auden [in the letter cited in footnote 17] had predicted."

16. Christopher Palmer, "The Colour of the Music," in Patricia Howard, ed., *Benjamin Britten: The Turn of the Screw* (Cambridge University Press, 1985), 101–25, especially 110–13 and 124. It is worth noting that a connection between sensuality/sexuality and Bali had been made in a different, but equally revealing, way by Colin McPhee in letter to William Mayer (postmarked 2 September 1942 and preserved in the Britten-Pears Library at Aldeburgh):

> I remember that at nineteen I was filled with the idea that I had something precious to say, and that at twenty-three I no longer believed it. I already felt lost, filled with despair, and took refuge in living completely for the moment. Many times there was a decision to be made between some important opportunity and a sexual (homosexual) relationship which was purely sensual. I never hesitated to choose the latter. This I did deliberately and would do again and again, for it seemed the only thing that was real. The Balinese period was simply a long extension of this.

17. Saturday (31 January 1942), printed in Mitchell and Reed, *Letters from a Life,* vol. 2, 1015–16.

18. Patricia Howard goes so far in not seeing/hearing it as to claim that the theme "first occurs in Act I scene 1 at a significant point in the governess's musings"—the passage seven measures after figure 3 ("O why, why did I come?"); see "Structures: An Overall View," in Howard, *Benjamin Britten: The Turn of the Screw,* 82.

19. Palmer, "The Colour of the Music," 106.

20. Michael Moon, "Disseminating Whitman," *South Atlantic Quarterly* 88 (1989): 255.

21. Moon, "Disseminating Whitman," 256.

22. Humphrey Carpenter, *Benjamin Britten* (London: Faber & Faber, 1992), 20–25; Carpenter is extremely judicious in handling these accounts given to him by Eric Crozier and Myfanwy Piper. The second story hinges on Piper's statement, "He did say this his father was homosexual and that he used to send him out to find boys" (23).

23. Myfanwy Piper, "Writing for Britten," in David Herbert, ed., *The Operas of Benjamin Britten* (New York: Columbia University Press, 1979), 11.

24. It was after I conceived this passage that I came across the extracts from Michel Poizat's *L'Opéra, ou le cri de l'ange* (Paris: A. M. Métailié, 1986) trans. Arthur Denner under the title "'The Blue Note' and 'The Objectified Voice and the Vocal Object,'" *Cambridge*

Opera Journal 3, no. 3 (1991): 195–211; Poizat usefully analyzes just such effects—the proleptic effects—of the "blue note" conceived in a wider sense than I originally intended here, as applying themselves in opera "towards a supreme mark of the failure of speech and the signifying order, namely, the cry" (201). In connection with the other presymbolic experience, not the first cry of the infant but the voice of the mother, it is interesting that one of Britten's early playmates has observed that Peter Pears's voice sounded like that of Britten's own mother. See Donald Mitchell's preface to Mitchell and Reed, *Letters from a Life*, vol. 1, 14.

I am indebted to Roger Parker for pointing out to me the similarity *as gesture* of this moment in Britten's score to the introduction to the famous Bell Song from act 2 of Delibes's *Lakmé*, an orientalist opera if ever there was one. What Carolyn Abbate says about this piece in the opening discussion of *Unsung Voices* applies equally to Quint's vocalizing: "Such moments enact in pure form familiar Western tropes on the suspicious power of music and its capacity to move us without rational speech." The differences between the two passages are revealing. If Lakmé's "overtly seductive performance... extracts one erotically fascinated listener from the crowd [Gerald, the besotted British officer]," Quint's song is more powerfully focused on its one onstage auditor, Miles. If Lakmé, whose music dissolves into fragments, "becomes *explicitly* a body emanating sonority," Quint is a disembodied vocal threat from the start. See Carolyn Abbate, *Unsung Voices: Opera and Musical Narrative in the Nineteenth Century* (Princeton: Princeton University Press, 1991), 4–9.

25. Harewood's observation appears in Gustav Kobbé, *Kobbé's Complete Opera Book*, edited and revised by the Earl of Harewood, 9th ed. (London: Putnam, 1976), 1494. It is confirmed by Rosamund Strode; see her "Reverberations," in Marion Thorpe, ed., *Peter Pears: A Tribute on His 75th Birthday* (London: Faber Music/The Britten Estate, 1985), 89–90. Strode identifies the piece in question as *Beata viscera Mariæ virginis*, printed in the widely used Archibald T. Davison and Willi Apel, eds., *Historical Anthology of Music* (Cambridge: Harvard University Press, 1949), no. 17c; and she points to Pears's performance of the monody to open the Purcell Singers Concert (conducted by Imogen Holst) on 16 June 1954 at the Aldeburgh Festival as the one that "suggested to Ben exactly what he wanted for Quint's unearthly and alluring calls to Miles" on the grounds that he was writing *The Turn of the Screw* that summer. But Myfanwy Piper "vividly remembers 'amazing crashes' accompanying Quint's calls to Miles" when Britten played through the work in progress during a mid-May visit, according to the account in Carpenter, *Britten: A Biography*, 337, where it is also reported (a) that Britten wrote to Lennox Berkeley on 6 July saying that "rehearsals start in a month & I have 5 scenes still to write—O Law!" and (b) that the composition sketch was finished on 23 July (355). Wilfred Mellers, "Turning the Screw," in Palmer, *The Britten Companion*, 149.

26. Clifford Hindley, "Why Does Miles Die? A Study of Britten's *The Turn of the Screw*," *The Musical Quarterly* 74 (1990): 11.

27. Oja is reticent with details of McPhee's sexual tastes and partners in Bali, but she notes that his marriage to Jane Belo, who financed the venture, foundered partly on his relationship with an indigenous male: "I was in love at the time with a Balinese, which she knew, and to have him continually around was too much for her vanity" (letter to Sidney Cowell, in Oja, *Colin McPhee*, 142). McPhee was also devoted to Balinese children, particularly the talented dancer, Sampih, a boy of about eight when they first met in 1932, who subsequently lived at the McPhee house and whom he loved intensely (op. cit., 88–89); McPhee founded a children's gamelan—*gamelan angklung*—as related in McPhee, *A House in Bali*, 195–201, and in his children's book, *A Club of Small Men* (New York: John Day, 1948), copies of which Britten possessed. Britten's feelings about McPhee

must have soured when the latter descried the *Seven Sonnets of Michelangelo* as "baroque and pompous show-pieces, pastiches that hold little interest" in *Modern Music* 21 (1943): 48–49; writing to Elizabeth Mayer on 13 May 1944, Britten comments, "I know how fickle the musical public is, & how superficial their judgements (although I was bit grieved by Colin's attack on the Michelangelo Sonnets);" see Mitchell and Reed, *Letters from a Life*, vol. 2, 1201–1202. If the music associated with McPhee nevertheless remained in Britten's composing consciousness, as Mitchell, Cooke, and others argue convincingly, why are these same commentators so fastidious about the characteristics of the person behind the music, especially the homoeroticism that was so strongly intertwined with his love of Bali?

28. Wilfred Mellers, "The Truth of the *Dream*," in Palmer, *The Britten Companion*, 191.

29. "The Queen's Throat: (Homo)sexuality and the Art of Singing" in Diana Fuss, ed., *Inside/Out: Lesbian Theories, Gay Theories* (New York: Routledge, 1991), 217–23.

30. Piper, "Writing for Britten," 11.

31. Henry James, *The Art of the Novel: Critical Prefaces by Henry James*, ed. Richard P. Blackmur (New York: Scribner's, 1934), 176. The argument here is indebted to George Haggerty's discussion of the tale in *Gothic Fiction/Gothic Form* (University Park: Pennsylvania State University Press, 1988).

32. Nor when we turn to the opera is Clifford Hindley's "third story"—of a blameless Quint offering Miles the fulfillment of his "true nature," the Governess the victim of the delusion that such relationships are all evil, and such evil as there is being projected onto Miss Jessel—a fully acceptable alternative. My "Britten's Bad Boys: Male Relations in *The Turn of the Screw*," in *repercussions* 1, no. 2 (Fall 1992): 5–25, addresses this and other issues raised by Hindley's "Why Does Miles Die?"

33. Mitchell and Reed, *Letters from a Life*, vol. 2, 1016.

34. Carpenter, *Benjamin Britten*, 341–55. The criminologist D. J. West distinguishes between the pedophile and "ephebophile," a category into whose broad outline Britten fits remarkably well, see *Homosexuality Re-examined* (4th edition. of *Homosexuality* [1960]), (London: Duckworth, 1977), 211–15.

35. For the process of transformation in this opera, see my "'Fiery Visions' (and Revisions): *Peter Grimes* in Progress," in Brett, ed., *Benjamin Britten: Peter Grimes*, 47–87.

36. Joseph A. Boone, "Mappings of Male Desire in Durrell's *Alexandria Quartet*," *South Atlantic Quarterly* 88 (1989): 102. Marjorie Garber proposes for "Boone's salutary substitution" of the homosexual male dancer that Said overlooks or represses, the further substitition of an irreducible transvestic spectacle, suggesting that "transvestism... *that* is the taboo against which Occidental eyes are veiled" in *Vested Interests* (New York: Routledge, 1991), 341–42.

37. Mitchell and Reed, *Letters from a Life*, vol. 2, 1015.

38. Carpenter, *Benjamin Britten*, 355, quoting a letter from Percy Elland, editor of *The Evening Standard*, to his proprietor, Lord Beaverbrook.

39. For a full account, including Plomer's note and Britten's letter, see Peter F. Alexander, *William Plomer: A Biography* (Oxford: Oxford University Press, 1989), 299–306. I am indebted to Mervyn Cooke for this reference.

40. Sara Suleri, *The Rhetoric of English India* (Chicago: University of Chicago Press, 1992), 147.

11

QUEER THOUGHTS ON
COUNTRY MUSIC AND k.d. lang

Martha Mockus

I HAVE NEVER BEEN A FAN OF COUNTRY MUSIC. I find I am vaguely aware of who's who in country, but I have never experienced a great desire to listen to country tunes or cultivate a taste for any particular country musicians. I was not attracted to the nasal and twangy sounds of country music, nor was I interested in its strict presentations of gender and sexuality; I just could not be bothered to give country music a fair shake.

Then there was k.d. lang. Since I did not follow country music in the first place, I did not become aware of lang until the release of her 1989 album *Absolute Torch and Twang*. Some of my lesbian and gay friends raved about her, but I only halfheartedly paid attention. I was also suspicious of the lesbian hero-worship of lang that often appeared in the queer press. Why were so many dykes drooling over a *country* music singer? It just did not make sense to me, nor did it appeal to me. I did not care if she created a powerful lesbian aura onstage or sported a cute butch style; I was not interested in her music. However, when I finally listened to her tune "Pullin' Back the Reins," I was amazed and deeply moved by her voice. I had to have more. I was fascinated not only by the power, range, and depth of her voice, but by the wonderful mixture of passion and mischief in her singing; and I thoroughly enjoyed the tight and playful sound of her band, the reclines. Country music—in the hands of lang—could be fun after all. I realized I had taken myself a bit too seriously, and I had taken country music too seriously. I was not necessarily inclined to listen to other country artists, but I was certainly excited about spending more time with lang's music.

So I did. And the pleasure I experience with lang's music has a great deal to do with my lesbianism *and* my previous distaste for country music. Thus, motivated by both suspicion and affection, I will engage some of her tunes within a context that includes lesbian identity and sexuality (mine and hers), the aesthetics of lesbian camp and the butch-femme dynamic, the reception of lang in the country music industry, and the fairly recent appropriation of country music by lesbian and gay bar culture.

steering clear of "the queer"

> I still receive a lot of resistance about the way I look. Particularly from the traditional country quarters. Still, I think it's loosened up a bit. Unfortunately, human beings evolve slowly. (k.d. lang, 1990)[1]

In the final chapter of *Country Music, U.S.A.*, Bill Malone describes the various trends that developed in country music in the 1970s and early 1980s.[2] He begins his discussion by noting that debates about country music—what it is, to whom, and why—have played a significant role within country music scenes since the 1970s, and the various sides of these debates are played out in the music, marketing strategies, and political alliances of the country artists themselves. He states:

> Musicians, industry leaders, and fans have been confused about what the music is or where it should go. The country music industry has discovered that its best interests lie in the distribution of a package with clouded identity, possessing no regional traits. The industry has striven to present a music that is all things to all people: middle-of-the-road and "American," but also southern, working-class, and occasionally youth-oriented and even rebellious in tone.[3]

According to Malone, many country musicians in the 1970s and early 1980s worked to revive "traditional" country music—and thereby protect it from the poison of pop music—while others successfully developed "progressive" sounds and crossover strategies.[4] The discussions of country musical style(s) published in the bimonthly magazine *Country Music* indicate that issues of "traditionalism" are still debated and fiercely defended.

However, even though musical "traditionalism" was not a central concern for all country musicians and critics in the 1970s and early 1980s, the traditional representations of gender and sexuality in country music certainly remained unchallenged. If other genres of mainstream popular music allowed for a minimal queer presence, country music made no such allowance whatsoever. Guys are guys, gals are gals, and anything queer is entirely exscripted. Even if many country tunes valorize "cheatin'" or other forms of illicit sex, the scenario is *always* heterosexual. Furthermore, the ideologies of patriotism and the nuclear family merge in the world of country music and intensify its homophobic practice. Of course, I speak as one who has been resistant to personal participation in country music, but the discourse of country music as I read it remains decidedly antiqueer.

This homophobic discourse has been thrown into total confusion by the fairly recent appropriation of country and western music in the lesbian and gay bar scenes. Cultural critic B. Ruby Rich argues that lesbian androgyny was expressed quite comfortably in country and western bars:

> In the '70s, when lesbianism took androgyny as both principle and style, the country-and-western bar was one of the only welcoming sites outside of the womyn's community. It was there, to those honky-tonk joints, that women could always go in flannel shirts and jeans and no makeup, raise no eyebrows, even dance with a girlfriend alongside all the straight country gals doing the same.[5]

Since the mid-1980s, gay and lesbian bars in major American cities have featured "country music nights" complete with line dances, square dances, and two-stepping. Although this was never unusual in cities such as Denver, Austin, and Houston, the trend reached new heights particularly in Chicago, Los Angeles, New York, San Francisco, and the Twin Cities. The Rawhide II in San Francisco and the Town House in St. Paul are completely country and western gay bars (and the Town House claims a clientele of half gay men and half lesbians). For many lesbians and gay men, hanging out and dancing to country music was and is a preferable alternative to the disco scene (either classic 1970s disco or its various 1980s derivatives). As DJ and general manager of the Townhouse, Steven Anderson puts it:

> Like the disco phenomenon, country music rekindled an interest in dancing—albeit to a different beat and a different style. The Texas two-step. Yes, it was the style of dance that seemed particularly appealing. And in the age of AIDS—when people are becoming more and more afraid to touch—I find it especially encouraging that country-western dancing incorporates an acceptable format for tactile pleasure...for being sensual without being sexual.[6]

And unlike the elaborate and far-flung fantasies of disco, the themes and scenarios presented in many country songs are often quite square, conservative, and downright sentimental.

What interests me in particular about this penchant for sentimentality, which one will not find in great doses in rap or metal, is that it coincided with the rise of the Reagan/Bush era and its propagandized image of America as morally upstanding, respectable, white, family-oriented, and hardworking: a "traditional," back-to-basics homophobic conservatism that wished the 1960s and 1970s had never happened. Thus, I find the queer participation in country and western music, as it exists in the bars, both disturbing and quite wonderful. Disturbing because it seems to buy right into the conservative project of Reagan/Bush "American traditionalism," which consequently erases queerness and allows straight society to continue to ignore and/or bash gay people. Wonderful because it enacts a massive critique of this project, seeing through its ridiculous falseness by delighting in the dorkiness of country music—in short, turning country into camp. For instance, the strict gender definition presented in country music provides excellent material for queer drag and butch-femme role-playing among both lesbians and gay men. Furthermore, the queer appropriation of country and western music in the bars has intersected with gay and lesbian rodeo folks, providing a space for them to meet and celebrate queer rodeo together. (In the United States, there is the National Gay and Lesbian Rodeo Association as well as numerous regional chapters. And of course, country and western music and dancing is the primary form of bar entertainment for these folks.) In these respects, to queerify country is, in a sense, to expose and even undo its homophobic deeds.

double crossing

> I think the time has come for me to let go of the idea of being a "country singer." Country will always be a major influence on me, but I've also been influenced by everything from opera to Ofra Haza; and I'm not prepared to make the kind of compromises that would be necessary for me to be accepted by those people [in Nashville]. At one time I did very much want to prove to them how much I honestly loved country music, but they make their own assessments whether you're honest or not. (k.d. lang, 1990)[7]

lang coined the phrase "torch and twang" to describe her particular musical style. "[T]he reason I chose the words 'torch' and 'twang' is that I would love to marry ballad jazz and country. Those are the types of music I'm most passionate about. People have incorporated jazz into country before, but I don't think anyone's dedicated their life to it."[8] As a crossover artist, lang has never enjoyed acceptance and airplay from the Nashville establishment or from rock radio, although she has a big following from both country and noncountry fans. A significant proportion of her fandom consists of lesbians and gay men, particularly lesbians.

Within the dyke subculture, lang has been thoroughly celebrated for a number of reasons. The lyrics of nearly all her songs contain no masculine pronouns; rather she employs an "I-you" mode of address that invites lesbian hearings. Second, her voice is admired for its range and shades of color. For me, what gives her vocal artistry a dykish quality is its depth and power, and her remarkable ability to take advantage of many of the conventions of country singing while simultaneously critiquing them. Lastly, lang's visual menu is enormously appealing. She challenges stereotypical presentations of gender by flaunting a consistently androgynous, if not overtly lesbian, image: nudie suits, short spiky hair, no wigs, and no makeup whatsoever. To dykes, lang's particularly bold vocal and visual styles suggest lesbian identification.

In her cover of Wynn Stewart's "Big Big Love," lang assumes a masculine subject position, and yet her performance invites a number of various dyke-oriented readings.

> Can't you feel my love a-growin'
> Can't you see it, ain't it showin'
> Oh you must be knowin'
> I got a big big love
>
> It's not the kind to be concealin'
> It's the type to be revealin'
> You must be feelin'
> I got a big big love[9]

The text of this song could suggest the "big big love" is simply that, or that it refers to a huge erection. lang's energetic and sassy performance implies the latter, yet plays on the fact that the "big big love" can be taken several ways. Indeed, to anyone familiar with Stewart's 1962 recording of this tune, originally entitled "Make Big Love," lang's version sounds deliberately raucous.[10]

Formally, the tune works within a standard AABA structure, and the harmony moves in a completely straightforward fashion: a I-V-I progression in each A section and a brief half cadence on V in each B section. The upbeat tempo and consistent rhythmic patterns in the guitars create a playful, intentionally innocent backdrop for the provocative image described in the vocals. In other words, the entirely regular form, harmony, and accompaniment play against the more explicit reading of the text, creating an ironic tension.

(Is she saying what I think she's saying? How can a girl have a hard-on, and why is she telling me about it?)

The shape of the melody, with its rhythmic push emphasizing the final word of each line, and the playful predictability of the rhymes ("growin,'" "showin,'" "knowin,'" "concealin,'" "revealin,'" etc.), set up an ironic potential that can either be subdued or celebrated. Indeed, lang's vocal delivery becomes increasingly tongue-in-cheek throughout the tune. Never shying away from the double entendre of the lyrics, she maintains a consistent volume level and gradually creates a mischievous effect during the repetitions of each verse. The "walkin'" and "talkin'" under the "great big moon above" in verse three are totally camped up by the "oohs" and "ahs" in the background, and by the nearly shouted a cappella delivery of the words "I got a big big love." Similarly, lang sings lines two through four in the repeat of verse one in a single breath; the exaggerated growls and the melodic glides on "showin'" and "knowin'" are anything but innocent.

What does it mean that lang sings in a drag role, appropriating both male imagery and a masculine subject position? On one level, she conveys that women do indeed get "hard-ons," but that descriptions of sexual arousal are too often constructed solely in terms of male anatomy. On another level, she sidesteps drag and, by toying with the notions of visibility and size, seems to suggest quite playfully the delights of female orgasm. But I hear this tune in yet a fourth way. In her article "Toward a Butch-Femme Aesthetic,"[11] Sue-Ellen Case argues that lesbians who dress and behave within a butch-femme dynamic do not reinforce heterosexual models of gender, but rather subvert them for their own lesbian purposes. The butch woman appropriates various codes of masculinity and displays them to the femme who simultaneously aims her "femininity" to the butch; both women contribute to the creation of a uniquely *lesbian* gender system. In addition,

> [T]hese women play on the phallic economy rather than to it. Both women alter this masquerading subject's function by positioning it [the phallus] between women and thus foregrounding the myths of penis and castration in the Freudian economy...In other words, these penis-related posturings were always acknowledged as roles, not biological birthrights, nor any other essentialist poses...These [lesbian] roles qua roles lend agency and self-determination to the historically passive subject, providing her with at least two options for gender identification and, with the aid of camp, an irony that allows her perception to be constructed from outside ideology, with a gender role that makes her appear as if she is inside of it...These roles are played in signs themselves and not in ontologies.[12]

Although Case discusses the butch-femme aesthetic primarily within the realm of theater, her conclusions can be adapted to critique the work of women performers in popular music.[13]

lang invites me to occupy the femme role suggested by the "you" in the lyrics of "Big Big Love." Much like the butch lesbian in the butch-femme aesthetic, her version of this tune juxtaposes conventional *musical* signs— standard form, regular harmony, and predictable rhythms—with a wonderfully mischievous vocal performance, enacting a radical and dykish twist in *gender* signs.[14]

"Big Boned Gal" presents a far more overt expression of a woman's affection and admiration for another woman. Apart from "women's music," it is highly unusual in any style of popular music to hear a woman sing about another woman who is not a mother, daughter, or sister:

> put her blue dress on
> and she'd curl her hair
> oh she'd been waiting all week
> with a bounce in her step
> and a wiggle in her walk
> she'd be swinging down the street
>
> you could tell she was ready
> by the look in her eye
> as she slipped in through the crowd
> she walked with grace
> as she entered the place
> ya, the big boned gal was proud[15]

lang sings about this "gal" with such high-spirited enthusiasm that it is no wonder that this tune never fails to generate a lively response from dykes, especially in the bars. It resonates with lesbians for a number of reasons. The narrative of dressing up, going out to dance, and being "proud" parallels the *fun* part of the coming out process—the act of coming out and flaunting it to other queer people (as opposed to straight folks), which is liberating as well as exhilarating. Furthermore, the description of the big-boned gal in verse three ("you could tell she was ready/by the look in her eyes") recalls cruising, both on the part of lang as well as the gal: the pleasure of looking and being looked at.

Musically, lang's vocal hiccups, yodels, quirky changes of register, and growls give this tune its exuberance and inspire my lesbian reading of it. Such vocal antics upset a rigid contour of melody thereby creating a rebelliousness that underscores the tune's daring premise of queer affection and desire. The control and boldness with which lang jumps from high to low and back again hardly resemble the ladylike vocal styles of Tammy Wynette, Brenda Lee, or Dolly Parton. The image of the big-boned femme and her playful attention to visual detail is met by lang's butch manner of singing.[16] "Big Boned Gal" carves a space for lesbian sensibility in *sound* and heralds one of the queerest moments in country music.

camping up the corn

> To be completely fair to those hostile country conservatives, lang's visual imagery has, at times, seemed like an elaborate parody of cowboy culture. She's appeared in publicity pictures striking the corniest Lone Ranger poses imaginable. "Sure," she concedes, "but to respect and to love something is also to understand the humour and absurdity in it. It is important to have fun with what you do" (Dave Jennings and k.d. lang, 1990).[17]

lang's sartorial statements are not all that "country conservatives" have found distasteful: her political commitment to animal rights, for example, resulted in a ban of her music on country radio stations in Kansas, Nebraska, Montana, Missouri, and Oklahoma during the summer of 1990.[18] The radio stations feared a withdrawal of financial support from members of the beef industry in both Canada and the United States because lang's vegetarianism and her views in favor of animal rights were perceived as potentially harmful to the industry's well-being. She appeared in a television commercial promoting vegetarianism that was sponsored by People for the Ethical Treatment of Animals.[19] Nothing in her *music*, however, reflects her political stance on animals. The censorship controversies surrounding 2 Live Crew and the NEA's defunding of performance artists John Fleck, Karen Finley, Holly Hughes, and Tim Miller also occurred during the summer of 1990. These debates concerned the content of art, not the beliefs of an artist expressed *outside* of her work.

However, within the country music network, a performer's image forms a central part of her reception, and radio airplay is vital for album sales. Don Gillmor of *Saturday Night* has written of k.d. lang's image: "She looked, depending on the night, like Stompin' Tom Connors or Buddy Holly on a cross-dressing spree; she didn't look like she would stand by her man. She bore no traces of country femininity, no signs of acquiescence prized by male listeners."[20] In 1989, Larry Nelson, owner of country music station WAUR in Aurora, Illinois, admitted that "a lot of country music fans are more conservative...They like a girl to look like a girl and a guy to look like a guy."[21]

Likewise, Warner Brothers's senior vice president of national country sales and promotion, Nick Hunter, acknowledged that "the image lang projects...intimidates people."[22] As lang summarizes, "It's just the media's way of saying, 'God, is she gay?' without having to actually say the word."[23] Thus, while the animal rights issue functioned as a convenient excuse to ban lang from country radio, an implicit homophobic reaction to the perceived queerness of lang was also at work in the radio boycott, allowing country conservatives to push her even farther out of the country music circuit.

lang's music, too, was perceived as a threat to "traditional" country music tastes. Critics claimed that her style was disrespectful and mocked the "honesty" of country music.[24] lang herself admits her attitude toward recent trends in country music and justifies her own approach:

> I think that there has been a continual phase in the urbanization of country music. It started with countrypolitan, which happens to be the music that I really like.
>
> But in the development of country music, I think it went through a period of urbanization which closeted, or ignored, the real humor or twang of it. You know, the early, early stuff—the stuff that created rockabilly. They got embarrassed about it and it has never been able to come out of the closet totally. It became a parody of itself.[25]

lang's use of the language of queer liberation to describe her view of urbanized country music is telling indeed and offers insight into the camp sensibility she employs in some of her tunes. For lang, to restore, or uncloset, the "real humor or twang" of country music is to engage with a camp musical strategy.

I return to Case's brief discussion of the aesthetics and practice of camp in which she concludes that the irony, wit, and artifice of camp work to reveal the constructedness of the conventions of straight sex and gender systems and liberate queers from the "regime of realist terror."[26] Although the irony and wit of k.d. lang's particular brand of camp is intended affectionately, it can be taken offensively by those country conservatives whose "regime of realist terror" camp means to dismantle.

In lang's cover of "Three Days" she camps up her performance and consequently invites a reading relevant particularly to women.

> Three days that I dread to see arrive
> Three days that I hate to be alive
> Three days filled with tears and sorrow
> Yesterday, today, and tomorrow[27]

"Three Days" moves in a regular sixteen-bar blues form and undergoes a half-step modulation before the repeat of verse two. The circular sixteen-bar form and the repetitions of each verse (with their internal repetitions of "three days") underscore the bluesy sentiment of this tune, particularly as it is expressed in the last line: "these three days start over again." As the song progresses, lang's boisterous vocal inflections exceed the boundaries of the accompaniment. On one level, her performance conveys the "tears and sorrow" of missing the absent (or former) lover. She "cries" with her voice with increasing intensity throughout the tune. On another level, what starts out as an aural tribute to Patsy Cline is soon camped up: the frequency and exaggeration of her vocal cries, glides, whimpers, and hiccups in the final statement of each verse reinterpret the three days much more physically. The three days now suggest menstruation. lang's campy vocal maneuvers re-present the "dread," the "tears and sorrow," and the knowledge that it will "start over again" to form a menstrual narrative, so to speak, and pokes fun at the cultural taboos surrounding menstruation. In so doing, she boldly parodies both the tune itself—its corny, clichéd formulas—and those who scorn camp in country music.

star starvation:
lang thangs and "real dyke" politics

> Lesbians have been the rudest to me on the road...They think I owe them something. They want me to go out to a club with them, but I don't like clubs, gay or straight. I've been to lesbian and gay conferences. I've worn a pink triangle. Where did it get me? I admire gay activists, but I'm an artist. (k.d. lang, 1992)[28]

If the country music establishment resents k.d. lang for her androgynous image, antibeef politics, and "dishonest" music, the lesbian establishment has criticized her for not being out enough in her work. Although many lesbians are wildly enthusiastic fans (lang thangs), they have had to grapple—until only very recently—with lang's refusal to come out as openly lesbian. To lesbians and queer-sensitive people who instantly recognize a lesbian sensibility and behavior, lang's dykeness is obvious.[29] In her account of a k.d. lang show at Caesar's Lake Tahoe (Nevada), lesbian critic Susie Bright writes: "She [lang] doesn't make any admission to her adoring girl fans, but she certainly teases us to death...If only I was a mysterious talent who never said a word about her private life but fulfilled every dewy-eyed homosexual crush!"[30] An

On Our Backs reader responded to Bright's article most unsympathetically:

> I hate to be a sourpuss, but all this lesbian hero-worship of k.d. lang really
> irks me. Lesbian celebrities who stay firmly wedged in the closet are bad
> enough, but lesbian celebrities who tease and prance and flirt just barely
> on the wrong side of coming out make my blood boil!...They're willing to
> soak up our love and money, but won't take the risk of coming out.[31]

Similarly, a Santa Cruz reviewer who praises k.d. lang for "her bold defiance
of the c.w. tradition" also felt that during her show lang unfairly "manipulated" and "teased" the lesbians in the audience.[32] And Stacy D'Erasmo of
the *Village Voice* bemoans lang's semisecret identity: "What makes girls in
the real world go crazy is lang's self-consciousness, an awareness of the tropes
she's manipulating that suggests she could, at any minute, say the words we
long to hear."[33]

Arlene Stein has discussed the problem of the varying degrees of outness
among lesbians in popular music, including lang:

> The arrival of the new breed of androgynous pop women [k.d. lang, Tracy
> Chapman, Michelle Shocked, Phranc, Indigo Girls], propelled in large part
> by an increasingly self-conscious lesbian audience, signals the fact that
> women can now defy conventions of femininity in popular music and still
> achieve mainstream success. But at what cost? Are "androgynous" women
> performers cowering to a homophobic industry, enacting a musical form
> of passing? Or are they pushing the limits of what is possible and, along
> with it, lesbian visibility?
>
> A growing debate pits those who would stand outside the dominant
> culture and openly name their lesbianism (even if that naming restricts
> their audience) against those who, in search of broader appeal, represent
> their sexuality more covertly.
>
> ...For the new breed of women are not particularly heterosexually
> identified, and many are no less out than their women's music predeces-
> sors [Alix Dobkin, Meg Christian, Cris Williamson]. Phranc and Two Nice
> Girls are the two most obvious examples, but much the same could be said
> for k.d. lang, probably the butchiest woman entertainer since Gladys
> Bentley (even if she'd rather support animal rights than say the "L-
> word").[34]

Obviously, at issue here is the need for positive, clear-cut lesbian representation in mainstream popular music. The visibility of lesbians in popular
culture is so thoroughly minimized that when it does surface, it is often in
hatefully negative terms, or it is enticingly suggested only to be firmly denied.
It was not until 1985 that Donna Dietch's film *Desert Hearts*, which enjoyed

mainstream circulation, presented portrayals of lesbians who finally remain lesbians (that is, they do not convert back to heterosexuality).[35] In other words, dykes are starved for representation in popular culture, particularly in music. lang satisfies this hunger to a significant, but limited, extent. The criticism levelled against her by other lesbians suggests that representation is not enough: lesbians seem to need the Perfect Star. As Lily Braindrop puts it:

> While no artists are obligated to wear their sexuality on their sleeve, it's disheartening how few major-label queers buck the stigma and address their sexuality at all. We're all tired of songs with suspiciously gender-vague lyrics and pussyfooting interview quotes like "My focus is on my art, not on my sexuality," "I keep my personal life separate," and "Oh, I would never categorize my sexuality. Who cares about that stuff anyway?" You want to know who cares about "that stuff"? Millions of queers in this country who are aching to see a mainstream performer stand up and say "Yes, I am!"[36]

And, of course, it really is not fair to insist that lang be the Perfect Star, but this need stems from the grim fact that lesbians are still a terribly oppressed minority. The ironic mechanisms of oppression work simultaneously to instill an intense desire for lesbian visibility while maintaining a need to vigorously criticize the very woman who is visibly and audibly lesbian.

I think k.d. lang has a much larger political project on her hands than most lang thangs acknowledge. Perhaps the expectation or promise to satisfy the social and political needs of her "adoring girl fans" was not even set up by lang. Rather, I perceive her as an artist who admirably attempts to bring the discourses of lesbianism and country music into some sort of mutually compatible coexistence, and it is country music that will have to shape up, not the lesbian nation.

postscript:
from country to cuntry

> It's taken me a long time to say yes to *The Advocate* because I know the repercussions are gonna be there. It's like, I want to be out. I want to be out! Man, if I didn't worry about my mother, I'd be the biggest parader in the whole world. (k.d. lang, 1992)[37]

The public comings out of Debra Chasnoff, Sandra Bernhard, and k.d. lang certainly marked 1992 as an illustrious year for lesbians. Chasnoff, who won an Academy Award for her documentary *Deadly Deception: General Electric,*

Nuclear Weapons, and Our Environment, thanked her lover, Kim Klausner, during her nationally televised acceptance speech.[38] Bernhard, who had previously maintained a smug secrecy about naming her sexuality, loudly declared, "I'm out! I'm out!" during her show *Giving till It Hurts,* which toured North America in mid-1992. In early June, k.d. lang came out officially in an interview in one of the most celebrated issues of *The Advocate.*[39] On 10 August, she appeared as a guest on *Arsenio Hall* and spoke about her decision to come out in the *Advocate* interview. She seemed relieved to have come out and yet firmly concluded that she would rather that "people focus on my music, which is ultimately the most important to me." However, about her music and her lang thangs, she remarked in a Bay Area interview that "I'm a lesbian, but my music isn't lesbian music. They [lesbian fans] have to realize that's the way I feel, and respect it."[40]

I think lang's obvious concern with *how* her audience interprets the connection(s) between her lesbianism and her music is perhaps not as crucial as the larger issue of confronting homophobia within the popular music industry. Perhaps lang's disclosure will make it a bit easier for other queers in mainstream popular music to come out, especially those who choose to come out before they have gained any success.[41] The miracles that lesbians and gay men work by coming out every day, and in everyday places, must never be underestimated, but when celebrity types come out, our existence can be validated and celebrated beyond the queer subculture. k.d. lang's disclosure marks an important historical moment for women who seek and enjoy wide-ranging presentations of gender and female sexuality— especially lesbianism—in popular culture.

Notes

This essay owes its existence to Nancy Newman. I also want to thank Lydia Hamessley and Lynn Mickelson for their encouragement and enthusiasm, and my brother, Joe Mockus, for introducing me to k.d. lang's music.

1.   "Lesley Gore on k.d. lang...and Vice Versa," *Ms.* (July/August 1990): 30.

2.   Bill Malone, "Country Music, 1972–84" in *Country Music, U.S.A.* (Austin: University of Texas Press, 1968, revised 1985), 369–416.

3.   Malone, 369.

4.   Malone, 374–412.

5.   B. Ruby Rich, "On Standing by Your Girl," *Artforum* 30 (Summer 1992): 19.

6.   Steven Anderson, "The Power of Country Music," in Al Borcherding and George

Holdgrafer, eds., *Pride Guide 1992* (Minneapolis: Twin Cities Lesbian-Gay Pride Committee and International Gay/Lesbian Archives, 1992): 82.

7. Interview with Dave Jennings, "The Twang's the Thang: k.d. lang," *Melody Maker* (26 May, 1990): 41.

8. Jennings, "The Twang's the Thang," 41.

9. Wynn Stewart (JAT Music Publishing Co., 1968), recorded on *Love's Gonna Happen to Me,* Capitol Records ST-2849.

10. I am indebted to Jim Mannheim for sharing his recording of Stewart's "Make Big Love" with me.

11. Sue-Ellen Case, "Toward a Butch-Femme Aesthetic," in Lynda Hart, ed., *Making a Spectacle: Feminist Essays on Contemporary Women's Theatre* (Ann Arbor: University of Michigan Press, 1989), 282–99.

12. Case, "Toward a Butch-Femme Aesthetic," 291–92, 297. In the anthology *The Persistent Desire: A Femme-Butch Reader,* ed. Joan Nestle (Boston: Alyson Publications, 1992), many of the essays—too numerous to cite here—discuss butch and femme not only as subversive role-playing, but as central features of lesbian gender and sexual identification.

13. See Judith A. Peraino, " 'Rip Her to Shreds': Women's Music According to a Butch-Femme Aesthetic," *repercussions* 1 (Sping 1992): 19–47.

14. I might add that the butch-femme aesthetic in country music was probably first set in motion by Dolly Parton, whose self-consciously excessive femininity can be read as a humorous critique of gender stereotyping. Needless to say, Parton also enjoys a huge lesbian and gay audience.

15. k.d. lang/Ben Mink (Bumstead Publishing/Zavion Music 1989) recorded on *Absolute Torch and Twang,* Sire Record 4–25877.

16. As many critics of k.d. lang have noted, some of her butch mannerisms, vocal and visual, resemble those of Elvis Presley. This was especially apparent in her performance of "Jingle Bell Rock" on the 1988 Christmas special of *Pee Wee's Playhouse,* which, I must say, was one of the queerest of Pee Wee's episodes: Little Richard, Grace Jones, the DelRubio Triplets, Charo, Whoopi Goldberg, and Cher, among others, were all featured guests. For other particularly lesbian fascinations with Elvis, see Sue Wise, "Sexing Elvis," Simon Frith and Andrew Goodwin, eds., *On Record: Rock, Pop and the Written Word* (New York: Pantheon, 1990), 390–98; and Phyllis Christopher, "Elvis Herselvis," *On Our Backs* 7 (July/August 1991): 23–27.

17. Jennings, "The Twang's the Thang," 41.

18. Jeffrey Abelson, "Industry Should Defend k.d. lang's Rights: Radio Boycott Sets Bad Precedent," *Billboard Magazine* 102 (18 August, 1990): 11.

19. Abelson, "Industry Should Defend k.d. lang's Rights: Radio Boycott Sets Bad Precedent," 11.

20. Don Gillmor, "The Reincarnation of Kathryn Dawn," *Saturday Night* 105 (June 1990): 30.

21. Quoted in Katherine Seigenthaler, "Hot Singer, Cool Reception," *Chicago Tribune* (12 September, 1989), section 5: 2.

22. Quoted in Sean Ross, "No Absolutes for Lyle & Lang: Country PDs Resist Grammy Winners," *Billboard* 102 (10 March 1990): 14.

23. Quoted in Linda Kohanov, "k.d. lang," *Pulse!* (April 1992): 74.

24. See the scathing review of *Absolute Torch and Twang* by Rich Kienzle in *Country Music* (Sept/Oct 1989): 59. In this review, Kienzle also vents his spleen over lang's previous album, *Shadowland*. He claims that "*honesty* is what country music has always been about, and in [lang's] case, I don't hear much" (emphasis mine). See also Ross, "No Absolutes for Lyle & Lang," 14; Tom De Savia, "k.d. lang's Truly Western Experience," *Cash Box Magazine* (10 June 1989): 7.

25. De Savia, "k.d. lang's Truly Western Experience," 7.

26. Case, "Toward a Butch-Femme Aesthetic," 287–88.

27. Willie Nelson and Faron Young, Pamper Publishing, 1962, Capitol Records 4696.

28. Quoted in Adam Block, "k.d.: Lesbians Have Been the Rudest to Me," *The Advocate* 595 (28 January 1992): 66.

29. Julia Sweeney's "Pat" on *Saturday Night Live* can be read in much the same way. Pat's wonderful insistence on not naming her gender or sexuality puzzles her (presumably) straight officemates, even though the lesbian subtext of Pat's behavior is quite apparent.

30. Susie Bright, "Famous Lesbian Dilemmas," *Susie Sexpert's Lesbian Sex World* (Pittsburgh and San Francisco: Cleis Press, 1990), 148–49.

31. Christina Winter, Letters, *On Our Backs* (March/April 1990): 5.

32. Joan Edwards, "k.d. lang Blazing Trails," *Matrix Women's Newsmagazine* 13 (October 1989): 19.

33. "Canadian Love Call," *Village Voice* 37 (2 June 1992): 78.

34. Arlene Stein, "Androgyny Goes Pop: But Is It Lesbian Music?" *Out/Look* 12 (Spring 1991): 26–33.

35. I find it very interesting that this film, the story of which takes place in Reno, Nevada, 1959, features the music of Patsy Cline. This complicates my earlier assertion that queerness and country music stand discursively opposed to one another.

36. Lily Braindrop, "Pop Goes Queer," *The Advocate* 587 (8 October 1991): 37.

37. Brendan Lemon, "Virgin Territory: k.d. lang," *The Advocate* 605 (16 June 1992), 44.

38. For queer coverage of this event, see Robin Stevens, "Dykes' Night out at the Oscars," *Out/Look* 17 (Summer 1992): 31–34.

39. Lemon, "Virgin Territory," 34–46. lang also discusses her tortured relationship with the country music industry as well as her recent musical style shift to "postnuclear cabaret" on her latest compact disc, *Ingénue*.

40. Barry Walters, "k.d. lang: it's a little bit fun being oppressed," *San Francisco Examiner* (2 August 1992), D1.

41. Currently thriving in North America is an active nonassimilationist queer music scene led by openly gay and lesbian performers and recording labels. See Braindrop, "Pop Goes Queer"; Adam Block, "Gary Floyd, Rockin' Bear"; Lily Braindrop and Adam Block, "Tribe 8 and Bay Area Acts"; Doug Sadownick and Stuart Timmons, "Drance and the Amoeba Artists"; Jim Fouratt and Victoria Starr, "The Best of the Big Apple"; Michael Bronski and Jim Provenzano, "Adult Children and a Foxx"; Adam Block, "Queer Music by Mail"; all in *The Advocate* 587 (8 October 1991): 37–44.

Part Three

CONSORTS

12

LESBIAN COMPOSITIONAL PROCESS
One Lover-Composer's Perspective

Jennifer Rycenga

To be swept up by the dialectic is
to experience a plunge to freedom...
(but) thought cannot
be allowed to dissolve into a
"Bacchanalian revelry"...Free creative
power assures the plunge to freedom.[1]

—Raya Dunayevskaya

$\mathcal{B}$EING A LESBIAN MAKES A DIFFERENCE, transforms the thought/action process that is composition. To make such a claim is not an invitation to an old essentialism/constructionism debate, but to be in movement beyond static and deterministic categories. The attitude to the world made possible by both music and lesbian sexuality opens routes to an involved, attentive materiality/temporality. This calls forth discussion of three subjects that are normally taboo by themselves, let alone in combination: sexuality, the process of creativity, and ontology. By ontology I do not mean any closed system, but an active sense that the experience/process of Be-ing[2] and know-ing—i.e., living—is real: "It has all the meaning we can make of it."[3]

For me, touching overlapping sources of power—music, lesbian sexuality, political creativity, and a sense of the ever-changing modes of Be-ing—rendered manifest how they were identical/identified and yet distinct.[4] As analogies and connections multiplied, the situation called forth honesty about my own self, a deep critical analysis of my self and the culture(s) in which I live, and a realization of the very nature and complexity of power, both positive and negative. I came out as a lesbian because of my compositional and creative work. The music I was hearing and feeling in my body, the projects I wanted to accomplish musically, the relation of music to the rest of the human situation—all of these summoned a strongly physical response from me. If it had not been for the ways in which music acted upon me, music acted with me, music touched me, it is unlikely that I would have been able to act as decisively in a physical sense as I did. There is no reason to dismiss the *active* role of music herSelf in this process.

In my compositional biography, there are three key pieces that I wrote by "listening" to what the *music* was giving as direction, rather than insisting on my own preconceived ideas of ordering. The first two of these were written (in 1980 and 1984, respectively) before I came out and marked high points in the sensuality of my writing. Significantly, both of these times I subsequently ran away from this "irresponsible" approach and freedom, which seemed alarmingly "nontechnical." While I have now acknowledged this sensuality and freedom in my music and in myself, an increasingly honest relationship with music creates its own fears, promises, and potentials. In this article I outline some of my feminist reflections as a composer and musician. These include the politics of composition, the ontological condition of music,[5] the relationship of lesbian tactility to musical-temporal thinking, and a particular set of ruminations pertaining to my current compositional project.

Philosophically, my positionality resides with radical feminism, and especially its utopian ontology based on relational interplay, on dereifying quality and experience,[6] and on attentiveness to the ways of reality made manifest. My political philosophy—not really a separate category from philosophy, of course—has been particularly influenced by Hoagland's *Lesbian Ethics*, Audre Lorde's essays and poetry, and the dialectical Marxist-humanism of Raya Dunayevskaya.[7]

The Human Politics of Music

The human politics of music are concerned with the cooperative nature of musical art. Discussions with other women musicians and composers, particularly in the San Francisco Bay Area ensemble Ovaryaction,[8] helped to reveal to me the hierarchy of composers to performers. Most of the women identified primarily as performers, but no one of them was lacking in compositional/creative abilities. We each had had different experiences with the authoritarian and patriarchal organization of Western art and popular musics, but one of the most illuminating differences between us concerned my attitudes toward music as a composer and those of the performers. My performer friends spoke of being "controlled by expectations of what the music was supposed to be" exclusive of their own subjectivity.[9] Performers are placed in situations where they are structurally acting as cogs in a machine, where they are only intended to "play a part" in the larger scheme of someone else—that someone else being the composer.[10] A schematic view of the hierarchy suggested by these discussions would be: composer—composer's intentions—abstract idea of "Music"—written music as a text[11]— the instrument[12]—the physical performer[13]—the performer as individual. To subvert this hierarchy, I have been working to establish a noncoercive and nonpatronizing (and nonmatronizing) creative relationship with my musicians—writing with specific women and men in mind,[14] and working with their creative input, be that improvisation, interpretation, or precompositional discussion of what the performer wants in—and from—a piece. The approach is meant to value the subjectivity of all musicians in as many ways as possible.[15] The performer's creative input is part of the compositional process, and the performer is no longer just a replaceable part in a larger labor scheme devised by the composer.

The analogy I now prefer is that of a seamstress—both the performer/friend and her instrument are naked bodies[16] for which the composer designs an article of clothing. The piece/garment should highlight both the performer/instrument and itself, not so much to expose their peculiarities, but to reveal their underlying life.[17] This means that the player and her instruments are not "mere instruments"—either for the composer, the composer's ideas, or the performer's own virtuosity. Composition can thus approximate friendship, discourse, and dialogue.

Another way of viewing the situation is to redefine the nature of composition. Western art music relies on compositions having fixed formats; thus *Grove's Dictionary* can say that composition "is a term usually referring to a piece of music embodied in written form."[18] Obviously, this is ethnocentric, anachronistic in the age of sound recording (let alone oral culture), and extrinsic to the sound itself—implying that music composition only takes place in the alienated mode of writing. But if we drop the offensive "written" part, the value that guides this definition is one of preservation, the sense that a composition is a finished product which can be repeated in performance. This concept of repetition is based on the idea that any performer who can "handle the part" will be adequate—no further creative input is designated from the performer. Furthermore, the etymology of the word "composition" turns on the concept of "putting together" and "putting in proper form or order." This is implicit in a Western art music understanding of composition: it involves planning, technical skill and knowledge, and a grasp of the whole as it is exhibited in the ordering network of form.

However, these definitions *all eliminate the performer.* They are endemic to the division of intellectual and physical musicality that runs as a mind/body dualism through much of Western intellectual history.[19] The kind of human politics that I cultivate in compositional situations among women would fit a broader definition, in which composition consists of *the establishment of a musical matrix with some established elements/directions, for the purpose of facilitating interactions with musical materials.*[20] Such a definition encourages everyone—composers, performers, listeners—to participate in the materiality of music itSelf rather than to have music depend on external systems of validation.[21]

It can also establish what I have referred to elsewhere as situations of composer-performer trust.[22] For instance, musical systems that integrate composition and improvisation, such as the two classical systems of India— Hindustani and Karnatic— or bebop and postbop jazz styles, presuppose ongoing *musical agency* on the part of the performers. Lesbian compositional process, at least for this composer, has to create situations that have similar parameters, though they may not imitate this exact compositional/ improvisational dynamic.[23] Situations of musical trust will not only deconstruct the composer's presumed authority and prestige, but stress the agency, interaction, and extension of the situation, over time, of all involved.[24] Thus the human politics of music can become a location for an ethics that is not judgmental, but relational.

The Ontological Condition of Music

The ontological condition of music is centrally related to my lesbian musical reflection. Suzanne G. Cusick suggestively names the idea of music as a lover;[25] my own thought proceeds on similar lines: that music is alive within the network of connectivity in which it participates. Thus it has a life and sacrality[26] as autonomous and interconnected as anybody else's.[27]

Such a claim sounds initially preposterous, but there are crucial ethical reasons why it should be considered. Our ability to conceptualize such possibilities is blocked by dualism and binary thinking. It is my contention, as a scholar of religion, that "objectivity" and "dualism" are not only the root causes of all oppression, but that, in their modern Western secular guise, they represent a specifically *Christian heresy* that has effectively emptied the world of significance. In the transcendent worldview of Christianity, the world was never inherently sacred, but was made so (temporarily) by association with the creator-deity. When the European Enlightenment and post-Enlightenment thinkers eliminated that deity, or made that deity disappear (into the infamous "watchmaker" role), they did not rethink the rest of the metaphysical system on which it was based. Having eliminated the transcendent source of sacrality (i.e. "God"), the world was no longer sacred by association. But the possibility that the world was meaningful (in a dynamic sense) in and of itself was also dismissed. In other words, much of the last two centuries in Western philosophical thought has been built on a beheaded transcendent system.

The result of this is that the very possibility of reality—and with it concepts such as freedom and agency—have been rendered nearly impossible in the logocentric disciplines of philosophy in this century. This ranges from the analytic philosophy of midcentury to current trends in postmodernism. The underlying assumption is that language can—either through increased "scientific" precision or through adroit wordplay—construct or deconstruct a world that "makes sense." The power of language to name, to articulate, to define/redefine/unmask, is not fundamentally questioned. Yet some of our experiences—most notably our tactility and our musicality—do not fit any linguistic model, and, therefore, language alone is incapable of containing or expressing or *even breaking up* the entirety of reality.[28]

> Music cannot be described adequately in language.
> But few refrain from *trying* to define music in words.

Musical analysis provides a compelling example. There are two basic types of methodology in present-day academia. The first is the time-honored analysis that is taught under the titles of musicology and music theory, in which music is considered exclusively in its own terms, but in such a way that it is reduced to the point of meaninglessness—its connectivity with social/historical, erotic, personal, and expressive dimensions is scorned and virtually ignored. The second is represented by ethnomusicology, and by the burgeoning research into gender and sexuality studies in music. This works from the basis that music is socially organized sound and that music is a product of, and producer of, human culture. In the rush to understand how music is structured—be it in formal analysis or through approaches that consider social organization and the production of music—music itSelf, as a Self, as the living result of human interactions, is not listened to or heard.

When music itSelf is not given its full import, then its significance becomes instrumental to something else, be that social structures or formal structures. I will stridently maintain otherwise, that *music needs no external system for its validation and significance (in order to reveal the materiality in the world that is music). Music, in its network of connections to physical reality, living musicians, and historical/social situations, is its own validation and significance.*

Thus, in protest, I call mySelf not a philosopher *of* music, but a philosopher *with* music—likewise a composer not *of* music, but *with* music, and not a lover *of* music, but lovers *with* music. The change of preposition implies an attempt to think *with* or think *along with* music, rather than to think *about* music in the abstract or at a distance.

I am *not* suggesting a New Age philosophy here, since that movement has shamelessly treated music as background atmosphere, or as a high road to meditation, health, metaphysics—anything but music as music. I *am* suggesting that the way out of dualism—and out of similarly unfruitful debates such as essentialism versus constructionism —is (a) to combine the two ideas (so that, for example, music has both immediate and mediated qualities) and (b) to at least tentatively assume life qualities in all we know.[29] Foremost among these qualities are dynamism, autonomy, and interrelation. Thus, what I refer to as "life qualities" are not unchanging, quantifiable static "essences" or even "categories"—for these would lack growth. Likewise, the given materials of our lives—be they gender roles, clothing, art forms, etc.— are not empty lifeless toys, which are only given breath by human activity—for these would lack autonomy. Rather I am suggesting that it is in the constant interaction between living entities, between existents, that significant (ontological) process occurs.

This discussion is informed by two crucial radical feminist philosophical concepts. The first is Mary Daly's *Nag-Gnosticism*, which she defines as "the philosophy of those who Sense with certainty the reality of transcendental knowledge and at the same time never cease to Nag our Selves and Others with recurrent awareness of questions and uncertainties; the philosophy of those who overcome the pseudodichotomy between transcendence and immanence, between otherworldliness and worldliness."[30] The second is Sarah Hoagland's *autokeonony*. She defines autokoenony as "a self who is both separate and related, a self which is neither autonomous nor dissolved: a self in community who is one among many."[31] "She does not merge with others, nor does she estrange herself; she *interacts* with others in situations."[32] This principle illustrates an intersection where questions of significance, ethics, creative activity with matter and with each other as women come together. The final clause of the second quotation contains all of this rather succinctly: "She [a lesbian] interacts [is therefore an active agent with other active agents (*not* 'things') who can act] with others [acknowledging otherness and, by implication, calling forth an ethic of recognition and respect] in situations [meaning the world exists in time, space, and matter, in specifics, in details, *not* in the abstract, but in concrete situations]."

Similarly, relationships between women call for ethical responses that entail recognition and respect: recognition of the other's existence and her attendant joys and sufferings, and respect for both her autonomy and the ways in which she is connected (necessarily *and* by choice)[33] to the whole. If music has ontological status as a kind of living be-ing, or if we are willing to approach it in this manner by analogy because of its connectivity and dynamic existence in time, then the relationships of women evoked in lesbian community (both erotic and not) parallel the compositional relationship to music I am trying to live—they each call for ethical, political, and spiritual/material *attentiveness.*

Both lesbian activity and musical activity are direct ways of engaging our tactility with the physicality of the world. I refer to this as *materiality,* by which I mean a thorough and complete involvement in the matrix of the physical world. Lesbianism is no detached political ideal—it is an embodied tactile/political/erotic/personal activity. It is a way in which our physical Selves interact with women, and with women in/to the world. I believe that our lesbian creativity as lovers and musicians[34] involves a direct interplay and intimate contact with materiality[35] in a manner that implies that material can be and is a location for relationship. Materiality characterizes those interactions where, to speak (non)metaphorically, one's hands get dirty in the soil.

As a lesbian creative artist/philosopher, I can no longer responsibly discuss anything called metaphysics.[36] No longer should we refer to what we do philosophically as "going beyond physics," but instead start from the physical. Therefore I call what I am thinking here *panenphysicality*—a neologism based on panentheism. It means that all is matter/energy,[37] but matter/energy is more than we can know. I should clarify that I do *not* mean that the totality of the universe is in some sense comprehensible, but is regrettably so vast that it is beyond our limited abilities to understand it. What I am suggesting is that the physical/dynamic world we are in is infinite in extension, specifically as it is changing, transforming, becoming.

Panenphysicality encourages a simultaneity of monism and pluralism. One corollary of such an approach is that "difference"—that much-touted and little-actualized value—is neither erased in a false unity (that would be monism, in which all perceived difference is, in the final analysis, illusion), nor rendered divisive (that would be dualism, in which resolution of difference is only achieved by defeat/elimination of the Other), nor made incomprehensible (that would be a radical pluralism—tolerably close to postmodernism—in which there is no shared ground, and all perceived similarity or identity is, in the final analysis, illusion). What this can mean for lesbian theory and creativity is that our different[38] experiences of the physical are generative of our "spiritual" world, so lesbian experience—sexual, affectional, artistic, political—based in our tactility, results in a radically different sense of how matter is perceived, what its creative potential is, and how to *communicate with* it, than we find in heterosexuality, gay male sexuality, asceticism, or negative oppressive systems such as heterosexism, patriarchy, or imperialism.[39]

This also means that music, in its physicality, takes on the quality of a heirophany—it reveals the sacrality of the universe (that is, its monistic side), of the particular moment/piece/voice we are hearing (that is, its particularity and pluralism—the infinitude of moments of interaction), and of itSelf (the music as matrix/mediatrix). Music is not mute, but dialogic with us.

Temporality

Music composition entails actively engaging with time—entering into it, experiencing it, working with it, trying to comprehend how it can be, is, and will be experienced by others. And it is in this relation to temporality that lesbian compositional process is present. This is because women's bodily experience of time is different from men's, both in terms of a life course (i.e., a greater number of physical life changes such as menstruation, menopause, pregnancy, etc.) and, even more to the point, in terms of lesbian sexuality. In lesbian sexuality, there is a participation in time in a radically different sense than any sexuality that involves the phallus. Beginnings, endings, plateaus, goals, climaxes, interactions, uses of the body, ways of pacing—all are, in my experience, suggestive of a musical texturing of temporality, and a texturing that is distinguishable from sexualities that involve men.[40]

Susan McClary discusses issues of time, music, and gender in relation to Janika Vandervelde's composition *Genesis II*.[41] McClary suggests that the piece re-presents the historical conflict between a stable, cyclical sense of "timelessness" and a narrative-driven struggle that seeks the eventual "transcendence and obliteration of time."[42] She further speculates, on the basis of in-class gender-based reactions, that these two approaches to time reflect two different experiences of sexuality:

> many women students recognize in the clockwork an image of female
> erotic pleasure—pleasure that is not concerned with being somewhere
> else...By contrast, many of the men in the classes often report having heard
> the clockwork as a "void," and they tend to be relieved when the strings
> rush in to "make something happen."[43]

McClary is contrasting linear, quantitative, successive, "teleological," spatialized,[44] measured time with an overlapping, "cyclical," intensive, qualitative
experience of time—what Bergson called the *durée*. McClary summarizes this
contrast in her essay on Laurie Anderson: "Narrative is...sacrificed for the
sake of sustained pleasure."[45] I certainly agree with McClary's basic analysis of
a *historical* conflict between a stable cyclical sense of timelessness and a narrative-driven struggle that seeks the eventual transcendence and obliteration
of time. I further agree that this struggle can be heard in a great deal of
Western music(s), and that it has roots in gendered approaches to sexualities.

However, all of this is based on a logocentric and visual philosophic
ground—almost a literalizing and spatializing of time, indeed a reification
of it into lines, points, "timelessness", etc. We have, as musicians, a unique
philosophical opportunity to interact with time—the musical question, it
seems to me, is whether or not music is conceived as being *about* time (i.e., a
commentary on time) or as *be-ing time*. I am suggesting that time itself—
not a reification of it (which almost all literary attempts to describe it
are)—is an essential, intrinsic element of music, is a part of its be-ing. In
saying this, I am not denying the social constructedness of music. But
acknowledging construction does not mean denying that music has its own
nature, any more than acknowledging the atmospheric and geological conditions of the earth takes away from the dynamic nature of particular plants.
The ecological network makes distinct plants possible, and distinct natures
of plants make the dynamic growth of the ecological network possible.
Similarly, music *is* time, has its be-ing in time, is connected to the network
of the universe at the node of temporality.

As a composer, I have found lesbian sexuality to create ideal atmospheric
and geological conditions (to be a hothouse, even) for the growth of time.
What is most telling for me is the way in which two women can use their bodies to *cocreate* time and *develop*[46] telos. It is the experience of being enwrapped
in time, inseparable from it, a part of it, that links music and lesbianism. It is
not a matter of translating sexual experience into a narrative structure or
antinarrative structure—that is only part of the whole.[47] Furthermore, narrative structures, distinguished from immersion in temporality, introduce a

specter of literalism between eroticism and its musical expression. While both language and sight can play a key role in erotic situations, as a lesbian composer, I feel that I have the philosophicomusical liberty/ability to becloud and erase—through temporality—the lines between experience and story, between experience and expression. Love-making is simultaneously experience and expression, and music can be too. While narrative is an important part of our universe, it is *not* temporality—it is *about* time, *about* memory, *about* re-counting.[48] Of course music is erotic because of culturally encoded signals, but it is just as much erotic at root because it is involved in the substance of life—temporality—and when you are involved in music (e.g., dancing, performing, singing along, etc.) you cannot be detached from the movement of time.[49] It is this that I believe Pauline Oliveros means when she says that "music in any of its multitudinous manifestations is a sign of life. Sound *is* intelligence."[50] Music is life, because it inherently involves motion, perception, reflection, separation/connection, materiality, process, relationality—it is, at root, *involved.*[51]

Briseis and Penthesilea: An Opera Project

Given these philosophic roots, it may at first seem incongruous that the project I am currently working on is a large-scale narrative opera, based on a most famous story in Western civilization—the Trojan War. The opera primarily concerns two women who are very much in the midst of the Trojan conflict, and yet who remain marginalized in the traditional telling of it. The first is Briseis, the war slave of Achilles who is taken by Agamemnon in order to punish and humiliate Achilles, therefore setting in motion the action of the *Iliad.* Her own subjectivity is virtually ignored in the *Iliad*—she is tokenistically granted one speech in the poem.[52]

The other major female character in the opera is the Amazon, Penthesilea. Her story is not Homeric but is included—most likely to fill out the heroic résumé of Achilles—in all synopses of the war. Interestingly, no two versions tell it in precisely the same way, but all ancient sources agree that Achilles[53] slays her and, after killing her, takes a "romantic" interest in her: necrophilia seems a more precise description. Within the opera I am writing, I have adopted an ancient telling in which Penthesilea at first slays Achilles, but the Olympian gods are so shocked by this reversal of fate that they resuscitate Achilles, who returns to slay Penthesilea.

As I have conceived the plotting in the libretto, these two women appeal to me both because they had the strength to resist patriarchy in its baldest forms, and because, while they were both critical of the war, they did not have (or take) the option of detaching themselves from the horror around them. Briseis, as a slave and rape victim, has been dragged into the conflict against her will; Penthesilea feels a mixture of compulsion and free will taking her to Troy—but neither of them succumbs to the litany of complaint that marks Euripides's *Trojan Women*. Likewise, neither of them presume that the men might listen to them, as Berlioz's Cassandra does (to her perpetual frustration).[54]

Given the subject matter, the musical tone is rarely of the ecstatic character of lesbian love-making. Relations between the Amazons provide some occasions for eroticism, but the focus of the piece is on the entire scope of relations between women. This includes women's hostility toward each other (e.g., the reaction of the Trojan women to the Amazons), as well as the full range of what would fall under Janice Raymond's conception of "Gyn/affection."[55]

This does not mean that the compositional insights enunciated above are invalid. On the contrary; I never intended to imply any literalism or translation of lesbian sexuality into musical expression. Rather, lesbian compositional process refers to a way of interacting with materiality and temporality that permeates my musical thinking in such a way as to be inclusive of a lesbian-feminist identity: an identity that enthusiastically includes, but is not limited to, genital activity, reflecting an orientation toward the universe.

The three basic topics that I addressed above are very much present in my thinking about this piece. First, I have worked closely with my performers, especially singers, from the beginning of the project and have tried to understand their input both before pieces are written and afterward, to give them broad interpretive scope in the finished works. Second, my own attentiveness and recognition of music's autonomy and relatedness to myself has led me into an intensity around the very act of composing that is, in some ways, like a love affair— exhilarating, exhausting, and time-consuming. I have always been a composer who will attempt to play the instruments I am writing for, to test the sensations of blowing air through them, or pulling a bow across strings. This kind of materiality now extends into every rhythmic and melodic gesture; I want to feel these as part of entire body motions, to experience the pull of their own direction. Third, my participation in compositional temporality is radically different. I used to find myself planning the lengths of pieces before I embarked on a new work, but this is no longer the case. Individual pieces seem to suggest their own time frames. I sincerely doubt that the completed work will be amenable to a single-night performance, or to any type of linear presentation. This is not to deny the veritable arrowlike trajectory of narrative in the plot—these women are constantly involved in action and activity, enmeshed in it. But each moment, each number, is not defined

Example 1

Example 1, continued

solely by its historical placement, by its relation to sequential time. The immediate experience of *durée*—even (always) in the midst of succession—is the act of be-ing/becoming.

As an example, in one of Briseis's first pieces—when she is trying to touch her own despair at being a war slave, realizing that her body is not her own—the musical temporality reflects an emptiness of time in which thought simply goes around in circles, seeing dilemmas, but unable to solve them. While the piece can be understood in an abab-coda form, its sense of proportion is not a major formal consideration, and there are literally "dead spots"—temporal quicksand that threatens to make the music immobile. The instrumentation—electric guitar, electric bass, and trombone—maintains a rather austere and sparse contrapuntal texture and only makes unified rhythmic statements at moments of negative self-declaration by Briseis ("Not I, not I, but men live in me").[56] The transition from the first a section to the b section shows much of what I have discussed (example 1)—the moment of stillness that, in this case, suddenly produces the chordal guitar entrance, Briseis's vocal range and logic moving in small circles, the overlapping counterpoints that keep the rhythmic framework out of focus, the harmonic progression itself, which is cyclic rather than telic, and so on. While it is not for me to say if I have achieved what is possible in this regard, I do know that my involvement with the material of the piece (both musical and topical), my strong gyn/affection with Ellen McDonald (the singer cocreating this role) and my own musical and physical/erotic knowledge of temporality helped to make this piece what it is.

While Briseis has, throughout the opera, a kind of self-contained metaeroticism, Penthesilea has an overt erotic charisma. She is a lesbian, from a land of women, leading an army of women who kill men. Briseis, having been repeatedly violated physically, does not trust touch of any kind, while Penthesilea has been nearly invulnerable physically. Touch is always clear for her—either agonistically combative or consensually erotic. Penthesilea's eroticism is simply a part of who she is. But her stage presence is not that of a "dyke on the make"—her eroticism is a fount of energy, not looking to exploit, but to enspark. In her first solo piece (analogous to the one discussed for Briseis), Penthesilea sings with only one instrument, a cello, which is wrapped around her like a garment—the two lines breathing as one. The sense of temporality reflects what happens to the overenthusiastic Amazon when she is hit with the kind of sensory and psychic chaos that greets her on her arrival in Troy: the scene includes sobbing women, the body of the recently slain Hector, the gloomy prophecies of Cassandra, the lesbophobic contempt of Andromache, and the unique strength of Briseis

Example 2

(who resists Penthesilea's attempts to initiate friendship). When Penthesilea is alone, her mind races faster than the subjects can be considered, she flits from mood to mood, and the music only expands when she is ready to concentrate her energy in some direction for a short time. This restlessness is not so much a wandering desire for a goal as it is the living impossibility of being fully who she is in a linear world. She cannot sing everything at once, so she sings everything consecutively (and therefore contradictorily) and not fully, because she doesn't have the time (or leisure) to do that. Formally, this means that the unity of the piece comes from what Penthesilea does to transform her energy, her musical materials, rather than from the imposition of order upon those materials. The entire piece is, in a sense, explosive, but not because it is headed toward a climax. Penthesilea (as befits an Amazon lesbian) is always "on the edge." Example 2 shows the sweep of an accelerating passage, which threatens to climax in anger (circa measure 72 to 75) before Penthesilea recalls the principle of duality (continuum) over dualism (oppositional poles), and the anger melts into amazed awe (measure 76 to 79). Her sense of temporality is here telescoped, but it reflects the basic principle of tension, release, and warmth coexisting, rather than tension leading to release.

The singer who is cocreating this role, Elaine Valby, and I have ardently discussed the possibilities and avenues open to a character such as Penthesilea on the operatic stage. The challenge of simultaneously being focused and diffused, both musically and dramatically, could not be merely an invention or a projection strictly from compositional intellect. Both Briseis and Penthesilea provide cases where the input of the women singing these roles has been essential *in expanding the creative possibilities.* Neither compositional solipsism nor performer disinterest is tolerable in such a situation. I am fortunate and grateful to have these collaborators, who have spurred the growth of the process described in this article.

Conclusion

Among our modes of being in the world, music and physical contact with others (especially in their heightened conscious and consensual modes, respectively, of performance and sexuality) grant us munificent insight into time, and how we can feel and live it. This does not mean that any piece of music needs to succumb to a literalism of reproducing the temporal experience of sexual love. But it can mean that the ways in which we choose to know time will be reflective and reflexive of our transformative musical and sexual power.

As I engage the process of composing this opera, I find that it is giving me the opportunity to live out some of the impulses of a lesbian compositional project. Various decisions reflect this, including my preference for smaller orchestrations[57], contrapuntal intimacy between singers and instruments, and a sense of form that is both fluid and structured. There are problems and inconsistencies in the attempt to live authentically what I have proposed here. Some of these are caused by singer-collaborators being located in distant geographic ports, and others are caused by the time constraints of having to compose while also teaching full-time, or of having to prepare for imminent performances. But overall, I have been transformed by the self-consciousness with which I examine my compositional craft.

Recognizing the subjectivity of all women/performers, relying on a panen-physical worldview, and basking in temporality are direct results, for me, of being both a lesbian and a creative musician. Lesbian sexuality and artistic creativity have elicited a heightened awareness and potential for both my attentiveness to women and the world and my freedom to live authentically. This attentiveness and creative freedom have operated both in conjunction with each other and along parallel paths. The complexity of identities that each lesbian/musician brings to shared encounters with body/sound/time can exact from each of us both exhaustive thinking and exhausting ecstasy.

Notes

My thanks for this paper include most of the women musicians in my life, but for specific help and discussion I would like to acknowledge Ruth Charloff, Michelle Landau, Staphanie Dumoski, Mari Gasiorowicz, Laura Kopase, Clara Rycenga Marchese, Ellen McDonald, Maggie McNaught, Anne Pagliarulo, Yamuna Sangarasivam, Jane Sheperd, Elaine Valby, and David Alan Black. A version of this paper was presented in Minneapolis in June 1991 at the Feminist Theory and Music Conference. I appreciate comments received from Catherine Roma, Karen Pegley, J. Michelle Edwards, Mitchell Morris, Paul Attinello, Suzanne G. Cusick, Judith Peraino, Philip Brett, Elizabeth Wood, and Gary C. Thomas.

1.   Raya Dunayevskaya, "Hegel's Absolute as New Beginning," (Chicago: News and Letters Reprint; originally published in Warren E. Steinkraus and Kenneth L. Schmitz, eds., *Art and Logic in Hegel's Philosophy*, Atlantic Highlands, N.J.: Humanities Press, 1980), 3, 7.

2.   Mary Daly, *Beyond God the Father: Toward a Philosophy of Women's Liberation* (Boston: Beacon Press, 1973), 183.

3. Judy Grahn, "Here in the Sunrise," in *The Queen of Wands* (Trumansburg, N.Y.: Crossing Press, 1982), 2.

4. This is, of course, the philosophical question of the One and the Many. The dialectical tension *and* connection between unity and multiplicity is what makes both diversity and unity (in a political situation, or in the given situation of Life itSelf) possible. I deal with this question in greater depth below, but I also recommend the reader to Mary Daly, *Pure Lust: Elemental Feminist Philosophy* (Boston: Beacon Press, 1984), 352–53, and the unifying telos of human freedom in relation to the historic forces for revolutionary change as detailed by Raya Dunayevskaya in all her work; the reader may be especially recommended to *Rosa Luxemburg, Women's Liberation, and Marx's Philosophy of Revolution* (2nd edition, Urbana, Il.: University of Illinois Press, 1991), wherein the argument is embedded in the very nature of dialectics. What needs to be maintained in any feminist reflection on the One and the Many is that the One is not a static category (nor one deserving of hierarchic superiority), and that the Many are neither disparate, nor collapsible, reducible fragments.

5. This article does not really attempt to deal with the epistemology of music. If some of my theories here are correct, it would be contradictory to attempt an epistemology of music in language.

6. In fact, as I read and interpret these ideas, radical feminism *deifies* quality and experience, as long as one remembers that "deity" is not a static or separate entity, but a dynamic, immanent verb.

7. See Sarah Lucia Hoagland, *Lesbian Ethics: Toward New Value* (Palo Alto, Calif.: Institute of Lesbian Studies, 1988); Audre Lorde, *Sister Outsider: Essays and Speeches* (Freedom, Calif.: Crossing Press, 1984); Raya Dunayevskaya, *Philosophy and Revolution: From Hegel to Sartre, and from Marx to Mao* (3rd edition, New York: Columbia University Press, 1989); and *Marxism and Freedom from 1776 to Today* (4th edition, New York: Columbia University Press, 1988).

8. The members of Ovaryaction at the time when I was involved with the group included Nina Egert, Gila Rayberg, Deborah Katz, Carol Adee, Anne Pagliarulo, Ellen McDonald, Carla Atkins, Johanna Johnson, Mantra ben-Yaakova, and Thea Farhadian.

9. Personal communication with Ellen McDonald.

10. This is, of course, akin to a labor analysis. As Dunayevskaya points out in her humanist reading of Marx's analysis of capitalism, exploitative conditions produce situations in which "relations between men [sic] appear as relations *between things* because that is what '*they really are*'" (Dunayevskaya, *Marxism and Freedom*, 111, emphasis mine). The extent to which the authoritarian relations between composers and performers mirror similar structures in all of society cannot be overlooked or dismissed. Composers often act as though they are the people with the master plan, who organize how, when, where, and what performers will do.

11. The written musical text then becomes an icon *against which* the performer is evaluated. Thanks to Philip Brett for recalling this to my attention.

12. The instrument, too, can become an icon that receives far more attention than the player. When this is extended to singers, the instrumentality and lifelessness of it become obvious; to say that someone's voice is a "beautiful instrument" is to refer to a person's own voice (their physicality and its sonic embodiment) in a distanciated manner. To compliment any instrument rather than (or above) the player is to similarly divorce the intelligence/passion of musicality from living human beings. Such iconicity is seen in the fetishism of technology, when there is less concern with how a new synthesizer can be used musically than with the machine itself.

13.   Here I am referring to the way in which "star status" or canons of physical beauty take precedence over the subjective interactions of performer, music, and listener. This is not to say that presentation and performance are unimportant. It is simply to state the basic principle once again—that the performer's actual interaction with music is given a very low priority and low status in relation to the composer's, and that when performers are lionized it is often for reasons distant from their musical inventiveness.

14.   I should add that I had been deeply involved in these issues before coming out, but that my own role in the process and hierarchy were not fully analyzed, and so what I tried to accomplish was often ill-conceived or patronizing. Still, the ongoing experiments of the Composers' Cafeteria in the San Francisco area were crucial for me in rethinking these matters. Thanks especially to those musicians who brought these issues to the fore, especially Daniel Plonsey, whose unpublished master's thesis from Mills College, *Delayed Counterpoint* (1988), is an excellent work on musical politics.

15.   By subjectivity I mean the sense in which musicians are subjects in their own life and musicality, and not objects of music; I am not trying to imply that individuals are unitary subjects with limitless unchanging extension in time. Key to this notion of subjectivity is that of agency, and thus it is intimately tied to a political understanding of women's oppression. As a composer, I cannot participate in sustaining a power relationship that, in Western art music, has limited the creativity of both performers and women. The principle I try to maintain as a feminist is to seek out how women articulate their will to create and define their own freedom. In the case of music, as I am suggesting, one can equate the position of performers to women. The task is how all of us—as human beings or within the subset of musicians—can and must oppose all attempts to narrow our range of thought, our range of possibilities, and our ability to create. See Hoagland, *Lesbian Ethics*, especially 9–13.

16.   Naked bodies are, of course, fully adequate unto themselves, and do not *have* to be clothed. However, we usually *do* wear clothes—*and* perform certain pieces—and this does not have to be undertaken simply from a sense of modesty...of course, clothed bodies can be as erotically stimulating, if not more so, than naked ones (thanks to Staphanie Dumoski).

17.   I should add that I have been critiqued by two friends of mine who are dancers—Amelia Rudolph and Yamuna Sangarasivam—for not considering the *visual* component of tactility in my work. One opening for me to continue my work in this direction comes from this image. But I believe that the temporalities touched through music and through movement are not necessarily identical.

18.   Mark Lindley, "Composition," in Stanley Sadie, ed., *New Grove's Dictionary of Music and Musicians* (London: Macmillan, 1980), vol. 4, 599.

19.   In music this mind/body dualism begins with Pythagoras, is buoyed by Boethius and Augustine, and is solidified by religious documents that explicitly value words (text) over music. One should note that none of these men is ever reclaimed as a protofeminist!

20.   "Directions" here is meant more in the sense of "trajectories" than a "set of instructions."

21.   Incidentally, composers, performers, and listeners are not necessarily different people.

22.   See my dissertation, *The Composer as a Religious Person in the Context of Pluralism* (Graduate Theological Union, 1992).

23.   For instance, the virtuosic brinkmanship of jazz and Indian classical musics may not be of interest to all feminist musicians.

24.   By this I mean both a mutual trust between composers, performers, and listeners

concerning the immediate and mediated qualities of music's temporality and the extension of time in the sense of history.

25. See Suzanne Cusick, "On a Lesbian Relationship with Music," in the present volume.

26. By sacrality I do not mean a religiousness conferred by organizational authority, nor a special status in relation to any external deity. I am referring to the significance and power of music, especially as this is known in the experience of it. Since I adhere to an immanent worldview—articulated more fully in the concept of panenphysicality cited below—I do not conceive of sacrality as a privileged category, but rather as a present potential (perhaps even an active potency!) in everything/everyone.

27. I chose here between "anybody," "anyone," and "anything." This should also not be misunderstood as a Platonic reification of music into an Idea.

28. This is not intended to be a condemnation of language per se, but an attack on language as a transcendent or exclusive explanatory system. The best counterexample is in poetry, the form of language least susceptible to the logocentric pitfalls of distinction and judgment, and closest to music in its attempt to reawaken a life inherent in words themselves. Some writers who provide examples would include Judy Grahn, Audre Lorde, Gloria Anzaldúa, Adrienne Rich, Joy Harjo, Dionne Brand (especially *No Language Is Neutral* [Toronto: Coach House Press, 1990]), and Janice Gould.

29. This is not the same thing as maintaining that music is an autonomous living being in precisely the same sense as human beings, but it is meant to force us to reconsider the ease with which we interact with the world in a mechanistic "I-it" manner. See Martin Buber, *I and Thou* (a new translation with a prologue, "I and You," and notes by Walter Kaufmann, New York: Charles Scribner's Sons, 1970). Also, see my analysis of this work in *The Composer as a Religious Person in the Context of Pluralism*, chapter 2.

30. Mary Daly in cahoots with Jane Caputi, *Websters' First New Intergalactic Wickedary of the English Language* (Boston: Beacon Press, 1987), 83. Daly is using the word "transcendental" here as a play on the definition of gnostic—but I still find it bothersome (as I do when she uses it in other contexts as well).

31. Hoagland, *Lesbian Ethics*, 12.

32. Hoagland, *Lesbian Ethics*, 145.

33. The contrast here is between those connections we can choose (like lesbian separatism/connectionism) and those we cannot (such as the state of our health, our living conditions under patriarchy/racism, etc.)

34. Incidentally, lovers and musicians are not necessarily different people.

35. Materiality is not the same thing as materialism; in fact, they may be opposites.

36. It is worth noting, however, that the etymology of the word metaphysics was originally merely the title of one of Aristotle's treatises, meaning (roughly translated) "the book that follows 'Physics'" (an earlier volume of his)!

37. Physicality includes both that which is material and that which is dynamic within it, which is energy.

38. I *do* mean *different* here, not better or opposed to heterosexuality, gay male sexuality, etc. I think that one necessary correlate of a philosophy based on monism/pluralism is that the infinite is not infinitely knowable, but knowable in its particularity; thus emphasis and difference define knowledge, but never exhaustively. I would welcome similar explorations by people with different physical experiences of sexuality and/or tactility, and would not be surprised or disappointed by the existence of either overlaps or radical differences.

39. Note that the oppressive systems of heterosexism, patriarchy, and imperialism all hate matter and seek to destroy it or transform it into wealth (an imaginary construct).

40. The very terms used to describe phallus-based sexualities—even something as seemingly innocent as "How many *times* have you had sex?"—become nonsensical in a lesbian temporal framework, as Marilyn Frye describes, in Jeffner Allen, ed., *Lesbian Philosophies and Cultures* (Albany: State University of New York Press, 1990), 305f.

41. Susan McClary, *Feminine Endings: Music, Gender, and Sexuality* (Minneapolis: University of Minnesota Press, 1991), chapter 5.

42. McClary, *Feminine Endings*, 118, 119. It is interesting that both the drive to obliterate time and the desire for timelessness seem to call for the *marginalization of time itself,* either by destroying it or abandoning it. What I suggest as philosophic parameters of temporality could well include the kinds of musical textures found in *Genesis II*, but it is unlikely that I would characterize them in this same fashion.

43. McClary, *Feminine Endings*, 124.

44. "Spatialized" is both a technical term and a metaphoric term in this context. This is because it conveys both the act of measuring time and the visual (i.e., not musical) model on which such a conception of time is based. Many of these terms are from J. T. Fraser *The Voices of Time* (Amherst: University of Massachusetts, 1981), 23–5 (re: Bergson). Victor Zuckerkandl's discussion of time in *Sound and Symbol* (trans. Willard R. Trask and Norbert Guterman, Princeton: Princeton University Press, 1956) is also crucial to my understanding of music and temporality. See my *The Composer as a Religious Person in the Context of Pluralism*, chapter 2, for further analysis.

45. McClary, *Feminine Endings*, 145.

46. I use "develop" here in contrast to "moving toward," i.e., goal-oriented telos.

47. Especially when antinarrative is a reaction against narrative within a schema ordered by narrative; i.e., when antinarrative is part of a closed system defined by narrative.

48. Of course I am aware that narrative exists in time and is often dependent on time for a sense of suspense, or for the simple act of reading or listening, and therefore is, in some sense, also temporality itself. Likewise, since successive, linear time coexists with *durée,* any musical composition or sexual experience can be given a narrative, "blow-by-blow" (so to say) description.

49. If you are detached from the activity of making music, you are in danger not only of inauthenticity, but, to make a sexual analogy, of not remembering the name of the piece you played last night in the morning! I utilize this principle in much of my music, employing technical difficulties (especially rhythmic ones) as a way of insuring that the music will open itself more to people who care than those who don't. To play my music calls for concentration at a high level of discipline. If a player doesn't concentrate, disaster inevitably ensues. The music cannot be played "by ear" (no matter how "natural" it may sound to the listener). Each player hears her part in order to create the whole (individual diversity forming community), which, hopefully, gives each one a sense of Self worth in relation to the coconstruction of the music.

50. Pauline Oliveros, *Software for People: Collected Writings 1963–1980* (Baltimore: Smith Publications, 1984), 179, emphasis Oliveros's.

51. Just to repeat the point, this is not essentialism because to say that the *essence* of something/someone is *a verb*, a motion, change/growth, is the opposite of the reification process that is essentialism. If essentialists, determinists, and constructionists could agree on this, we could proceed with the business of lesbian-feminist philosophizing.

52. Homer, *The Iliad*, Book 19, ll. 333–358.

53. Medieval European versions actually cast Penthesilea against Achilles's son, Pyrrhus, but these represent a different brand of Trojan legend—the beleaguered Trojan underdogs being cheered on by their descendents. See Christine de Pizan, *The Book of the City of Ladies* (trans. Earl Jeffrey Richards, N.Y.: Persea Books, 1982), 47–51, for a medieval, woman-centered version of the battle between Penthesilea and Pyrrhus.

54. I do think, though, that Berlioz's Cassandra is one of the few defensible male portrayals of a woman in opera. It seems significant that Clément does not mention this (French) work in her study of opera—see Catherine Clément, *Opera, or the Undoing of Women* (trans. Betsy Wing, Minneapolis: University of Minnesota Press, 1988). Cassandra's eventual choice of suicide is regrettable, but, like the lead characters in *Thelma and Louise*, once she is backed into a corner, it is unclear what other choices she may have. While this is frustrating, it may be an accurate portrayal of patriarchy—the final place where women can stand on their own agency and subjectivity is in taking their own lives. But this is an unattractive—and extreme—analysis; it is lamentable that these situations occur (in drama and in life) as often as they do. I have a similar choice to make in my opera, concerning Penthesilea. When she is injured and trapped in battle, Achilles plans to take her alive, for breeding purposes. Faced with that prospect, Penthesilea kills herself. But the ambivalence of such a decision is not only excruciating to me as composer, but is likewise paradoxical for the character Penthesilea herself.

55. Janice Raymond, *A Passion for Friends: Toward a Philosophy of Female Affection* (Boston: Beacon Press, 1986), 7ff; see especially 14–18 for distinctions between gyn/affection and lesbianism.

56. This is a purposeful paraphrase of Paul's "Not I, but Christ lives in me…"

57. Actually, I may have an *orientation* toward chamber-music-like orchestrations…

13

GROWING UP FEMALE(S)
Retrospective Thoughts on Musical Preferences and Meanings

Karen Pegley and Virginia Caputo

The interface
between feminism
and various disciplines
provides a forum within which many
previously silenced voices can be heard.
Within musicology, this interrelationship has
warranted a rethinking of the way one both objectively
and subjectively approaches/listens to/analyzes music.
The present work seeks to bring together perspectives from
both feminism and musicology in order to articulate notions
of consumption, interpretation, and performance
in the musical lives of two women.[1]

The work of feminist theorists
in another of the expressive arts—namely
the visual arts—locates our study. At issue
is the musical parallel of what some feminist theorists
have defined as the "male gaze": a unit of analysis that
informs much of their work. For many feminist
film theorists, "the gaze" became an important
concept in narrative cinema. Laura Mulvey's
1975 work was one of the first to explore
the notion of "the gaze" by focusing
specifically on sexual difference in relation to
cinematic pleasure. Mulvey suggests that the

form of narrative
cinema itself is complicit
with the psychocultural repression of women.
In her article, she develops a model emanating from
the work of Freud and Lacan in examining the
ways in which cinema, through voyeurism,
empowered men who consciously and
unconsciously controlled the production
and reception of film images.
By examining the act of looking itself,
she renders this act as
active/male and passive/female.
As Mulvey states:

> the determining male gaze projects its fantasy onto the female figure,
> which is styled accordingly. In their traditional exhibitionist role women
> are simultaneously looked at and displayed, with their appearance coded
> for strong visual and erotic impact so that they can be said to connote *to-be-looked-at-ness*.[2]

Mulvey argues that by aligning the
male viewer in the audience with the
male character on the screen, this complicity holds
the power of "the look" which in turn excludes women.
Similarly, E. Ann Kaplan in *Women and Film*[3]
addresses the way in which the gaze, encoded with culturally
determined components of male sexual desire,
perceives "woman" as a sexual object.
This entire process excludes women from
the role of the subject. The result is that women
become fixed in the position of object of the
gaze, rather than as the subject directing it,
resulting in the representation of woman as "other"
in the male gaze. As Kaplan posits, "woman" is
held within the patriarchal system of signs,
unable to construct herself as the subject
rather than the object because of this containment.
Any representation of "woman"
    carries the values and belief systems
        of patriarchal culture that are
            encoded in these signs.

Extending this work on visual organization,
Kaja Silverman explores the acoustic
elements of cinema. In particular, her work
identifies the presence of the aural in
combination with the visual in the
construction of "reality." As Silverman
states: "...what is at stake within cinema's acoustic
organization, as within its visual organization,
is not the real, but an 'impression of reality.'
Cinema creates this 'impression of reality' by
participating in the production and maintenance
of its culture's dominant fiction..."[4] By pointing to
the participation of sound in the production
of this "reality," Silverman argues convincingly for the
aural complement to the notion of the active eye.
In its application to music, Beverley Diamond
extends further the notion of the active ear,
positing that the ability to hear music may be
articulated through a framework sensitive
to the concept of gender.[5] Diamond states that:

the strong essentialist arguments of many schools of music critics and
music theorists—those that build an argument on the undeniable abstraction of many of the parameters of musical language, especially instrumental
musical language, posit the meaning in music as "integral" and independent of contextual considerations. In place of this I query whether we hear
and explain what we hear with a "male ear," the musical analogy of the
"male gaze" identified in feminist film and art history studies.[6]

The concept of difference
as suggested by Diamond is important,
not only in terms of male and female ways
of hearing and responding, but also in that
sameness must not be presupposed
among varying women and men.
In turn, our questioning
of the musical analogy of the "male ear"
allows the possibility of hearing and explanation
from a female perspective—a "female ear" —
that is itself pluralistic.
It is the apparent singularity and

homogeneity by which the consumption of
musical sound and musical experiences
within a context of power relations
has been articulated that underlies our concerns.
Assuming that these relations of power
inform part of a creative, lifelong process,
our methodology addresses the relationship
between power and music, and the impact it
has had on the lives of the informants
in our study. Through the conjuncture of
perspectives from feminism and musicology,
we have been able to create a space within our
academic discourse to address these issues.

By locating our argument
within this space, we have attempted to
define the subject of the gaze as no longer centered,
bounded or seen in relation to an "other."
As Vicki Kirby states in "Capitalizing
Difference: Feminism and Anthropology,"

the problem becomes one of just how to conceptualize difference differently. A critique of the binarism which harnesses thought into an
either/or division must ask whether difference can be understood outside
an oppositional economy. In other words, must difference (cultural, sexual, class, etc.) always be understood or "othered" as the complement,
inversion or negation of/from a defining reference point (Western, male,
white, bourgeois, etc.)?[7]

Accordingly, from our informants' anecdotes,
we look for the ways they articulate their
differences differently. In our analysis of these
vignettes of musical experiences, their musical
choices may be seen to be both resistant to
hegemonic forces around them and, on the other hand,
ironically, part of the reproducing forces
that shape their lives.

During the course of a seminar
on music and gender in 1989, our
informants attended sessions in which they

examined the construction of gender
in children's songs and games.
One session in particular was spent
viewing a collection of video tapes of
children's interactions within music
classroom settings. Our informants
spontaneously shared recollections
of their own childhood experiences.
One of our informants recollected
skipping rhymes performed exclusively
by girls' groups, yogi elastic games,
and tunes accompanied by ball-bouncing.
She was surprised to find through
these conversations with her colleague that
assumptions she held regarding the universality
of these girls' experiences were unfounded.
They did not have parallel recollections.
In fact, they found that many of their
experiences were quite dissimilar both with regard
to the repertoire of songs and social interaction.

In light of this dialogue, it became apparent
that the plurality of their responses
could not be accommodated by the concept of difference
as understood from the literature
on gender and music available to the authors.
The sources presented instead a picture
of homogeneous female musical experience
in negative contrast to the male experience—
a picture that in turn helped to sustain
the binary opposition of male and
female in the musical field.
Simon Frith's *The Sociology of Rock* serves
as an example of an analysis of music consumption
carried out during the time of our informants'
adolescent years. In this work, Frith makes a clear distinction
between "girls' and boys' culture" in the 1970s:
whereas boys participate in "complex and hi-fi" music,
girls have less interest in this form;
they play about on guitars but are generally

more interested in singing than in
instrumental music production.[8]
Accordingly, Frith suggests a greater degree of
individuality in boys, who actively explore their own
creativity. Girls' culture, however,
is described as passive, with a remarkable degree
of homogeneity.

To challenge stereotypical notions of
girls' culture as articulated by authors
such as Frith, our methodology consisted
of, first, asking our informants to produce
a list of ten musical selections from
various genres that figured prominently
in their socialization and, second,
interviewing our informants
based upon these selections. Some of
these experiences as recounted to us by
our informants form the basis of our analysis.
These vignettes are considered in light of notions
concerning difference within relations of power that include
resistance, conformity, and negotiation.

To begin, Informant A
recalled an important musical experience
beginning at the age of twelve. She talked about
her life at this time as divided between wanting to be
included in girls' groups and yet feeling an
awkwardness with such a relationship.
Belonging exclusively to a girls' group in
this informant's opinion meant being
excluded from interacting with boys,
which was important for her at the time.
Music provided her with a way to
maintain her position within the girls' groups
without jeopardizing her ability to
interact with boys who were
excluded from this musical group.
This informant's first musical selection
was taken from the repertoire of a popular

teenybopper Scottish band, the Bay City Rollers.
For a preteen at this time,
acceptance into this fan club meant
vocal participation in the music,
adopting a style of dress, and participation in
ownership of the group's records, posters, and
memorabilia. As my informant stated,
"I really enjoyed singing their music,
collecting information on the groups' members
from teen magazines, and plastering my walls with pictures."
The text from the first musical example, the Bay City Rollers'
"Rock and Roll Love Letter," is provided:

> Hey says the poet, dear brother poet too,
> These tears are words I make, I wanna be with you,
> 'Cause I need to spend my body, I'm a music makin' man,
> I know this can release it like this amplifier can...
> This is my Rock 'n Roll Love Letter to you [repeat].
> Gonna sign it, gonna seal it, gonna mail it away,
> Gonna mail it today.[9]

The way in which this informant
described her experience suggests that
she met the criteria of Frith's definition of
one who conforms in girls' culture.
Singing was an integral activity for her
and, like the girls described in Frith's studies, she put
singing before
instrumental activities. This form of
participation by girls seems to be interpreted
by Frith as a lack of interest in the music itself,
a perhaps unfortunate result of girls' culture
which "starts and finishes in the bedroom."[10]
According to Frith, this activity
prepares the girl for marriage,
the adolescent females' true career.[11]
The informant recollected that
her singing experience was not
disempowering, and, as a young lesbian,
the connection to marriage was, for her, problematic.
Jennifer Giles and John Shepherd

have examined this issue of empowerment
through singing. Their 1986 study, for example,
looks at individual music consumption
as experienced and interpreted by four
English-speaking girls in Montréal, Québec.[12]
In particular, they discuss two important steps in this
process of musical empowerment:
(1) internalization of music within their bodies and
(2) claiming ownership of an important component of musical
production—namely vocalizing—as their own.
First, with regard to the issue of music
within the body, Giles and Shepherd posit that sound
(and therefore the musical text) is:

> the only major channel of communication that actively vibrates inside the
> body...sound is felt in addition to being heard...It is, in the form of popular
> music, a way in which we possess others and are possessed by others...[The
> four girls were aware] of these empowering and possessive qualities of
> music.[13]

Accordingly, the practice of singing
popular music by girls is seen here as an
empowering experience; it is a felt
musical practice that connects the group.
The second issue addresses ownership
of the music. Frith attributes girls' singing to their
lack of interest in instrumental performing;
they were more interested in the words
than were boys. From this statement,
Frith seems to imply that singing is a
less valued activity that is associated
with females. Adopting the practice of
singing, however, has been explained more
positively by Giles and Shepherd, who describe it as
"a rejection of an encompassing masculine identity...the
exclusion of a foreign, encompassing and potentially
threatening musical reality is matched by an
active affirmation of self through the
'other' (the text) of music."[14] Again,
Giles and Shepherd discern resistance,
not disempowerment, through vocalizing.

Frith also identifies male-objectification as a
criterion of girls' culture and claims that
this form of idol worship—which includes activities
such as purchasing magazines and hanging posters—
unites young females. Informant A agreed that
the activities united her group of friends;
they were, however, more important for providing an
entry into the group than solely for worshipping idols.

In their article "Girls and Subcultures,"
Angela McRobbie and Jenny Garber identify
a number of other "negotiative processes"
at work with regard to "idol-worshipping."[15]
These include: (1) few requirements in association with this
commercially based subculture—as the informant stated,
"one only needed to sing and purchase relevant
merchandise to be part of the group"—and
(2) few personal risks, i.e., sexual risks, once a member of the group.
Informant A felt that sexual activity, which
seemed to her to be part of the image of heavy rock groups,
was not a requirement for her membership in
following the Rollers; her status as a Rollers fan
sheltered her from this peer pressure.
In discussing the sexual implications of the idol-fan relationship,
McRobbie and Garber state:

> a function of the social exclusiveness of such groupings is to gain private,
> inaccessible space...teeny bopper subcultures could be interpreted as ways
> of buying time, within the commercial mainstream, from the real world of
> sexual encounters.[16]

Participation in "girls' culture" allows for the
exploration of different personal spaces than those
occupied by boys. Informant A's
selective participation points to how,
   through resistance, she established
      her personal space
         within teenybopper culture.

Our second informant, Informant B,
recalled that as a fifteen-year-old

her time was split between formal
music studies and trying to be
a "normal" high school student:
"I was always set apart from my peers because
I was so involved in performing and studying music.
In one way, I wanted to be part of the girls' group,
but, on the other hand, the kinds of things
they liked to do didn't really interest me."
This is significantly different from
the experience articulated by Informant A.
For her, music provided a way
into the group, whereas for Informant B,
music provided an escape from
involvement in stereotypical girls' culture.
Informant B stated that she preferred to
listen to solo female acoustic artists.
This performer-fan relationship is
different from the idol-fan relationship
described by Informant A:
an identification rather than an objectification.
Informant B recollected experiences at
two different points in her life that
hinged upon one particular song.
Carly Simon's "That's the Way I've Always
Heard It Should Be" describes the
expectations of being "female"—
as someone's child, lover, wife, and mother:

You say we'll soar like two birds
through the clouds,
But soon you'll cage me on your shelf.
I'll never learn to be just me first, by myself.
Well, O.K. it's time we moved in together,
and raised a family on our own, you and me.
Well that's the way I've always heard it should be
You want to marry me, we'll marry.

For this informant, the female roles
defined in this song coincided with those
she had been socialized to accept.
McRobbie articulates this process as

"the way girls experience[d] all the pressures imposed on them
to aspire to a model of femininity and how
they live[d] this ideology on a day-to-day basis."[17]
In addition, the informant discussed the
vocal quality and instrumentation of Simon's songs,
which she described as light and breathy,
with no direct, pointed sounds.
The effect, as the informant explained,
was nonthreatening and adhered to
her image of femininity.
McRobbie and Frith concur with this argument
when they discuss solo female artists, stating that
"whatever the ability, integrity and toughness
of [these musicians], their musical appeal,
the way they were sold, reinforced...the qualities
traditionally linked with female singers—
sensitivity, passivity, and sweetness."[18]
By following these female artists, as opposed to
popular teen idols or groups that would
require more active participation,
Informant B marginalized her position
within her own peer group, yet remained
safely within the boundaries
of female expectations.

This particular Carly Simon song
was brought up again in the informant's account
of her life at age twenty.
At that time, she began to play popular music
herself as a solo performer in clubs in her hometown.
She began her first set of every performance
with Simon's song. As she stated:
"Singing this song first made me feel more
comfortable in that situation,
and the audience accepted this image
and the sound right away
Yet at this stage in her life, she was no longer comfortable
with the stereotypical image expected of her,
and the song became a vehicle
to subvert the image.

The personae of the solo female artists
became a site of empowerment rather than conformity,
for in them Informant B described finding her strength.
She saw the women as aggressive/strong figures
that were able to successfully carve out a niche for themselves
in the male-dominated world of recorded music.
The informant
noted the assertion of strength on the one hand,
and the maintenance of femininity on the other.
As Informant B stated: "The irony lay in the fact
that someone like Rikki Lee Jones could appear onstage
complete with an oversized man's cap,
blue jeans and a cigarette in hand—
an appearance that I was socialized to define
as more of a masculine image
Yet she sounded very feminine to me."
The artists challenged the notion of
women's passivity in music
and stereotypical notions of "femaleness"
that imposed uniformity on their lives.
No longer did the phrase "That's The Way
I've Always Heard It Should Be"
evoke notions of compliance for this informant.
She had moved to a different stage
in her identity as a female.

Informant A's second selection was
significant for her at the age of seventeen.
Enrolled in a university music program, she .
recalls being fascinated with Stravinsky's music,
particularly his Symphony in C. She
immediately responded to the first movement
and its sonata form features and sought
to understand why Stravinsky's interpretation
of sonata form was so fascinating.
This informant recalled a metaphor
that influenced her initial perception
of this work. A classmate saw sonata form
as an appropriate model for life.
It is in three stages:

the exposition (youth and education),
development (marriage, parenthood, and career)
and recapitulation (retirement).
After painstakingly making a chart that
mapped out the music's formal development,
Informant A felt that this work in particular reflected
the way in which her life
was going to develop as a lesbian:
it could be graphed within a rigid box
(analogous with her strict environment)
and sections "developed,"
but not in the traditional sense (family or children).
Finally, and most importantly, she did not sense
closure at the end of sections.
Instead, she heard juxtaposed areas that functioned
as interruptions—
a pattern that she thought was
inevitable in her life. She recalled being struck
by Edward T. Cone's analysis of the work: he describes it
as having a "peculiar phrase structure: extended,
repetitive developments over an ostinato...clear
phrase divisions achieved by interruption
and even by interpolation."[19] Stravinsky utilized
rhythm, phrasing, and articulation to create patterns,
which, as noted by Alan Lessem,
"relentlessly disrupt continuity and closure."[20]
Informant A sensed continuity
in Stravinsky's work but was more interested in its
discontinuity; his manipulation of sonata form seemed
    more befitting as a musical model for life
        than any she had
            experienced previously.

The second piece recalled by Informant B
            as especially important in her experiences was
        Rachmaninoff's Elegie op. 3, no. 1. At this time, she
    was a student in a university music performance program.
        As she recalled, "The Rachmaninoff was chosen
            for many reasons. First, it was a way for me
        to negotiate my place in a male-centered environment.

The piece was demanding emotionally,
but not so much technically. I liked it because
I used my entire body in performing it.
The sound was heavy, the tone was full
and required the full weight of my arms."
Recall Giles and Shepherd's notion of the
empowering nature of singing in the use
of the body as an instrument.
Their definition is extended in this informant's
account to articulate the notion that the body
joined with an instrument
is equally empowering as singing,
but in a different way.
In singing Carly Simon on the one hand
and playing Rachmaninoff on the other,
Informant B felt that she could mediate her
vulnerability and strength within the female image
that she wanted to create for herself.

She went on to discuss the ironic fact that
the pieces she preferred did not conform to the sound
she thought of as "feminine."
Yet this musical preference was in direct contrast
to the kinds of music she played away from the
confines of the music school.
By moving back and forth between
what she was socialized to accept
as a model of femininity
on the one hand, and what did not comply on the other,
she created what she later described
as a fragmented persona rather than a unified whole.
From the examples chosen by this informant, one sees that
it is critical to recognize her plurality as a woman.
To quote Luce Irigaray, "'She' is indefinitely other in herself."[21]
For Informant B, music helped develop
this pluralistic expression—she chose music that
resisted forces of containment in her life.
Irigaray provides an insight into the process
articulated by Informant B when she addresses a similar issue
with respect to women's words:

"One would have to listen with another ear,
as if hearing an 'other meaning' always in the process
of weaving itself, of embracing itself with words,
but also of getting rid of words in order not to become fixed,
congealed in them."[22] Within the rigid confines
of the music institution, Informant B was able
to create her own space.

The various examples presented
    illustrate that
        there exists a…**multiplicity**…of female differences and
            demonstrate the complexity
      of the "female ear."
         Within each of the particular
         moments we have described,
     we have found
   that our informants' choices
both upheld and manipulated
  the existing structures
    of music and negotiated **space** within the relations of power.
            It is only through the
        conjoining of
    musicological and feminist
   thought that we have been able
to locate these positions.
   Due to this **rethinking** of music
      consumption, interpretation,
        and performance as women,
          we have tried to make audible
           what has previously been,
             for our informants,
              silenced.

It is usually a feature of qualitative research
to conceal the identities of your informants,
and we acknowledge this responsibility.

The model that has developed
from our work, however, modifies this criterion
and makes necessary the disclosure
of our informants' identities.

Karen Pegley, Informant A   Virginia Caputo, Informant B

Notes

This paper was first presented at the conference "Feminist Theory and Music: Toward a Common Language," Minneapolis, Minn., June 1991. In preparing this article, the authors have sought to replicate the performative nature of the original aural presentation, which included the interplay of their voices as well as playing taped excerpts of musical examples. Accordingly, the presenter's voices are represented in print by contrasting alignments and typefaces.

1. While this work represents only two perspectives, one lesbian and one straight, the authors have sought to lend voice to different, yet equally significant, experiences of women. In preparing this work, we would like to thank Beverley Diamond for her encouragement and helpful insight.

2. Laura Mulvey "Visual Pleasure and Narrative Cinema," *Screen* 16, no. 3 (1975): 11; reprinted in Mulvey, *Visual and Other Pleasures* (Bloomington: Indiana University Press, 1989), 19.

3. See E. Ann Kaplan, *Women and Film: Both Sides of the Camera* (New York: Methuen, 1983), 10.

4. Kaja Silverman, *The Acoustic Mirror: The Female Voice in Psychoanalysis and Cinema* (Bloomington: Indiana University Press, 1988), 44.

5. Beverley Diamond, "Aesthetics and Canadian Women's Music," paper presented at the Feminist Theory and Aesthetics Conference, Toronto, Ontario, October 1990.

6. Diamond, "Aesthetics," 2.

7. Vicki Kirby, "Capitalizing Difference: Feminism and Anthropology," *Australian Feminist Studies* 9 (1989): 4.

8. See Simon Frith, *The Sociology of Rock* (London: Constable & Co., 1978), 65.

9. These are the lyrics as recounted by the informant. As she recalled, the exact words were not known to the members of her peer group, but this was not an important issue when performing the song.

10. Frith, *Sociology of Rock*, 65.

11. Frith, *Sociology of Rock*, 66.

12. Jennifer Giles and John Shepherd, "Theorizing Music's Affective Power," in Robert Witmer, ed., *Ethnomusicology in Canada* (Toronto: Institute for Canadian Music, 1990): 19.

13. Giles and Shepherd, "Theorizing Music's Affective Power," 21.

14. Giles and Shepherd, "Theorizing Music's Affective Power," 20.

15. Angela McRobbie and Jenny Garber, "Girls and Subcultures," in *Feminism and Youth Culture: From "Jackie" to "Just Seventeen"* (Boston: Unwin Hyman, 1991), 12.

16. McRobbie and Garber, "Girls and Subcultures," 14.

17. Angela McRobbie, "The Politics of Feminist Research," in *Feminism and Youth Culture: From "Jackie" to "Just Seventeen"*, 63.

18. Simon Frith and Angela McRobbie, "Rock and Sexuality," *Screen Education* 29 (Winter 1979): 9.

19. Edward T. Cone, "The Uses of Convention: Stravinsky and His Models," in Paul Henry Lang, ed., *Stravinsky: A New Appraisal of His Work* (New York: W. W. Norton, 1963), 26; cited by Pieter C. van den Toorn, *The Music of Igor Stravinsky* (New Haven: Yale University Press, 1983), 260.

20. Alan P. Lessem, "Schoenberg, Stravinsky, and Neo-Classicism: The Issues Reexamined," *The Musical Quarterly* 48, no. 4 (October 1982): 535.

21. Luce Irigaray, *This Sex Which Is Not One*, trans. Catherine Porter (Ithaca: Cornell University Press, 1985), 28.

22. Irigaray, *This Sex Which Is Not One*, 29.

14

AUTHORITY AND FREEDOM
Toward a Sociology of the Gay Choruses

Paul Attinello

Introduction

*T*HE ABRUPT PUBLIC REVELATION of a gay American community in 1969 led rapidly to a unique transitional social structure. This structure— what is known as the "gay subculture"—is a complex field of values and relationships that is suffused with both traditional American middle-class values and intense reactions against those values. Contemporary French cultural critics have claimed that homosexuality, because of its uniquely subversive relationship to Western values, has a crucial social function in breaking down repressive structures. In spite of this idealistic concept, the gay subculture reacted to the awareness of its own existence by creating both rigid and diffused social structures in an atmosphere often fraught with tension and social uncertainty.[1]

Into this atmosphere, and before the onslaught of AIDS began to alter the new social structure, the groups now incorporated as the Gay and Lesbian Association of Choruses (hereafter referred to as GALA) began to appear. In 1978, in San Francisco, the new San Francisco Gay Men's Chorus gave its first performance at the memorial service for Harvey Milk and George Moscone. Within the next year, choruses appeared in Los Angeles, Seattle, and Chicago, and thence rapidly throughout the United States.[2] In the summer of 1986, GALA included thirty-eight choruses located in most of the country's larger cities and a surprising number of smaller ones; other choruses have also appeared in Canada and Europe. The second triennial festival of GALA choruses was given in June 1986 in Minneapolis. Fifteen gay men's choruses, one lesbian chorus, and a small mixed ensemble performed in five concerts, culminating in a presentation by the host chorus, three commissioned works each performed by several choruses in combination, and a finale performed by all of the festival members.[3] As might be expected, the festival was rich in potential sociological data.

The first part of this paper consists of references and speculations in philosophy and sociology related to the study of gay society in general and gay chorus structure in particular. At the end of that section, questions for future study are brought up. This section is followed by an empirical section consisting of the results of a questionnaire sent out to five choruses. Finally, the appendices include the actual questionnaire and charts of selected results.

I would like to thank Jon Bailey and Glen Banta of Los Angeles, Kevin Ames, Dick Kramer, and Gregg Tallman of San Francisco, and Kip Snyder of Chicago for their help in designing and distributing the questionnaire; without them, this study would be far more incomplete than it is. This paper is dedicated to Jerry Carlson, conductor of the Gay Men's Chorus of Los Angeles, who died of AIDS on 23 November 1987; and to Jon Sims, founder of the gay band and chorus movement, who died of AIDS on 16 July 1984.

History, Concepts, Aims, Problems

In the past, two major approaches have been made in the problem of studying the gay subculture. One of these is complex in nature, being related to the modern French trend toward intertwining philosophical, sociological, and political thought; the other is the relatively straightforward American empirical approach. A third stream, the German psychopathological approach, has been out of favor since the 1940s, although it produced an enormous amount of sophisticated work in its day; since that approach is now considered largely outdated, it will be ignored here.

History: France

The late George Stambolian pointed out the historical importance of French writing on the broader subject of homosexuality:

> The French possess a strong tradition of writing on homosexuality which since the late eighteenth century has nurtured its own growth. In the

perspective of history one can now say that the proliferation of critical and biographical studies on Gide and Proust, the emergence of Genet, the rediscovery of Sade, and the rise of Sartrean existentialism mark a moment in the middle of the twentieth century when this accumulated tradition attained a "critical mass" in France and became an inescapable presence to a degree not reached in other countries. [4]

However, that history is chiefly literary; up to a more recent point in time, French writing on homosexuality was confined to the particularity of belles lettres and personal revelations. For work of wider applicability, a newer form of writing was required, one tied to the social sciences and involving the tools of the structuralist/poststructuralist project.

The history of this particular aspect of poststructuralism begins in May 1968 with the French student revolutions and the abrupt shift of emphasis in that country's intellectual studies. What had begun with Lévi-Strauss in the 1950s as an attempt to excavate the structures of human existence developed into a specific plan, i.e., the undermining of the existing political structure. Suddenly, the apparently outdated Marxism of the Frankfurt school was rediscovered, with new psychological and social studies appearing as evidence for its viability. The French rapidly extended these studies from economics into the deep structure of psychoanalysis, suggesting that the problems of the "administered society" had as much to do with the discoveries of Freud as with those of Marx.

Two important books on the problems of sexuality in the administered society appeared in 1972. Guy Hocquenghem's powerful, complex monograph *Homosexual Desire* considers the problem of the homosexual as a threat to the existing society at the very deepest level. His point is that the current structure of Western society is specifically heterosexual and phallic, and that homosexuality's literal inversion of values is a more powerful force against the status quo than any merely political ideology, as such ideologies always recreate the phallic structure:

> The homosexual situation which has been created by the gay movement, as opposed to those which have long been established in society, has the inestimable advantage of being located in fact rather than in principle, in the reality of everyday life where the division between the public and the private is abolished. Some left-wing elements may well have been outraged at Jean Genet's remark: "Perhaps if I had never gone to bed with an Algerian, I would never have approved of the FLN."[5]

The second book has become a major and frequently cited work in poststructuralism. Cowritten by philosopher Gilles Deleuze and psychologist

Félix Guattari, *Anti-Oedipus: Capitalism and Schizophrenia*[6] is based on an extraordinary thesis: that all of our perceptions can be arranged in a polarity ranging from paranoia to schizophrenia. Deleuze and Guattari claim that paranoia and schizophrenia are only identified as mental illnesses when they pass a certain point, but that these conditions are not innately different in quality from those of "normal" people. In this polarity, we can discover a choice of which we have been unaware; Freud's Oedipus complex and the resultant authority problems are based only in the paranoia end of the polarity and are not universal to all human beings. Out of this structure appears a new approach to politics, society, sexuality, and psychology, where paranoia is associated with the right wing, fascism, and phallic authority, while schizophrenia is associated with the left wing and anarchic desire; as a result, anarchy and free desire are rediscovered as viable alternatives to authoritarian systems. This book can be seen as a broader theory that explains Hocquenghem's relatively localized phenomena.

Anti-Oedipus has led to a major expansion in the study of society in sexuality, as opposed to the more traditional approach of studying sexuality in society. The extraordinary wave of feminist theory has actually created the possibility, perhaps for the first time in Western history, of reading and discussing texts without taking phallic authority for granted. In addition, studies by Foucault and Boswell in the history of sexual concepts have shown that, quite simply, things were not always as they are now in the sexual/social sphere.[7] This set of new concepts of society is extremely useful in examining the institutions of gay culture, including, of course, the choruses.

History: America, and a Synthesis

American studies of homosexual society are less breathtaking in their implications. In line with the American insistence on empiricism in the social sciences, the interdisciplinary speculations of the French have few counterparts in gay studies on this side of the Atlantic;[8] instead, various statistical studies have been made of gays as a population. These studies chiefly concentrate either on simply defining the population, or on specific *individual* problems, pair bonding and alcoholism being favorites. These problems, however, have nothing to do with gay institutions; they are based on an atomized view of the gay man as an isolated deviant in a society apparently unrelated to him.

The limitations of empirical studies that ignore larger structures in the formation of individual experience can be illustrated with the issue of pair bonding. Personal observation suggests that the structures of pair bonding in gay society break down rapidly in groups that have any ongoing identity. When a new member joins a gay chorus, there is a commonly observed phenomenon lasting only a few weeks in which the new and existing members are briefly but intensely aware of each other as potential sexual or romantic partners. Actual liaisons are extremely few, and the socialization of the new member involves a dramatic shift in which other chorus members become "just sisters," and inappropriate for most sexual contact. Humorous references to incest are made in such circumstances, and any pair-bonding structure tends to fall apart under social pressure. The few chorus members who attempt to continue sexual activity with other members receive a great deal of adverse comment, and existing pairs of lovers are expected to avoid expressing their relationship physically or emotionally when they are with the group.

As a result, I believe that pair-bonding studies fail to account for certain aspects of gay institutions. The atomistic studies, of which one of the better earlier examples is C. A. Tripp's *Homosexual Matrix,*[9] are of use in socially flexible areas of gay life that do not involve group identity, such as bars and discos. However, important as these areas are, they have no bearing on institutions that do have such an identity, including the gay choruses.

It should be possible to employ current French thought to fill the existing vacuum in American studies; nevertheless, these studies must be tempered with an awareness of the more commercial, "administered" aspect of American society. It is interesting to note that, in spite of the importance of gay philosophy and gay individuals in French society, the French gay subculture is not known for being remarkably large or self-identified. The truly powerful gay subcultures are currently situated in urban America and Germany; both of these nations are perhaps more rigid economically and socially than France, which results in some difficult questions that should be applied to the basic tenets of a gay sociology. However, if one uses the French studies as a background, it is possible to create some hypotheses that can be used on the subculture in this country.

Gays and Authority

If modern society is seen as an *administered* society, i.e., as paranoid/fascist, it becomes clear that contemporary revolutions in thought as well as various social upheavals are a natural reversion to schizophrenic/anarchist thought. Thus, the polarity of the two states is a battle rather than a compromise, with contemporary society as the battlefield; any individuals or organizations clearly stating their allegiances will be forced into a defensive position. However, the very act of being gay is an ambivalent statement, with an allegiance to both ends of the polarity. The gay male is often more male-oriented than his heterosexual counterpart;[10] many of his desires and obsessions are ultimately phallic and authority-centered. The fetishes of uniforms and leather, the common attraction to sadomasochism, and the extreme conformity within many sectors of the subculture suggest an unusually fascist state of existence. However, the gay male does not necessarily identify with or support those things that fascinate him. Any phallic, authoritarian society will necessarily reject the gay male, and he is often sharply aware of this. Certainly, the ambivalent status of gays in the Third Reich recalls a complex and uncomfortable situation in which secret homosexuality was common in the controlling oligarchy, but open homosexuality in the controlled masses led to extermination. Particularly in American society, where values of democracy, civil rights, and liberalism are associated with the very idea of minorities, the gay male is brought into the realization that the authoritarian point of view is not safe for his subculture. Righteous anger directed at authoritarian repression becomes the normative reaction in any public situation, although fetishistic repression fantasies are acted out in a purely private arena.

This righteous anger leads to a strong, if mostly symbolic, identification with other minorities or any group that is perceived as oppressed.[11] One of the more unusual actions taken by various GALA choruses is the addition of someone onstage at a concert signing for the deaf. This practice has become widespread, although it may seem rather odd; one's initial puzzled reaction might be to ask why a deaf person would want to come to a concert in the first place, and how interesting can musical lyrics or texts be? This signing is not merely, however, a practical action, but also a symbol of inclusion; although the institution is dedicated to the production of music, which is based on sound, it encourages participation by those who cannot perceive sound. More importantly, signing is seen as a gesture of solidarity with intensely emotional implications. At the 1986 GALA festival, the Rochester Gay Men's Chorus, a group of about thirty singers, signed and sang the pseudo-African "Kumbaya." The musical arrangement was simple, and the delivery straightforward; however, both at the festival and in questionnaire responses, people referred to this performance as "the emotional high point of the festival." Later that year, a Christmas concert given by the Los Angeles chorus ended with the entire group signing "White Christmas," introduced in a speech by the guest conductor referring to the gift of sound and its loss. This final song came soon after a group of spirituals performed with a black female guest soloist—an attempt, of course, to integrate a symbol for blacks and women into the predominantly white male group.

   Solidarity of minorities seems ideologically related to the overthrow of established authority, but can actually have a distinct and even very different intention. A fascinating event in the breakdown of authoritarian structures occurred just after the final communal concert at the GALA 1986 festival, which involved over 1,400 singers performing an inflammatory selection from Randall Thompson's "Testament of Freedom." Outside the concert hall is a large, landscaped fountain terrace, beautifully clean as is everything in Minneapolis. It is a strong temptation to wander from the path stones to the similar stones in and around the fountain, but most people in the vicinity do not do so; in five days of walking past the fountain and spending a certain amount of time reading under a nearby tree, I only saw two children in shorts dare to run through the water. It may thus be clear how cheerfully anarchic the social situation on the terrace became after the final concert: as members of the Denver Women's Chorus and a number of men from various choruses sang "Kumbaya" and other communal songs, some of them dove into the fountain in their concert pants and tuxedo shirts. The entire situation was clearly led by the women, who were, however, in the minority at the festival.
   On the basis of this and other observations, I would suggest that "gay anarchy" as a concept underlies many actions by lesbians, but rather few by gay men. I suggest that public resistance to authoritarian structures, which comes quite naturally to homosexual women, is conceptually a strong value for gay men, but that they more rarely act in accordance with the concept. I also suggest that such resistance is admired by gay men but often considered rather vulgar. The arena where resistance to authoritarian structures appears for gay men is usually in secret, private, and/or sexual circumstances, such as those detailed in the fascinating but conflicting stories surrounding the collapse of the Jacuzzi in our hotel. Evidently, a number of authoritarian rules were broken (in addition to the Jacuzzi itself), but these rules were broken in secret and semiprivate circumstances that involved a few men at a late hour. However, the concept of breaking those rules led to a great deal of gratified and rather proud gossip over the ensuing days of the festival, even when the hotel management closed the Jacuzzi and pool areas for the duration.

Implicit Structures of Gay Choruses

A chorus designed on traditional lines is a highly authoritarian structure, requiring strict allegiance to the sole figure of the director, from whom all power flows. Although most professional and many amateur groups are run by some kind of board that actually employs the director and holds most of the administrative power, even administrative decisions are virtually always made in accordance with the director's wishes. Situations in which an administrative board wrests the main power away from the director remain unusual and problematic; generally, in such a case, a new director must be found as soon as possible to avoid the institution's complete collapse.

Adorno made the following statements about conductors in orchestral situations:

> [C]onductor and orchestra in themselves constitute a kind of microcosm in which social tensions recur and can be concretely studied…A conductor does not owe his fame to his ability to interpret scores, or certainly not to this ability alone. He is an imago, the imago of power, visibly embodied in his prominent figure and striking gestures…[T]he conductor demonstrates his leadership role visibly: the orchestra really must play the way he commands…Experiments with conductorless orchestras were made in the first years of the Russian Revolution, and however naïve those may have been in a purely musical sense, they were merely calling the conductor figure to account for permanent debts incurred in social psychology. The conductor symbolizes dominance even in his attire: it is that of the master class and of the whip-wielding ringmaster in a circus.[12]

It is suggested that in a choral situation, although the conductor has a slightly lower status in relation to the general public, his relation to the performers is even more dominating than in an orchestra.[13] Any voice teacher is aware that telling a person how to make vocal sound and how to pronounce words attacks certain very basic aspects of his or her presentational identity. Instrumentalists are able to objectify their skill as a function of time and work, external to their personal worth; the vocalist is constantly returning to the problem of judging the way he expresses himself through speech, which is identified closely with the social persona. The choral conductor tells performers not only how to perform the music, but how to stand, breathe, and talk; the conductor's administration extends to very personal areas of their self-expression.

A comment by Attali extends the sociopolitical aspect of this situation to the music itself:

> [M]usic appears in myth as *an affirmation that society is possible.* That is the essential thing. Its order simulates the social order, and its dissonances express marginalities. *The code of music simulates the accepted rules of society.* It is in this connection that the debate on the existence of a natural musical code and an objective, scientific, universal harmony takes on importance…If such a code did in fact exist, then it would be possible to

deduce the existence of a natural order in politics and a general equilibrium in the economy.[14]

The musical organization is thus seen as an extremely structured authoritarian body, very high on any list of paranoid/fascist groupings; the unpaid
(nonprofessional) chorus is an even more extreme case, as allegiance must
substitute for the performers' economic needs. Given the fascist/antifascist
ambivalence of gay males as suggested above, it will come as no surprise that
the relationship between director and performers is complex and often
uncomfortable in gay choruses. Adorno's concept of the "force field"
(*Kraftfeld*) made up of various social forces comes in handy here; the forces
involved are often barely balanced, and the authoritarian relationship
changes rapidly from moment to moment.

The act, or the apprehension, of replacing the conductor creates an arena
of intensely contested change in this relationship. Many of the choruses have
gone through at least one major trauma in impeaching, replacing, or
battling with a director; the divisions of the gay choral communities of San
Francisco, Chicago, and New York into pairs of ideologically antagonistic
choruses is chiefly based on identifiable historical events centering on
particular directors. Stable dynastic periods are identified by the name of the
director. These periods are sometimes alarmingly short, and, when they end,
the general body of communication in the chorus can become violently
emotional and even confrontational. A chorus whose director leaves or
becomes ill[15] is faced with the remarkably difficult task of finding an
adequate authority figure to replace him; this task is faced with all
the equanimity and business sense of a traumatized orphan seeking a
new parent. The chorus becomes a replacement for the usual authoritarian
structures of the heterosexual world, particularly the extended family. In this
sense, the gay chorus member has on some level accepted a new authoritarian structure to replace the one he has implicitly, or explicitly, rejected;
naturally, there is ambivalence in this acceptance.

On the subject of implicit aspects of gay choruses, it should be pointed
out that the relationship of the chorus to the community is an extremely
positive one. The one aspect of the administered society that gay choruses
generally escape is that of exchange value. The choruses do not have an
economic base for existence; as in other American musical organizations,
concert tickets do not begin to pay the costs of the musical commodity
involved, and, of course, members are unpaid. Individual choruses are
generally either impecunious or pay their operating costs out of a seemingly
inexhaustible fund of private contributions. Other sectors of the gay male

subculture manage to merchandise all of its important aspects, including physical beauty, sexual pleasure, and home comforts. The costs of gym memberships, sophisticated home furnishings, commercial entertainment, drinks, drugs, and adult toys are all highly inflated; paying these prices is virtually mandatory in the subculture for an accepted member. The choruses are often beloved by the gay community as its least exchange-oriented organizations, as places to rest from the financial rat race and small havens from the constantly proliferating traps of the administered society.

Potential Study Problems in the Sociology of Gay Choruses

Several other problems come to mind in connection with the above speculations. A study of rigidity of format in rehearsals might be productive in analyzing the authoritarian ambivalence of the choruses; there is wide variation in adherence to strict schedules or appropriate behavior, and individual directors hold widely differing policies at different times. It could also be useful to analyze the programming of the GALA festivals, noting how much traditional and new music is performed, how many commissions are created within the subculture, and the like. The polarized opposition of values between the performance of classical music and popular arrangements has been a standing area of argument in most of the choruses since their inception; the questionnaire included responses related to this, but a clear consensus was not reached. It is also important to notice, in the area of traditional structures, a very strong identification with traditionally performed common-practice music; the desire on the part of the directors to commission new works is rarely matched by the performers' enthusiasm. Finally, it would be useful to consider the social forces that are generated by individual jealousy and egotism, and expressed in and around performance, particularly by small ensembles or soloists; this is a major topic of conversation in the gay choruses, leading to unusual negotiations, confrontations, and disagreements.

An important subject that is more distant from the above concerns would be a comparison of the gay male choruses with the vigorous subculture of lesbian music, which is rarely choral or traditional in nature. The most common musical style in lesbian society is a sort of folk/pop, generally concentrating on romantic ballads and communal songs performed by a single woman with keyboard. The lesbian repertoire is also much more original than the gay male one, consisting almost entirely of new songs, as opposed to traditional music. There are strong forces involved that may go to the roots of gender socialization and differentiation.

Methodology, Results, Analyses, Considerations

One might suppose that the speculations that make up the first part of this paper would benefit from empirical backing. Unfortunately, many of the more important or interesting points are in areas where it is difficult to quantify or even to extract responses. The defensiveness of subcultures is a serious problem, and the powerful human desire to avoid examination of one's deeper motives constantly gets in the way of open discussion of these areas. The design, handling, and results of the questionnaire are thus of some interest, if only as an example of mistakes to be avoided; unfortunately, the responses pale in comparison with live conversations that can be heard in the groups studied and are limited in scale in comparison to the above speculative questions.

Population

For the empirical study, the population under consideration consists of choruses in Los Angeles, Chicago, and San Francisco. All results are based on 172 questionnaires received (about 48 percent of the total membership of the four choruses involved). I had intended to establish a balanced structure in two parallels—the San Francisco pair of the San Francisco Gay Men's Chorus (SFGMC) and the Dick Kramer Gay Men's Chorale (DKGMC) and the Chicago pair of the Chicago Gay Men's Chorus (CGMC) and the Windy City Gay Chorale, with the Gay Men's Chorus of Los Angeles (GMCLA) as a control group. The ideological disagreements between the two parallel groups, compared with the relatively "middle-of-the-road" reputation of the Los Angeles group, could result in a fascinating study. Unfortunately, both of the San Francisco groups returned relatively few responses, and the Windy City Gay Chorale did not respond at all; as a result, the study is not balanced. I have restructured the answers into a tripartite set of Los Angeles, Chicago, and San Francisco, where the responses from both San Francisco choruses are combined, ignoring the ideological differences that may distinguish them.

The Questionnaire

Questionnaires were distributed at rehearsals, supposedly anonymously, but with a vague statement implying institutional backing of some sort (possibly by GALA itself).[16] This seemed safe at the time, but may have backfired: responses to many of the questions were made on "best behavior," with an attitude of solidarity and positive image. This is probably a stronger comment on survival in a paranoid "administered society" than on any specific aspect of the choruses. In addition, due to some of the unusual and vitriolic responses from San Francisco chorus personnel, I am led to wonder about the actual distribution and resultant discussion that may have occurred in those choruses; as is true of all questionnaires, any doubt, uncertainty, or disapproval expressed, however subtly, by the person distributing them may have led to a generalized disinterest in answering the questions. In addition, the San Francisco choruses apparently did not have the leisure to easily fill out the forms during rehearsal, which could have led to a generalized dissatisfaction that would skew opinion responses.

The questionnaire (see p. 327) was designed with several goals in mind. The task of the first section (questions 1 through 4) is to create an accurate social profile of the members who responded. This section consists of questions on age, race, profession, salary, and neighborhood; it also brings up points on musical professionalism and begins to delve into the problem of gay identification or ghettoization. The second section (questions 5 through 9) attempts to divine the educational background and musical taste of participants. I had hoped to be able to analyze the responses in accordance with a typology approximately derived from Adorno's set of musical types,[17] but this became difficult for reasons that will be explained below. Perhaps the clearest result is an extension of the idea of musical professionalism mentioned above; it is quite clear what the participants' economic and educational relationships are to their positions on musical performance.

The third section explores the subject's relationship to his chorus, considering socialization, reasons for joining, intolerance of heterosexual presences, and judgment of music performed. Question 11 was a resounding success in supplying information that enabled me to create a matrix of analyzable and comprehensible data on reasons for being in the group, and question 13 also had very clear results. Unfortunately, question 14, which was of special interest, came up with virtually no interesting results; one would guess from it that the chorus members like all of the music they perform and that there is never any argument about musical values, which does not appear to be the actual case. Question 15 was as ambitious, and almost as unsuccessful, as question 14; it asked for the subject's opinions on various GALA festival participants. I would suggest that this section, more than any other, suffered from the anonymity of distribution of questionnaires; answers were guarded and vague, and mostly similar, so that most of the people who answered this question at all responded as though they had had the same reaction to all choruses. It is possible to establish some correlation of chorus skill, style, and repertoire with notations of "great" as opposed to "good," but this seems risky as an interpretive tool.

GALA QUESTIONNAIRE

Please answer as many questions as you can. Thank you for your time and attention.

1. Age: Under 20 [ ]   21-25 [ ]   26-30 [ ] 31-35 [ ] 36-40 [ ]   41-50 [ ]
    51-60 [ ]   Above 60 [ ]
2. Race: White [ ]   Asian [ ]   Hispanic [ ]   Black [ ]   Other [ ]
3. What is your profession or vocation?

    _____

    How are you making you living, if it is different from the above?

    _____

    What is your yearly salary range?
    Under 15,000 [ ]   15,000-25,000 [ ]   25,000-35,000 [ ]   35,00-50,000 [ ]
    Above 50,000 [ ]
    If you are a professional musician, but it is not your main income source, how
    much is your music income per year?
    Under 1,000 [ ]   1,000-5,000 [ ]   5,000-10,000 [ ]   Over 10,000 [ ]
4. What city, town and/or neighborhood do you live in?

    _____

    Do you live in a neighborhood that is:
    mostly gay? [ ]   partly gay? [ ]   tolerant of gays? [ ]
    unconscious or intolerant? [ ]
    Do you have a job or place of employment that is:
    mostly gay? [ ]   partly gay? [ ]   tolerant of gays? [ ]
    unconscious or intolerant? [ ]
5. Were you involved in musical organizations during your school years?
    Which ones?
    Choral [ ] _____
    Instrumental [ ] _____
    Popular/show [ ] _____
    None [ ] _____
6. Have you ever taken, or are you taking now, private music lessons?
    Voice lessons [ ] How many different teachers have you had? _____
    How long? Less than 1 year? [ ]   1-2 years[ ]   2-3 years [ ]
    3-4 years [ ]   Over 4 years [ ]
    Piano lessons [ ] Other instrument lessons? [ ]   Instrument: _____
    How long? Less than 1 year? [ ]   1-2 years[ ]   2-3 years [ ]
    3-4 years [ ]   Over 4 years [ ]
    Are you taking lessons now?   Yes [ ]   No [ ]
7. Do you hold any academic degrees?
    High school [ ]   Bachelor's [ ]   Master's [ ]   Doctorate [ ]   Other [ ]
    Are any of them in music? B.A./B.F.A. [ ]   M.A./M.F.A. [ ]
    Ph.D./D.M.A. [ ]   Other _____
    If you have a music degree, what field is it in?
    Performance [ ]   Composition [ ]   Education [ ]   Musicology [ ]
    Therapy [ ]   Other [ ] _____

8. What kind(s) of music do you go to concerts to hear, or listen to on records or radio?
   Classical [ ]   What kind(s)? (opera, baroque, etc.)
   Popular [ ]   What kind(s)? (rock, show, etc.)
   Other [ ] _____

9. Do you socialize with other members of this group? Where?
   Constantly [ ]   Often [ ]   Sometimes [ ]   Seldom [ ]   Never [ ]
   Restaurants [ ]   Bars [ ]   Parties [ ]   Trips [ ]   Other [ ] _____

10. How important to you were the following reasons in first joining this group?
    (On a range of: 1 = very important, to 5 = unimportant.)
    Musical excellence: 1 [ ] 2 [ ] 3 [ ] 4 [ ] 5 [ ]
    Community service: 1 [ ] 2 [ ] 3 [ ] 4 [ ] 5 [ ]
    Being in a gay group: 1 [ ] 2 [ ] 3 [ ] 4 [ ] 5 [ ]
    Performance opportunity: 1 [ ] 2 [ ] 3 [ ] 4 [ ] 5 [ ]
    Political identity: 1 [ ] 2 [ ] 3 [ ] 4 [ ] 5 [ ]
    Having a good time: 1 [ ] 2 [ ] 3 [ ] 4 [ ] 5 [ ]

11. Which of these reasons is important to you now?
    Musical excellence: 1 [ ] 2 [ ] 3 [ ] 4 [ ] 5 [ ]
    Community service: 1 [ ] 2 [ ] 3 [ ] 4 [ ] 5 [ ]
    Being in a gay group: 1 [ ] 2 [ ] 3 [ ] 4 [ ] 5 [ ]
    Performance opportunity: 1 [ ] 2 [ ] 3 [ ] 4 [ ] 5 [ ]
    Political identity: 1 [ ] 2 [ ] 3 [ ] 4 [ ] 5 [ ]
    Having a good time: 1 [ ] 2 [ ] 3 [ ] 4 [ ] 5 [ ]

13. How would (or do) you feel about someone straight (male or female) in the group?
    Like the idea [ ]   No opinion [ ]   Don't like the idea [ ]
    In a support of staff position?   Like the idea [ ]   No opinion [ ]
    Don't like the idea [ ]
    Directing the group?   Like the idea [ ]   No opinion [ ]   Don't like the idea [ ]

14. Do you feel the music that you have done in this group over the past year is, in general:
    too difficult [ ]   difficult but learnable [ ]   not difficult [ ]   easy [ ]?
    appropriate [ ]   inappropriate [ ]   too political [ ]   too trivial [ ]
    too sophisticated [ ]   other [ ] _____

15. If you were at the GALA Festival II, please share your opinions: what was your
    reaction—musical, social, political, emotional—to the following choruses?
    (If you want to write about other groups, or have more to say, please use the back.)
    Chicago GMC _____
    Denver Women's Choru _____
    Dick Kramer GMC (San Francisco) _____
    GMC of Washington, D.C. _____
    Los Angeles GMC _____
    Madison GMC _____
    New York City, GMC _____
    Portland, GMC _____
    Rochester, GMC _____
    San Francisco, GMC _____
    Seattle Men's Chorus _____
    Twin Cities Men's Chorus _____
    Windy City Gay Chorus (Chicago) _____

Results

Discussion of the results of the questionnaire will be handled as follows: first, a basic profile of the subjects will be built up, followed by analysis of education and musical taste. Questions 10, 13, and 14 will then be considered as determining the relations between subject and group, and finally questions 11 and 15 will be considered as indicating basic commitments of the chorus members (see appendix A for full results).

Age and race responses are unsurprising; 87 percent of members are between the ages of twenty-six and fifty, and 93 percent are white. The racial demographics suggest that gay white solidarity with minorities is mostly of symbolic value; in fact, black members of the GMCLA met with bigoted statements and antisocial behavior from several members of the CGMC when they visited Chicago. It is undeniable that the choruses are essentially white institutions producing performances of white music. Salary responses are slightly lower than expected, as more than half of respondents made less than $25,000 annually.

Question 3d indicates that these choruses must be classified as nonprofessional groups, as only 11 percent of their members have any musical income, and none of them makes over $5,000 per year from musical work. The "ghettoization" questions (question 4) include minor variations between cities; as might be expected, gay men in Los Angeles experienced somewhat more intolerance than those in San Francisco, and Chicago men much more. Generally, subjects live in "partly gay" neighborhoods and have "tolerant" jobs; more repression in the workplace than at home is probably normal.

Question 5 begins the analysis of musical background and education. It shows that 92 percent of respondents were involved in musical performances (often of all three types) during their school years, but many members stopped music performance after that time, and virtually all of them stopped being involved with instrumental performance. This is important, as an instrumental background leads to much greater precision in pitch and rhythm for most vocalists. Voice lessons are in the background of only about half of the subjects; the number currently taking voice lessons seems remarkably low (10 percent), since voice lessons are generally regarded as useful throughout a singing career. However, the musical professionalism of the population seems higher if the responses on length of study are considered, which indicate that those taking voice lessons have spent an appreciable amount of time and effort. Responses on instrumental lessons are parallel to, but lower than, responses on vocal lessons.

The more sophisticated attitude toward "high culture" commonly noted in San Francisco is indicated in a distinctly higher profile of musical education (although the sparsity of San Francisco responses makes analysis difficult). By reputation, the DKGMC is regarded as a proponent of "high culture" and the SFGMC as more "mainstream," though both perform more classical music than the other choruses; in fact, the CGMC is considered a "popular" chorus and rarely performs classical music. General academic statistics are fairly consistent between the choruses, and do not seem out of line with national norms. Statistics on music degrees are, however, surprising: the number of people with an academic background in music is extremely low among those responding. Question 9, on personal listening preferences, also showed that the San Francisco members tend to prefer classical music.

The socialization question (number 10) indicates patterns that are made clearer in the more elaborate matrices of question 11. Socialization within the group is frequent; the slightly tongue-in-cheek answer "constantly" actually had some responses, and almost 90 percent of the respondents socialize at least "sometimes." When locations are divided into commercial (restaurants and bars) and personal (parties and trips), and comments added under "other" are included in this division, the results are fairly evenly split; there seems to be no strong preference for homes versus commercial establishments. A more detailed question that requested that answers be put in a hierarchy might come up with different results. Of interest is the relatively lower rate of socialization of the DKGMC, which might be compared to its emphasis on musical aims. In addition, the extremely high response to socialization specifically in bars in the CGMC (83 percent) may reflect a particular aspect of that chorus, but more probably reflects a noticeable aspect of Chicago gay society—that it is even more centered on bars and alcohol consumption than the California gay subculture.

Question 13, on potential heterosexual members of choruses, showed strongly aligned results with interesting implications. If "no opinions" are excluded, responses are about equally divided on the idea of a heterosexual member of the group (although, as a member of the CGMC pointed out, "we have one"). However, responses are very positive about the idea of a heterosexual support or staff person, and very negative about being directed by heterosexuals. This supports certain aspects of the theory of authoritarian structures and the ambivalence of the gay male toward phallic dominance. If gay males re-create a traditional authoritarian structure within a given group, they evidently prefer to do so only among themselves; straight "servants" are acceptable, even pleasant, but straight "masters" are out of the question, as such a configuration would make the situation identical to the structures of the outside world that the openly gay man is revolting against. In this context, it is interesting that the only known gay chorus that was not a member of GALA in 1986 was the Turtle Creek Chorale in Texas, which was then directed by a straight man; overheard comments indicate that the chorus had pariah status among GALA members at that time.

Question 14 had problematic results, which I believe do not reflect the real situation. Discussion of the difficulty and appropriateness of repertoire is common among the choruses, and a source of ongoing controversy; the overwhelmingly positive answers to this question suggest a sampling error to me. Probably questions 11, 14, and 15 also suffer from a problem detailed earlier, that of the apparent source of the questionnaire; since 14, particularly, requests a certain amount of self-criticism, it could create defensive responses in subjects uncertain of the ultimate destination of their answers.

Question 11: A Special Analysis

Question 11 is by far the most consistently answered of the "opinion" questions after question 9. Virtually every subject responded with six single values for six possible answers. The only problem responses are those who answered all six values as "one," or more rarely as "two"; these are common and added nothing to the usefulness of the responses. However, they do not skew the relationships between answers; the only result is that a disproportionate number of "ones" occur in each category, but each category retains a useful comparative relation to the others. It might be plausible to ignore all undifferentiated responses, as it is difficult to believe that anyone has exactly the same commitment to six very different activities.

Question 11 can be divided into 11a, which identifies reasons for joining the group, and 11c, which includes reasons for being in the group now. These are further interpreted into 11b and 11d, which group commitments in pairs as musical, political, or social. The results of 11d—the interpreted reasons for being in a chorus—are shown in charts in appendix B. Radical differences in values show up here, suggesting that this question indicates important aspects of differentiation between the choruses.

One of the original hypotheses of this study was that the various choruses are centered on different central commitments. If the existence of a heterosexual chorus has chiefly musical and secondarily social reasons for its existence, a gay chorus may have a more complex relation to social issues, and may have political commitments that do not even appear in a heterosexual group. More importantly, the gay choruses do not exist in a social vacuum; chorus reputations, as known among GALA groups, tend to become self-perpetuating, and are generally based on the strongest commitment of the group. This commitment will, of course, be related to the strongest commitment of its director, combined with the strongest values typical of a given city.

The general chorus commitment can become even stronger if it solidifies into an ideology, as it tends to do when there are two choruses in the same city. For example, the contrast between the two Chicago choruses—the CGMC and the Windy City Gay Chorale—is remarkably specific and widely acknowledged. The verbal battle between the two is best summed up by Windy City's frequently repeated assertion that they stand for "quality, not quantity," and in the CGMC's peculiar acceptance of such a malicious distinction. This may go a long way toward explaining the CGMC's unusually high commitment to social values, as can be seen in the second chart. On the other end of the spectrum is the DKGMC, whose high musical values and very low political values appear on the third chart; this contrasts with the values of the other San Francisco chorus, which are less extreme, perhaps for ideological reasons.

The responses to question 11 are more useful for differentiating choruses than for a general analysis of the gay choruses, as can be seen in the final chart; when all values are added together, they tend to become statistically similar (except for the low initial response to political values). I suggest that the total field of possible "highest commitments" is basically undifferentiated, and that the best way to analyze them is by the different patterns they form in different groups. It would seem that all sorts of values are initially important to all of the groups, but each group gradually develops its own ideology and value structure. In fact, "I suggest" that the gay choruses were started for political reasons, and then immediately continued for social reasons; however, as the entire system matured, it became clear that a chorus could only remain viable if a commitment to music and/or the socialization of performance were to be created. In other words, it makes sense to join a group for political reasons, and to stay for social reasons, but one can only get through years of weekly rehearsals if a commitment that is directly related to the material at hand (i.e., music) is emphasized on an ongoing basis.

A task that might be possible with the results of question 11 would be to corroborate the answers to this question with some sort of summary of the education and taste questions, so that individuals could be analyzed independently of the group structure. Thus, a given questionnaire could be considered as having a certain "educational/musical index" based on traditional "high culture" values, and this could be compared to the strongest commitment indicated on the same questionnaire. The results of such analysis could be useful in indicating minimal and maximal educational requirements for the needs of different directors.

Question 15

The results of question 15 are problematic; responses are vague and often overly similar, perhaps because the question itself required a certain amount of time and thought and came at the end of a long questionnaire. It is often difficult to get people to put their opinions on paper, particularly when they are uncertain as to who will read them; also, of course, the subjects were being asked for opinions on an event five months after its end. It is unfortunate to be unable to record the many elaborate and specific judgments that were aired during the festival. Most individuals verbally expressed strong valuations for or against the various performances, citing precision, musicality, sincerity, and other criteria. Interestingly, the GMCLA responses subtly reflect the director's opinions, which were publicly expressed to the group after the festival; since these opinions did not tally with the general discussion as it had developed until then, I suggest that many members reformed their opinions in conformity with the director's. This may also have happened in other choruses, and it reflects both the authority of the director and the ideological homogenization of opinion.

Question 15 faintly indicates certain patterned reactions. This raises the interesting idea: Can such patterns be accurately discovered, if the question is phrased differently? Optimally, the question should give a sharper picture of the values of the individual; it would reveal, for instance, if he felt that his chorus were excellent musically, but wished he were in another group that would meet higher social requirements. The danger of such a question, aside from that of insulting the directors and half of the performers (a very real risk), is that answers may become tautological: if the larger group ideology establishes that a certain chorus is very skilled, finding out that an individual thinks the chorus is very skilled is useless. More valuable would be a questionnaire that, without appearing to do so, would ask: Do you think chorus "x" is very skilled? Do you think this is good, neutral, or bad? Is it enjoyable to watch them perform? Do you think this is good, neutral, or bad? et cetera. It would be valuable to find a phrasing that would be both useful to the questioner and plausible to the subject.

Epilogue

In conclusion, I suggest that authority structures and individual commitments are important subjects of study, that they can be analyzed in a useful way, and that this applies to any organization. The conflict between a lack of musical sophistication typical of contemporary American culture, a survival-based need for strong political identification, and an instinctive attempt to revive traditional authoritarian musical goals created a complex and sometimes uncomfortable social structure in the gay choruses during their first decade. It is dangerous to create powerful authority structures in the absence of a clearly stated commitment (i.e., social versus musical), as such structures tend to become both self-perpetuating and unrelated to outside goals. This is shown in frequent minor skirmishes over power, where the group commitment to either gay identity or musical skill is so unclear or unarticulated that individuals fight for ascendancy in the group, regardless of the damage done to its social fabric.

Perhaps there is not a best answer, or even a strongest commitment, and if the need is for an ongoing dialectic between different commitments, this must finally be acknowledged. What is perhaps the most interesting aspect of the problem is that, in line with Attali's comments, the gay chorus is not merely a microcosm of an existing society; it can be seen as the only existing microcosm of a potential gay society, which does not yet exist. If it is possible to learn from the various successes, mistakes, and uncertainties, the kind of nonauthoritarian society envisioned by the writers of *Anti-Oedipus* may be a realizable goal.

Appendix A

Quantifiable Questionnaire Results

Question	GMCLA #	%	CGMC #	%	DKGMC #	%	SFGMC #	%	SF Total #	%	Total #	%
Current membership (approximate)	85	100	120	100	55	100	100	100	155	100	360	100
Responses received	60	71	72	60	24	44	16	16	40	26	172	48
1 Age:												
21-25	6	10	6	8	2	8	2	13	4	10	16	9
26-30	9	15	19	26	7	29	2	13	9	23	37	22
31-35	15	25	23	32	1	4	5	31	6	15	44	26
36-40	13	22	12	17	3	13	5	31	8	20	33	19
41-50	13	22	11	15	10	42	2	13	12	30	36	21
51-60	3	5	2	3	1	4			1	3	6	3
Above 60	2	3									2	1
2 Race:												
White	52	87	71	99	21	88	16	100	37	93	160	93
Hispanic	1	2			2	8			2	5	3	2
Black	5	8			1	4			1	3	6	3
Asian			1	1							1	1
Other	1	2									1	1
3c Salary:												
Under 15,000	10	17	12	17	2	8	4	25	6	15	28	16
15,000-25,000	15	25	25	35	8	33	4	25	12	30	52	30
25,000-35,000	18	30	13	18	4	17	5	31	9	23	40	23
Above 50,000	9	15	10	14	1	4	2	13	3	8	22	13
3d Musical income:												
Under 1,000	8	13	4	6	1	4	2	13	3	8	15	9
1,000–5,000	1	2	2	3	1	4			1	3	4	2
4b Neighborhood:												
Mostly gay	7	12	15	21	4	17	1	6	5	13	27	16
Partly gay	30	50	35	49	13	54	7	44	20	50	85	49
Tolerant of gays	14	23	15	21	5	21	6	38	11	28	40	23
Unconscious/intolerant	11	18	9	13	2	8	1	6	3	8	23	13

Question	GMCLA #	GMCLA %	CGMC #	CGMC %	DKGMC #	DKGMC %	SFGMC #	SFGMC %	SF Total #	SF Total %	Total #	Total %
4c Job:												
Mostly gay	8	13	8	11	3	13	2	13	5	13	21	12
Partly gay	10	17	14	19	8	33	6	38	14	35	38	22
Tolerant of gays	32	53	21	29	8	33	6	38	14	35	67	39
Unconscious/intolerant	10	17	28	39	4	17			4	10	42	24
5a Music in school years:												
Choral	51	85	58	81	19	79	13	81	32	80	141	82
Instrumental	24	40	29	40	12	50	4	25	16	40	69	40
Popular/show	26	43	34	47	7	29	9	56	16	40	76	44
None (interpreted)	5	8	6	8			3	19	3	8	14	8
6a Music after school years:												
Choral	41	68	33	46	16	67	12	75	28	70	102	59
Instrumental	6	10	5	7	2	8	1	6	3	8	14	8
Popular/show	17	28	16	22	9	38	3	19	12	30	45	26
None (interpreted)	15	25	32	44	4	17	3	19	7	18	54	31
7a Voice lessons	28	47	39	54	17	71	12	75	29	73	96	56
7b Number of teachers:												
1	6	10	13	18	7	29	2	13	9	23	28	16
2	11	18	6	8	2	8	2	13	4	10	21	12
3	4	7	8	11	4	17	3	19	7	18	19	11
4 plus	5	8	12	17	3	13	5	31	8	20	25	15
7c Years:												
Less than 1	5	8	11	15	6	25	2	13	8	20	24	14
1–2	7	12	7	10	4	17	2	13	6	15	20	12
2–3	7	12	4	6	4	17	1	6	5	13	16	9
3–4	1	2	4	6	1	4	1	6	2	5	7	4
Over 4	8	13	10	14	2	8	4	25	6	15	24	14
7d Currently taking voice lessons	2	3	13	18	1	4	2	13	3	8	18	10
7e Piano lessons	33	55	22	31	11	46	7	44	18	45	73	42
Other instrument lessons	23	38	18	25	6	25	2	13	8	20	49	28

Question	GMCLA #	%	CGMC #	%	DKGMC #	%	SFGMC #	%	SF Total #	%	Total #	%
7f Years:												
Less than 1	7	12	3	4	1	4	1	6	2	5	12	7
1–2	8	13	4	6	3	13	3	19	6	15	18	10
2–3	5	8	5	7	3	13			3	8	13	8
3–4	3	5	2	3	1	4			1	3	6	3
Over 4	19	32	17	24	6	25	3	19	9	23	45	26
7g Currently taking instrument lessons:	2	3	1	1	2	8			2	5	5	3
8a Academic level:												
High School	7	12	12	17	6	25	4	25	10	25	29	17
Associate	4	7	2	3	2	8			2	5	8	5
Bachelors	29	48	31	43	9	38	8	50	17	43	77	45
Masters	13	22	22	31	5	21	4	25	9	23	44	26
Doctorate	8	13	4	6	2	8	1	6	3	8	15	9
8b Music degrees:												
Associate	1	2									1	1
Bachelors	9	15	2	3							11	6
Masters	2	3	1	1							3	2
8c Field of music degree:												
Education	5	8	2	3							7	4
Performance/conducting	2	3									2	1
Composition	1	2	1	1							2	1
Musicology	1	2									1	1
9a Music heard:												
Classical	53	88	56	78	24	100	13	81	37	93	146	85
Popular	49	82	62	86	18	75	14	88	32	80	143	83
9b Music heard exclusively:												
Classical (interpreted)	12	20	9	13	6	25	1	6	7	18	28	16
Popular (interpreted)	7	12	15	21			2	13	2	5	24	14
10a Socializing:												
Constantly	3	5	6	8	3	13	1	6	4	10	13	8
Often	22	37	36	50	5	21	8	50	13	33	71	41
Sometimes	25	42	23	32	13	54	4	25	17	43	65	38
Seldom	9	15	2	3	4	17	2	13	6	15	17	10
Never							1	6	1	3	1	1

Question	GMCLA #	%	CGMC #	%	DKGMC #	%	SFGMC #	%	SF Total #	%	Total #	%
10b Location:												
Restaurants	39	65	39	54	7	29	8	50	15	38	93	54
Bars	25	42	60	83	5	21	8	50	13	33	98	57
Parties	38	63	56	78	14	58	12	75	26	65	120	70
Trips	26	43	32	44	7	29	8	50	15	38	73	42
10c Location, commercial (interpreted)	67	112	100	139	13	54	17	106	30	75	197	115
Location, personal (interpreted)	68	113	92	128	26	108	21	131	47	118	207	120
13a Straights in group:												
Like the idea	20	33	15	21	10	42	4	25	14	35	49	28
No opinion	18	30	31	43	9	38	6	38	15	38	64	37
Don't like the idea	21	35	26	36	4	17	5	31	9	23	56	33
13b Straight support:												
Like the idea	35	58	38	53	11	46	9	56	20	50	93	54
No opinion	18	30	27	38	11	46	6	38	17	43	62	36
Don't like the idea	5	8	6	8			1	6	1	3	12	7
13c Straight direction:												
Like the idea	11	18	7	10	3	13			3	8	21	12
No opinion	21	35	21	29	9	38	6	38	12	30	57	33
Don't like the idea	26	43	40	56	9	38	10	63	19	48	85	49
14a Music:												
Too difficult	2	3			2	8	1	6	3	8	5	3
Difficult but learnable	37	62	33	46	20	83	11	69	31	78	101	59
Not difficult	16	27	23	32	1	4	1	6	2	5	41	24
Easy	2	3	11	15			1	6	1	3	14	8
14b Appropriate	42	70	54	75	19	79	10	63	29	73	125	73
Inappropriate	1	2	1	1							2	1
Too political	2	3	2	3							4	2
Too trivial	3	5	5	7			2	13	2	5	10	6
Too sophisticated	2	3									2	1
14c Positive answers from "other"	2	3	2	3	1	4			1	3	5	3
Negative answers from "other" plus total from 14b	13	22	10	14	2	8	4	25	6	15	29	17

GMCLA	**One** (most imp.)		**Two**		**Three**		**Four**		**Five** (least imp.)	
	#	%	#	%	#	%	#	%	#	%
11a Reason for joining:										
Musical excellence	19	32	16	27	14	23	5	8	5	8
Community service	12	20	19	32	18	30	6	10	4	7
Being in a gay group	34	57	8	13	5	8	3	5	9	15
Performance opportunity	23	38	16	27	13	22	5	8	(2)	(3)
Political identity	17	28	15	25	12	20	12	20	(0)	(0)
Having a good time	24	40	12	20	13	22	9	15	(2)	(3)
11b Musical excellence + performance opportunity	42	35	32	27	27	23	10	8	(7)	(6)
Community service + political identity	29	24	34	28	30	25	18	15	(4)	(3)
Being in a gay group + having a good time	58	48	20	17	18	15	12	10	(11)	(9)
11c Reason for staying:										
Musical excellence	37	62	12	20	1	2	2	3	7	12
Community service	22	37	19	32	11	18	3	5	4	7
Being in a gay group	29	48	12	20	8	13	1	2	8	13
Performance opportunity	31	52	12	20	9	15	6	10	(0)	(0)
Political identity	23	38	14	23	14	23	4	7	(0)	(0)
Having a good time	22	37	11	18	15	25	9	15	(2)	(3)
11d Musical excellence + performance opportunity	68	57	24	20	10	8	8	7	(7)	(6)
Community service + political identity	45	38	33	28	25	21	7	6	(4)	(3)
Being in a gay group + having a good time	51	43	23	19	23	19	10	8	(10)	(8)
CGMC										
11a Reason for joining:										
Musical excellence	11	15	19	26	29	40	11	15	4	6
Community service	26	36	20	28	15	21	7	10	6	8
Being in a gay group	41	57	17	24	6	8	6	8	5	7
Performance opportunity	23	32	30	42	11	15	4	6	5	7
Political identity	13	18	18	25	12	17	12	17	18	25
Having a good time	40	56	18	25	5	7	7	10	5	7

CGMC (continued)	One (most imp.) # %	Two # %	Three # %	Four # %	Five (least imp.) # %
11b Musical excellence + performance opportunity	34 24	49 34	40 28	15 10	9 6
Community service + political identity	39 27	38 26	27 19	19 13	24 17
Being in a gay group + having a good time	81 56	35 24	11 8	13 9	10 7
11c Reason for staying:					
Musical excellence	30 42	23 32	9 13	4 6	3 4
Community service	39 54	20 28	5 7	3 4	3 4
Being in a gay group	42 58	12 17	6 8	7 10	2 3
Performance opportunity	27 38	25 35	6 8	5 7	5 7
Political identity	13 18	19 26	18 25	5 7	12 17
Having a good time	38 53	15 21	8 11	3 4	5 7
11d Musical excellence + performance opportunity	57 40	48 33	15 10	9 6	8 6
Community service + political identity	52 36	39 27	23 16	8 6	15 10
Being in a gay group + having a good time	80 56	27 19	14 10	10 7	7 5
DKGMC					
11a Reason for joining:					
Musical excellence	13 54	5 21	4 17		2 8
Community service	1 4	6 25	6 25	8 33	2 8
Being in a gay group	10 42	7 29	4 17	1 4	1 4
Performance opportunity	12 50	4 17	6 25·	1 4	
Political identity		1 4	7 29	9 38	6 25
Having a good time	7 29	10 42	6 25	1 4	
11b Musical excellence + performance opportunity	25 52	9 19	10 21	1 2	2 4
Community service + political identity	1 2	7 15	13 27	17 35	8 17
Being in a gay group + having a good time	17 35	17 35	10 21	2 4	1 2

DKGMC (continued)	One (most imp.) # %	Two # %	Three # %	Four # %	Five (least imp.) # %
11c Reason for staying:					
Musical excellence	15 63	5 21	3 13		
Community service	1 4	9 38	8 33	2 8	2 8
Being in a gay group	6 25	9 38	4 17	2 8	1 4
Performance opportunity	11 46	3 13	10 42		
Political identity	1 4	2 8	7 29	7 29	6 25
Having a good time	9 38	7 29	7 29		
11d Musical excellence + performance opportunity	26 54	8 17	13 27		
Community service + political identity	2 4	11 23	15 31	9 19	8 17
Being in a gay group + having a good time	15 31	16 33	11 23	2 4	1 2
SFGMC					
11a Reason for joining:					
Musical excellence	7 44	5 31	1 6	1 6	1 6
Community service	6 38	3 19	2 13		4 25
Being in a gay group	11 69	1 6	2 13		2 13
Performance opportunity	8 50	3 19	2 13	1 6	1 6
Political identity	3 19	3 19	2 13	1 6	5 31
Having a good time	6 38	5 31	4 25		1 6
11b Musical excellence + performance opportunity	15 47	8 25	3 9	2 6	2 6
Community service + political identity	9 28	6 19	4 13	1 3	9 28
Being in a gay group + having a good time	17 53	6 19	6 19		3 9
11c Reason for staying:					
Musical excellence	10 63	3 19	1 6		1 6
Community service	5 31	5 31	2 13	1 6	1 6
Being in a gay group	7 44	4 25	1 6		3 19
Performance opportunity	8 50	3 19		1 6	2 13
Political identity	4 25	2 13	2 13	1 6	5 31
Having a good time	4 25	5 31	4 25		2 13

SFGMC (continued)	One (most imp.) # %	Two # %	Three # %	Four # %	Five (least imp.) # %
11d Musical excellence + performance opportunity	18 56	6 19	1 3	1 3	3 9
Community service + political identity	9 28	7 22	4 13	2 6	6 19
Being in a gay group + having a good time	11 34	9 28	5 16		5 16
San Francisco combined					
11a Reason for joining:					
Musical excellence	20 50	10 25	5 13	1 3	3 8
Community service	7 18	9 23	8 20	8 20	6 15
Being in a gay group	21 53	8 20	6 15	1 3	3 8
Performance opportunity	20 50	7 18	8 20	2 5	1 3
Political identity	3 8	4 10	9 23	10 25	11 28
Having a good time	13 33	15 38	10 25	1 3	1 3
11b Musical excellence + performance opportunity	40 50	17 21	13 16	3 4	4 5
Community service + political identity	10 13	13 16	17 21	18 23	17 21
Being in a gay group + having a good time	34 43	23 29	16 20	2 3	4 5
11c Reason for staying:					
Musical excellence	25 63	8 20	4 10		1 3
Community service	6 15	14 35	10 25	3 8	3 8
Being in a gay group	13 33	13 33	5 13	2 5	4 10
Performance opportunity	19 48	6 15	10 25	1 3	2 5
Political identity	5 13	4 10	9 23	8 20	11 28
Having a good time	13 33	12 30	11 28		2 5
11d Musical excellence + performance opportunity	44 55	14 18	14 18	1 1	3 4
Community service + political identity	11 14	18 23	19 24	11 14	14 18
Being in a gay group + having a good time	26 33	25 31	16 20	2 3	6 8

Total	One (most imp.)		Two		Three		Four		Five (least imp.)	
	#	%	#	%	#	%	#	%	#	%
11a Reason for joining:										
Musical excellence	50	29	45	26	48	28	17	10	12	7
Community service	45	26	48	28	41	24	21	12	16	9
Being in a gay group	96	56	33	19	17	10	10	6	17	10
Performance opportunity	66	38	53	31	32	19	11	6	(8)	(5)
Political identity	33	19	37	22	33	19	34	20	(29)	(17)
Having a good time	77	45	45	26	28	16	17	10	(8)	(5)
11b Musical excellence + performance opportunity	116	34	98	28	80	23	28	8	(20)	(6)
Community service + political identity	78	23	85	25	74	22	55	16	(45)	(13)
Being in a gay group + having a good time	173	50	78	23	45	13	27	8	(25)	(7)
11c Reason for staying:										
Musical excellence	92	53	43	25	14	8	6	3	11	6
Community service	67	39	53	31	26	15	9	5	10	6
Being in a gay group	84	49	37	22	19	11	10	6	14	8
Performance opportunity	77	45	43	25	25	15	12	7	(7)	(4)
Political identity	41	24	37	22	41	24	17	10	(23)	(13)
Having a good time	73	42	38	22	34	20	12	7	(9)	(5)
11d Musical excellence + performance opportunity	169	49	86	25	39	11	18	5	(18)	(5)
Community service + political identity	108	31	90	26	67	19	26	8	(33)	(10)
Being in a gay group + having a good time	157	46	75	22	53	15	22	6	(23)	(7)

Appendix B

Question 11d

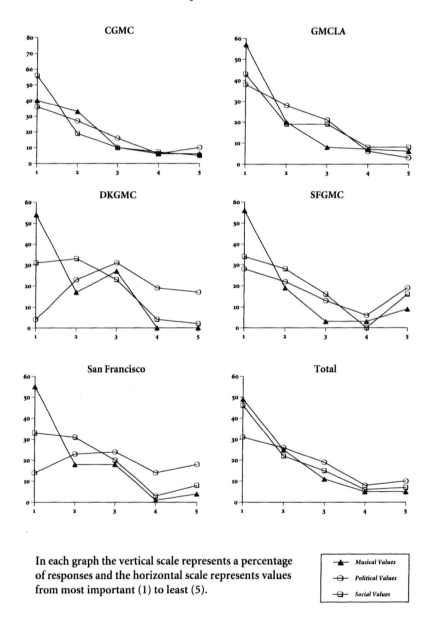

In each graph the vertical scale represents a percentage of responses and the horizontal scale represents values from most important (1) to least (5).

- ▲ *Musical Values*
- ⊖ *Political Values*
- ⊟ *Social Values*

Notes

I am indebted to Sue DeVale for supporting me in writing this paper at a time when its subject caused evident discomfort in a number of colleagues; to Philip Brett for kindly encouraging me to exhume it; and to Philip, Carol Robertson, and Elizabeth Wood for their valued comments. Shortened versions were read at the first Feminist Theory and Music conference in Minneapolis on 29 June 1991, and at the national conference of the Society for Ethnomusicology in Chicago on 13 October 1991.

1. The original version of this paper was researched and written in the fall of 1986. Its assertions and observations are embedded in social situations that were current at the time; various social and ideological patterns in the gay choruses and in gay culture in general have changed since that period. As it would be impossible to adequately expand the ensuing theory and data to cover queer/activist culture, lesbian choruses, and the stable bourgeois infrastructure that has developed in many gay institutions in the wake of the AIDS crisis, I have chosen to leave my ideas mostly in their original form; I believe the paper is best viewed as a snapshot of a particular, and interestingly volatile, historical moment, accompanied by a theoretical structure that remains viable, if in need of qualification. The researcher interested in the gay choruses may wish to examine the growing literature on lesbian choruses, notably Catherine Roma's article originally titled "Women's Choral Communities—Singing for Our Lives: The Women's Choral Movement in the USA Since 1975," which is scheduled to appear in *Signs*; and Carol Robertson's "Power and Gender in the Musical Experiences of Women," in Ellen Koskoff, ed., *Women and Music in Cross-Cultural Perspective* (Urbana: University of Illinois Press, 1989), 225–44.

2. Jon Sims founded the San Francisco Gay Freedom Day Marching Band in June of 1978 and the San Francisco Gay Men's Chorus in November of that year. Other choruses and instrumental groups appeared in rapid succession in major American cities. A more detailed biography and historical overview by the present author appears in *Baker's Biographical Dictionary of Musicians*, eighth edition (New York: Schirmer Books, 1992) under "Sims, Jon Reed."

3. GALA has continued to expand with remarkable speed. As of 1993, there are 188 member choruses in North America and Europe; the 1992 triennial festival included performances by more than sixty ensembles.

4. George Stambolian and Elaine Marks, eds., *Homosexualities and French Literature* (Ithaca, N.Y.: Cornell University Press, 1979), 25. George Stambolian died of AIDS in 1991.

5. Guy Hocquenghem, *Homosexual Desire*, trans. D. Dangoor (London: Allison & Busby, 1978), 126. The FLN is the *Front de libération nationale*, or Algerian freedom movement.

6. Gilles Deleuze and Félix Guattari, *Anti-Oedipus: Capitalism and Schizophrenia*, trans. Robert Hurley, Mark Seem, and Helen R. Lane (Minneapolis: University of Minnesota Press, 1983).

7. Michel Foucault, *History of Sexuality*, vol. I, trans. Robert Hurley (New York: Random House, 1980); John Boswell, *Christianity, Social Tolerance, and Homosexuality* (Chicago: University of Chicago Press, 1980).

8. In the face of recent American publications that cite a great deal of French theory, this assertion is somewhat dated. Philip Brett has also pointed out that although French homosexual theorists such as Foucault, Derrida, Deleuze, Wittig, and others have had a major effect on French intellectual culture, they inhabit a country that has a much less powerful gay subculture than America or Germany. Perhaps this leads to a distinction between theorists who are permanent outsiders and theorists involved in processes of assimilation; in any case, American cultural criticism has been severely limited by its avoidance of the questions raised in French discourses.

9. C. A. Tripp, *The Homosexual Matrix* (New York: McGraw-Hill, 1975).

10. As is often the case in psychological and cultural analysis, the opposite is true for a portion of the population: drag queens and images of feminization are an important part of the subculture and a reminder of the historically powerful "inversion" model of homosexuality. However, the significant aspect of post-Stonewall gay culture seems to be the creation of alternatives to pre-Stonewall choices of assimilation or effeminacy, including the construction of a partly traditional masculinity that is exaggerated and re-marked to signify gayness (e. g., the "clone" look). This "third choice" was long employed by the most visible members of the subculture in urban centers, as "queerness" is employed today. In any case, all of these polarities, whether construed as positive or negative, indicate the importance of these signifiers and their implications to the members of the subculture.

11. Such identification is extremely common among groups that purport to represent the general gay population—although, of course, there are some subject-specific groups that tend toward the political right.

12. Theodor Adorno, *Introduction to the Sociology of Music*, trans. E. B. Ashton (New York: Seabury Press, 1976), 104–106.

13. My use of gendered pronouns is not unintentional, given the context and implications of the discussion.

14. Jacques Attali, *Noise: The Political Economy of Music*, trans. Brian Massumi (Minneapolis: University of Minnesota, 1985), 29.

15. If that illness is AIDS, as it frequently has been, the lengthy, gradual, and unpredictable shifts in ability and well-being suffered by the director are agonizing for the chorus as a social institution, paradigmatically as the familiar situation of a strong parent suffering the slow deterioration of aging is widely regarded as agonizing for adult children of any sexual persuasion.

16. The questionnaire itself is included here for reference. The alert reader will notice no question 12; this was true of the original.

17. Adorno, *Introduction*, 1–20.

INDEX

A

Absolute Torch and Twang (lang), 257
Achille Lauro, the, 107
Acis and Galatea (Handel), 187
Adams, John, 97
Adorno, Theodor, 216, 322, 323, 326
Advocate, The, 269
AIDS, 10, 21, 89, 94, 96, 102, 103, 104, 110, 169, 315, 345n
Albee, Edward, 90, 106
Albert Hall, the, 239
Albert Herring (Britten), 105
Alceste (Gluck), 39
Aldeburgh Festival, 239, 254n, 255n
Alexandria Quartet, The (Durrell), 249
Allatini, Rose, 24n
Amazons, the, 284-85
Ameling, Elly, 94
American Musicological Society, 15, 205
Anderson, Laurie, 283
Anderson, Steven, 259
André, Lucrezia d', 163, 193-94n
Anna la Bonne (Cocteau), 88
Anniversary, The (Rorem), 88
Anti-Oedipus (Deleuze and Guattari), 317-18, 334
Antonioni, Michelangelo, 91
Antony and Cleopatra (Barber), 99
Aphrodite (Erlanger), 41, 42
Arcadia, 175, 177-79, 188, 198n
Ariane et Barbe Bleue (Maeterlinck/Dukas), 42
Ariosti, Attilio, 174
Armgart (Eliot), 58n
As Music and Splendour (O'Brien), 36, 37
Atherton, Gertrude, 33, 54, 60n
Attali, Jacques, 322-23, 334
Attinello, Paul, 207
Aubrey, Mary, 117
Auden, W. H., 240, 249, 250
Augier, Emile, 42
Augustine, St., 11
Austen, Jane, 212

B

Babbitt, Milton, 97
Bach, J. S., 14, 77-78, 93
Baldwin, James, 227
Balinese Ceremonial Music (McPhee), 238
Balzac, Honoré, 139-51 passim
Bantock, Granville, 237
Barber, Samuel, 75, 97, 99, 100
Barney, Natalie, 28-29, 37, 40, 42, 66n
Barthes, Roland, 140-42, 144-47
Bartlett, Neil, 23
Bartók, Bela, 16, 95
Bartoli, Cecilia, 57n
Bay City Rollers, the, 303
BBC Music Magazine, 26n
Beaver, Harold, 198-99n
Beecham, Thomas, 55
Beeson, Jack, 108
Beethoven, Ludwig van, 76, 90, 93, 208-233 passim, 229n, 231n, 232n
Beethoven Op. 127, 213, 232n
Beethoven Op. 130, 213, 232n
Beethoven Third Symphony, 213
Bellini, Vincenzo, 37, 38, 44
Beni Mora (Holst), 237
Berg, Alban, 16, 44, 91, 97, 103-104
Bergson, Henri, 283
Berkenhead, John, 121, 124, 134n
Berlioz, Hector, 29, 285, 296n
Bernede, Artur, 42
Bernhard, Sandra, 268-69
Bernstein, Jane, 51-52, 65n
Bernstein, Leonard, 92, 116, 236
Bertha (Rorem/Koch), 88
Bizet, Georges, 41, 43
Black Mask, The (Penderecki), 102
Blitzstein, Marc, 86-87, 97, 253n
Bloom, Allan, 12
Blount, Teresa, 178
Bolcom, William, 100
Bononcini, Giovanni, 156, 174
Boone, Joseph, 249, 250, 256n
Boosey & Hawkes, 235

Boris Godunov (Mussorgsky), 238
Boswell, John, 318
Boulanger, Nadia, 25n
Boulez, Pierre, 93
Bowles, Jane, 90
Boyle, Richard (Earl of Burlington), 177-80
Brahms, Johannes, 165
Braindrop, Lily, 268
Brando, Marlon, 92
Bray, Alan, 168-70, 172
Brecht, Bertolt, 102
Bredbeck, Greg, 25n
Breslin, Herbert, 94
Brett, Philip, 38, 82n, 120, 148-49, 207, 346n
Brewster, Harry, 45, 47, 49, 53, 55
Briggs, Donald, 102
Bright, Susie, 266-67
Britten, Benjamin, 18-21, 25n, 52, 65n, 93, 98, 101, 105, 106, 235-56
Bronski, Michael, 13
Brooklyn Academy of Music, 92
Brooks, Romaine, 42, 47
Brown, Malcolm, 210
Brydges, James (Earl of Carnarvon), 180
Buckley, William F., 105
Bülow, Bernhard von, 48
Bulteau, Augustine, 51
Burlington House, 169, 177-80
Burney, Charles, 165, 166
Butt, Clara, 43
Buxtehude, Margreta, 192-93n
Byrd, William, 120
Byron, Lord, 52

C

Cage, John, 97, 238
Cain and Abel (Goodman), 88
Cain, Henri, 42
Calamus (Whitman), 110
Caldwell, Sarah, 92
Callas, Maria, 58n, 92
Calvé, Emma, 29-32, 33, 37-55 passim, 57n, 62n, 64n
Cambridge Opera Handbook, 239
Cannons, 179, 180
Canonic Variations on "Vom Himmel hoch" (Bach), 77-78
Carmen (Bizet), 41-42, 43-44, 46, 52, 53-54, 236
Carpenter, Humphrey, 250

Carter, Elliott, 95, 97
Cartwright, William, 134-35n
Casanova, 147-48
Case, Sue-Ellen, 13, 262-63, 265
Cather, Willa, 33-36, 38-39, 40, 41, 43, 54, 59n, 60n, 61n
Chambers, Ross, 232n
Chasnoff, Debra, 268-69
Chaucer, 87
Chéri (Colette), 90
Chicago Gay Men's Chorus, 325-44
Childhood Miracle, A (Rorem), 87
Chocolate Soldier, The, 94
Chorley, Henry, 31
Christopher Street, 16
Chrysander, Friedrich, 162-63, 187
Clap, Margaret, 172
Clause 28, 20
Clément, Catherine, 44, 63n, 93n, 296n
Cléopâtre (Massenet), 41, 42
Cline, Patsy, 266
Cocteau, Jean, 88
Colette, 40, 90
Cone, Edward T., 226, 233n, 309
Consul, The (Menotti), 99
Cooke, Mervyn, 237, 238
Copland, Aaron, 22, 25n, 87, 97, 237, 253n
Corelli, Arcangelo, 174-75
Corsaro, Frank, 93
Country Music, U.S.A. (Malone), 258
Covent Garden, 46, 50, 51, 55
Cowell, Henry, 16, 238
Cowley, Abraham, 126-27
Coxe, William, 161-63, 165
Crosby, John, 88
Curlew River (Britten), 239, 250
Curzon, Clifford, 238
Cushing, Mary, 35, 40, 41
Cusick, Suzanne G., 278

D

Dahlhaus, Carl, 13, 216, 222-23, 227
Dallas Opera, 87
Daly, Mary, 280, 294n
Dame, Joke, 36
Daudet, Alphonse, 42, 43
Daudet, Lucien, 42, 47
Davenport, Marcia, 33, 54, 59n
David, Félicien, 236
Davies, Peter Maxwell, 94
Davis, Peter G., 104

Dean, Winton, 184, 187
Death in Venice (Britten/Mann), 19, 21, 239, 251
Debussy, Lily, 101
Deleuze, Gilles, 317-18
Delius, Frederick, 237
Deller, Alfred, 139
de Musset, Alfred, 64n
Dennis, John, 185-86
Denver Women's Chorus, 321
de Nyvelt, Hélène, 28
D'Erasmo, Stacey, 267
Dering, Sir Edward and Lady, 134-35n
Desert Hearts (Dietch), 267-68
Despised and Rejected (Fitzroy), 23n
Dialogues de Carmélites, Les (Poulenc), 99
Diamond, Beverley, 299
Dick Kramer Gay Men's Chorus, 325-44
Dietch, Donna, 267-68
Domingo, Placido, 99
Donne, John, 116, 117-18, 126-27
Dukas, Paul, 43
Dunayevskaya, Raya, 276, 292n
Durrell, Lawrence, 249-250

E

Eagleton, Terry, 212
Easton, Celia, 127
Edel, Leon, 89
Edlestone, John, 52
Elegies for Rod (Monette), 102
Eliot, George, 33, 58n
Ellman, Richard, 104
Elmslie, Kenward, 88
Englander, Roger, 109
Enlightenment, the, 169-70, 189, 279
Entertaining Mr. Sloane (Orton), 90
Epstein, Matthew, 94
Erlanger, Camille, 41
Eroica Symphony (Beethoven), 213
Eugénie, Empress, 63n, 65n
Eulenberg, Phillip, 48
Euripedes, 285
Evans, Peter, 242
Exposition Coloniale de Paris 1931, 239

F

Faderman, Lillian, 125-26
Fables (Rorem), 88
Fantasio (de Musset), 64n

Fantasio (Smyth), 48, 49
Farinelli, 144
Fauré, Gabriel, 49, 98
Favola d'Orefeo, La (Monteverdi), 149
Felsenstein, Walter, 92
Finley, Karen, 264
Fischer-Dieskau, Dietrich, 94
Fitzroy, A. T., 23n
Flaubert, Gustave, 249, 250
Fleck, John, 264
Fliegende Holländer, Der (Wagner), 52
Flower, Newman, 164, 165-66, 179, 190, 193n
Floyd, Carlyle, 96
Fone, Byrne, 198n
Forester, E. M., 251-52
Foucault, Michel, 9, 156, 167, 172, 196n, 203n, 210, 230n, 318
Four Indian Love Lyrics (Woodforde-Finden), 235-36
Four Saints in Three Acts (Thomson/Stein), 97
Fragoletta (Latouche), 43
Frank, Anne, 107-108
Fremstad, Olive, 33, 35, 38-55 passim, 59n, 60n, 61n, 63n
Freud, Sigmund, 167, 298, 317, 318
Frith, Simon, 301-302, 303, 304, 307
Frost, Robert, 110
Furman, Nelly, 44, 54
Fuss, Diana, 10

G

Gallop, Jane, 142, 147
Ganymede, 89, 90
Garber, Jennie, 305
Garber, Marjorie, 52
Garden, Mary, 40-42, 61n, 62n, 101
Gardiner, John Eliot, 30
Garland, Judy, 92
Gautier, Théophile, 42, 43, 211, 224-25
Gay and Lesbian Association of Choruses, 315-44
Gay, John, 177-79
Gay/Lesbian Study Group Newsletter, 207
Gay Men's Chorus of Los Angeles, 325-44
Gelbert, Bruce-Michael, 100, 111
Genesis II (Vandervelde), 282-83
George II, 157-58, 166, 191-92n
George III, 193n
Gershwin, George, 97

Giannone, Richard, 38
Gide, André, 227
Gideon, Miriam, 107
Gilbert and Sullivan, 235
Giles, Jennifer, 303-305, 310
Gilman, Sander, 32
Girotti, Massimo, 92
Giving till It Hurts (Bernhard), 269
Glass, Philip, 97
Gluck, Christophe von, 29, 39, 42, 49
Gluck, Alma, 33, 59n
Glück, Robert, 225
Glyndebourne, 21
Goethe, Johann Wolfgang von, 147
Gombert, Nicholas, 211
Goodman, Paul, 88, 108
Gordon, Eric, 86-87
Gounod, Charles, 42
Goya (Menotti), 98-99
Graham, Martha, 92, 97
Gramit, David, 209, 229n
Gramm, Donald, 94, 100
Grand Tour, the, 173-75, 177, 180, 188
Griffes, Charles, 109
Grau, Maurice, 33
Grove, George, 214
Guardian, The, 239
Guattari, Félix, 317-18

H

Habock, Franz, 144
Hall, Radclyffe, 47, 59n, 66n, 227
Halperin, David, 9
Hammond, Tom, 30
Handel, George Frideric, 151n, 155-190, 190-203n
Hanslick, Eduard, 13, 225, 227
Harewood, Earl of, 245
Harrison, Lou, 96, 110, 238
Harvey, Elizabeth D., 128
Hauptmann, Gerhard, 102
Hawkins, John, 158, 159-63, 171, 174, 192-93n, 201n
Hawthorne, Nathaniel, 87
Hearing (Rorem), 88
Hemmings, David, 249
Henahan, Donal, 99, 105
Henry Wood Promenade Concerts, 25n
Hepburn, Katherine, 111
Hérodiade (Massenet), 41, 42
Hérritte-Viardot, Louise, 29

Hicks, Anthony, 164
Hicks, Michael, 16
Hindemith, Paul, 109
Hindley, Clifford, 245, 256n
Hoagland, Sarah, 276, 280
Hocquenghem, Guy, 317, 318
Hoffman, William M., 89, 110
Hoffmann, E. T. A., 13
Hogwood, Christopher, 155, 158, 164, 179-80, 190, 199n
Hoiby, Lee, 99
Holiday, Billie, 92
Holland, Bernard, 207, 229n
Holmès, Augusta, 48-49
Holmes, Jim, 88, 89
Holst, Gustav, 237
Holston, James, 126
"Hope, Laurence" (Amy Woodforde-Finden), 235-36, 250
Horowitz, Joseph, 206
Houston Grand Opera, 102
Hudson, Rock, 103
Hughes, Holly, 264
Humm, Andrew, 111
Hunter, Nick, 264

I

Illiad, The (Homer), 284-85
Imeneo (Handel), 183
In C (Riley), 76
Incoronazione di Poppea, L' (Monteverdi), 97, 148, 149-51
Irigaray, Luce, 310
Israel in Egypt (Handel), 186
Ives, Charles, 16, 22, 208

J

Jackson, Earl, 223-24, 225
James, Henry, 89, 244, 247
Jolas, Betsy, 107
Jonah (Beeson/Goodman), 108
Jones, Rikki Lee, 308
Jongleur de Notre Dame, Le (Massenet), 41

K

Kantrowitz, Arnie, 87
Kaplan, E. Ann, 298
Karayannis, Plato, 87
Keates, Jonathan, 157, 158, 163, 167, 170-71, 192-93n, 199n

Kent Education Committee, 21
Kent, William, 178-80
Kenyon, Nicholas, 183
Kessler, Jascha, 88
Key, Stevan, 238
Keyser, Dorothy, 143
Kingsbury, Henry, 13
King's College, Cambridge, 235
Kirby, Vicki, 300
Kit-Kat Club, 177, 199n
Klinghoffer, Marilyn, 107
Klausner, Kim, 269
Koch, Kenneth, 88
Koestenbaum, Wayne, 31, 61n, 247
Kolb, Barbara, 107
Kosman, Joshua, 183
Krafft-Ebing, Richard, 32
Kramer, Larry, 111
Kramer, Lawrence, 223, 226

L

Lacan, Jacques, 12, 73, 81n, 199n, 244, 298
Lady of the Camellias, The (Dumas), 91
La Fontaine, Jean de, 88
Lakmé (Delibes), 255n
lang, k. d., 257-71
Lang, Paul Henry, 143, 149, 156, 158, 163,
    164, 165, 166, 171, 178, 179, 182, 190,
    194n
Laredo, Jamie, 87
La Scala, 92
Last Tango in Paris, 92
Latouche, Henri, 43
Laura, Donna, 163
Lawes, Henry, 115-38
Least of My Children (Briggs/Linnard), 102
Leblanc, Georgette, 42
Lee, Brenda, 264
Lee, Vernon, 49, 51
LeFanu, Nicola, 16
Legrand, Clotilde, 42
Lehmann, Lilli, 33, 35
Lehmann-Haupt, Christopher, 104-105
Leppert, Richard, 186
Lessem, Alan, 309
Levine, James, 100, 105, 106
Lévi-Strauss, Claude, 317
Lewis, Anthony, 105
Linnard, Loren, 102
Lizst, Franz, 79
loca, La (Menotti), 99

Locke, Ralph P., 236
Lombardo, Guy, 75
London, 172-73, 196n
Lorde, Audrey, 276
Louÿs, Pierre, 41
Lover in Damascus, A (Woodforde-Finden),
    236
Ludlam, Charles, 90-91
Lulu (Berg), 44, 91, 92, 97, 100, 102, 103-
    104

M

McCarthy, Mary, 105
McClary, Susan, 15, 44, 76, 236, 282-83
McEwen, Terry, 95-96
Machlis, Joseph, 109
McIntosh, Mary, 9, 10-11, 16
McNally, Terrence, 91
McPhee, Colin, 237-39, 245, 253n, 255-56n
McRobbie, Angela, 305, 307
Madonna, 79
Maeterlinck, Maurice, 42, 101
Mahler, Gustav, 55
Mailer, Norman, 105
Mainwaring, John, 158-59, 162, 163, 164,
    171, 190, 192n, 193n, 194n
Maitland, J. A. F., 50
Malcolm X, 102-103
Malone, Bill, 258
Mamelles de Tirésias, Les (Poulenc), 239
Manhattan Opera House, 42, 46, 50
Mann, Thomas, 21
Manon, (Massenet), 93
Marchesi, Blanche, 55
Marchesi, Matilde, 55, 57n
Marvell, Andrew, 126
Marx, Karl, 317
Mass, Lawrence D., 16, 85-111
Massenet, Jules, 41, 42, 43, 64n
Matheson, John, 171, 175, 192n
Mayer, Andreas, 208, 229n
Mayer, Elizabeth, 237
Mead, Margaret, 253n
Medici, Gian de', 174, 197n
Medici, Ferdinand de', 174
Medium, The (Menotti), 99
Meistersinger von Nürnberg, Die (Wagner),
    86
Melba, Nellie, 57n
Mellers, Wilfred, 245
Menotti, Gian Carlo, 97-99

Mercier, Philipp, 171
Mérimée, Prosper, 43, 63n
Messager, André, 46
Messiah, The (Handel), 179, 182, 186
Metastasio, Pietro, 176
Met Opera Studio, 88
Metropolitan Opera, 88, 93, 94
Metropolitan Opera House, 34
Midsummer Night's Dream (Britten), 245-48, 251
Midsummer Night's Dream (Shakespeare), 136n
Milk, Harvey, 315
Milk Train Doesn't Stop Here Any More, The (Williams), 90
Miller, D. A., 18
Miller, Tim, 264
Milton, John, 126
Mishima, Yukio, 89, 90
Miss Julie (Rorem/Elmslie), 87-88
Miss Ogilvy Finds Herself (Hall), 66
Mitchell, Donald, 237, 238
Mohr, Richard, 195n
Monette, Paul, 102, 110
Money, John, 32
Montagu, Lord, 250
Montaigne, Michel, 124
Monteverdi, Claudio, 97, 148, 149-51
Moon, Michael, 244
Moore, Douglas, 97
Moore, Marianne, 88
Montaigne noire, La (Holmés), 49
Morrison, Toni, 110
Moscone, George, 315
Mother of Us All, The (Thomson/Stein), 89, 95
Mozart, Wolfgang Amadeus, 41, 97, 213, 214
Mulvey, Laura, 297-98
Munich Opera House, 36
Muraro, Lisa, 67
Musgrave, Thea, 107
Mussorgsky, Modest, 238
Mustafa, Domenico, 31
My Mortal Enemy (Cather), 38

N

Nathan, Isaac, 31
National Gay and Lesbian Rodeo Association, 260
National Review, 105

Native, The, 104, 108
Naufrageurs, Les (Smyth), 46-55 passim
Nazimova, 92
National Endowment for the Arts, The, 264
Near, Holly, 79
Neilson, Francis, 50
Nelson, Larry, 264
Nettl, Bruno, 15
New York City Gay Men's Chorus, 102, 109
New York City Opera, 88, 95
New York Times, The, 50, 93, 105, 207
Nietzsche, Friedrich, 54
Ninety-Second Street Y, 206-207, 226
Ninth Symphony (Beethoven), 213, 232n
Nono, Luigi, 97
Norma (Bellini), 37, 38
Northcott, Bayan, 238
Nozze di Figaro, Le (Mozart/da Ponte), 102, 103

O

O'Brien, Kate, 36, 37-39
O'Brien, Sharon, 36, 43
Oedipus Rex (Sophocles), 89
Of Lena Geyer (Davenport), 33-36
Old Testament, the, 108, 187
Oliveros, Pauline, 284
On Our Backs, 267
Orfeo ed Euridice (Gluck), 29, 37, 39, 42, 49, 56n, 58n
Organization for Lesbian and Gay Action, 20
Orpheus, 29-30, 56n
Orton, Joe, 90-91
Ottoboni, Cardinal, 174-75, 176
Ovaryaction, 276-77
Owen, Anne, 118
Owen Wingrave (Britten), 251

P

Pagoda of Flowers, The (Woodforde-Finden), 236
Palmer, Christopher, 238, 239-40, 242, 244
Paris Opéra, 49
Paris Opéra Comique, 42
Parker, William, 94, 106
Parsifal (Wagner), 41
Parton, Dolly, 264
Pasatieri, Tom, 96
Paul Bunyon (Britten), 238

Pavarotti, Luciano, 94
Pee-Wee's Playhouse, 270n
People for the Ethical Treatment of
    Animals, 264
Pears, Peter, 19, 20, 65n, 239, 245, 250,
    253n, 254n, 255n
Pelléas et Mélisande (Debussy/Maeterlinck),
    100
Penderecki, Krzysztof, 102
Penelope Brandling (Lee), 51
Pergolesi, Giovanni, 37, 38
Perle, George, 91, 104
Pérotin, 245
Peter Grimes (Britten), 19-21, 52, 238, 249
Petronius, 88
Philips, Katherine, 115-38
Phillip V, 144
Piaf, Edith, 92
Pietschmann, Kurt, 143
Piper, Myfanwy, 242, 254n, 255n
Pitt-Rivers, Michael, 250
Plomer, William, 250-51
Polignac, Prince Edmond de, 47
Polignac, Princesse de, (Winnie Singer),
    46-47, 49, 51, 54, 55
Ponnelle, Jean-Pierre, 93
Ponsonby, Maggie, 50
Ponsonby, Mary, 50
Ponticello, Il, 32
Pope, Alexander, 169, 177-79
Porgy and Bess (Gershwin), 97
Porter, Andrew, 95
Poulenc, Francis, 87, 90, 98, 238-39
Presley, Elvis, 79, 92, 270n
Price, Leontyne, 99
Prince of the Pagodas, The (Britten), 239,
    251
Proust, Marcel, 99, 227
Puccini, Giacomo, 53

R

Rachmaninoff, Sergei, 309-10
Radio Three, 183
Raj Quartet (Scott), 236
Rawhide II, 259
Raymond, Janice, 285
reclines, the, 257
Reflections in a Golden Eye (McCullers), 92
Rice, Ann, 61n
Rich, B. Ruby, 259
Riley, Terry, 76

Ring Cycle (Wagner), 93
Ring des Nibelung Der (Wagner), 86, 93
Rise and Fall of the City of Mahagonny
    (Brecht/Weill), 100, 103
Robbers, The (Rorem), 87
Robbins, Cynthia, 95
Rochester Gay Men's Chorus, 320
Rockwell, John, 95
Rodrigo (Handel), 164
Roethke, Theodore, 109
Rogers, Howard, 25n
Rome, 175-77
Rorem, Ned, 18, 85-111
Rosenkavalier, Der (Strauss), 41, 103-104
Rosolato, Guy, 12
Rosselli, John, 143
Rothstein, Edward, 207
Rousseau, George S., 157, 173-74, 175, 176,
    191-92n

S

Said, Edward, 236, 249-50
St. Marks Baths, 2
Saint-Säens, Camille, 62n, 236, 252n
Salome (Strauss), 41, 43-44, 62n
Salome (Wilde), 225
Samson (Handel), 187
Samson et Dalila (Saint-Säens), 62n, 236
Sand, George, 33, 64n
San Francisco Gay Men's Chorus, 315, 325-
    44 passim
San Francisco Opera, 96
Santa Fe Opera, 88-89, 102
Sapho (Gounod), 42
Sapho (Massenet), 42
Sappho (Daudet), 43
Sappho (Glanville-Hicks), 62n
Sappho of Lesbos, 27, 42, 48, 56n, 109, 126-
    27
Sarrasine (Balzac), 139-51 passim
Saturday Night, 264
Saul (Handel), 182
Sayão, Bidu, 101
Sbülens, Mme., 163
Scarlatti, Alessandro, 60-61n
Scarlatti, Domenico, 196n
Scheman, Naomi, 202-203n
Schenker System, 14
Schoenberg, Arnold, 16, 239
Schor, Naomi, 141-42
Schubert, Franz, 15, 98, 205-33

Schubertiade of the 92nd Street Y, 206-207, 226
Schulman, Sarah, 102
Schumann, Clara, 1, 46
Schumann, Robert, 209, 229n
Scotland Yard, 250
Scott, Paul, 236
Second World War, 106
Sedgwick, Eve Kosofsky, 10, 18, 167, 188, 189, 215, 230n
Semele (Handel), 187
Serauky, Walter, 191-92n
Sessions, Roger, 109
Setting the Tone (Rorem), 107
Settling the Score (Rorem), 85
Shakespeare, William, 136n, 247
Shaw, George Bernard, 41
Shawe-Taylor, Desmond, 31
Shepherd, John, 303-305, 310
Sikov, Ed, 104
Sills, Beverly, 94
Silverman, Kaja, 12, 299
Simon, Carly, 306-307, 310
Simon, John, 105
Sinatra, Frank, 92
Smith, John Christopher, 158, 162, 184
Smyth, Ethel, 44-55, 62n, 63n, 64-65n, 65-66n
Solomon (Handel), 182
Solomon, Maynard, 15, 205-33 passim
Sondheim, Stephen, 96
Song of the Lark, The (Cather), 33-36, 39, 59n
Songs of the Springtide (Swinburne), 48
Sonnambula, La, 92
Sophie, Electress of Hanover, 164
Spink, Ian, 119, 120-21, 136n
Souzay, Gerard, 94
Stabat Mater (Pergolesi), 37, 38
Stambolian, George, 316-17
Steakley, James, 48
Streber, Eleanor, 109
Steblin, Rita, 208, 229n, 230n
Steffani, Agostino, 174
Stein, Elliot, 87
Stein, Gertrude, 88, 109
Stevens, Wallace, 110
Stevenson, Robert Louis, 88
Stockinger, Jacob, 177
Stone, Lawrence, 173
Stonewall, 9, 11, 16, 18, 171

Strasberg, Susan, 91
Stratas, Teresa, 101
Strauss, Richard, 41, 53, 98
Stravinsky, Igor, 16, 25n, 90, 308
Streatfeild, R. A., 165, 187
Strohm, Reinhard, 148-49, 186
Stubbes, Phillipp, 185, 201n
Styron, William, 105
Suddenly Last Summer (Williams), 90
Suicide Club, The (Stevenson), 88
Suleri, Sari, 251
Sumidagawa, 250-51
Summer and Smoke (Hoiby/Williams), 99
Susanna (Handel), 183
Sussex Education Committee, 21
Sutcliffe, Tom, 239
Swinburne, Algernon Charles, 48

T

Talma, Louise, 107
Tarquini, Vittoria, 163, 194n
Taylor, Deems, 97
Tchaikovsky, Pyotr Ilyich, 3, 15, 44, 210, 252n
Telemann, Georg Philipp, 166-67
"Tennessee Waltz, The," 75, 82n
Teorema, 92
Théâtre de la Monnaie, 46
Théâtre Lyrique, 29
Thelma and Louise, 296n
Theodora (Handel), 183, 200n
Third Reich, 320
Thompson, Randall, 321
Thompson, Tommy, 94
Thomson, Virgil, 97, 98
"Three Days" (Nelson/Young), 265-66
Three Sisters Who Are Not Sisters (Rorem/Stein), 88
Ticklish Acrobat, The (Rorem/Elmslie), 88
Tippett, Michael, 106
Tobin, Robert, 88
Torke, Michael, 92
Toscanini, Arturo, 105
Tourel, Jenny, 94
Tower of Ivory (Atherton), 33
Town House, the, 259
Traviata, La (Verdi) 100
Tripp, C. A., 319
Trojan War, 284
Trojan Women (Euripedes), 285
Trumbach Randolph, 196n, 197n, 200n

Turgenev, Ivan, 32
Turn of the Screw (Britten), 238-45
Turn of the Screw (James), 244-45
Turtle Creek Chorale, 330
2 Live Crew, 264
Tyler, Parker, 111

U

Ulrich, Karl H., 22
Umbrellas of Cherbourg, The, 91
Universal Deluge, 169, 170, 189
Updike, John, 105

V

Valby, Elaine, 290
Valente, Benita, 87
Vandervelde, Janika, 282-83
Van Vechten, Carl, 33
Verdi, Giuseppe, 30, 98
Viardot-Garcia, Pauline, 29-32, 33, 38-40,
    46, 56n, 57n, 58n, 62n
Village People, The, 206
Village Voice, The, 267
Vincer se stesso è la maggior vittoria
    (Handel), 183
Visconti, 92
Vivien, Renée, 28, 40
von Binitz, 174, 197n
von Schober, Franz, 232
von Stade, Frederike, 100

W

Wagner, Richard, 13, 15, 33, 49, 86, 97-98,
    101, 103, 223
Wald, Der (Smyth), 46-55, 63n
Waller, Edmund, 125-26, 132, 133
Walter, Bruno, 55
Waltz, Gustave, 156
Warner Brothers, 265
War Requiem (Britten), 101

"War Scenes" (Rorem), 101
WAUR Radio, 264
Weaver, William, 92
Webern, Anton von, 16
Weill, Kurt, 100, 102, 109
Weisgall, Hugo, 96
Well Tempered Clavier, The (Bach), 93
West Side Story (Bernstein), 236
What the Butler Saw (Orton), 90
White, Edmund, 108
Whitman Cantata (Rorem), 110
Whitman, Walt, 89-90, 97-98, 99-100, 109, 111
Wigman, Mary, 92
Wigmore Hall, 238
Wilamowitz-Moellendorf, Ulrich, 48
Wilde, Oscar, 43, 48, 225
Wildeblood, Peter, 250
Willets, Pamela J., 121, 136n
Wilhelm II, Kaiser, 48
Williams, C. F. Abdy, 175, 197n
Williams, Tennessee, 90, 93, 99, 227
Williams, William Carlos, 110
Wilson, Lanford, 99
Windy City Gay Choral, 325, 332
Winter Words (Britten), 251
Wood, Elizabeth, 207
Woodforde-Finden, Amy, 235-36, 245
Wreckers, The (Smyth), 46-55
Wulp, John, 89
Wynette, Tammy, 264

Y

Yaddo, 237, 253n
Yeats, W. B., 242
YMCA, 206
YMHA, 206
Young, Percy, 166, 194n

Z

Zeffirelli, 91
Ziegler, Marion, 175, 176, 198n

CONTRIBUTORS

Paul Attinello is a doctoral candidate in systematic musicology at UCLA whose research focuses on the interpretation of modernist and avant-garde music.

Philip Brett teaches music at the University of California, Riverside. He is general editor of *The Byrd Edition*, and compiler of the Cambridge Opera Handbook on Britten's *Peter Grimes*.

Virginia Caputo is a doctoral candidate in social anthropology at York University, Toronto, Canada.

Suzanne G. Cusick teaches music history and criticism at the University of Virginia. She is currently writing a book on 17th-century composer Francesca Caccini.

Joke Dame works as a research assistant at the Music Department of the University of Amsterdam where she is currently preparing her Ph.D. on the singing voice in western classical music. She teaches feminist musicology at Utrecht University.

Lydia Hamessley, Assistant Professor of Music at Hamilton College, has written extensively on manuscript compilation and the reception of the Italian madrigal in Elizabethan England.

Wayne Koestenbaum teaches English at Yale University. He is the author of *The Queen's Throat: Opera, Homosexuality and the Mystery of Desire, Ode to Anna Moffo and Other Poems*, and *Double Talk: The Erotics of Male Literary Collaboration*.

Lawrence D. Mass, M.D., is a co-founder of Gay Men's Health Crisis and the author of *Dialogues of The Sexual Revolution, Volumes I and II*. He is compiling a book, *Confessions of a Jewish Wagnerite*.

Susan McClary is professor of musicology in the Faculty of Music, McGill University. Her most recent books include *Feminine Endings: Music, Gender, and Sexuality* and the Cambridge Opera Handbook on Bizet's *Carmen*.

Martha Mockus received her M. Mus. in historical musicology from King's College, London, and is working toward a Ph.D. in Comparative Studies in Discourse and Society at the University of Minnesota.

Karen Pegley is a doctoral student in music at York University, Toronto.

Jennifer Rycenga teaches religious studies and women's studies at Pomona College. She is also a composer and performer.

Gary C. Thomas teaches in Cultural Studies and Comparative Literature at the University of Minnesota. He has published on 17th-century German music and poetry.

Elizabeth Wood, a musicologist and writer, teaches Gay and Lesbian Studies on the Literature Faculty of Sarah Lawrence College.